THE ACADEMIC MIND

A Report of the Bureau of Applied Social Research,
Columbia University

RECENT BOOKS FROM

THE BUREAU OF APPLIED SOCIAL RESEARCH, COLUMBIA UNIVERSITY,

PUBLISHED BY THE FREE PRESS

COMMUNITY CONFLICT
by James S. Coleman

POLITICAL SOCIALIZATION
by Herbert H. Hyman

UNION DEMOCRACY
by Seymour Martin Lipset, Martin A. Trow,
and James S. Coleman

DEVELOPMENTS IN MATHEMATICAL PSYCHOLOGY
R. Duncan Luce, Editor

THE VOLUNTEERS
by David L. Sills

MATHEMATICAL THINKING
IN THE MEASUREMENT OF BEHAVIOR
Herbert Solomon, Editor

THE
ACADEMIC
MIND

SOCIAL SCIENTISTS IN A TIME OF CRISIS

BY PAUL F. LAZARSFELD

AND WAGNER THIELENS, JR.

WITH A FIELD REPORT BY DAVID RIESMAN

THE FREE PRESS OF GLENCOE, ILLINOIS

6002056290
LC58006486

C

234313 Sociol

Grateful acknowledgment is made to:
   Harcourt, Brace and Co., for permission to quote from T. S. Eliot's
   Four Quartets.
   Chappell & Co., for permission to quote from the lyrics of My Fair Lady,
   copyright © 1956 by Alan Jay Lerner and Frederick Loewe. Chap-
   pel & Co., Inc., Publisher and owner of allied rights throughout
   the world.

PREFACE

During the years following the Second World War this country was faced with the difficult problem of balancing its need for national security with its traditional desire to respect individual rights and aspirations. Government employees, for example, found their private opinions scrutinized for signs of disloyalty, sometimes so sharply as to weaken their professional initiative. The secrecy necessarily imposed upon scientists at work on modern weapons threatened to hamper the general progress of the natural sciences. In this period, too, the opinions and associations of college professors received much critical attention.

The present study was set up to investigate some ramifications of this spotlight on college teachers. We have focused on social scientists, for it was they who dealt directly in the classroom with the very issues over which the larger community was concerned. How did the general tension affect social science teaching? The search for a careful answer to this question could point in more than one direction. It might lead to a study of the impact of the times on the curricula of social science, comparing, say, course offerings in 1940 with those in 1955. Or the investigations to which individual teachers were subjected might be the object of research. Either course would require a type of study using documentary evidence, such as college catalogs and the dossiers of investigating agencies. Analysis of this kind can be done at any time; competent historians, it is to be hoped, will one day go back to these records. But there is one aspect of a crisis situation which is very difficult to reconstruct later on: the immediate reactions, attitudes, feelings, and expectations of the people involved. Such information is available in any detail only near the time of its occurrence.

Is it really necessary to know how people feel? Aren't events and acts all that matter? No one can yet be sure how the episodes of these years will affect American education in the long run. But to understand the outcome eventually, the positions generally taken by college teachers at the time will have to be known. What actually happens is always the resultant of both the forces which impinge upon people and the way they look at and feel about them. If in addition one wants to affect the course of events, an understanding of attitudes may be even more important. How, for instance, can procedures for the preservation of academic freedom be developed as long as no one knows how much it is really wanted by professors and how resistant they are to its infringement?

We therefore decided to arrange for personal interviews with a considerable number of American teachers. We wanted to know their experiences and attitudes while the wave of accusations was still going on. A number of further decisions was necessary. We could have selected for detailed study a group of schools at which major controversies over academic freedom had occurred. This, however, would have precluded more general statements relating specific reactions of social scientists to their basic attitudes and the environment in which they taught. Only a sampling survey covering a representative number of colleges and professors could provide such information. The expenses involved imposed another limitation. To learn the attitudes of trustees, university presidents, and deans at the schools in our survey would undoubtedly have been very revealing. But this would have required a division of both effort and budget between professors and administrators, depriving us of reliable information about either group.

We thus present in this book some salient attitudes of a representative cross-section of social science professors regarding the events of the post-war decade, a picture which was obtained in the spring of 1955. The study was sponsored by the Fund for the Republic. Their purpose was to obtain information which could form the basis for intelligent social action. The authors have three additional objectives in mind. Belonging ourselves to a college community, we hope that the study will help to interpret the academic mind to the outsider. Chapters I, V, VI, VII, and X, especially, provide basic information about the world of the teaching profession which was not heretofore available. We are also aware that the social research methods used in this type of study are still little understood. At various points we have therefore explained in some detail the strategy of the investigation and the procedures for analyzing the data. Finally, since no figures are available for any earlier period, we have not been able to make conclusive comparisons with the past. So we have tried with this study to set a benchmark: once the data in this survey have been recorded, future investigations can be made much more revealing.

The formulation of the questions, the research techniques, the analysis of the data, and the presentation of conclusions in this volume have been carried out by the authors, their consultants, and the staff of the Bureau of Applied Social Research at Columbia University. An effort has been made to be as impartial as possible in the presentation of results. Whenever a broader interpretation or an expression of opinion seemed appropriate, they have been clearly separated from the factual findings. The authors believe that social scientists, if they are to contribute to the progress of the country, need an atmosphere of free inquiry and full expression of ideas. Some of the teachers included in this study take a more conservative stand; we have given their point of view what we hope is a fair hearing.

The directors of a sampling survey like this one do their best to write a sound questionnaire, select good interviewers, and instruct them properly. But they never quite know what happens when interviewer and respondent meet. In the present case the problem was of special concern because college professors are clearly different from the typical subjects of large-scale surveys. Therefore, shortly after the interviews were completed, Professor David Riesman was invited to talk at length with a considerable number of respondents and interviewers, and to analyze the complexities of their encounter. His report is included in this volume.

PAUL F. LAZARSFELD
WAGNER THIELENS, JR.

New York, August, 1958

ACKNOWLEDGMENTS

THIS STUDY would have been unmanageable without the collaboration of a large number of associates. Our main debts are to the following men and women:

Louis Harris: who supervised the sampling and the field work of the two organizations which carried out the interviewing, Elmo Roper and Associates, and the National Opinion Research Center of the University of Chicago, and helped greatly in the development of the questionnaire.

Clara Shapiro: who was in effective charge of the project's administration from beginning to end. Her devotion in coordinating the many facets of a complicated endeavor was accompanied by a warmth which sustained the morale of the staff for three years.

Helmut Guttenberg: who efficiently organized the difficult task of statistical tabulation. In his hands highly intricate data-processing operations became an intellectual accomplishment.

Jeannette Green: who patiently and imaginatively scrutinized individual cases which would not fit the statistical mold. Her numerous memoranda based on these materials were consistently illuminating.

David Caplovitz: who gave special attention to the colleges, their statistical characteristics, and their individual deviations. His helpful comments on our several manuscript drafts deserve separate mention.

Patricia Kendall: who continuously gave us the benefit of her interpretative skill and her editorial experience.

We are also indebted for competent and faithful assistance during the analysis to the following members of Columbia's Bureau of Applied Social Research: Jeanne Bilby, Jane Emery, John Meyer, Bobbetta Mladen, Florence Ruderman, Robert Somers, and Ilse Zeisel.

In addition to these individuals, who were the backbone of the project's full-time staff, we want to offer our grateful thanks to a number of others who gave help.

In preparation for the study a group of Fellows at the Center for Advanced Study in the Behavioral Sciences, composed of Arthur Brodbeck, Richard Christie, Frank Pinner, Arnold Rogow, and Louis Schneider, collected and digested material from California high schools which provided us with important leads. James Coleman developed the sampling scheme. Edward Shils gave expert advice during the development of the final questionnaire. Throughout the analysis David Riesman generously shared with us his wide familiarity with American colleges. Earlier drafts of the manuscript were read by William Evan, Richard Hofstadter, Stanley Schachter, Gerhart Wiebe, Logan Wilson, Hans Zeisel, Morris Zelditch, and Hans Zetterberg, all of whom contributed ideas which have been incorporated in the present version.

Two advisory committees gave us considerable aid. One, composed of Marie Jahoda, Frank Stanton, Samuel Stouffer, and Ralph Tyler, assisted substantially in the planning of the project. During the last revision of the manuscript we received help and advice from William Fels, Robert Merton, and Samuel Stouffer.

Obviously the study would not have been possible without the cooperation of the college teachers who were interviewed. We can only hope that when they read this report, they will feel their time was not wasted.

CONTENTS

(xi)

+ + +

Some Observations on the Interviewing
in the Teacher Apprehension Study
(*by David Riesman*)
    AN OVER-ALL ASSESSMENT; THE NATURE OF THE INVES-
    TIGATION; THE PROBLEM OF CONSCIOUS EVASION OR
    DECEIT; THE COLLEGIATE SETTING OF THE INTERVIEWS;
    THE INTERVIEWERS; THE INTERVIEWERS' PREPARATION;
    SOME CONCLUDING REMARKS

+ + +

THE ACADEMIC MIND

Chapter I

THE SOCIAL SCIENTIST
AND HIS COLLEGE

WHENEVER ONE DISCUSSES a social group, be it lawyers or Middle Westerners or Frenchmen, there is a recurrent danger of oversimplification. For professors and colleges this is especially true. Most people attend one college at most, and have encountered only a small number of teachers. These are the associations which come to mind whenever a reference to higher education is made. Our first effort, therefore, is to provide some notion of the remarkable variety that prevails among American colleges. We shall start by describing the sample of individual teachers who were interviewed, and then will characterize the schools in which they work.

Our study is based on information provided by 2,451 social scientists. This is admittedly a somewhat vague term. Our intention was to include those teachers who were likely to deal with controversial topics in their courses. Historians were therefore included, although they are usually classified as humanists. We also interviewed social geographers because we thought that the problems of underdeveloped countries and of colonial policy, which play such an important role in current events, might very well come up in their teaching. Actually, this was rarely the case, although, as will be seen later, the few examples we have are especially revealing. In any event, the geographers had rather different attitudes from the rest of our respondents. In a way this is fortunate, because the findings suggest possible differences between social scientists and teachers in other sciences. We might have been justified in omitting the 160 geographers from the final picture. However, as the decision about the sample had been made deliberately, it seemed better to include them in our computations.

Among psychologists, we chose only those who, according to the college catalogues, were teaching at least one course that might be included in a curriculum of social psychology. It should be remembered, therefore, that when we talk of psychologists, we refer to only a small part of the constituency, say, of the American Psychological Association. Our sample of anthropologists was small because, in many colleges, anthropology courses are taught by men who classified themselves as sociologists during their interviews. There were also several respondents, usually from smaller institutions, whom we were forced to classify as "general social scientists" because they taught such diverse topics that it was not possible to allocate them to any specific discipline.

A word may be said about groups excluded from the sample. Teachers of literature and of Slavic languages might well have met our qualifying criteria. The decision to exclude them was made on pragmatic grounds: it seemed preferable to interview a larger number of respondents in what we considered core groups. We made another restriction in regard to economists: only those who taught in liberal arts colleges were selected; this excluded, for instance, economists who taught exclusively in business schools. The same was true for an occasional sociologist whose teaching was confined to a journalism school.[1]

The professional activities of our respondents were distributed as shown in Table 1-1.

Table 1-1
The Departmental Affiliation of Our Respondents

	Number	Per Cent
History	681	28%
Economics	565	23
Sociology	405	16
Political science	384	15
Geography	160	7
Social psychology	141	6
Anthropology	65	3
General social scientists	26	1
Not classifiable (subjects too varied, or insufficient information)	24	1
Total	(2451)	100%

1. A complete record of all the steps in the sampling procedure is kept at Columbia University's Bureau of Applied Social Research. The general execution of the sample was under the supervision of Louis Harris.

The Sample

WE FEEL CONFIDENT that our sample is reasonably representative of the sector of American college teachers we set out to study. In fact, it is safe to say that our cross-section of social scientists is as good as the cross-sections of the total population obtained by the better public opinion polls. We selected our respondents in two steps, the details of which are explained in Appendix 1. There are some 900 accredited four-year undergraduate colleges in this country; these were classified according to information available in published records. Among the types of schools so formed, 182 colleges were chosen at random. The president of each of these schools was then sent a letter stating the purpose of the study, its sponsor, how it would be conducted, and requesting permission to have our interviewers work on the college premises. Twenty schools refused to participate, and six others were dropped for lack of current accreditation or for other reasons. Last minute substitutions were made for nine colleges; this brought the total of participating schools to 165.[2] They are listed in Appendix 7.

The respondents were selected from the latest obtainable catalogues of the colleges in the sample. In the smaller schools every social science teacher was included; in the larger schools, depending on their size, between a half and a third were chosen at random. About 90 per cent of the original list were actually interviewed. Whenever a respondent could not be reached, the interviewer had recourse to a definite procedure for finding a substitute similar to the absentee in age, rank, and field of teaching. About 8 per cent of those on the original list refused to participate or obviously

---

2. For details, see Appendix 1. We thought it would be enlightening to investigate the situation in the colleges which did not grant permission. During the summer of 1955, therefore, we commissioned a number of social scientists, familiar with the regions, to make field trips to several of these colleges.

We plan to publish later a group of papers which will take up a number of matters that deserve more attention than can be given in this volume. These will cover, besides an examination of the refusal colleges, such things as a history of the development of the questionnaire, a comparison of the results obtained by the two interviewing agencies, a special study of women teachers, etc.

escaped being interviewed. (The figure cannot be precise because it was sometimes difficult to decide, for instance, whether a professor was really ill or just did not want to be reached.) As far as we can see, these refusals were not concentrated within a specific group of schools or professors.

The actual interviewing was carried out in April and May, 1955, by the trained personnel of two nationally known interviewing agencies: the National Opinion Research Center and the firm of Elmo Roper and Associates. The questionnaire schedule they administered is shown in Appendix 2. The shortest interviews lasted about forty-five minutes; the longest, well over five hours; on the average, interviews took between one and a half and two hours.

Women made up 11 per cent of our sample, Negroes 3 per cent. Two-thirds of the respondents were Protestants, 12 per cent Catholics, and 5 per cent Jews; 3 per cent were in other denominations, 13 per cent stated they had no religious affiliations, and we had no information for 1 per cent. The median age of the sample (a variable of some importance, as we shall see) was slightly over forty; 8 per cent were thirty or younger and 8 per cent sixty-one or older.

Closely related to age is the rank of the respondents. More than one-third, 881, were full professors, and 516 were associates; 964 were assistant professors and instructors, in a ratio of about 2:1. The meaning of rank is not quite the same for every college, since tenure must also be considered. It was held by 93 per cent of the associate and full professors, about half of the assistant professors, but only a few of the 334 instructors. It is possible that our sample may overweight the higher ranks somewhat: we took the names of our respondents from printed catalogues; but some universities make last minute appointments on the instructor level, and the names of these staff members might not be included on the official lists.[3] If this is true, our figures would somewhat exaggerate the extent of tenure, which is surprisingly high.[4]

As many as 8 per cent of our respondents are the sons and daughters of teachers. Nearly half come from other professional

3. As explained in Appendix 1, recent appointments were systematically listed and interviewed only at colleges with less than 2,500 students.

4. For further details on rank, age, tenure, and length of teaching, see Appendix 8A.

or managerial backgrounds, while somewhat less than one-third are the children of farmers or manual workers. The relatively high status of these family backgrounds may come as a surprise to some; the details are therefore presented in Table 1-2.

Table 1-2
Over Half of the Respondents Come from
Professional and Managerial Backgrounds

Father's Occupation	Per Cent
Teacher	8
Other professional	23
Managerial	25
White collar and small business	15
Farmer	13
Manual labor	15
No information	1
Total	100% (= 2451 respondents)

We now turn to some aspects of the academic scene which have special importance for our main problem.

Productivity and Professional Leadership

IN STUDYING any professional group it is important to be able to classify individuals according to their achievement. For one, it is likely that the successful members of the profession set the standards of conduct which are followed by the less success-ful. Also, they are likely to display most clearly the attitudes that are characteristic of their profession. More specifically, we will see that professional eminence plays an important role in the particular problems examined in this study.

The achievement of a member of the academic profession can be judged on at least three grounds: his publications, the recogni-tion he has received from his peers and from the community, and his ability as a teacher. An evaluation of this last is impossible with-out knowing the opinions of administrators and students, but neither of these groups was interviewed for our study. On the other hand, we had varied information on professional productivity.

Furthermore, prestige is often determined by the quantity of a professor's published and unpublished contributions. We therefore set up a classification based on these items.

The following facts were available: 82 per cent had written a dissertation; 72 per cent had published papers—half had published three or more. Two-thirds had delivered papers at professional meetings, 40 per cent presenting three or more. One-third of the sample was credited with at least one book beyond the dissertation. This information was combined to form a rough index of productivity. One score point was assigned for a dissertation, another for publishing one or more papers, a third for publishing one or more books, and a final one for having delivered at least three papers at professional meetings.[5] Thus a respondent who qualified on all four criteria received 4 score points, one who qualified on three received 3 points, and so on down to a score of 0 for a teacher who lacked a Ph.D., had published neither a paper nor a book, and had delivered fewer than three papers at meetings. Only 9 per cent of our respondents fell into this last group. About one-quarter were in the top group, and about half had scores of 3.

As we proceed, we shall use our productivity index repeatedly to single out leading social scientists. We can do this with some confidence because other indicators of leadership are closely associated with productivity. Figure 1-3, for example, relates productivity to the proportion of teachers who have held office in professional organizations and to the proportion who have been called in as consultants to non-governmental agencies. We see that the higher the productivity of a teacher, the greater this kind of recognition. The relation holds up, incidentally, even when it is examined separately for different age groups.

We might add in passing that after the age of fifty the likelihood of holding professional office increases very little. Apparently

---

5. The reader should not think that we consider quantity of pages the main aim of scholarship; nor do we overlook the role of quality in academic work. If we wanted to characterize individual social scientists, we would certainly not use our crude index. But for classifying a large number of teachers it is acceptable. Actually alternative indices were considered and tried out. We show in Appendix 3 how representative results reported in the subsequent pages of the report would remain the same if other indices of professional eminence were used. The whole problem of this kind of index formation and its bearing on empirical findings is taken up in considerable detail in this Appendix. All indices used in the book are listed in Appendix 9.

Figure 1-3
The Likelihood that a Professor Holds a Prestigeful Off-Campus Position Increases with Productivity*

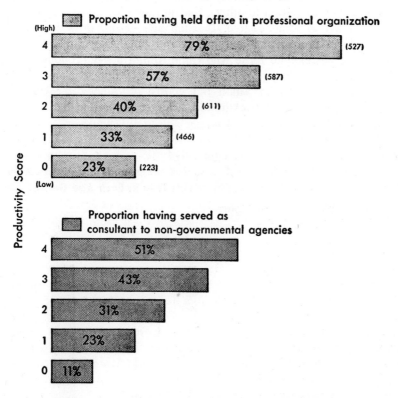

* For thirty-seven respondents not enough information was available to form a productivity score. The total number of respondents in each productivity category is given at the right of the top set of bars; the same figures apply to the lower set of bars.

the "elder statesman" does not play the same dominant role in academic organizations as he seems to in the top levels of public life—in the American Senate or the British Cabinet, for example.

We can link productivity to two other factors. The more productive teachers on each age level had made more moves from one campus to another than had their less productive colleagues. (The difference is consistently about 11 per cent.) This suggests that the man who stays at the same college for a long time may often do so only because he has not received enough professional attention to bring an attractive invitation from another institution.

It will come as a surprise to some readers, and as evidence for a social conviction to others, that productivity and social origin are related to some degree. In each age group, professors who came from professional and managerial families were somewhat more successful than those who came from a lower economic and social stratum. Figure 1-4 shows the extent of this relationship.

The differences are small but consistent. Among teachers of higher socio-economic background, a larger proportion had a high productivity score.[6] In the younger age group, however, this may

Figure 1-4
Professors from High Socio-Economic Backgrounds are More Likely to be Highly Productive. This Holds True in Each Age Group.

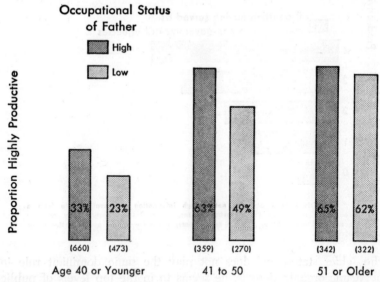

6. The productivity index increases strongly with age as can be seen if one compares figures for the three age groups in Figure 1-4. This is an artifact, due to the cumulative nature of the index: as a man grows older his total output cannot decrease; it can only stay constant or increase. Therefore, it will often be necessary to make comparison within age groups, as is done in Figure 1-4.

be due partly to mere availability of time. Many younger people from a low income group have had to work their way through college and graduate school. This would delay their writing a dissertation—a special tabulation shows a consistent social difference in the proportion of our respondents holding a doctorate. In addition, a more sophisticated background probably fosters an early ability to write, while it may take a lifetime to develop this ability on one's own. Whatever the reason, the result deserves attention because of the role which professional leadership will play in our study.

Occupational Self-Esteem

THE ACADEMIC MEN and women covered by our study felt that they were not especially appreciated by the outside world. These people had spent many years becoming specialists in their fields. They held positions of considerable authority on the campus. Although poorly paid, they had greater job security than most other professional men and women. Nevertheless, they had what one might call a feeling of being put upon. The important consequences of this will be discussed somewhat later in our report. At this point the fact itself must be established.

We asked our respondents to compare their occupation with three others: the manager of a branch bank, an account executive of an advertising agency, and a lawyer.[7] These three occupations share an important characteristic with the work of a professor: none of them produce tangible goods, and all deal in symbols, either verbal or monetary.

We were not interested in finding out what image college teachers themselves had of these three occupations. Some may have regarded them as occupations inferior to the profession of teaching; others may have considered them superior occupations. Be that as it may, we asked respondents to tell us how, in their opinion, significant members of the outside community compared professors with men engaged in the three other pursuits. One of the questions read as follows:

7. This questionnaire item was suggested by Professor Edward Shils of the University of Chicago.

Suppose a typical businessman were to rank these four occupations by the esteem he holds for each—in what order do you think he would rank each?

The same question was then asked twice more, making the imaginary judge in turn a "typical congressman" and a "typical trustee of your college." Our respondents thus were asked to say how they thought the four test occupations would rank in the eyes of a businessman, a congressman, and a trustee. In each instance they could visualize professors as having one of four possible ranks. The results are reported in Figure 1-5.

Figure 1-5
Professors Usually Think Themselves Ranked in Low Esteem by Leaders of the Community, Especially by Businessmen and Congressmen

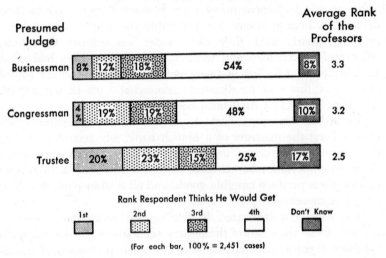

It is clear that professors do not feel they are much appreciated by businessmen or congressmen. Social psychologists have given considerable attention to what they call the mirror image: they have found that individuals are strongly affected by what they believe others think of them. In a sense it matters relatively little what the political and business leaders of the community actually think of professors. If the professors themselves are convinced that they are not accorded the prestige they deserve, then this feeling will strongly color their own attitudes.

Trustees are assigned a more favorable role. Since many trustees are actually chosen from the business community, professors might be expected to experience the two as allied. But it turns out that trustees were considered more friendly than either of the other two groups of judges. This probably reflects an element of reality: it is doubtless the more understanding businessman who becomes a trustee, and contact with the academic world is likely to make him even more susceptible to its traditions. Figure 1-5, incidentally, contributes an interesting sidelight on the nature of stereotypes. Most of the respondents claim to know what the typical business-man and the typical congressman feel; but 17 per cent say that they do not know how the trustee would rank a college professor on their own campus. Of course, this is partly due to the fact that, in many colleges, professors have relatively little contact with their trustees. But there cannot be many professors who know a con-gressman personally, and yet only 10 per cent say that they could not guess his attitude. The differences in the trustee rankings of Figure 1-5 are probably best explained in psychological terms: the more closely connected people are with our lives, the more hesitant we are to express stereotyped opinions about them.

For later reference, it might be added that the image which pro-fessors attributed to trustees varied considerably according to the type of school. In Catholic schools over half the respondents be-lieved that trustees would put the college teacher in first or second place, while in tax-supported schools only a little over one-third did so. Privately endowed colleges, as well as teachers colleges and Protestant institutions, fell in between the two extremes.

It is worth while to speculate how the rank of a teacher affects this mirror image. A full professor has more prestige than an in-structor, almost as a matter of course. One might therefore expect the higher ranks to attribute a more friendly opinion to trustees. But the opposite is also conceivable: as a teacher ascends in the professorial hierarchy, he may expect a greater increment in pres-tige than he actually finds accorded to him; as a result, his mirror image may become increasingly deflated. The data seem to sup-port this second alternative: the higher ranks felt less appreciated.

Only 22 per cent of the instructors, against 34 per cent of the full professors, said that a typical trustee would rank the professor fourth. (Assistant and associate professors fell neatly in between, with 29 per cent and 31 per cent respectively.) This is a type of result which helps to clarify the functions of social research. As we have already indicated, the opposite finding would have sounded equally "obvious." Indeed, it often happens, as it did in this case, that common sense is equally willing to believe either of two contradictory alternatives. It is the purpose and merit of empirical investigation to find out which of the two is true.[8]

In a way, then, professors, at least social scientists, seem to consider themselves an occupational minority toward which significant sectors of the community hold relatively contemptuous attitudes. This has an unexpected implication.

American social scientists have a voting pattern which is quite different from that of the population at large. In 1952, 58 per cent of the teachers interviewed voted for Stevenson and 30 per cent for Eisenhower, while 10 per cent did not vote at all.[9] This becomes even more significant if one remembers the relatively high social background from which these professors come. In general, the progeny of an occupational distribution similar to that described in Table 1-2 would have a strong Republican majority.

The major reasons for these teachers' political choices will be considered in Chapter VI. Here we wish to submit that in part they are voting for the party which is traditionally the rallying place for protesting minorities. Two facts support this interpretation. One goes quite directly to the point: the Democrats have a slightly higher occupational inferiority feeling than the Republicans, as can be seen from Figure 1-6. There the two groups of voters are compared as to how often they think powerful people rank the professor fourth among the four test occupations.

---

8. To round out the picture, we mention here the average rankings which, in the opinion of our respondents, the three types of judges would give the four occupations: lawyer 1.79, bank manager 2.34, account executive 2.58, professor 3.02. The only time that a professor was thought to be ranked above the advertising man was when the respondents were imputing the answers to a college trustee.

9. For the remaining 2 per cent, forty-seven cases, either we had no information, or they claimed they couldn't remember, or they voted for a third party.

Figure 1-6
Democratic Voters are More Apt to Consider Themselves Held in Low Esteem by Community Leaders

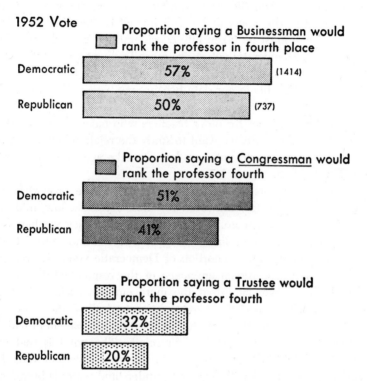

1952 Vote

Proportion saying a <u>Businessman</u> would rank the professor in fourth place

Democratic 57% (1414)

Republican 50% (737)

Proportion saying a <u>Congressman</u> would rank the professor fourth

Democratic 51%

Republican 41%

Proportion saying a <u>Trustee</u> would rank the professor fourth

Democratic 32%

Republican 20%

A higher proportion here means greater pessimism regarding the status of the teacher in the larger community. The Democratic voters are consistently more inclined to think that nobody loves the professor.

The second argument is more indirect. It is known that if a minority group tends to vote for the Democratic party, the tendency is especially marked among those members who identify more strongly with the group.[10] We have no explicit measure of how

10. For evidence, see Suchman and Menzel, "The Interplay of Demographic and Psychological Variables in the Analysis of Voting Surveys," in *The Language of Social Research*, Lazarsfeld and Rosenberg, eds. (Glencoe, Ill.: The Free Press, 1955).

central their professional role as social scientists is to our respondents, but for the moment the productivity index can serve
as a substitute. Taking just the two-party vote, the Democratic proportion increases from 59 per cent to 69 per cent as the productivity
score rises. But this conceals the full impact of the difference, for
the role of age must be taken into consideration. As in the population at large, Democratic voters are more frequent among younger
teachers. (There seems to be a recent reversal of this trend, but
it is barely noticeable in our data because we have so few respondents below the age of twenty-five.) At the same time our productivity
index has to be higher for older teachers who have had more time
to publish. If, therefore, we want to study the relation between professional leadership and vote, we have to take age into consideration. This leads to Figure 1-7.

First, respondents are divided by age. Then the proportion of
Democrats is separately indicated for those having a low, middle,
or high productivity score. For our present purposes we have to
look at each of the three lines in Figure 1-7. We find indeed that,
in each age group, the proportion of Democratic voters is greater,
the higher the professional eminence of the respondent.[11]

It will be shown later that the more eminent social scientists
most often exhibit certain characteristics typical of their profession. We do not claim that a protest against the low esteem in which
they are held is uppermost in their minds. The point is that an
occupational inferiority feeling can be inferred from our data in
a variety of ways and will help us to understand many subsequent
findings.

---

11. Figures like Figure 1-7 will appear often in our report, and it is important that the reader see how easily they can be absorbed in spite of their
somewhat formidable look. The simple trick is to remember that to each of
the nine points shown belongs a base number. These appear in parentheses
beneath the Figure. They represent the number of teachers who were found
to be in each of the nine possible combinations of the three age groups with
the three productivity groups. For instance, 284 voters are highly productive
and in the youngest age group. For each of these combinations, we now want
to know what proportion are Democrats. This is the case for 79 per cent (226
respondents) in the class of lowest age and highest productivity. This percentage is printed beneath the chart, and is also represented by the right-hand
point of the top line in the chart. (The remaining 21 per cent, of course,
voted Republican.)

So far we have described the individual professor: his social background, his age, and other characteristics. What about the college he teaches in?

Figure 1-7
The Proportion of Respondents Voting Democratic Increases with Productivity in Each Age Group (Two-Party Voters Only)

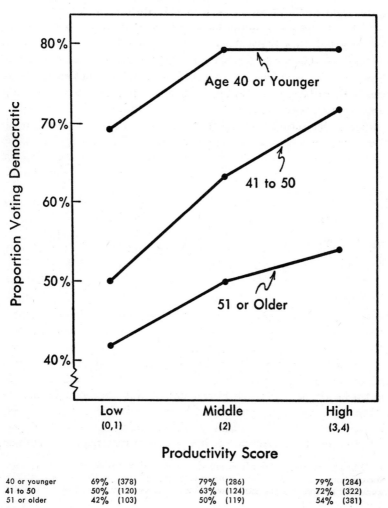

	Low (0,1)	Middle (2)	High (3,4)
40 or younger	69% (378)	79% (286)	79% (284)
41 to 50	50% (120)	63% (124)	72% (322)
51 or older	42% (103)	50% (119)	54% (381)

Some Ways
of Describing Colleges

WHAT CHARACTERIZES a college? Obviously, its size is relevant. Relations between administration, trustees, and faculty are
likely to be more intimate in a small college than in a large one;
this ought to be of importance in a study where the question of
possible interference with the activities of the faculty is a focus
of attention. In a big college the faculty works with greater individual anonymity; it is also more likely to exercise the power
conferred by its bigness in a controversy with the administration
and the trustees. Also, the small college is more often located in a
small community, and therefore its activities are likely to come
under closer scrutiny by local community organizations—although
there are, of course, notable exceptions. Finally, in many cases the
big college is apt to be richer and therefore able to attract a higher
proportion of teachers who have achieved the professional distinctions mentioned earlier.

For our purposes it is sufficient to distinguish between four size
classes of colleges. The first class is comprised of schools having
fewer than 700 students; the second and third classes include those
ranging from 700 to 2,500, and from 2,500 to 9,000; and the fourth
is made up of the largest schools, with over 9,000 students.[12]

The second dimension is somewhat more complex; we shall call
it "type of organization." Some colleges are tax-supported; others
are privately endowed. Some of the privately endowed institutions are closely affiliated with a religious denomination, either
Catholic or Protestant. Thus, a simultaneous classification by source
of support and denominational control leads naturally to four groups
which are mutually exclusive. But it seemed advisable to single
out a fifth type: the teachers colleges. It was important to include
them in our sample, for what happens today in a teachers college is bound to affect primary and secondary schools tomorrow.
At the same time, however, it did not seem reasonable to combine

---

12. The sources from which our data were taken and how they were used
for the purpose of our classification are described in detail in Appendix 4. This
appendix also covers the other two dimensions which we are about to sketch
briefly.

them with liberal arts colleges. Teachers colleges have a distinctive purpose and curriculum; the training of their faculty members is therefore likely to be different from that prevailing in other institutions. But this situation created a certain logical difficulty. By far the largest number of American teachers colleges are tax-supported; of the twenty-nine in our sample, only three were privately endowed, one by a Catholic order. Another four teachers colleges were in the process of developing liberal arts divisions. However, it seemed that the dominant function of all these institutions was to train teachers, and we therefore made them a separate group.[13] This then gave us the following five types of institutions: tax-supported by state or municipality; privately endowed; affiliated with the Catholic Church; affiliated with a Protestant denomination; teachers colleges.

A word must be added about the Protestant colleges. It is not easy to identify this group, and the reason is historically interesting. Originally, almost all American colleges were founded by a religious denomination.[14] But, for the past hundred years a steady trend toward secularization has been operating. Today, some Protestant colleges are denominational in the same sense in which Catholic institutions are; others are so more as a vestige of their past and are actually on the borderline of secularization. Thus, some arbitrary decisions had to be made. We were able to obtain three types of information from printed records to help us in making these decisions: we found out whether religious education or religious chapel attendance were compulsory, and whether the bylaws of the college required a considerable number of its trustees to be chosen from ministerial ranks. If a college conformed to at least two of these three policies, it was classified as being affiliated with a Protestant church.[15]

There is a close relationship between the size of a college and its type of organization. The very large institutions are found most

---

13. Only teachers colleges not affiliated with universities were included in our sample; thus, for instance, Columbia University's Teachers College, or the Harvard School of Education, were treated like the other professional schools in these institutions, and were excluded from our study.

14. Richard Hofstadter and Walter P. Metzger, *The Development of Academic Freedom in the United States,* pp. 346 ff. (New York: Columbia University Press, 1955).

15. A more refined classification of Protestant colleges is being made in an on-going study.

frequently among the state universities; Protestant-affiliated schools and teachers colleges are usually quite small.[16]

We turn now to the most difficult, but perhaps the most important, dimension of our classification: the *quality* of a college. This is a characteristic which comes to mind quite readily; it is not easily defined or measured. However, foundations that make grants to colleges distinguish between those of higher and those of lower achievement. Families today worry about whether their children will be admitted to a really good college. How can such a classification be established with reasonable assurance? From published sources we obtained information on both the size of the college library and the ratio of books to undergraduate students. We knew the annual budget per student and the tuition fees; the proportion of Ph.D.'s among the faculty members is also a matter of public record; and finally, previous studies of many colleges had determined what proportion of their graduates received scholarships and other honors after leaving college. Putting all of this information together, an index was formed which permitted us to assign an objective quality rating to each college. This is a complex procedure, and the reader who is interested in the details of such operations will be able to follow the steps in Appendix 4. Most important, we shall be able to show presently that these ratings, which are based on published records, are substantiated by evidence collected in our own survey.

For the moment our main purpose is to relate these quality ratings to the other two dimensions—size and type of organization. To simplify matters as much as possible, we distinguished nine groups of schools. Among the public schools we formed three size classes: small colleges with a student body of less than 2,500, large schools with 2,500 to 9,000 students, and very large institutions with more than 9,000 students. Among private schools we distinguished only smaller and larger colleges, again with the line of separation at 2,500 students. The few very large private colleges in our sample were combined with the large schools. The same division into small and large schools was made for the Catholic colleges, among which there were no very large institutions. De-

---

16. For details see Appendix 4.

tailed scrutiny of many tabulations induced us not to divide the Protestant schools or teachers colleges by size; it appeared that in these institutions type of organization completely overshadowed differences in size, which were small to begin with. Table 1-9 shows how these nine groups differ in their quality ratings.

Table 1-9
Quality Ratings of Various Types of Schools

TYPE OF SCHOOL	QUALITY RATING			
	Low (Score: 1.0-1.9)	Medium Low (2.0-2.9)	Medium High (3.0-3.9)	High (4.0-5.0)
Private				
Large	2	6	7	7
Small	0	6	5	11
Public				
Very Large	0	0	5	6
Large	1	6	8	4
Small	2	5	3	0
Teachers Colleges	11	18	0	0
Protestant	11	11	9	3
Catholic				
Large	2	3	1	0
Small	3	8	1	0

The quality score varies from 1 to 5. Among the privately endowed schools, the smaller ones have a tendency to rate somewhat higher on our index. In the tax-supported colleges the relation is markedly in the other direction: the larger the institution, the higher the rating. With the exception of about one-third of the Protestant colleges, most of the teachers colleges and denominational schools receive "low" and "medium low" quality ratings.

These three basic dimensions of classification will stay with us for the remainder of the report. They are also related to most of the information discussed earlier; many characteristics of teachers vary greatly as we compare different groups of colleges. A summary of some of these relations will give more vivid meaning to our classification of schools and will also help in interpreting our subsequent findings.

The Role of Size

THREE of the characteristics of individual social scientists which we introduced earlier are associated with the size of the college in which they teach. These are their productivity, their social background, and their vote. The data are presented in Figure 1-10.

Size alone does not explain these variations; only after having introduced further dimensions of classification can we acquire real understanding. Even so, the trends are not without substantive interest. We have already guessed at the average tendency of more distinguished professors to teach in larger schools; this is now corroborated in the top part of Figure 1-10. The trend in the figures for socio-economic background is less strong, but it reinforces an earlier finding. If, for various reasons, the sons and daughters of more privileged families have a better chance for success, and if teaching at a larger school is considered more desirable, then we should find, as we do, a larger proportion of teachers with higher socio-economic background in the larger schools. The voting data we shall leave undiscussed at this moment. They will acquire considerable significance in a subsequent context. In quite a number of respects size made no difference even on this merely descriptive level: the average age, the frequency of movement from one campus to another, and what we have called the occupational inferiority feelings were the same in all size classes.

We can provide a rough idea of the atmosphere in which our respondents worked by presenting their opinions on three matters: the working conditions (teaching burdens, salaries, etc.) in their schools, the relations among faculty members, and the relations between the faculty and administration. They were asked in each case to appraise the situation at their own school in the light of "what you know about other institutions." Answers were obtained by using a predetermined checklist. Figure 1-11 reproduces the wording of this list and gives the over-all statistical results.

By and large, the feelings are not gloomy, especially in regard to the sentiments which the faculty members seem to have for each other. Eighty-four per cent of the respondents consider these

Figure 1-10
Certain Characteristics of Social Scientists Vary with the Size of Their College

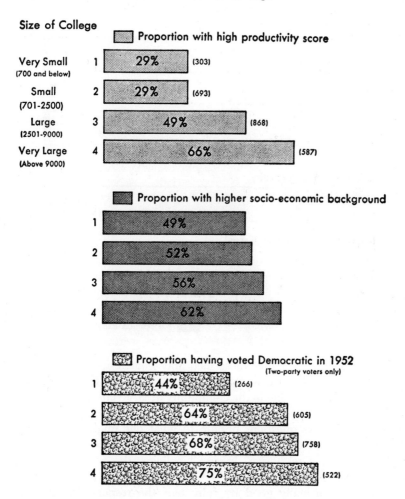

Size of College

Proportion with high productivity score

Very Small (700 and below)	1	29% (303)
Small (701-2500)	2	29% (693)
Large (2501-9000)	3	49% (868)
Very Large (Above 9000)	4	66% (587)

Proportion with higher socio-economic background

1	49%
2	52%
3	56%
4	62%

Proportion having voted Democratic in 1952 (Two-party voters only)

1	44% (266)
2	64% (605)
3	68% (758)
4	75% (522)

relations either good or unusually good. Even the attitude toward the administration is obviously not hostile. Working conditions were most likely to provoke some dissatisfaction: 29 per cent described them as fair at best, and only 17 per cent considered them unusu-

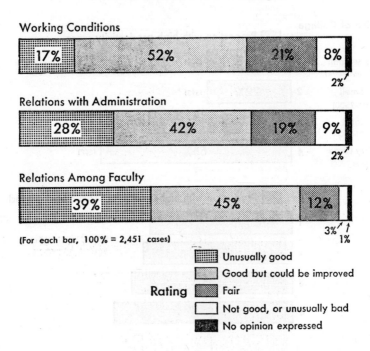

Figure 1-11
Answers Regarding Working Conditions and
Personal Relations at the Colleges

Working Conditions

| 17% | 52% | 21% | 8% |

2%

Relations with Administration

| 28% | 42% | 19% | 9% |

2%

Relations Among Faculty

| 39% | 45% | 12% |

3%   1%

(For each bar, 100% = 2,451 cases)

Rating

- Unusually good
- Good but could be improved
- Fair
- Not good, or unusually bad
- No opinion expressed

ally good. (The fact that these men and women are by no means always of a mind to complain puts the pessimism they exhibited regarding their prestige in the community at large into even stronger relief.)

Two of these questions pertain to what one might call human relations within the college community, and these show an interesting variation with size. In small colleges the relations among faculty members and between faculty members and administration are called unusually good by fully half the respondents. As the size of the college increases, the proportion of teachers who give their college this top rating declines, especially with regard to relations with the administration.

Figures 1-10 and 1-12 provide an interesting contrast. The

Figure 1-12
Unusually Good On-Campus Social Relations Are Most Frequently Reported at the Smaller Colleges

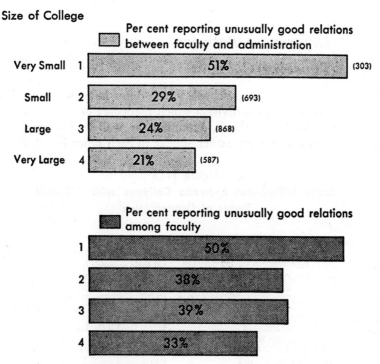

Size of College

Per cent reporting unusually good relations between faculty and administration

Very Small	1	51% (303)
Small	2	29% (693)
Large	3	24% (868)
Very Large	4	21% (587)

Per cent reporting unusually good relations among faculty

1	50%
2	38%
3	39%
4	33%

former shows that the larger colleges can be more selective in the composition of their faculties. Yet we now see that at the same time there is less feeling of satisfaction with interpersonal relations on these campuses.[17] This might in part explain why no uniformity can be found in the appraisal of working conditions; it is about the same in schools of all size classes. This is a somewhat surprising result, because the salaries at the large institutions are certainly higher; their research facilities are probably better and their teaching burdens lighter. What intervenes could be the ex-

17. For a general discussion of the decrease in intimacy characteristically found as groups increase in size, see K. H. Wolff, ed., *The Sociology of Georg Simmel* (Glencoe, Ill.: The Free Press, 1950), Part Two.

pectations of the teachers. In the small colleges there are likely
to be some who prefer a less hectic life; the larger colleges may
not always have satisfied the high hopes with which their appointees
came.

Differences Between
Types of Colleges

AS ONE COMPARES schools which differ in type of organization, one is struck by a division which reappears in many tables.[18]
The denominational schools, Protestant as well as Catholic, and
the teachers colleges are rather similar to each other but different

Figure 1-13
Some Differences Between Colleges with Different
Types of Organization

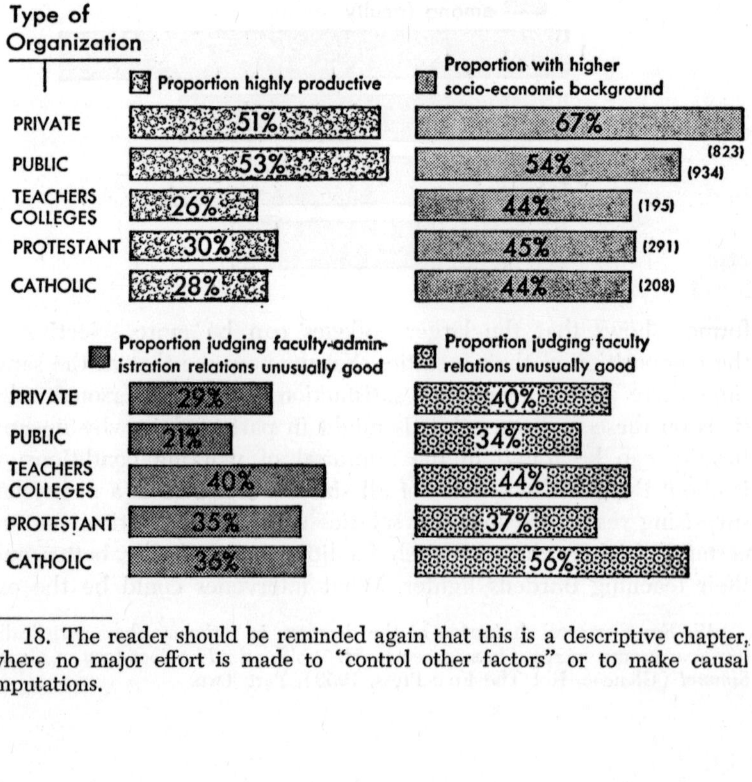

Type of
Organization

	Proportion highly productive	Proportion with higher socio-economic background	
PRIVATE	51%	67%	
PUBLIC	53%	54%	(823) (934)
TEACHERS COLLEGES	26%	44%	(195)
PROTESTANT	30%	45%	(291)
CATHOLIC	28%	44%	(208)

	Proportion judging faculty-administration relations unusually good	Proportion judging faculty relations unusually good
PRIVATE	29%	40%
PUBLIC	21%	34%
TEACHERS COLLEGES	40%	44%
PROTESTANT	35%	37%
CATHOLIC	36%	56%

18. The reader should be reminded again that this is a descriptive chapter,
where no major effort is made to "control other factors" or to make causal
imputations.

from the privately endowed and tax-supported institutions. Figure 1-13 provides some typical examples.

In the upper half of the Figure, the proportion of professors with high productivity and higher socio-economic family background is reported: the private and public schools show proportions well ahead of the remaining three groups. The last two parts of the Figure deal with social relations within the college community: teachers in the Catholic, Protestant, and teachers colleges consider themselves better off than the others do; they are clearly more at ease with their administrative superiors, and on the average also more close to each other. Such results suggest the existence of a common quality which would, if not explain, at least summarize the meaning of the differences. One is reminded of a distinction which anthropologists and sociologists often make when they compare social units. They talk about the traditional ways of life that are found in rural communities or in societies not yet invaded by industrialization. They stress certain characteristics shared by these traditional social organisms: close social ties, belief in authority, distrust of change. In societies at the opposite extreme one finds more division of labor, greater emphasis on personal success and achievement, and on intellectual values. These distinctions are relevant to our present problem. It seems appropriate to describe denominational schools as being more or less tradition-minded. And it is not too surprising to find that teachers colleges belong to this traditional group; after all, their central task is not to carry out research along the frontiers of knowledge, but instead to train their students to transmit the cultural heritage.[19] It is more difficult to find a good descriptive term for the other group. We say that the tax-supported and privately endowed colleges—especially the larger ones—show more secular tendencies. In using this term, however, we are aware of an inconsistency: in the narrow sense of not being affiliated with religious groups, practically all teachers colleges are, of course, also secular. But we shall use the term in a somewhat broader sense. Then the distinction between relatively traditional and relatively secular colleges seems well justified by results like those in Figure 1-13.[20]

19. See Footnote 13, page 19, of this chapter.
20. A more complete analysis shows that sometimes the small state universities (those with a student body of less than 2,500) are more similar to

Earlier in this chapter we suggested that the voting behavior
of social science teachers can take on symbolic significance, indicating a broader attitude. This possibility finds corroboration in
a different context when we compare the voting record of respondents in different types of schools.

Figure 1-14
**Variations in the Voting Record of Professors from Different Types
of Colleges (Two-Party Voters Only)**

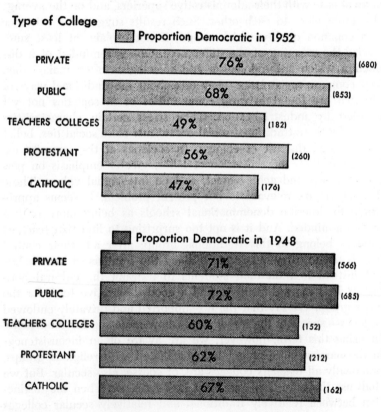

the traditional schools than to the rest of the tax-supported institutions. However, this group is very small. It therefore seems justifiable to neglect them
when it comes to broader generalizations and to characterize the public colleges by the large majority of their type. Occasionally, however, we shall return to this point.

The 1952 vote discloses the same grouping that was just discussed. Given the image which the two candidates presented in the 1952 campaign, it is not farfetched to say that Eisenhower stressed more traditional and Stevenson more secular values. This interpretation finds further support in the 1948 figures; in that campaign the candidates did not differ so much with regard to the traditional-secular values they represented, and the voting figures in our five groups of schools were roughly similar. There are, however, two changes which deserve attention. The sharpest decrease in Democratic votes occurred among professors in Catholic schools; this parallels what happened in 1952 in the country at large. The increase of Democratic votes in the private colleges is more simply explained: in 1948 there were eighty-one Wallace voters in our sample, most of them found in this group of schools; in 1952 a majority of these men returned to the Democratic fold.[21]

The Quality Rating
of the Colleges

MANY OF OUR MAJOR RESULTS will be related to differences in quality between schools. In order that the reader may have confidence in this classification, an anticipated objection must be met. Several items in our index, such as those dealing with the college budget and library, pertain to the resources of the institution.[22] How do we know that a school with greater resources actually renders better educational services—even if we accept a rather vague meaning of the notion of quality? It would be easy to find in our sample a few instances in which a college with small resources has high scholastic standards while another much better endowed institution is, by common consent, a degree mill. The question is whether, apart from such exceptions, our quality index reflects educational and academic distinction beyond mere resources.

Fortunately, we can give an affirmative answer by drawing on some of the material from our own survey. One crucial test is whether the colleges with a high objective quality rating turn

21. Thirteen of them, however, voted for Eisenhower.
22. The term "socio-academic rating" was suggested by David Riesman.

out to have a higher proportion of productive professors. This is
indeed the case. Figure 1-15 classifies colleges into four quality
groups just as Table 1-9 did. Within each group the professors
themselves are divided into four groups ranging from those who
have a high productivity score of 4 to those who have a low one
of 1 or 0.

Figure 1-15
**The Higher the Quality Rating of a College, the Greater the
Proportion of Highly Productive Social Scientists on its Faculty**

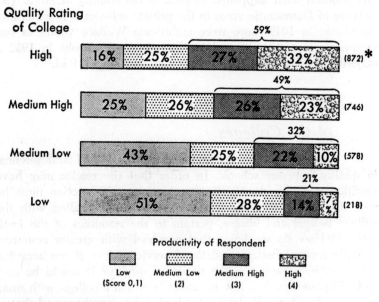

Quality Rating
of College

High — 16% | 25% | 27% | 32% — 59% (872)*

Medium High — 25% | 26% | 26% | 23% — 49% (746)

Medium Low — 43% | 25% | 22% | 10% — 32% (578)

Low — 51% | 28% | 14% | 7% — 21% (218)

Productivity of Respondent

| Low (Score 0,1) | Medium Low (2) | Medium High (3) | High (4) |

* See Footnote to Figure 1-3.

The proportion of scholars who are at least moderately productive is 59 per cent in the best schools and only 21 per cent in the
least distinguished institutions.[23] However, the relation between
the quality of a school and the quality of its social scientists is

---

23. Incidentally, it is interesting that even in the low quality schools 7 per
cent of the teachers are highly productive. In the most distinguished schools
16 per cent have published very little, but they usually turn out to be very
young teachers.

even stronger than Figure 1-15 indicates. If we divide the schools into more detailed quality groups, we find that in the colleges with a rating of 4.5 or higher, 61 per cent of the professors are productive, while this is true of only 15 per cent if the quality rating of the school is less than 1.5. We would point out that there is no overlapping of the data which goes into the quality index of the college and the information used to establish the productivity index of our respondents. The college rating covers, for instance, the number of books in the library, while the measure of individual productivity uses the books written by our respondents. Hence Figure 1-15 provides a true corroboration.

If better schools have a better faculty, then this should make social contact with one's colleagues more attractive. Some information on this point is available; one of the questionnaire items asked:

Are the people you see the most of socially mainly from your department, from the faculty generally, or from the community?

In the sample as a whole, 62 per cent said that their main social contacts are confined to the university. This answer was probably affected by the size of the college, but it is difficult to predict just how. It could be that the availability of a larger faculty makes it more likely that friendships form within the college. On the other hand, larger colleges are often in or near larger communities, which would make more off-campus people available for social contacts. Therefore, in Figure 1-16, we have tabulated answers to this question simultaneously for schools of varying size and varying quality.

Among colleges of the same size, we find that as the quality of a school increases, there is a clear-cut tendency for its social scientists to center their social life around their colleagues.[24]

---

24. From time to time the reader should be reminded of the difference between two types of Figures. In Figure 1-15 we dealt with two factors: quality of school and productivity of professors. The entries within each bar reveal essentially the number of respondents who are characterized by each combination of the two variables. Consequently per cent figures add up to 100 in each bar. In Figure 1-16, and also in charts like Figure 1-17, we deal with three variables. In Figure 1-16 these are quality, size of school, and the social habits of the respondents. In each bar we learn the proportion of respondents who have in-school contacts for each type of school. No per cents add up to 100

Figure 1-16
The More Distinguished the College, the Higher the Proportion of Social Scientists Who Have Their Main Social Contacts within the Faculty

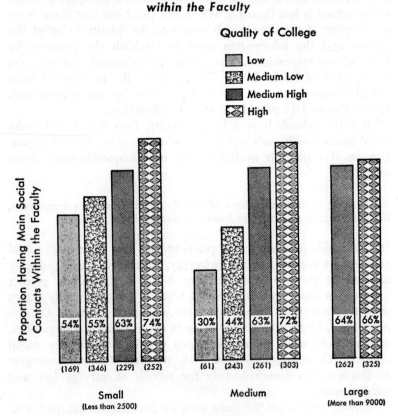

Quality of College

- ▨ Low
- ▩ Medium Low
- ▦ Medium High
- ▧ High

Proportion Having Main Social Contacts Within the Faculty

Small (Less than 2500)				Medium				Large (More than 9000)	
54%	55%	63%	74%	30%	44%	63%	72%	64%	66%
(169)	(346)	(229)	(252)	(61)	(243)	(261)	(303)	(262)	(325)

Size of College

Usually, quality differences between colleges have the same meaning in all types of schools. But this is not always the case. An example of a more complex relation is provided by the average length of time a social scientist teaches in an institution. A fairly

in this more complex type of table. For each bar, however, one could reach a total of 100 per cent if one were to include the professors who have most of their contacts off the campus. This would be, for instance, 26 per cent in the small colleges of highest quality.

competent professor, if he is not removed after a very few years, can usually stay at a college as long as he likes, or until a more lucrative offer draws him elsewhere. Length of teaching can

Figure 1-17
Average Length of Teaching Reported by Our Respondents in Various Types of Colleges

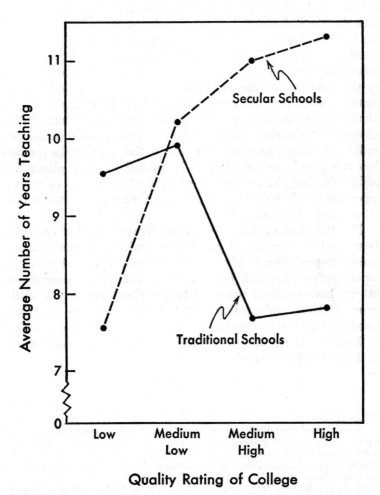

	Low		Medium Low		Medium High		High	
Secular schools	7.6	(53)	10.2	(273)	11.0	(586)	11.3	(845)
Traditional schools	9.6	(177)	9.9	(316)	7.7	(166)	7.8	(35)

therefore be taken as a reasonable indicator of satisfaction, and we would expect it to be higher in the more distinguished colleges. But again, Figure 1-17 shows that this is true only for the secular institutions.

In the secular group the average length of teaching in the high quality schools is half again as great as in the colleges of low quality. Among traditional institutions, by contrast, the more distinguished schools show a slightly shorter duration of service than their less distinguished sister colleges. With two exceptions the traditional schools of high and medium high quality are Protestant institutions. It is quite possible that in these colleges, various difficulties develop because professors who were attracted originally by the resources of the institution find themselves under cross-pressures when they are expected to conform to its traditions; the administration, in turn, may face a corresponding dilemma.[25] The relatively high average length of service in the less distinguished traditional colleges may in part be due to the fact that the teachers they can afford are not likely to be invited to other places. We might add that the average age in the eight groups of schools appearing in Figure 1-17 is not very different and certainly does not account for the main finding.

The President of the University of Texas remarked once that there are few occupational groups about which so little is known as college professors.[26] About the subspecies of social scientists, our survey provides rich information indeed. In the present context we have confined ourselves to a preliminary picture of the group we have studied. Our next task is to describe what happened to these teachers and their colleges in a postwar era marked on the international scene by a cold war and on the domestic by great concern for internal security.

---

25. We emphasize these schools here because of a special study under way of the thirty-three Protestant schools included in our sample. There the specific denomination and the degree of relative secularization are being investigated in considerable detail. The preliminary findings point in the direction mentioned above.

26. Logan Wilson, *The Academic Man* (New York: Oxford University Press, 1942).

Chapter **II**

THE DIFFICULT YEARS

THE DECADE following the end of the Second World War in 1945 was a period of unusual stress for American colleges and universities. Suspicion and attack were directed at many institutions during these years. Yet there has been considerable disagreement about how widespread these attacks were and about their impact. With this chapter we begin our report on these matters. To provide a backdrop for our central findings on the attitudes and behavior of teachers, we shall first describe some of the pressures felt by American colleges in this period. Necessarily, since this is not our main focus, it must be a sketch rather than a completely developed picture.[1]

The National Academic Scene

HAS THE GENERAL POSITION of American intellectuals and college teachers deteriorated in recent times? Two questions provide an indication of our respondents' over-all impressions on this subject. One of these concerned long-range changes in the status of intellectual activity in our society.

Do you feel that there is a greater threat to intellectual activity in America than there was a generation ago, less of a threat, or don't you see any difference?	Greater threat	63%
	No difference, uncertain	32
	Less of a threat	5
	Total	100%

1. As the reader will observe, the questionnaire items on which this chapter is based were intended only to obtain a rough report of the events of this decade, rather than a detailed and comprehensive account. Still, the material collected from our respondents offers unique leads as to what happened in many kinds of American colleges (although historians of the post-war academic scene will want to obtain additional evidence from other sources).

About a third of the teachers see no noticeable change from the past in the present situation, and a small group of 5 per cent see an improvement. Nevertheless, a clear majority of present-day social science teachers believe that the position of the intellectual is in greater danger than it was a generation ago.

The second question about general trends dealt with a shorter time span and a different aspect of the matter. During the postwar period, according to many observers, there was a widespread growth of concern among the general public regarding the political opinions of college teachers. The results of our second question show that four-fifths of our respondents concur in this observation.

Is it your impression that there is greater concern these days than 6 or 7 years ago on the part of the public and groups outside the college over teachers' political opinions and what political matters are taught in the classroom, or not?	Greater concern	79%
	Undecided	3
	No greater concern	18
	Total	100%

It would be easy to conclude that teachers who noticed a greater public concern over their own politics or those of fellow teachers would consider the development a harmful one. But when we asked teachers about this, they were by no means in unanimous agreement:

(If teacher sees greater public concern:) In general, do you feel this greater concern has caused any harmful effects on the climate of freedom in the country or do you think this charge of harmful effects has been overdone?

	PERCENTAGE	
	Of total sample	Of those noticing greater concern
Harmful effects	52%	66%
Undecided	6	8
Charge overdone	21	26
Total	79%	100%

We can look at the answers to this question in two ways. In terms of the total sample of 2,451 respondents, just over half (52 per cent) see the public concern with teachers' politics as having harmful effects. Or if we consider only those who have noticed greater public interest, a two-thirds majority believes it has been damaging. However, a substantial minority do not agree. A segment of the teachers, in fact, when asked to explain their views in a follow-up question, felt that the public attention has been beneficial to colleges. Some pointed to the elimination of Communists or other radical groups they considered dangerous and applauded this consequence. Others found that, as a result of the criticism, teachers have been led to think their own personal positions through more carefully and responsibly. And some added that a public which has marched on a college, determined to root out subversion, may depart instead with a new respect for the integrity and ability of its teachers. Perhaps more surprisingly, there was also a sizeable segment (8 per cent) who saw as the benefit a new recognition of potential dangers to civil liberties and academic freedom.

The majority of our respondents take another view, however. Broadly speaking, from either the long- or short-range point of view, American social scientists felt in the spring of 1955 that the intellectual and political freedom of the teaching community had been noticeably curtailed, or at least disturbingly threatened.

This conclusion provides little clue, though, to the spread of this threat within the academic world. Were all colleges affected, or only relatively few? How many of our 2,451 teachers had observed the impact of new pressures on their own school administrations, on their colleagues, and on themselves?

Outside Pressures on the School Administration

USING OUR RESPONDENTS as a large corps of on-the-spot reporters, we can obtain a more detailed picture of the total scene.

A considerable share of the pressures directed at a college will be borne by the school administration. We did not conduct interviews with these officials, so we cannot explore in any detail their role as intermediaries between faculty and community or their attitudes and opinions on matters of academic freedom. But it did not seem unrealistic to ask teachers a few general questions about their administrations, if provision was made for those who felt unqualified to answer.[2]

We wanted to know whether the generally noted increase in public attention to colleges and universities had appeared at the respondent's own school. In particular, had the difficult years brought increasing pressures on his administration, perhaps to drop dangerous courses, or to fire controversial teachers and hire safe ones? Again using the six or seven year time span as the period for comparison we asked four questions that took this form:

Is it your impression that the administration of this college is under more pressure to avoid controversy from trustees than it was 6 or 7 years ago, less pressure, or that there hasn't been much change?[3]

Identically worded questions were asked about pressure from "alumni," "the community right here," and "the legislature or local politicians."[4]

In each case, just over half of the respondents see no new

2. Throughout this chapter we shall make use of interview questions which asked respondents to describe and evaluate aspects of the situation on their campuses rather than their own experiences and feelings. For a general discussion of this type of data, see Appendix 5.

3. The reader will find that a number of other questions in our interview asked about changes in the past "6 or 7 years." Putting questions in these terms implied two decisions. For example, here we could have asked our informants directly how much pressure their administration appeared to be under at the time of the interview. But this might have made the question more difficult to answer; on many matters it is easier to compare two time periods than to make a categorical judgment on the situation of the moment. Furthermore, we were mainly interested in finding out whether teachers had observed changes in their schools during recent years. For these comparisons we chose, after considerable experimentation, the period "6 or 7 years ago." (If a teacher had not yet taught for six or seven years, the interviewer asked him to give, nevertheless, his general impression.) This referred approximately to the time when the concern with national security had begun to be acute. A comparison with the pre-war period might have put the contemporary difficulties into even sharper relief, but to many respondents the longer-range comparison would have been psychologically difficult.

4. Clearly we might have drawn up a more extensive and specific list of pressure sources. We could have separated the legislature from local politicians, and spelled out some of the elements which make up the community, such as patriotic groups, religious groups, and newspapers. But while we wished to differentiate to some degree between the various sources of pressure, such detailed questions might have been difficult for many respondents to answer responsibly. As it was, between 20 per cent and 29 per cent felt unqualified to express an impression concerning the four sources we used.

Figure 2-1
Observed Changes in Pressure Compared
to Six or Seven Years Earlier

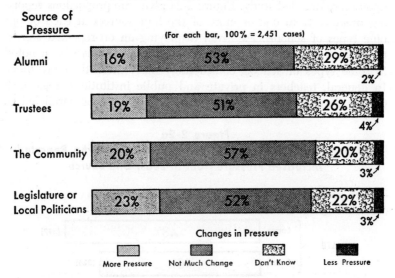

Source of Pressure

(For each bar, 100% = 2,451 cases)

Alumni	16%	53%	29%	2%
Trustees	19%	51%	26%	4%
The Community	20%	57%	20%	3%
Legislature or Local Politicians	23%	52%	22%	3%

Changes in Pressure

More Pressure   Not Much Change   Don't Know   Less Pressure

pressures. Among those who notice a change, it is almost invariably in the direction of increased rather than decreased pressure. Almost five times as many respondents notice more pressure from trustees than report less; the ratio is even higher for the three other sources.[5]

These answers reinforce our earlier impression that approximately half of American social science teachers detected a decline in intellectual and academic freedom. For if we count the teachers who detect a noticeable increase in pressure from *at least one* source, the resulting figure is 40 per cent. This means that approximately half of the 70 per cent to 80 per cent of our sample who have formed any kind of definite impression about pressures on their school administration say that they increased in the last six or seven years.

5. All through the report there will appear a small number of teachers who do not share the prevailing "pessimism." Their answers may reflect such things as a change of administration, an incident which led to countertendencies among the faculty, or a feeling that the situation had noticeably improved in the few months just before the interviews in May, 1955.

Figure 2-1 might seem to reflect a rather stereotyped set of responses, since the pattern of answers for each of the questions is quite similar. But a number of clear-cut distinctions appear upon more detailed study. Figure 2-2a gives the proportions reporting pressure from one or more of the four sources at each of our nine types of schools. Far from displaying an oft-repeated stereotype, these summary figures show that pressures have been noted in some types of schools considerably more often than in others. In general, teachers in private and public institutions, regardless of size, have observed an increase in pressures not paralleled in

Figure 2-2a
Percentages at the Different Types of Colleges who Reported Increased Pressure from at Least One Source

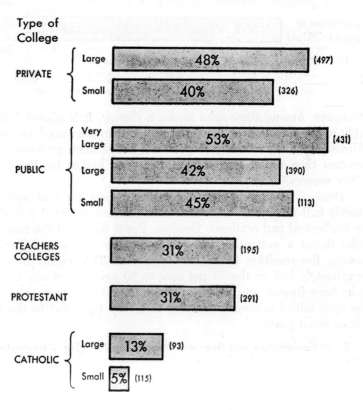

any of the traditional institutions. In the case of the Catholic schools, in fact, little if any change is noticed. Also, in each case where comparison is possible (that is, within the private, the public, and the Catholic schools) it is always the larger institutions which report the greater increase of pressures.

Furthermore, as Figure 2-2b makes clear, trouble does not always come from the same source. Teachers at the large private schools described increased pressures from three of the four sources —alumni, community, and politicians—in about equal degree. The trustees at these institutions, however, appear to have held back somewhat from the general impulse to question and scrutinize. Much the same can be said of the smaller private schools. In addition, these are the only colleges whose teachers felt that alumni had taken the lead in urging a new pattern of conformity on their schools. It seems likely that the alumni of private colleges are better organized than those of other types of institutions. And the growth of their financial contributions in recent years also undoubtedly brings them increased influence. The alumni of private schools, indeed, may feel entitled to a share of the regulatory power exercised by the state legislature over public schools and by organized religion over denominational schools.

At the public schools, including the teachers colleges, the patterning of pressures is different. Here it is the politicians who were most widely described as exerting new pressures. During this period, a number of state legislatures created special committees to inspect the loyalty and fitness of faculties at tax-supported institutions, and others debated or passed new special loyalty oaths for these teachers. The public schools reported pressures from the regents and from the community in which they are located less often. In each of the four groups, the alumni exerted less pressure than the other three sources.

At the Protestant schools, rather surprisingly, it was the outside community which seemed most interested in urging conformity on the schools. For the most part these are small institutions which depend largely on the members of their denomination in nearby communities for sufficient enrollment to keep the school going. During the post-war decade it was often a conservative or religious parent, rather than an organized group of alumni, who

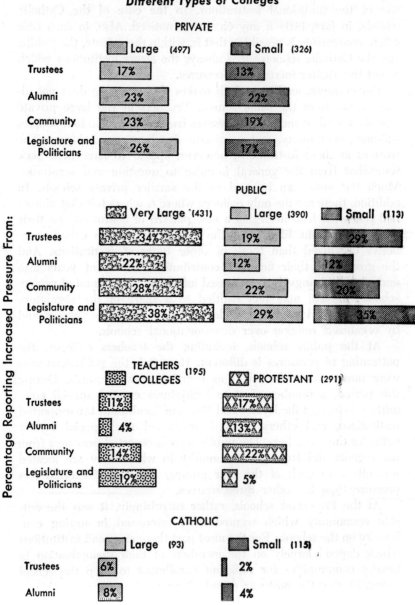

Figure 2-2b
Details on Pressures upon the Administration at Different Types of Colleges

Percentage Reporting Increased Pressure From:

PRIVATE

Large (497)   Small (326)

	Large	Small
Trustees	17%	13%
Alumni	23%	22%
Community	23%	19%
Legislature and Politicians	26%	17%

PUBLIC

Very Large (431)   Large (390)   Small (113)

	Very Large	Large	Small
Trustees	34%	19%	29%
Alumni	22%	12%	12%
Community	28%	22%	20%
Legislature and Politicians	38%	29%	35%

TEACHERS COLLEGES (195)   **PROTESTANT** (291)

	Teachers Colleges	Protestant
Trustees	11%	17%
Alumni	4%	13%
Community	14%	22%
Legislature and Politicians	19%	5%

CATHOLIC

Large (93)   Small (115)

	Large	Small
Trustees	6%	2%
Alumni	8%	4%
Community	4%	2%
Legislature and Politicians	0%	0%

set out to make sure that his child was not exposed to unwanted ideas; local newspapers, churches, and fraternal groups also sometimes kept an eye on these institutions.

Incidents on the Campus

WE HAVE DESCRIBED a widespread impression among social scientists that the post-war decade brought increased pressures on the administration at many of our schools. To what extent was this accompanied by pressures experienced directly by teachers themselves?[7] We inquired into this matter much more extensively. In a series of questions spread through the interview, each respondent was requested to describe in detail any episodes in which either he himself or his colleagues at school had been subjected to accusation and attack. Two of these inquiries were phrased very broadly, so that any experience of this kind might provide an appropriate answer. We asked in one about instances in the past few years in which the respondent felt his own academic freedom had "been threatened in any way"; the other dealt, in parallel language, with similar experiences among his colleagues. A second very broad pair of questions asked directly for instances of campus "civil liberties cases" or "problems," and of "local events that had stirred up strong feelings" in recent years. These questions were all designed not to limit in any way the kind of complaint or charge which could be described. A further pair of items was somewhat more specific. Could the respondents recall any occasion at their school when an individual who was of superior ability but "unconventional" had been bypassed for permanent appointment in favor of another of lower professional merit, and, in a different vein, had there been instances in which they themselves "were being watched in a classroom"? Two more questions referred to politics. Had teachers been "reported unfavorably to higher authorities" for their views on a political subject, and had they encountered "pressures to conform" to the prevailing local political patterns?

---

7. Pressures can of course take many forms. A teacher might experience "an unfriendly atmosphere in the country at large" as a source of pressure on himself. Our description here, however, will be limited to more direct and concrete manifestations of pressure on professors.

Finally, in order to study one problem area more closely, we inserted a question which asked specifically whether anyone on the faculty had been accused "of being subversive or of engaging in any un-American activities." This item, with its considerably more limited focus, will be treated somewhat differently in our discussion.[8]

In answering each of these questions, the respondents were requested to describe as many separate episodes as came to mind. Often in replying to the later questions they added details about events described in earlier replies. Every effort was made, by asking questions from widely varied points of view, and by providing repeated opportunities for further examples and additional details, to obtain the respondent's full store of information about campus incidents.[9]

For each school we collated the answers given to these questions by all the teachers interviewed, and reconstructed a composite account of the various incidents at the school. This means that at larger schools the observations and recollections of as many as sixty respondents were pooled to form an over-all picture of campus events. Of course, individual incidents were often described by more than one professor; a Congressional investigation accompanied by specific accusations against a faculty member might well be discussed by every teacher in our sample at a college. Frequently, also, we have the evidence of central participants, and can learn about their reactions to an incident first hand.

We should be clear about the word "incident." We use it in a broadly inclusive, but definite, sense: it describes an episode, long or short, in which an attack, accusation, or criticism was made against a teacher, a group of teachers, or a school as a whole. This means that in the report of an incident an *overt act*, the making of a charge or criticism, was described. This act might be a listing of the names of supposedly "pink" professors in the gossip

---

8. The exact wording of questions can be found in Appendix 2. The questions described here, in order of their appearance in the schedule, are numbers 2, 11, 13, 20, 28, 29, 31, 35, and 44.

9. Nevertheless, it remains true, particularly on the larger campuses, that, in view of all the other questions we asked, it might be physically impossible in a two- or three-hour interview for a well-informed respondent to recall and describe in detail all the incidents he knew of in which he and his numerous colleagues had been involved.

column of a local newspaper, a student going to a dean with a charge against a teacher, or a teacher reporting that another man had been passed over for promotion because of his politics. (To be on the safe side we have completely excluded all cases where an individual reports *himself* unfairly passed over for promotion.) This means that many descriptions of pressures, no matter how strongly or widely felt among a faculty, are excluded here. Widespread reports at a college of "considerable tension" in the 1952 election between faculty and community would not qualify as an incident unless respondents went on to add, as accounts at one school did, that "Someone strewed garbage all over the lawn of our faculty Democratic committeeman." The incident must directly involve the college or a teacher on its campus. Remarks about teachers in general or colleges in general, and episodes affecting nearby campuses or other outside groups, have been disregarded. Attacks against students, parents, or college employees who do not teach (except administrators, whom we consider to represent the college as a whole) are also omitted. Situations which obviously might develop into incidents, as for instance when a student was known to be reporting regularly on a teacher's classroom comments to a local patriotic group, are included only after an actual charge or criticism ensues.

A single organic episode is considered one incident, regardless of the number of teachers involved and of the complexity of the immediate reverberations.[10] Repeated accusations from the same source have been lumped together. Furthermore, a few teachers in our study reported a number of personally experienced attacks. To count these separately might in some cases double the total number of incidents at a school. We felt that giving so much weight to a local *enfant terrible* would distort the meaning of a school's count, and so established the arbitrary rule that these too were to be combined and counted as one incident only. Finally, since this is a study of American schools after the Second World War, we have excluded from our count all incidents which, according to respondents' reports, occurred before 1945.

---

10. Suppose a Congressional committee charges five teachers at a school with subversive activities. Two are fired at once, and a third suspended from teaching following intervention by the board of trustees. Faculty committees are formed, a fund-raising campaign postponed—and years pass before the entire episode ends. We consider this a single incident.

One further limitation of a different sort should be made clear. Accusations against teachers which were directed to a school administration and disposed of without faculty knowledge, and any other cases which occurred outside the awareness of the teachers who took part in our study, of course cannot appear here.

Altogether, the combined responses to twelve different questions in our interview, answered by 2,451 respondents at the 165 schools in our sample, yield a total of 990 incidents.

These incidents vary widely in a number of respects. They may have been instigated by a Congressional committee, a trustee, a fellow teacher, a student or a student's parent, or a local citizen—by hundreds of letters from an aroused public or by a petulant complaint from an old lady down the street. A teacher may have been charged with past membership in the Communist Party or present "un-Americanism," with misrepresenting the position of the Catholic Church concerning purgatory or endangering the morals of his students by discussing the sociology of prostitution. (The only kind of charge which might be placed against a teacher, without being counted an incident, would be of professional incompetence; this we consider outside the scope of our study.) Furthermore, the history of an incident, once launched, can vary greatly. The letter complaining to the dean may just be mentioned to a professor, or lead to years of conflict and to wholesale firings and resignations.

Before going into these matters, however, we need to discuss further our manner of counting incidents.

The Meaning of
the Incident Counts

THERE CAN BE little doubt that if we had asked even more questions than we did, or if our interviewers had been instructed to probe relentlessly for further examples, the crop of incidents would have been augmented; a shorter set of questions obviously would have produced fewer reports.[11] The total figure

---

11. A more intensive array of questions might also have produced more frequent and more detailed accounts of the incidents which did get reported. For we see in Table 2-3 that 62 per cent of the incidents were described by

we have presented cannot therefore be relied upon *in itself* as providing more than an approximation of the correct over-all picture. Yet we believe that we have missed little of importance for this study. The frequency with which the questions we did ask merely turned up second and third versions of incidents already described, and the mere fact that the entire social science faculty of the smaller colleges and a considerable segment of those at the larger schools contributed to our depiction of incidents, are intrinsic safeguards against gross errors in our results. But even if the final figure were known to be total and exact, it would be of little value, because we have no figures from different periods or other lands with which to compare it.

The total number of incidents found at any one school varied from zero to more than twenty. No incidents were reported in twenty-four colleges, almost all of them among the very smallest in our sample. The largest number of incidents recorded at any one school was twenty-eight. A number of the largest and best-known universities in America are represented in this table; some of them are schools which, judging from the newspapers, seemed under almost constant attack during the post-war years. It may at first seem surprising that none had more than twenty-eight incidents. Yet the reader is asked to remember that many of the headlines from a particular school, appearing sometimes over a period of years, dealt with what is considered here a single incident.

---

only one respondent at a school, while altogether only 11 per cent were mentioned by as many as a quarter of the respondents at a school.

Table 2-3
Less than Half the Incidents Were Reported by More than One Teacher

Incident reported by	Per cent
One respondent, the target of the incident	22%
One respondent, not the target	40
Two respondents	15
More than two, but under 25% of the respondents at a school	12
25% to 49% of the sample	5
50% or more of the sample	6
Total	100% (990 cases)

The authenticity of the incidents reported by only one respondent needs to be questioned, since we have no verification for these from other teachers. We have decided after careful study that there are good reasons for believing that few of these incidents were improvised by teachers; this point is discussed at length in Appendix 5.

Table 2-4
The Total Number of Incidents at a School
Varied from 0 to 28

Number of Incidents	Number of Schools
0	24
1	19
2	20
3-5	33
6-10	43
11-15	10
16-20	9
21-28	7

Although the over-all incident count has no absolute value in itself, the story is different when we begin to make comparisons within our sample. Since every teacher and every school answered

Figure 2-5
On the Average, Secular Schools Had More Incidents than
Traditional, and Large Schools More than Small

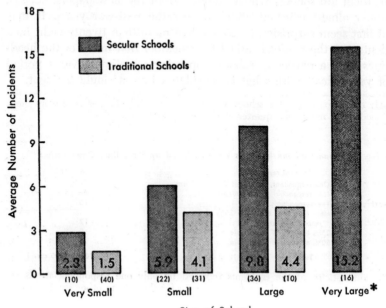

Size of School

* There are no very large traditional schools in the sample.

the same questions, any *differences* we may find are potentially meaningful.

At the secular colleges, the private and public schools, the frequency of incidents is higher than at the traditional. But the secular schools are on the whole larger than the traditional.[12] Their higher count may simply represent the fact that even if teachers who were targets of incidents had been attacked purely at random, the larger faculties would of course be tapped more often. In Figure 2-5 we therefore compare the secular and traditional schools, separated according to size.

In each of the three size groups where comparisons are possible, the secular schools have a larger average number of incidents. And as expected, we note in passing that in both types of schools the frequency of incidents is considerably greater in the larger schools.

The Charge

AT ITS CORE each incident contains some form of complaint —against a teacher, a group of teachers, or an entire school. Since a great many of these complaints take the form of an accusation, we shall call them charges. In the eyes of the instigator of a charge, his target has been guilty of a breach of proper or acceptable behavior. Of course, while one student may go to the dean of a college and report that a teacher's classroom remarks revealed him as a Communist fellow traveller, another student might have said only that the teacher was presenting an objective discussion of Russian political institutions. In short, we deal here with accusations which by no means are necessarily based on fact.

One of the questions about pressures on colleagues, dealing with accusations of subversion and un-Americanism, names a particular type of charge. For the time being we will omit those incidents which came to mind *only* when respondents were asked for instances of these particular charges, and present a comparison of the incidents mentioned spontaneously.[13] The various kinds of charges, and their frequency, are listed in Table 2-6.

12. For detailed figures see Appendix 4.
13. Altogether 192 incidents are therefore omitted in this tabulation.

Table 2-6
A Majority of the Charges Made in Incidents
Involved Political Issues

1. Charges involving political position and ideology		54%
a. Political extremism and disloyalty:		
Communism, subversion, and un-Americanism	29%	
b. Left-of-center political views	13	
c. Middle-of-the-road views	2	
d. Right-of-center views	2	
e. Miscellaneous political charges	8	
2. Specific nonpolitical issues: religion, segregation, economics, and others		19
3. Personal idiosyncrasy, immorality, unconventionality		7
4. Intramural issues: unusual teaching techniques, intellectual rivalries and hostilities, disobedience to authority		5
5. Incidents in which issues are raised but charges seldom made		7
a. Restrictions imposed by authority (gag rules about speakers, limitations on research, etc.)	5	
b. Loyalty oath incidents	2	
6. Information about the charge not given		8
Total	(798 incidents)	100%

While this subject was not the central focus of our study, we doubt that any other investigators have collected comparable information on such a widespread scale. It therefore seems worthwhile to present a more extended description of the material we obtained. Focusing on the charge as the central feature of each incident, we can illustrate the variety of forms which attacks and accusations took during this period.

1a. Extremist politics and disloyalty. In a majority of the incidents the charge was political in nature. This reflects the politization of education in recent years; a few generations ago most attacks against teachers would probably have been over evolution, religious issues, and other matters of contemporary controversy.

Among the political incidents, as one would expect, the major issue was that of Communism or related forms of extremist politics. A further breakdown of the charges in this group proves revealing. The figures are found in Table 2-7.

Table 2-7
Further Details on Charges of Political Extremism and Disloyalty

	Per Cent of Total Incidents	Per Cent of Extremism Incidents
Communist Party membership		
Target of charge took the 5th Amendment or otherwise refused to cooperate in investigation	3%	10%
Other charges of Communist Party membership	2	6
Communist sympathy	8	28
"Communism" (not further specified)	7	23
Subversion and un-Americanism	9	33
	(100% = 798 incidents)	(100% = 234 incidents)

During the post-war years the college incidents which most frequently made newspaper headlines were those in which professors were charged with Communist Party affiliations.[14] The general interest this reflected in these episodes is also mirrored in our data: the cases which draw the most widespread comment in our interviews are those in which a teacher has been charged with Communist Party membership, particularly when he has for any reason refused to testify under oath. Since these cases are well known, a brief summary of one will be a sufficient reminder.[15] In an incident at a large state university several months before the time of our interviews, three teachers were called before a legislative committee investigating un-Americanism and queried about past affiliations with the Communist Party. Two invoked the Fifth Amendment. One also refused to testify in private before a faculty committee set up to review the case and recommend administrative action. He was fired, with the approval of the great majority of colleague respondents. The second teacher admitted to the university group that he had belonged to the Party many years before, but said that he had long since resigned, specifically renouncing

14. In discussing these incidents, we shall make use of the additional information obtained in the special question about accusations of subversion and un-Americanism; it supplies useful details about incidents discussed elsewhere in questionnaires.

15. Many such episodes are reported in detail in Robert MacIver, *Academic Freedom in our Time* (New York: Columbia University Press, 1955); Russell Kirk, *A Program for Conservatives* (Chicago: H. Regnery, 1954); and George R. Stewart, *The Year of the Oath* (Garden City: Doubleday, 1950).

its program of overthrowing the government. The faculty committee recommended that he be retained. But he too was dismissed
—a pattern of administration rejection of faculty recommendations
followed in a number of other cases. The third professor testified
fully before the government committee, admitting his past membership and also talking freely in a long session with F.B.I. agents.
Suspended at first by the administration, he was finally reinstated,
but colleagues in his department felt that his chances for promotion
in the foreseeable future looked dim. It should be added that every
one of the very large sample of respondents at this university discussed this incident in some detail. A number were deeply per-
turbed by the handling of the affair by the administration; the
feeling is widespread that the faculty is vulnerable for lack of
administration support and understanding.

A frequent feature of these cases, even of those in which a
teacher invoked the Fifth Amendment, was the opinion of our
respondents that the teacher had not allowed his extremist or
leftist political orientation to color his classroom teaching; many
respondents who conceded their personal antipathy for the man
involved reported that they had found no evidence of unprofessional teaching practices. Of course many of the attacked teachers
taught in fields in which political bias would be difficult to bring
into the classroom, like physics, biology, or pharmacy. At one
Southern university, a botanist stated under questioning that he
had at one time been a member of the Communist Party. A questionnaire was circulated by the administration among all of his
students, asking if he had ever expressed his views in his teaching.
Not one reported that he had. Nevertheless, he was fired.

No matter how early the membership, how soon the renuncia-
tion, and how long-standing the public confession, teachers could
still be fired during these troubled years. In one case at an Eastern
privately endowed university, a professor had joined and then
renounced the Party while still a college student, and publicly
declared these facts intermittently ever since. Called to Washington in the early 1950's to testify before a Senate committee, he
invoked the Fifth Amendment when asked to name former associates. Although he was considered one of the best teachers in the
school, had taken a formal oath before university officials that
he was not now a Communist, and had been granted tenure, he

was discharged for "intellectual arrogance before a Congressional committee."

In a few cases it is possible to follow the path of a much-accused teacher who had by coincidence taught at two or more of the schools in our sample. One man charged with membership in the Young Communist League as a student was fired when he refused to cooperate with ex-F.B.I. men hired by the university to investigate charges of widespread subversion in the faculty. Employed later at another sample school nearby, he got into trouble again when the old charges received a fresh spate of publicity. Although not formally accused this time, he became a target for community recrimination: "Neighborhood children were told it was all right to throw stones at his children and call him a Commie." He eventually moved again, accepting a teaching position some distance away.

Sometimes, by contrast, incidents revolving about the issue of Communist Party membership received no official or public airing. At a large Midwestern school a young teacher up for reappointment privately informed department officials that he was a member of the party; his contract was quietly not renewed, and he departed with so little fanfare that few teachers in the school knew of the incident. Occasionally, in fact, a teacher who had been called a card-carrying Communist was unaware that the incident had occurred. In one case, the school authorities, having found on investigation that the charge was false and its instigator simply a crank, did not bother to tell the intended target about it, and the incident was reported only by a colleague who heard of it from other sources.

It seems appropriate to separate the cases where Communist Party membership is at issue from another group in which some form of Communist sympathy is charged. These include allegations of such things as "favoring a pro-Russian policy," "publishing an article which was pro-Communist," "having Red views," "voting the Communist ticket," "following the Party line," and "being a fellow traveller." In a few instances these incidents, too, created considerable stir on a campus. At one Southern school, an incident was of sufficient note to be reported by a majority of the respondents. A teacher wrote and presented on campus a play which sympathetically explored the thoughts of a conscientious objector. An aroused faculty member declared that the play followed the Communist line. Local American Legion officials joined in, calling it "un-American" or "pro-Communist" (reports differ on the exact word used), and requesting the president of the school to make a statement in which the play would be denounced and suppressed. When none was forthcoming, they repeated the request, again with no result. Interestingly enough, some respondents felt that by his failure to act, the president had backed up the playwright, but others decided he had not taken a firm enough stand in favor of the author's right to his opinions.

Most incidents in which the issue of Communist sympathy was raised attracted less attention. At a large Midwestern school, for example, only one respondent recalled an instance in which colleagues who had put out a new translation of the Bible had been called "Communist-inspired."

Incidents have occurred in which teachers were criticized for such things as inviting a group of touring Russian student editors to visit their campus or their classroom. Underlying the criticism would seem to be the implicit idea that by inviting proponents of a Communist way of life onto the campus, such teachers are symbolically expressing at least slight "sympathy" for Communists in the mere act of extending to them the use of college facilities. A small number of cases like this have therefore been included among these incidents.

Additional observations on charges of extremism. The cases in which there was at least some specification of the nature of Communist association or belief comprised less than half of those in which the issue of Communism was raised. In the remainder all we are told is that the individual had been called "Communist" or "a Communist." There is in fact no way of knowing whether the charge should be presented here as "Communism" or "communism" —as adherence to the Communist Party or to the intellectual philosophy. In such cases we shall arbitrarily use only the capitalized form of the word.

In some cases, of course, it is quite possible that if more complete information were available, we would find that the charge had indeed been more specific. But in others, it seems likely that "Communism" was actually the complete charge made. Often such an incident was described in considerable detail, sometimes by several teachers at a school, and still the charge was never further specified. Such cases illustrate an interesting general point. "Communism" is often associated with a wide variety of thoughts and acts which in themselves have no apparent immediate link to membership in the Communist Party or participation in the Communist movement, and no attempt was made by the accuser to establish such a link. The following are all the complete descriptions provided by teachers (or rather, the best single description) of a number of incidents of this nature.[16]

Sometimes the charges of "Communism" seem actually to be the accuser's way of saying he believes the teacher is more politically to the left than he and is therefore untrustworthy.

Dr. K., of our school of education, was appointed a member of a committee to draw up recommendations for the social studies curriculum in the state public schools. He helped to draft recommendations which included encouragement of discussion of controversial issues, such as United Nations activity, foreign relations of the United States, civil liberties, propaganda, censorship of the mass media, etc. For this he was accused by local professional patriots and some reactionaries of being a Communist.

One woman who lives nearby came on campus with an Eisenhower petition for faculty members to sign. A man with a Russian name refused to sign. So she denounced him as being a Communist.

Occasional comments indicated that underlying such an incident may be the belief that college teachers as a whole are politically untrustworthy. As a teacher at a small school on the West Coast commented, "There are groups of people who feel that college professors *per se* are un-American; in fact it has been levelled against me—I've been called a Communist." The remark of a Southern professor suggests that this can be almost a standard reaction in some college communities. Asked if he had felt any pressures toward political conformity, he replied off-handedly, "Oh, just that some people call you a Communist."

Sometimes the charge seems to stem from the idea that anyone who does not suitably decry and devalue all things Communist must himself be one. At a Southern technical college, an economics

---

16. Throughout this book, initials, disciplines, and other identifying facts about teachers have sometimes been altered to preserve anonymity.

teacher gave a talk on the subject, "Know your enemy," to a local business club, describing the "prevailing resources of Russia and indicating the strength of Russia." Objections were made forthwith to the president of the school that the speaker was a Communist. Similar logic appears to underlie the charge that Communism is behind opposition to anyone's anti-Communist activities, or unwillingness to shun the intellectual study of Communism. The chairman of the social science department of a small East Coast teachers college reported the following incident.

I took a field trip with a large number of students, the college president, and other faculty members. We visited a union headquarters, Communist headquarters, Social Democrats, and so on. We were addressed by a Communist, a Social Democrat, by an official of the cooperative movement, by a Nazi, and a Fascist. As a result, I was accused of being a Communist by the bishop of this diocese.[17]

Teachers who take unpopular views on racial matters may be called "Communist." When a teacher at a school near New York City objected to a minstrel show in his church as showing racial prejudice, a church member wrote to the school president accusing him of being a Communist. Of course, these incidents may reflect the fact that the American Communist Party actually has become involved in race problems in the past. Thus at a West Coast school, a teacher was called Communist because he shared views on race relations believed held by Communists.

In one case a faculty member was accused of being Communist. The president of the school stated, "After all, he has been interested in interracial relations, which the Communists are interested in." He was dismissed.

In some cases the charge of "Communism" was directly related to a teacher's criticism of local economic interests.

I have on occasion given a speech outside the college. (I once said:) "The tariff on oranges into the United States should be reduced," and was called a Communist. If I'd said potatoes, I wouldn't have been accused unless I had said it in Idaho.

I was charged by my opponents with an unfounded Communist charge.

---

17. Quite possibly this took place before the Second World War.

It gave me a feeling that would make me leery of working in forest products or the fishing industry. The action of their pressure groups that I encountered makes me feel very leery of them.

A teacher is a "Communist" in some eyes if he appears to suggest a criticism of *any* established American institution.

I had a student one summer who was very suspicious, a Gerald L. K. Smith follower. He gave a speech saying I was a Communist because I had said that the Constitutional Convention had ignored a suggestion that an amendment be made.

Such cases suggest that in this period an individual could be called a Communist for almost any kind of behavior, or for holding almost any kind of attitude. In them, we suspect, the word "Communist" became a vague and angry label, a "dirty name" with which an individual showed his disagreement with a teacher's thinking.

Three conclusions about this type of accusation are suggested by these cases. First of all, it would seem that Communism acquired a new over-all meaning in the post-war period. Once best described as an extremist economic and political philosophy, and as a splinter American political party dedicated to the overthrow of the existing political system, during this decade it acquired the connotations of a less definite but more widespread and threatening danger, covering all things from espionage for a foreign power to distasteful unconventionality.

Paralleling this, there appears to have been a considerable enlargement in scope of the kinds of thoughts and acts which were supposed to reveal an individual's hidden Communism. While unconventional and left-of-center political views on the part of a teacher became particularly open to such an interpretation, almost any kind of criticism of the past or dissatisfaction with the present American order of things could bring a charge of Communism.

There was, then, a double "spillover," both of the content of Communism and of the behavior which served to indicate it. Just as in the Salem of the 1690's good citizens were quick to see in many an act an evil intent, and in each evil intent the signs of witchcraft, so in the post-war decade many detected a lurking evil in the behavior of college teachers which must surely spring from a subtle and pervasive Communism.

The parallel with Salem suggests a third possible element. During the Salem witch-hunting fever, as, for instance, Arthur Miller re-creates it in his play *The Crucible,* some individuals found it possible to capitalize on the general hysteria of the times to achieve unrelated private goals; a personal antagonism could be settled by an accusation of witchcraft. While several of the episodes just described might be interpreted in this way, a detailed account of an incident in a small West Coast college offers a particularly clear instance.

Dr. A., our present professor of philosophy, chaperoned a group of students on a tour of Central Europe last summer. The parents of one of the students in the tour requested him to accompany their daughter back to her home in one of the Western states at the end of the tour. This Dr. A. did, and was forthwith accused of immoral conduct by the mother of another student, Miss K. Miss K. had been gaining a good deal of independence and maturity from her mother in the process of her college education, a fact which her mother resented. Inasmuch as Dr. A. was her advisor, Mrs. K. seems to hold him responsible for her daughter's growing maturity and independence. When Mrs. K. approached the president on this matter of immoral conduct, the parents who had requested the chaperonage and who were well satisfied that it was not immoral interceded on Dr. A.'s behalf. Mrs. K., who is slightly paranoic, then charged Dr. A. with Communist leanings, and stirred up a few professional patriots to raise the same hue and cry. The president threatened Dr. A. with immediate dismissal if any such charges should be made in the future. And this in the face of unparalleled hard work by Dr. A. in assiduously cultivating the aid and support of people in this state for the University, and in his classes an unquestionable and clearly demonstrated opposition to Communism and any form of totalitarianism.

In this episode, the mother was unable to make her first charge of immoral conduct stick. But when she then raised a charge of Communist leanings, she was able to obtain local support. As the episode is presented to us, she thus managed to capitalize on others' fear of Communists to cause trouble for a teacher whom it appears she actually disliked for personal reasons.[18]

---

18. There is also the suggestion in the incident that the spectre of Communism frightened the college president in a way that the charge of immorality could not. He either arbitrarily accepted the Communist charge, or considered it so dangerous that even if it were untrue its recurrence must be prevented.

1b. Charges of radical and leftist politics. In the second main group of incidents, individuals were charged with being radically to the left in political matters, but without any implication that the individual was Communistic, disloyal, or un-American.

A small number of these centered around a charge of socialism. These accounts have an almost classic ring, of familiar old issues being aired in the customary old way. Several schools, for instance, warmly debated whether or not Norman Thomas should be allowed to speak to student or faculty groups—a kind of debate which has been occurring on American college campuses now for many, many years.

Only one incident, in fact, had a more characteristic post-war flavor, with an invitation to students to report on teachers, exhortations to rout out subversive influences, and the like.

A young squirt was put on the Board, a cocky little guy. He addressed 4,000 students at a convocation, telling them that if they ever heard a professor talking about socialism in class they should write to the Board and the Board would see to it—the Board did not want socialism part of the University. It got into the newspapers, and some newspapers jumped on that Board member. He lost ten pounds in two weeks.

It is worth noting that the instigator of this incident followed the pattern of an unwarranted arrogation of powers which had been set by others in positions of responsibility during this period. And he openly invited students to violate the old unwritten code that informers are to be despised, not heeded. Finally, it is worth noting that in spite of the respondent's obvious sarcasm, he went on to add that "all of us felt a little bit threatened" by the incident. It does not necessarily take wholesale firings to alarm teachers.

This group also includes a scattering of incidents in which teachers were criticized for belonging to or supporting supposedly leftist or radical organizations. Thus a teacher at a small Midwestern Protestant college told how a colleague was fired from his job, ostensibly for other reasons, but actually for membership in Americans for Democratic Action. In fact, in some cases there was the implication that membership in such groups indicated Communist or subversive tendencies. At a Southern university, for example, when two teachers supported Wallace for president in 1948, the home of one was smeared with red paint.

Sometimes a teacher was charged with "liberal views," "being left-wing," "being too liberal," "radicalism," etc., without further specification of the charge. These incidents were, on the whole, skimpily reported by respondent or interviewer.

1c, d, e. Other political charges. Our records contain a small number of incidents revolving about adherence to the two major American political parties. At a small New England college, for instance, a teacher who was "heavily sold on New Deal philosophy" was by-passed for promotion in favor of a younger man. And at a Midwestern school, a father wrote a letter to the dean that his son was "getting too much Roosevelt in his classes." We have already referred to an incident at one New England college where there was some resentment among local citizens about the activities of the faculty on behalf of the Democratic Party; the culmination came on Election Night, when the lawn of the chairman of the faculty Stevenson Committee was strewn with garbage by parties unknown.

The most prominent incident in this group occurred at a large school in the Middle West. It began shortly before the 1952 election when more than fifty professors at the school endorsed the candidacy of Stevenson in a newspaper advertisement. This brought on a flood of letters ("a thousand," according to one respondent), opposing the teachers' action in a ratio of about 10 to 1, and sometimes demanding mass dismissal of the teachers. Trustees and officers of the school administration intervened: "We were told in no uncertain terms that it was an unwise procedure." It was frequently asserted that the teachers had no right to make such a statement in their capacity as faculty members, but a committee which worked for a year following the incident was unable, we were told, to find a formula by which the group might jointly declare their feelings in some "private" capacity.

In clear contrast with the hundreds of incidents in which teachers and colleges were charged with being politically left-of-center to a great or small degree (we include Communism here, perhaps arbitrarily, as "left"), there were a total of twelve incidents in which some kind of right-of-center, conservative, ultra-conservative, reactionary, or rightist behavior was charged to a teacher or school. Several of these took place immediately after World War II and involved charges of Nazi sympathy. There were altogether perhaps five instances in which simple "conservatism," uncomplicated by overtones of bigotry or authoritarianism, led to unfortunate consequences for a teacher. One respondent at a large private East Coast school, after telling how several individuals with socialist or leftist philosophies had been asked to leave the faculty or otherwise held back in their careers, went on to describe the following incident:

In contrast, there was a conservative here some years ago. He had been here 11 years without a raise, and was still getting $4,000 a year. He had several kids, one crippled, who had 7 or 8 operations. He couldn't live on $4,000. He was offered a job outside, and came to me about it, saying if they'd give him $5,000 a year, he could stay at the school. I took it to the provost. We couldn't afford to lose such a good man, I said. He looked me straight in the eye, and said, "How soon do they want him?" I told him by the first of December. He said, "I think we can get a replacement for him by then." It was cut and dried, without even taking it to a vote. That man is now with a successful organization, he's been making $12,000 a year and he's due to become treasurer at $25,000. An able man who would have stayed here for $5,000 a year. But they were getting rid of conservatives, then.

However, the small number of these incidents suggests that, whatever their experiences in earlier periods, the conservative wing of American college teachers have rarely found themselves endangered in recent years. We shall elaborate on this point in Chapter VI.

A few incidents were clearly of a political nature but hard to classify among the groups just described. A student complained to the administration at one school that his civil liberties had been violated when he was compelled to listen to a teacher's views on the firing of General MacArthur by President Truman. Senator McCarthy, most understandably, criticized a respondent for joining the "Joe Must Go" Club. A department chairman told one respondent that his membership in a group to study United States policy concerning Formosa was bad judgment. A minister objected to the use of Orwell's 1984 in the classroom. Our records contain a number of scattered incidents like these.

2. *Nonpolitical issues.* While somewhat more than half of the incidents involved political charges, as was shown in Table 2-6, the other 46 per cent of the cases were of a different nature. Since

in recent years the emphasis in newspaper reports and other publications on the topic has been almost exclusively on the political charges made against teachers, the numerous incidents of a different nature obtained in our study deserve a separate and detailed presentation.

A major segment of the nonpolitical incidents dealt with religious matters, economic matters, segregation problems, and a number of other specific issues. Of course these topics can and often do take on considerable political importance, but here this was not the primary focus.

About fifty incidents centered on religious matters. Frequently occurring, of course, in denominational schools, a number of such cases involved teachers considered unacceptably deviant from established norms in their views. An East Coast school teacher described a typical instance:

There was a case of an agnostic teacher about five years ago; the students took offense, and he was told to stop expressing such ideas and then he left the university.

Errant behavior in matters of dogma may bring trouble: a teacher at a Lutheran school was criticized for publishing an article in a Unitarian magazine (this matter brought considerably more comment from teachers at the school than an accusation of Communism made against the same teacher during this period); promotion was withheld from an active Quaker at a Presbyterian school. Some incidents of this nature may not have been reported in the survey because they did not appear to respondents to suit the phraseology of the questions. For instance, there is only one report in which a professor in a denominational school told of being called too fundamentalist when asked if his academic freedom had been threatened. Such considerations may help to account for the almost complete absence of reported disagreements over matters of dogma in our interviews at Catholic schools.[19]

Often a particular religious tenet is involved. Students, for in-

19. In Appendix A of *Academic Freedom in Our Time*, Robert MacIver points out some of the special problems which arise in denominational schools. The Catholic point of view has been discussed by Journet Kahn in "The Threat to Academic Freedom," *Proceedings of the American Catholic Philosophical Association*, 1957.

stance, may take offense for religious reasons over a teacher's views on certain problems of marriage, of the family, or of the basic nature of human beings. There are two incidents, one occurring at a prominent state university, in which teachers were taken to task for teaching evolution. Occasionally, even quite special and intricate matters of doctrine were at issue.

Someone . . . presumably representing the Catholic Church, objected to my stand on purgatory, that there was no such thing until 600 A.D. I have wondered how the living know when a person is released from purgatory. I wrote a pamphlet which my freshmen are using, and the Catholic Church has tried to get it out of circulation.

While clashes over specific religious beliefs were not too rare, our records show only one incident centering simply about the presence of a Catholic at a non-Catholic school, and one about non-Catholics at a Catholic school. Oddly, in both instances, it is the individual in the minority who appears to have won out. The following episode was reported by a Catholic historian at a private Eastern university.

Our chairman felt that a Roman Catholic can't be a good historian. He recommended my discharge every year for a period of seven years. But he's gone and I'm still here.

And at a Catholic college, respondents complain that the non-Catholic dean of one department tended to favor the small group of non-Catholic teachers in salary matters.

Another primarily nonpolitical set of incidents centered on economic issues. We have seen above that teachers' stands on economic problems have sometimes led to charges of Communism and subversion. But there were about thirty further incidents in which the issue was limited to economic matters. In one, a West Coast corporation executive accused the faculty of a school of supporting discount houses and encouraging the students to deal with them. It is not surprising that in some incidents of this nature, when a professor was known to oppose the views of certain local interests, the issue of his right to support his position actively outside the university, as opposed to his discussion of it in the classroom, was raised.

There was a controversy about public housing here in town. During a common council meeting, some of our men were told by attorneys representing special interests that we should confine our views and activities to the university campus, and not express them publicly despite the fact that we were citizens of the community. One attorney was an alumnus.

Particularly when the professor had stubbed important toes, a clash sometimes occurred with school officials.

A member of the faculty wrote an article showing how big business was buying space in small newspapers, obviously not to sell goods, but to get the support of the small newspaper editors. The *New Republic* printed it, which was somewhat damning—they put the heading as, "Small Newspapers Sell Out." The chancellor of the university called in the professor and gave him fits. But he sent a copy to C. C. [a well-known local newspaper editor] and C. wrote a very congratulatory letter. The chancellor was afraid of C. The professor took this letter to the chancellor, and the chancellor said he was a fine man.

In the remaining economic incidents, the issues were somewhat more abstract—one teacher criticized for advocating government spending, another for presenting Keynesian economics, and so on.

About twenty-five incidents dealt with race and segregation problems. Several instances from the border states in the South seemed to reflect the uneasiness and uncertainty of a time of flux. The major episode reported at one such school developed when a white girl danced with a Negro boy at a college social affair.[20] The occasion was still widely discussed at the time of our interviewing although it had occurred six to seven years before. At another border school, a teacher who went to a meeting at a Negro college learned the president of the school had told a colleague to "stay away from me." At a third, the school president asked a teacher about to accept a position as a consultant to the N.A.A.C.P. to hold off, since an important fund drive was about to begin. In the Deep South, typically, the tone of incidents was different. Here, for instance, a professor was bluntly told that he would be fired if he attended an N.A.A.C.P. meeting. Here, too, at

---

20. This episode is not counted as an incident, however, since no teacher came under attack or criticism.

the Negro schools in our sample, most professors were reluctant to discuss segregation problems. One Negro teacher, however, did vividly describe how white officeholders constantly tried to deter him in his efforts to get Negroes to vote.

Scattered incidents involving a great variety of other specific, nonpolitical issues also turned up. Teachers were taken to task for being too critical of society in their social science courses; assigning the Lynds' *Middletown* to his students brought this charge on one man. A metropolitan teacher was accused of teaching free love by a colleague later found to be mentally ill. Conscientious objectors occasionally created problems; at one major state university, when one who was a student went to his faculty advisor, the teacher was prosecuted by the government for advising him. Teachers got into hassles with community groups over fluoridation, the advisability of a local liquor store, the merits of oleomargarine, and many other topics. A Midwestern teacher was sharply criticized for using the school's sororities and fraternities to illustrate the concept of social strata. Finally, there were a few complaints that teachers have been indelicate in their treatment of sexual matters. One professor was called down for a graphic discussion of the pimp and prostitute as undesirable social types. Another was told to report to the school dean for putting the Kinsey report on his reading list. At a Southern women's college two art teachers were sternly rebuked for allowing the student magazine to carry a drawing of a nude male. And an instructor of criminology stirred up a spate of letters to the local newspaper when his students were permitted to attend the trial of a prostitute who had killed a madam and another prostitute.

3. *Personal idiosyncrasy, immorality, and unconventionality.* Altogether, 7 per cent of the incidents fall into a group which might properly seem outside the scope of this study. Cases of alcoholism, jarring personality, sexual deviation, and the like might ordinarily be passed by in a study like this. We include them here because concern over political unorthodoxy among college teachers seems sometimes to have spilled over into concern with *any* kind of unconventionality. Many respondents commented that signs of unorthodoxy are interchangeable; as one Midwestern teacher put it, "We are always getting letters from a woman saying the faculty is full of Communists and sex perverts—they

always go together." And a Midwestern professor who takes an active interest in politics reported an embarrassing episode along such lines.

I was once in a case myself. I had warts on my chin and couldn't get rid of them. I had had them taken off several times but they kept coming back. I paid a lot of doctor bills. I grew a beard to hide them and was almost fired because I was behaving in a strange fashion growing a beard.

When some teachers become the apparent repository of unfriendly political forces, this may be accompanied by a new distrust of others who grow beards, write books, stand up for a minority viewpoint, or in other ways set themselves apart. Teachers can thus achieve the status of inherently dangerous men, whose every act and utterance must be viewed as a potential threat. In one incident, when two professors at a Western school reported findings in the press about radioactive fallout, the governor of the state came out with an indignant statement that they should be arrested for scaring the public. Significantly, this episode involved a school where an unusually large number of much-publicized incidents had occurred in which faculty members were attacked as Communists or subversives. It seems apparent that the professors' statements about fallout might have been quite differently received in a less aroused setting.

4. *Intramural issues.* Our study would seem incomplete to any college teacher if it did not uncover signs of the normal and inevitable frictions of campus life that we will call intramural issues. Intellectual rivalries and hostilities are surely a common and sometimes fruitful part of academic life. There will always be teachers whose classroom techniques are sufficiently unusual or daring to evoke criticism and even dismissal. So it is inevitable that we should have had instances like that in which a music teacher stubbornly persisted in teaching the twelve-tone scale, a historian was reprimanded for writing an angry letter to the football coach, and a liberal arts faculty fought the administration over the establishment of a student book co-op.

5. *Incidents in which issues are raised without charges being made.* There are two types of incidents in which our standard method of description breaks down. Up to now we have defined

an incident as a situation in which an attack or accusation is made. An issue may be raised, however, and sometimes hotly contended, without derogatory charges being placed against teachers. This is true of the 5 per cent of incidents in which a restriction was imposed by authorities on a faculty or a teacher. The most widely discussed instances involved the right of administrative officials to screen guest speakers invited onto a campus; we have cases where administrations succeeded in passing such a rule and others where they did not. Also included here are a number of administrative efforts to limit research, bar controversial textbooks, control the handling of certain classroom topics, prevent teachers from accepting off-campus speaking invitations, and so forth. Needless to say, these incidents were reported by angry teachers. It would be particularly interesting to have the administration's viewpoint on these cases.

We come finally to the loyalty oath incidents. Altogether, 2 per cent of the cases, a total of thirteen instances, fall into this category. If this seems a surprisingly small number, it must be remembered that there could be only one at a school, and that it would seldom occur outside the seventy-four tax-supported schools in our sample. What is more surprising is that the special loyalty oaths were hardly considered worth comment at several schools. In California, the evidence from the state-supported schools in our sample demonstrates again that the well-known oath controversy was a major fight which is not yet completely resolved. In other states, such as one in the Middle West whose main university fell into our sample, our interviews suggest that although at the outset considerable discussion and contention was stirred up by the legislative passage of the loyalty oath requirement, the ferment died down relatively quickly. The small group of teachers who refused to sign were dismissed, and the whole matter had apparently been accepted and largely forgotten by 1955, some three years afterward. In some states, the oath seems to have raised scarcely a ripple of interest; at least, no lingering concern is revealed. At one Eastern state university, there is exactly one sentence in thirty-one interviews mentioning dismissals brought by the oath signing: "Two fellows were dropped after refusing to sign the loyalty oath." It is impossible on the basis of our interviews to say why such little importance is now attached to the oath at these schools.

Perhaps the initial victory of the pro-oath forces in California discouraged faculties in some other states from making a fight. Or it may be that they prefer to forget what they considered an ignominious episode.

The Patterning of Incidents

IT REMAINS now to trace some patterns which are noticeable in our aggregate of incidents.

We have shown earlier that such incidents are considerably more frequent in the secular private schools and public schools than at the traditional institutions. It is also true that charges of extremism comprise a larger share of the incidents at such schools. While 76 per cent of all incidents took place at these schools, 83 per cent of the charges of extremism were found there. It is worth mentioning that among the very few incidents occurring at Catholic schools, charges of Communism and subversion play about as much a part as they do at other traditional schools.[21]

We can also present some rough information about the sources from which incidents arose. Perusal of newspaper headlines during this period might have suggested that attacks on schools and teachers came almost entirely from visiting committees of the state or national legislature, right-of-center individuals and groups in the community, and other sources outside the school. As inspection of the cases described above suggests, many incidents, altogether 39 per cent of the total, did arise in this manner. But in an almost equal 36 per cent, individuals or groups who were in one way or another formally connected with the university—trustees, administrators, alumni, colleagues, students, and relatives of students—brought accusations against teachers. This figure is probably deceptive in one regard: while in many cases the college administration appeared to teachers reporting an incident to have been the original instigator, its action undoubtedly was often taken after complaints had been made from other sources. Because of lack of information, or sometimes due to bad interviewing, information about the originator is not available for the remaining 25 per cent of the incidents.

---

21. Detailed figures may be found in Appendix 8B.

Each type of source tended to originate a distinctive pattern of charges. While there was never complete uniformity in incidents of a given origination, there are marked differences in the frequency with which the different charges were made. A quarter of the accusations brought by governmental investigating committees against teachers involved past membership in the Communist Party, subversion, and other extremist political positions, compared to 2 per cent of those made by all other sources. Interestingly enough, a majority of the charges stemming from other sources not formally connected to the university, such as local groups and individuals, alleged some form of Communism or subversion, but very seldom made the specific accusation of Party membership.[22] When the school administration took a teacher to task politically, however, in most cases it was not with charges of Communism and subversion, but more often those of unacceptable radicalism; incidents originating with administrations also focused on nonpolitical issues—religion, segregation, limitations on speakers and research, and the like.

It is worth noting again that governmental committees initiated the bulk of the Communist Party membership charges. Of course, almost all such incidents involved charges of *past* Party membership, most often in the 1930's. We do not wish to revive here the arguments over the merits of firing or penalizing a college teacher because of such past affiliation, and, in any case, we are in no position to consider the detailed evidence for the truth or falsity of individual charges. Readers who wish to acquire further knowledge in these matters must obtain it from other sources. Our purpose has been only to show the relative prevalence of such cases and to indicate something of their origins.

We have now reported that in our aggregate of incidents, charges vary considerably according to the kind of school and according to their source. The detailed descriptions in the previous section also touched on another important fact about incidents, their outcome. The assumption all along in this chapter has been that pressures on schools and teachers sometimes ended in trouble for the target. Table 2-8 provides a rough summary of our information about how incidents turned out.

---

22. Again the complete figures are given in Appendix 8B.

Table 2-8
The Outcome of Incidents

Target was fired	18%
Resigned under pressure	4
Promotion withheld	12
Limitations imposed	
(e.g., classroom, research)	5
Reprimanded or warned	5
Cleared of charge	8
No action taken at all	13
Outcome not clearly described	35
	100% (990 incidents)

Because of the large number of cases for which information is missing, this Table must be read as revealing simply that more than a few incidents ended in firings, forced resignations, or promotions withheld. Whatever else may be said about them, the pressures against teachers in the post-war decade often got results.

Here, too, incidents followed different patterns depending upon the charge. Table 2-9, presenting the approximate percentages in each charge group of the incidents which ended with either firings or forced resignations, gives an indication of this.

Table 2-9
Approximate Frequency of Firings and Forced Resignations

Type of Charge	Case Resulted in Firing or Forced Resignation	Other Outcome	Outcome not Clearly Described	Total	Number of Incidents
Communist Party membership, took Fifth Amendment or otherwise refused cooperation	64%	36	—	100%	(25)
Other Communist Party charges	28%	60	12	100%	(25)
Communist sympathy	17%	45	38	100%	(100)
"Communism," "subversion"	8%	33	59	100%	(286)
Left-of-center politics	16%	38	46	100%	(108)
Miscellaneous political charges	16%	44	40	100%	(91)
Religious	18%	49	33	100%	(49)
Charge not known*	16%	46	38	100%	(69)

* The remaining groups are too small, or too heterogeneous, for meaningful percentaging.

The group of cases where teachers were accused of Communist Party membership and also failed to testify fully before governmental or faculty committees is small, but in about two-thirds of them the target of the accusation was shortly forced to leave the campus. Even in the remaining Party cases, though the departure rate was considerably less, it was still higher than for any other group of political charges. Incidents in which nothing beyond Communist sympathy was alleged ended in no more forced departures than the remaining political and nonpolitical incidents. Significantly, these figures indicate that it was the vague "Communist" and "subversive" charges which least endangered a teacher's status on the campus. This would seem to underline the suggestion made earlier: such charges appear frequently to have a special and specious nature. And, the figures suggest, the administrative officials who have the power to fire teachers and enforce regulations are perhaps aware of this.

— — —

In a democratic society institutions of higher education are not immune from scrutiny and challenge. Criticism of their objectives and of the means used to attain them is to be expected in the normal course of events. But the marked increase in the pressures and attacks experienced by American college teachers during the post-war decade reflects more than a mere wave in the regular flow of democratic debate. The information collected from our broad sample of schools does not indicate that they were inundated by attacks. But the number of schools which came under increased pressure, and the number of teachers who were fired or compelled to resign, can scarcely be considered ordinary or negligible.

We need to have a phrase which will serve to evoke for the reader something of the state of affairs described in this chapter. We have shown that the years of the post-war decade were for many colleges a time of considerable if not extreme stress. In the pages that follow, we shall call them the difficult years.

Chapter III

A MEASURE OF APPREHENSION

In the spring of 1954 Robert M. Hutchins, in a popular magazine, expressed the opinion that the spirit of the teaching profession was being crushed. A few months later the Fund for the Republic commissioned the present study. Russell Kirk and other conservatives voiced skepticism: How could one expect that a study financed by the Fund would do anything but confirm its president's conviction? In the liberal camp Sidney Hook felt that Hutchins' statement was exaggerated. Characteristically, no one raised the question of what the statement meant and by what devices it could be proved or disproved. To this topic, the present chapter is devoted.

Brief thought needs to be given first to the implications of such an undertaking. An extreme position would be that Hutchins' statement is self-evident, and that its meaning and intent would only be perverted by an empirical investigation. No one can deny that many professors were investigated. Quite a number were dismissed, several probably without justification. It is only common sense that if some members of a social group are singled out for attack, the whole group may become frightened. Besides, this argument might continue, statistical data would only veil the moral implications of the situation. There are fifteen million Negroes in this country; if fifteen were lynched, would it not be absurd to say that this is *only* .0001 per cent?

The moral issue and the descriptive effort should not be confused. Our task is to analyze, as accurately as possible, the feelings of social scientists during the difficult years and to spell out some of the implications of their attitudes and experiences. A call, if necessary, for remedial action must be left to other agencies. Just as chemists hope that their discoveries will not help people to poison each other, so the social scientist expects that his findings and his language will not be misused.

The Basic Material

CHAPTER I and Appendix 3 have acquainted the reader with the general ideas used to formulate classifications of our 2,451 teachers. Similar procedures were used to establish a measure of what we shall call apprehension. The first step was to conduct a series of detailed interviews with a number of college professors, who were prevailed upon to describe in detail any situation encountered in their capacity as teachers which had somehow made them feel uneasy. We asked them to remember as much as they could of both important and trivial experiences which create problems in a teacher's professional career, experiences they had already encountered or which might arise in the future.

From these preliminary interviews we selected a list of about twenty relatively specific experiences. Questions were then worded so that the respondent simply had to say whether or not these things had happened to him. It was necessary to present a large number of situations related to academic life which might cause a teacher concern or induce him to act contrary to his convictions; depending on personality and background factors, one man's apprehension might express itself in regard to his publications, while for another relations with students or with neighbors might be more indicative.

The strategy behind this procedure deserves a moment of reflection. Long before surveys like this one existed, philosophers wondered how to make distinctions between people and put them into different classes for analytical purposes. William James, for instance, in *The Meaning of Truth*, says:

Suppose, e.g., that we say a man is "prudent." Concretely, that means that he takes out insurance, hedges in betting, looks before he leaps. . . . As a constant habit in him, a permanent tone of character, it is convenient to call him prudent in abstraction from any one of his acts.

In the fifty years since this was written, the basic idea expressed
has become the pivot of much empirical research. But it has been
amended in three respects. For one, we would not expect a
prudent man always to hedge in betting or always to take out
insurance; we talk today about the probability that he will do
so. Secondly, we no longer assume that we can arbitrarily divide
people into those who are prudent and those who are not. We
accept the idea that all such traits or attitudes form a continuum
which may be divided into segments only for practical convenience.
Finally, we know that the number of indicators to be used for
such a classification may be very large, and various subsets of
indicators may be chosen according to the purpose of the study
at hand. Among college students, for instance, we would find
little betting and rare occasions for taking out insurance. Thus
we might use as indicators of prudence whether a student always
makes a note when he lends a book, whether he always locks his
dormitory room, and so on.

In the spirit of this tradition twenty-one items were included
in the questionnaire to gauge a professor's apprehension. But
further screening was necessary to select the items most suitable
for the classificatory task on hand. It developed that a few units
did not signify what we had expected. In one such case, we had
inquired as to whether in hiring a teaching assistant the respondent
would wonder about the candidate's political background; 40 per
cent answered in the affirmative. But the comments and explanations added by teachers revealed an ambiguity. For many, such
concern was indeed a matter of self-protection and a sign of apprehension. But for others, it was a policy based on long-established
convictions. Other items turned out to be too limited in applica-
bility. Almost half of the respondents, for example, had no opportunity to act as sponsors for student organizations, and so a question
regarding caution in accepting such sponsorship was discarded.

As a result of this sifting, eleven items remained suitable for an
index of apprehension. These were then subjected to a further
analysis. On the basis of their wording, they were divided into two
groups, one pertaining to feelings of worry about security, the
other pertaining to precautionary behavior. The singling out of
these two dimensions of apprehension will be described first.

Finally, we made use of statistical tests to pick the small group of items which were most appropriate for classifying all the respondents.

Worry

OF THE ELEVEN ITEMS remaining after the preliminary screening, six contained a phrase such as "have you worried," or "do you ever find yourself wondering," or "have you ever thought about the possibility," in connection with such matters as gossip, delayed promotion, or other difficulties resulting from an expression of political opinion. The term "political" was always explicitly used to shift the focus away from issues of professional competence, scientific controversy, or moral problems which might otherwise have overly guided respondents' answers. In Table 3-1 the wording of the questions is reproduced, together with the distribution in percentages of the 2,451 answers to each.

The variation in the number of affirmative answers to these questions is considerable and not without interest. The first three items, reported by about the same proportion of teachers, all have one element in common: once one has expressed an opinion events are set in motion over which one may not have control. The difference between the figures for the second and fourth items probably reflects an element of reality in the academic tradition: a teacher's opinions are undoubtedly more likely to keep him from getting a job than to cost him one he already has.

The last two situations in this list are much less frequently reported. The alumni are considered a more remote hazard, perhaps because they are less likely to learn what the professor says than the people resident in the community, and because in some schools the influence of the alumni is slight to begin with. The term dossier in the last item may well have a cloak and dagger implication to which only the especially distrustful are responsive. While the answers to each question are certainly affected by many elements in the wording, it is still worth noticing that the most frequently experienced item refers to damage caused "inadvertently"; the Machiavellian designs implied in the final item are much less often visualized by teachers.

An important way of understanding the meaning of such a list is to study the relation of answers to the various items to each other. The same amount of worry can be expressed by quite different indicators according to the specific circumstances in which a respondent teaches. Still, there are certain interrelations which prevail more generally. Gossip is most frequently paired with the other situations; it is, so to say, the most characteristic of all the worrisome eventualities in the list. The three items which specifically refer to jobs (items 2, 4, and 6) form an interrelated group;

Table 3-1
Distribution of Answers to a Series of Items Indicating "Worry"

1. Have you worried about the possibility that some student might inadvertently pass on a warped version of what you have said and lead to false ideas about your political views?

Yes	40%
No	58
Don't know	2
Never encountered	—
Total	100%

2. If you were considering a move to another college, have you wondered if that college would ask anyone at your present college about your political background and the political biases you might have in your teaching?

Yes	37%
No	57
Don't know	4
Never encountered	2
Total	100%

3. Do you ever find yourself wondering if because of your politics or something political you said or did that you might be a subject of gossip in the community?

Yes	37%
No	61
Don't know	1
Never encountered	1
Total	100%

4. Have you ever wondered that some political opinion you've expressed might affect your job security or promotion at this college?

Yes	27%
No	72
Don't know	—
Never encountered	1
Total	100%

5. Have you ever wondered if there was something political you said or did that would cause you to become unpopular with any group of alumni?

Yes	16%
No	82
Don't know	1
Never encountered	1
Total	100%

6. Have you ever thought about the possibility that the Administration of the college has a political file or dossier on every faculty member, including yourself?

Yes	17%
No	82
Don't know	1
Never encountered	—
Total	100%

an affirmative answer to one is especially likely to go together
with the two others. The suspicion of a political dossier kept by
the administration is particularly unlikely to be linked with the
fear of inadvertent misrepresentation by students. This suggests
perhaps that there are really two types of respondents revealed by
these questions: those who felt that the difficult years were the result
of unfortunate circumstances in which some people were almost
unintentionally victimized, and those who saw the world more as
a place in which bad people are deliberately out to hurt the
good ones.

The reader should not be misled by our choice of the term
"worry" to describe these questions. It is undoubtedly true that
in answering them affirmatively a teacher expressed concern for
his job security and uncertainty about his freedom of opinion.
However, it need not only mean concern with his own position.
It may also express a general sensitivity to academic freedom or
political constraint. A man who thinks the college administration
has a political dossier on the faculty might have nothing to fear
himself and yet worry considerably that such practices prevail.
Affirmative answers could therefore indicate worry about oneself
combined with concern about the civil liberties situation in the
college at large. (This idea will be further developed in the next
chapter.)

On the other hand these affirmative answers might not only
express worry about professional matters; they could well be the
result of broader personal anxieties, the responses of people who
also worry every day about whether they have left a lighted ciga-
rette in their office or whether their children will fall off a swing.[1]

Caution

THE REMAINING five questions had a different character.
In these, teachers were not asked whether they had worried, or

---

1. At an early stage of this study we contemplated the insertion of a
number of questions which would directly gauge this generalized anxiety for
each respondent. In pre-tests, however, it was found that social scientists,
well acquainted with personality tests, resented answering such questions. In
a mailed questionnaire subsequently sent to some of the teachers we had interviewed, Professor Riesman inserted an item of this type, and again met with
the same difficulty.

what they had felt, but whether they had actually done something to forestall some of the consequences which caused them concern. Had they toned down their writings in order to avoid controversy? Were they more circumspect in their discussions with other people? Just as the items of Table 3-1 are indicators of worry, those in Table 3-2 could be called indicators of caution.

Table 3-2
Distribution of Answers to a Series of Items Indicating "Caution"

7.	Do you occasionally go out of your way to make statements or tell anecdotes in order to bring home the point directly or indirectly that you have no extreme leftist or rightist leanings?	Yes No Don't know Total	27% 71 2 100%
8.	Have you occasionally refrained from expressing an opinion or participating in some activity in order not to embarrass the trustees or the college administration?	Yes No Don't know Never encountered Total	22% 75 2 1 100%
9.	Do you find yourself being more careful now and then not to bring up certain political topics with your colleagues in order not to embarrass them?	Yes No Don't know Total	18% 81 1 100%
10.	Do you find in your recommendations of reference materials to students that you are more careful today not to recommend something that might be later criticized for being too controversial?	Yes No Don't know Never encountered Total	12% 85 2 1 100%
11.	Have you toned down anything you have written lately because you were worried that it might cause too much controversy?	Yes No Don't know Never encountered Total	9% 85 2 4 100%

In comparing Tables 3-1 and 3-2, one notices that the proportion of affirmative answers for the caution questions is likely to be smaller than for the worry items. This may be partly because it requires more honesty to concede that one is actually "pulling in his horns" than to reveal a general mood of concern. But it also makes good sense to find that a general feeling of concern was more pervasive than were concrete precautionary moves.

Questions 8 and 9 in Table 3-2 have one element in common:

they give the respondent an opportunity to justify his careful behavior with the idea that free expression of opinion might embarrass others. Item 7, as we shall soon see, also has an alleviating
element: it can mean that one has the courage of one's opinions
but wants to be sure that they are clearly understood by others.
This probably explains why the first three precautionary situations
in Table 3-2 are more frequently asserted than the last two. As
noted above, it is not surprising that conceding real changes in
one's professional activities is acknowledged by only a small number of respondents.[2] It is quite possible that our figures underrate
the frequency with which this actually happens. It is therefore
important to remember that we don't mean to use any of these
figures by themselves for describing the social reality. They are
part of a larger set of indicators which, when taken together, will
permit us to distinguish various levels of apprehension. We will
provide a possible corrective in Chapter VIII on the specific subject matter of the last two items. Respondents were asked whether
their colleagues had changed their publication and teaching practices in the course of the difficult years. The number of affirmative
answers, when talking about others, was about 8 per cent higher
than when respondents referred to themselves, even though one
out of five respondents had formed no judgment. Many of the
reports professors gave about their own reactions will be matched
in Chapter VIII against the observations they made on their colleagues.

The caution items of Table 3-2 are related to each other. As
could be expected, teachers who affirmed one of the two final
professional items were also likely to affirm the other. Not so
strongly, but still quite noticeably, the second and third situations
which refer to avoiding embarrassment were likely to be reported
by the same respondents. Additional suggestive insight is gained
by tabulating the worry against the caution items. The highest
worry-caution interrelation occurs between the fear of misrepresentation by students, and the tendency to make sure that one is
not considered an extremist. Some respondents, it appears, are
especially concerned over having their views quite clearly under-

---

2. The item on toning down one's writing has a somewhat different meaning for productive professors than for those who do very little writing. Information on this point is given in Appendix 8C.

stood by others. The wish not to embarrass the administration is paired, relatively strongly, with concern for one's job; tact appears to have a certain practical utility.

Looking at the whole picture revealed by the eleven questions, we face a dilemma of interpretation. Should we say that "only" one out of ten professors have been affected in their writings, or should we be appalled by the fact that thousands of college teachers have taken such precautionary steps? A similar moral issue, if one less central to academic institutions, is raised by the first item in Table 3-2. Is it a token of awakened patriotism or a sign of weakened moral fibre when more than a quarter of an academic community feels obliged to go out of its way to express its loyalty? We leave these decisions to the reader.

The Interrelation
Between Worry and Caution—
The Apprehension Index

WE CAN DIVIDE respondents into those who give a "yes" answer to one worry item, at most, and those who concede two or more. The same can be done with caution items. These two divisions together classify our respondents into the four groups shown in Table 3-3. In the upper left corner are those who report neither worry nor caution (1,184 cases or 48 per cent); 719 people (29 per cent) express considerable worry but report at most one precautionary move. Seventeen per cent (423 cases) are both worried and cautious. Only 125 respondents affirm a sizeable number of caution items but hardly any worry.

We can look at Table 3-3 in the following way. If teachers are not strongly worried (first column), they very seldom have reason to be cautious; actually the 125 cases who feel differently are surprising and will be discussed later. If teachers are worried, they may or may not make concrete precautionary moves (second column). Worry and caution can be considered different levels of an underlying attitude which we call apprehension.

A relatively low degree of apprehension is expressed mainly in feelings of worry and uneasy anticipation; as apprehension increases, it affects one's external behavior and leads to actual changes in one's work and social conduct. It is this formulation which will now be converted into our definitive instrument, the apprehension score. Henceforth we will be interested in the distinction between worry and caution only for certain special purposes; in general, we consider them the inner and outer manifestations of an underlying attitude of apprehension.

Table 3-3
Our Respondents Cross-Classified According to the Number of Caution and Worry Items They Answer Affirmatively

NUMBER OF CAUTION ITEMS	NUMBER OF WORRY ITEMS		
	0, 1	2-6	Total
0, 1	1,184	719	1,903
2-5	125	423	548
Total	1,309	1,142	2,451

From our eleven items six were selected to form the final apprehension index. They include the first four of Table 3-1 (worry about misinterpretation by students, about one's future employment chance, about community gossip, and about security in one's present job) and the last two of Table 3-2 (being more careful about reference material, and toning down one's writing). The choice of these six items was first based on general considerations of content and then verified by a statistical procedure. The two caution items selected were those closest to a teacher's professional activities. We eliminated the last two worry items for substantive reasons. The one which referred to alumni was, as mentioned before, too dependent upon actual variations in the role which such groups can play in a college. And specific tabulations convinced us that the item referring to a possible administration dossier had an overdramatic implication which prevented a number of respondents from giving an affirmative answer.

There remained the final task of showing that the six items selected for our index really were indicators of an underlying sentiment of occupational apprehension, a latent dimension along which respondents could properly be classified. We can give here only the general idea of such a statistical test and its main outcome.

Suppose we were able to look into people's feelings and see directly the degree of apprehension they experience. Then we

would expect the following relationship between this basic measure
and the different items which we use as indicators: the more apprehensive a group of respondents, the more likely are they to
answer an item affirmatively. But each of the indicators will have
a somewhat different relationship to the underlying sentiment.
Some will readily come to the fore as apprehension increases,
others will be asserted only at a very high level of apprehension.
Obviously we don't have such a direct measure. Nevertheless it
is possible to derive mathematically the curves which relate general apprehension to the propensity of reporting each of the
specific symptoms. In Figure 3-4, the horizontal direction represents the basic underlying dimension. Along the vertical direction
we have plotted for each question the probability that teachers
give an affirmative answer. These curves are sometimes called

Figure 3-4

The "Tracelines" for Four Items of the Apprehension Index

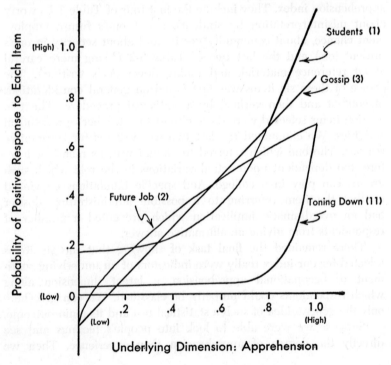

tracelines because they permit us to trace how characteristic an indicator is at various levels of basic apprehenison.

Take, for instance, the first three questions reported in Table 3-1. They are answered in about the same frequency. Forty per cent are worried about student misrepresentation, 37 per cent about their future job, and an equal 37 per cent about gossip in the community. Now, let us look at their tracelines in Figure 3-4.

The gossip item (3) is represented by a practically straight line. This must be understood as follows: people with little apprehension are very unlikely to be concerned about the repercussions of their political opinions in the community, but the likelihood increases in direct proportion to the degree of underlying apprehension. The concern about one's future job (2) presents a different picture. Its probability at the outset rises somewhat more sharply; at the lower degrees of apprehension people are a bit more likely to worry that an expression of opinion could jeopardize their chances to move elsewhere. But, on the other hand, at a high degree of apprehension this worry is less prevalent than the concern with gossip. After all, gossip is an ever-present danger while comparatively few people think far into the future or seriously consider that they will ever have to move to another college.

The item regarding student misrepresentation (1) is again quite different. First, we notice that at the onset its traceline is higher. This shows that even people who are not apprehensive at all reckon with student misrepresentation as part of the inevitable hazards of their occupation. And for quite a while, as apprehension rises, the probability of this concern doesn't increase very much. But then, at the higher levels of apprehension, it shoots up, and in the end becomes dominant.

For comparative purposes, we have added the traceline of the caution item which deals with the toning down of one's writing (11). The probability that a teacher will assert such a move appears only very late on the right side of our graph, but then it rises steeply. This confirms our general interpretation that such changes in professional practices are indicators of rather extreme apprehension, but even there they are not very likely to occur.[3]

3. The worry item on security in the present job (4) has a traceline lying between the gossip item and the one on student misrepresentation. Item 10 on reference material has a traceline very similar to item 11. In order not

Such an analysis of tracelines is the statistical method by which the meaning of an underlying concept is clarified. The kind of apprehension which our index measures is such that fear of community repercussions to one's opinions is what one might call the most typical expression; its probability increases proportionately to the increase of the underlying feeling itself. Concern about one's future job appears earlier than fear of local gossip. The harm students can do is taken more in stride, and worry about it characterizes only a rather advanced state of apprehension. Typically, the most acute form of apprehension is reflected in actual changes in professional activities.

The procedure we have just sketched could, if we wished, now also permit us to classify each respondent in a statistically precise way. But that would mean pushing the method to an extreme not warranted by the practical purpose of our study. Rather, we shall proceed as before, and classify our respondents simply by counting the number of items they answer in the affirmative. This leads to the distribution of scores presented in Table 3-5.

Table 3-5
Distribution of Scores on the Apprehension Index

Apprehension Score	Number of Respondents	Percentage of Respondents
0	742	30%
1	600	24
2	454	19
3	336	14
4	193	8
5	99	4
6	27	1
Total	2,451	100%

to crowd the graph, these two tracelines have been omitted. For an elementary introduction to this technique see: P. F. Lazarsfeld, ed., *Mathematical Thinking in the Social Sciences* (Glencoe, Ill.: The Free Press, 1954), Chapter 7. The reader should not be misled into the idea that we have an independent measure of apprehension against which the frequencies of the various items are plotted. The opposite is true. The statistician studies the interrelations of the items with each other. From those he derives the tracelines, and they in turn establish what the apprehension index actually means. The mathematical outcome never fits the empirical data completely. The degree of "misfit" can be seen from the fact that two of the tracelines show at the left side of Figure 3-4 slight negative probabilities, which of course should not occur; nor would the student item go above the probability 1.0 if the whole set of data fitted the model more closely. Still, the general trend of the tracelines remains valid.

We can compare the distribution of these scores with the types developed from Table 3-3. We may call unapprehensive all those with a score of 0 or 1. The rest (46 per cent) can be called apprehensive, with a very apprehensive group comprising those who have a score of 4 or higher. The picture presented in Table 3-6 ensues.

Table 3-6
Two Ways of Establishing Levels of Apprehension

Type			Apprenhension Score	
Neither worried nor cautious	51%		Low (0, 1)	54%
Worried but not cautious	31		Medium (2, 3)	33
Worried and cautious	18	Apprehensive	High (4-6)	13
	100%*			100%

* This excludes the 125 respondents who reported much caution but little worry.

The two classifications match fairly well, and the apprehension score turns out to be somewhat more conservative; it describes 46 per cent of all the social scientists as apprehensive. This classification is, of course, meant mainly for comparative purposes. We shall devote several chapters to reporting what types of social scientist are relatively more apprehensive and what situations make for a higher or lower frequency of apprehension in terms of this score. This is all an index should legitimately be used for. Indeed, this self-restraint is not confined to the kind of social research work to which this report belongs. The physicist can measure temperature by Fahrenheit, Celsius, etc. He can tell whether it is hotter in the suburbs or downtown. But he should not be asked how many hot days there were in New York City this year, because he does not know whether "hot" means above 90° or above 95°. Of course, there develops in each city a social tradition of what is considered "hot." In London newspapers the weather makes headlines if the thermometer rises above 85°. In this sense it would be a legitimate problem of empirical inquiry to ask what score people would consider the onset of dangerous or unusual apprehension. Repeated studies permitting comparisons over various historical periods would give a clue, but we have no such material. It is our impression, from reading numerous questionnaires in full detail, that two or more out of six items answered affirmatively do indeed indicate apprehension in the colloquial sense of the term. Whether or not this is correct must be left to future inquiries. One merit of our effort may be that it provides the first bench mark for a continued effort.

We turn to a more necessary task. The fact that people answer questions does not tell what the answers mean. The tracelines described earlier give some of the answers. Additional insights can be obtained in a variety of ways.

Additional Information

MANY OF OUR RESPONDENTS added comments of their own on the six questions after they had chosen between the alternatives presented to them. Quite often these remarks shed light on the interpretation given to questions by respondents. It is possible to show, by briefly summarizing this material, that any differences in understanding could not have markedly affected our statistical results.

A group of 400 questionnaires was selected at random and scrutinized for the observations added by respondents in the course of answering checklist questions. Altogether 315 comments were recorded by interviewers on the six items included in our index. About two-thirds of these reinforced or explained the interpretation of apprehension we gave to the checkmarks. For instance, one respondent, worried that expressing his political opinions might affect his job security, specified the area about which he was concerned:

You have to be careful in domestic and state politics. I avoid them. It is embarrassing.

Another professor, who said that he was now more careful regarding controversial reference material, explained his motivation:

This is because students are more apprehensive that readings will reflect on them.

Conversely, unapprehensive respondents often explained their "no" answers. In regard to misrepresentation by students, for instance, many respondents refused to be worried because they felt that such incidents were part of their job.

Any teacher who would worry about that should stop teaching—because I think that in teaching often people listen with half an ear and then go out and make statements about what you said. Also you should be strong enough in your own ideas to refute them if necessary.

Others were not worried because they had confidence in the administration.

It has happened to me but I have never worried about it. I am confident that the whole climate of administration is such as to discount warped student versions.

Conservative respondents often remarked that they didn't need to be cautious because their thinking was in tune with the opinion prevailing in the community.

About 10 per cent of the comments, however, indicate that the checkmarks which form the basis of the statistical treatment did not always catch the real meaning of the respondents' answers. In qualifying a "yes" answer, respondents sometimes said they were worried about the consequences of an expression of opinion, but then added that their worry shouldn't be taken too seriously.

I haven't lost any sleep over it. I'm young and mobile and not worried about security.

It's been just incidental thought on my part, as to what effect my words might have. But it has *not* been a sense of fear.

In most of these cases the qualifications centered around the interpretation of terms used in the question. These people wanted to say that they had considered the possibly dangerous implications of free expression of opinion but were not really worried about them.

The qualifications of "no" answers are somewhat more complex. Some of the respondents said that they had not refrained from frank expression in their writing although they could think of rather characteristic exceptions.

Wait a minute. I haven't toned down, but I have refrained from writing letters to editors, etc., that I would have written on segregation—some letters I have felt the urge to write.

Others said that they had already made protective moves. They said "no" to an apprehension item, but added remarks like these:

But I might point out to students that what they are going to read might be criticized by some people.

In a state college I have to be careful about socialized medicine. If I do refer to it, I refer to a conservative reference.

It should be remembered that in all these cases the response was statistically classified as not showing apprehension.

We found that when the 400 respondents were taken together, the qualifications tended to cancel each other. An affirmative answer which was qualified to a "no" occurred as often as a qualification in the other direction. This means that if we were to shift all the "misplaced" apprehension checkmarks and reclassify every teacher accordingly, the relationships to other factors, reported later in this volume, would remain much as they appear at present except that they might show slightly greater strength.[4]

We also have some statistical information which provides additional support for the apprehension index. The score should be higher among teachers who have a realistic reason for concern. This could occur either because they have actually been attacked, or because some previous association is open to misinterpretation. A commonsense classification of vulnerability in such terms should correlate well with the apprehension score. We know whether or not a professor had been involved in an incident; furthermore, our interviewer inquired as to whether the respondent had ever been a "member of a political group which advocated a program or a cause which has been unpopular or controversial."[5] The frequency

---

4. Characteristically, the qualitative remarks do indicate that the expression of worry is slightly exaggerated while the reports of cautious behavior underrate the actual occurrences.

A rather interesting sidelight can be added. As will be seen later, the colleges were divided into those where the administration protects the faculty against attacks from the outside and those where it doesn't. Respondents from unprotected colleges make about twice as many qualifications to their answers as those who teach at a more secure place. The tendency to feel ambivalent in talking with an outsider seems then in itself to be an indicator of a difficult situation.

5. Thirty-one per cent acknowledged controversial affiliations. Of these, one-fifth were involved in an episode of the kind described in the previous chapter. Among those who had not belonged to such an organization, only one out of twelve had been in trouble.

of apprehension among the four resulting groups of teachers is shown in Figure 3-7.[6]

Figure 3-7
Vulnerability as Related to Apprehension

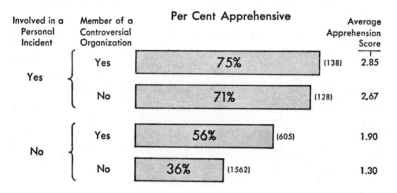

Involved in a Personal Incident	Member of a Controversial Organization	Per Cent Apprehensive		Average Apprehension Score
Yes	Yes	75%	(138)	2.85
	No	71%	(128)	2.67
No	Yes	56%	(605)	1.90
	No	36%	(1562)	1.30

If teachers were actually attacked, they were quite likely to be apprehensive; for these respondents the further effects of past membership were slight. Without a concrete incident, though, the potential dangers of a controversial membership made quite a difference. We report two kinds of measures in Figure 3-7 to show these results. In the bars the percentages of respondents with a score of 2 or more are recorded. The column at the right shows the mean score, the average number of items affirmatively answered by each group. Both measures verify our expectation and imply that the apprehension index is a reasonable and sensitive instrument.[7]

We can therefore accept a surprising finding with the confidence that it has substantive importance and is not due to the

6. Eighteen cases for which no information on past affiliation was available are excluded.

7. The mean score is more sensitive than the proportion with a high score; the latter, however, is much easier to compute and to understand intuitively. It will be used in this report except in a few cases where the mean score will help us to make finer distinctions. Also, since there are relatively few teachers reporting personal incidents and since past memberships make for little difference in their amount of apprehension, the 138 and 128 respondents will be combined henceforth as a single, most vulnerable group.

use of a faulty instrument. For if we compare the extent of apprehension in various groups of schools, we find small variations only, as can be seen from Figure 3-8.

Figure 3-8
Apprehensive Respondents in Nine Types of Colleges

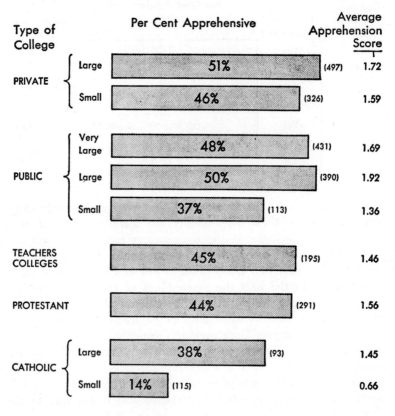

Type of College		Per Cent Apprehensive		Average Apprehension Score
PRIVATE	Large	51%	(497)	1.72
	Small	46%	(326)	1.59
PUBLIC	Very Large	48%	(431)	1.69
	Large	50%	(390)	1.92
	Small	37%	(113)	1.36
TEACHERS COLLEGES		45%	(195)	1.46
PROTESTANT		44%	(291)	1.56
CATHOLIC	Large	38%	(93)	1.45
	Small	14%	(115)	0.66

The small Catholic schools, it is true, have few apprehensive teachers.[8] Otherwise very little difference appears. The apprehension rate is the same in the smaller private schools as it is in Protestant and teachers colleges. Size, also, matters little. This is unexpected, because in Chapter I we saw how different these

---

8. They include a number of girls' colleges staffed by nuns.

groups of schools are in many respects, and in Chapter II that some had come under considerably more attack than others. If these same school groups are so similar in their apprehension rates, a congeries of factors ought to exist which results in such a relatively even distribution. For one, perhaps apprehension itself is a complex experience which might have different meaning in the context of various school types. Again, we must investigate what makes an individual professor apprehensive; maybe personal differences are large, but are balanced by differences between schools which need to be studied. The next four chapters will explore all of these questions.

Chapter IV

THE NATURE
OF APPREHENSION

W‌E HAVE CONSIDERED a teacher apprehensive if he was concerned with the consequences his political opinions might have for his professional reputation and his job security—a somewhat vague description. Apprehension conceived in such terms can find expression in a variety of ways. It can mobilize a person to face danger, or it can make him unfit for action. It can be the result of private experiences, or an attitude developed among groups of people about a common situation in which they find themselves. It can be the expression of a discerning mind, or it may result from an uneasy inability to understand what is going on in the world. What kind of apprehension emerges in this study?

Apprehension and Activism

A NUMBER of items in our questionnaire dealt with varying aspects of teachers' willingness to take an active stand on issues of academic freedom. We may make use of their statistical relation to apprehension to shed considerable light on its nature, and on the position of social scientists during the difficult years.

Two of these questions, given in Table 4-1, presented teachers with hypothetical situations. Those who favored the speech or the debate were then asked what they would do if the president of the college were to ban the event. In the case of the controversial speaker, 40 per cent of the whole sample said they would

Table 4-1
Two Questions to Gauge Resistance

"Suppose you were faculty advisor to a student organization here on this campus that proposed inviting Owen Lattimore, Far Eastern expert (now under indictment in Washington), to speak at a public meeting here. Do you think Lattimore ought to be allowed to speak here or not?"	Not allowed	14%
	Don't know or no answer	6
	Allowed	80
	Total	100%

"There has been a good deal of discussion recently about whether or not the proposed admission of Red China to the U.N. is a proper subject for intercollegiate debate. How do you feel about it—do you approve or disapprove of inter-collegiate debates on the admission of Red China to the U.N.?"	Disapprove	3%
	Don't know or no answer	2
	Approve	95
	Total	100%

protest vigorously to the president; regarding the debate on China, 55 per cent stated they would.[1]

While we cannot know whether the intention to protest would be carried out in a real situation, the mere claim indicates at least a teacher's impulse to act in defense of his convictions. Figure 4-2 shows that the intention to stand up for freedom of expression is more frequent the more apprehensive a person is.

Thus the apprehension of these social scientists did not prevent them from taking strong positions on civil liberties, even to a strange interviewer of whose discretion they could not be completely assured. However, this seems the case only up to a point. Once the degree of apprehension as measured by our index reaches a score of 3, the proportion of activistic responses flattens out; and at the highest level, in each instance, a slight reverse tendency sets in.

---

1. The alternatives offered were: "protest vigorously," "just say you disagree and leave it at that," or "accept his order and not say anything." The last alternative was chosen by 5 per cent on both questions. Just prior to our study President Eisenhower had made the statement that debate on Red China should not be prohibited even in military colleges. Doubtless as a result of this, only 3 per cent of our professors were in favor of such a prohibition, while 14 per cent would keep students from inviting a controversial speaker. Thus a comparison of the two questions contributes to our general knowledge of opinion formation. Seventy years ago a famous British political scientist, Dicey, argued that once a law has been adopted its underlying principle "acquires prestige from its mere recognition by Parliament." The power to confer legitimacy to ideas can rest with many forms of authority. In this case an utterance of the President seems to have done it.

One might, of course, speculate as to whether the two protest questions did not merely elicit fantasies of courage. But another set of questions dealt with what the teachers actually did, rather than what they might do. Our respondents were asked what maga-

Figure 4-2
Apprehensive Professors Are More Likely to Protest against Administrative Interference with Student Activities

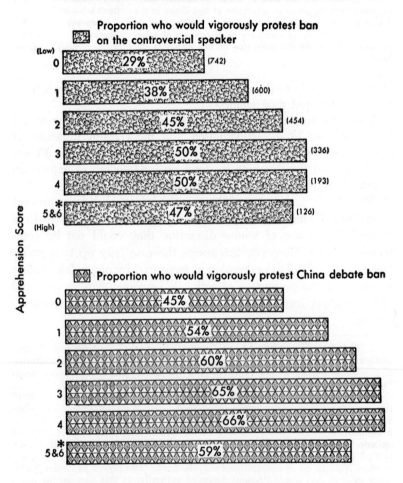

* Because they are so small separately, the two groups with the highest apprehension scores have been combined in this Figure and in those which follow.

zines concerned with public affairs they read. Let us select three magazines which are widely considered somewhat left-of-center and which, therefore, might at the time have been subject to censure by prevailing community opinion.[2] We see in Figure 4-3 that the liberal magazines were more often read by apprehensive respondents; and again for all three we find at the highest level of apprehension a slight decline much like that in Figure 4-2.

At another point in the interview we asked the following question:

Leaving aside Communist publications, which publications that teachers like yourself might receive do you feel are likely to be attacked as being subversive? Any others?

If a respondent indicated a periodical which he himself read as possibly dangerous, we took this as a token of defiance, for he was telling us that he continued to do something which might lay him open to attack. The upper part of Figure 4-4 shows that such behavior occurred much more frequently among apprehensive than among nonapprehensive teachers. But again, among the most highly apprehensive, there is a slight decline.

When similar questions on organizations were asked, no single group stood out enough to permit statistical counts. When we combined all those considered likely to be attacked, 13 per cent of the social scientists reported memberships. Once more, in spite of the danger involved, such membership was increasingly more frequent among those with higher levels of apprehension. The lower part of Figure 4-4 provides the evidence. (Here, incidentally, the decline sets in only at score 6, which is not separately shown.)

We thus arrive at a rather far-reaching conclusion. There is indeed widespread apprehension among these social science teachers, but in general it is hardly of a paralyzing nature; the heads of these men and women are "bloody but unbowed." Only for the respondents with the highest apprehension scores (about 5 per cent of the entire sample) is this perhaps no longer quite so true. While they too are considerably more activistic than the average, they show slightly fewer signs of resistance than the next most

---

2. There are, of course, other liberal magazines, but they are not read by a sufficiently large number of persons to yield meaningful results.

Figure 4-3
Apprehensive Professors Are More Likely to Read Liberal Magazines

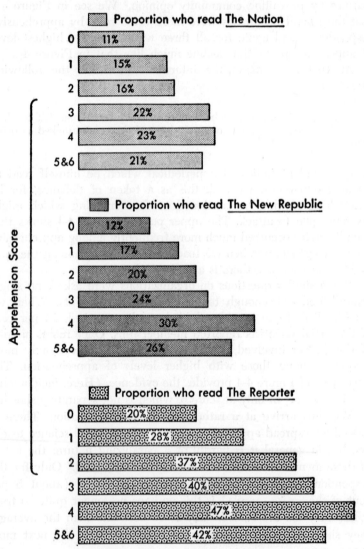

apprehensive group. It could be that on this high level of apprehension some paralysis has begun to set in.

The statistical relation between apprehension and activism, as
found in Figures 4-2 to 4-4, is undoubtedly the result of a complicated mechanism. We are dealing with a middle level of apprehension, so to speak. This is far from the atmosphere of security
in which one would expect a profession to do its best work; but
at the same time in the spring of 1955 it had not reached a level
of demoralization which would rule out resistance to restraints on
academic freedom. What might have happened if the situation

Figure 4-4
Proportions of Professors Who Read a Magazine or Belong to an Organization which They Consider Dangerous

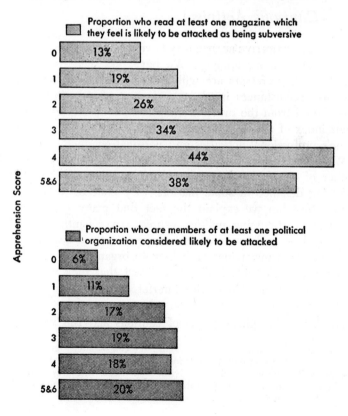

Proportion who read at least one magazine which
they feel is likely to be attacked as being subversive

Apprehension Score	
0	13%
1	19%
2	26%
3	34%
4	44%
5&6	38%

Proportion who are members of at least one political
organization considered likely to be attacked

Apprehension Score	
0	6%
1	11%
2	17%
3	19%
4	18%
5&6	20%

had become worse is, of course, impossible to say. Actually, at the time of our field work, the difficulties had passed their peak in some respects. The elections of 1954 and the censure of Senator McCarthy had brought a change in the tone in which legislative investigations were conducted. With the end of the Korean War, the feeling of the country at large calling for intense vigilance had somewhat slackened. Perhaps as a reflection of this calmer atmosphere, the sense of apprehension of the professoriate at the time of our study might be said to have reached a kind of uneasy equilibrium, with the pressures arising during the difficult years and the responding forces of moral resistance almost balancing each other. Some further observations about this can be made.

Cautious Activism

THE ATTENTIVE READER may have been struck by an apparent contradiction in our analysis. We have just seen that the more apprehensive professors are willing to engage in activities which in some circumstances involve an element of risk. But it will be remembered from the previous chapter than an important element in our index of apprehension was caution: a tendency to be wary in one's professional activities and personal conduct.

We are thus faced with the strange finding that a considerable number of our respondents are actually cautious activists. While professing defiance in some matters, they concede withdrawal in others. How can we explain the fact that many professors who refrain from discussing politics, express fewer controversial opinions in public, and are more circumspect in their writings, at the same time read magazines or belong to organizations which they know are controversial, and are confident that they would vigorously oppose a president who interfered in campus intellectual activities?[3]

To clarify this phenomenon of cautious activism we will first

---

3. The actual findings are beyond doubt. We can parallel Figures 4-2 to 4-4 in this chapter by using only the caution items (see Table 3-2) to classify our respondents. The frequency of the activism items either increases with the caution of the respondents or remains substantially the same. The figures have been relegated to Appendix 8D.

draw on the qualitative remarks volunteered by many professors when they themselves felt their pattern of replies might sound paradoxical. For some teachers the apparent contradiction is quickly revealed as no more than a separation between the attitudes and behavior appropriate to the campus and those befitting the larger community. These teachers felt that, while they are free to do and say what they please in the academic arena, considerable caution and restraint are necessary in off-campus activities if repercussions are to be avoided. A professor of political science at a West Coast state university was quite explicit:

There is no pressure put on me within the university about what I do in the classroom. There has been pressure outside the university on the administration by groups to get me fired because of public statements I have made. These activities and statements are off campus.

Sometimes such a position was accompanied by a feeling of considerable bitterness. One cautious activist told how he had been criticized for his membership in a controversial organization:

Not from the university. There my political activities are welcomed. It's the community—the ignorant and suspicious people who don't know the facts.

Corresponding to this difference in kinds of pressures, some professors were willing to take a stand on the campus as long as the matter could be kept within its confines. A political scientist at a state university, when asked whether he would protest a president's ban of a student discussion, answered:

I would not protest publicly, but would within the university. I would not issue a press release, but use the channels through which we go in the university.

At a college in the Mountain States a respondent said he had toned down some of his writing, and went on to explain:

I had to be careful because it would get beyond the university and people who read it would judge me entirely on what I wrote.

Here the idea seems to be that the mores of academia require that

a man's total intellectual personality be taken into account, while
in the outside world remarks might be torn out of context and
misinterpreted.

We shall see later that, generally, the professoriate feel safer
on the campus than outside its walls. No wonder then that they
would answer a series of questions in a cautious or a courageous
vein according to whether they interpret them in an intramural
or extramural context. This distinction has serious implications.
How can a teacher ever be sure which of his opinions will be confined to the campus? We should expect considerable uncertainty,
a tendency to surround what one says or does with all sorts of
precautions. And this is indeed a second element of which some
respondents were well aware. Many of them do want to stand up
for their convictions, but they become strategists who hold their
ammunition for situations where the aim seems attainable, and
make concessions on the issues which, in the present temper of
the time, they consider undebatable. A professor of government
at a New England university expressed this position quite clearly
in reporting an episode where he agreed with a restrictive move
of the president:

There may be circumstances under which the president might feel this
action a better way to protect academic interests in freedom. There are
times when we do need to make concessions to achieve some important
matter.

This attitude of "saving one's ammunition" was especially likely
to emerge when these cautious activists wanted to be sure that
they were not misrepresented as Communists. A professor of political science in another New England college made the following
statement:

When I was a member of the Progressive Party many critics equated
support of the Progressive Party with sympathy toward Communism.
It therefore became necessary for me and other academicians supporting
the Progressive Party to explain repeatedly that our support had nothing to do with sympathy toward Communism.

At a state university on the West Coast a professor of economics
was deeply disturbed that a display of loyalty became necessary
in order to clarify his true position:

I nearly got fired because of the loyalty oath. I resented very deeply the fact that it had to be signed and before the Korean War refused to sign and helped lead the opposition. Then South Korea was invaded and I was afraid the issues would get mixed up with patriotism and Communism, so I signed.

One should not overlook the difficulties implied in this position. Men and women who oppose Communism may find it quite degrading if they feel forced to reiterate their private convictions in order to satisfy suspicious critics. While they agree with the condemnation of Communism, they fear they may be setting a dangerous precedent on the broader issue of the free expression of opinions. If forswearing heresy becomes general practice, they may some day find themselves in a precarious position if they should deviate from the prevailing mood of the time. As a result, professors often feel embarrassment and even guilt. They are not extremists, but they dislike having to prove it. This came out particularly clearly when we asked respondents whether they occasionally went out of their way to demonstrate that they had no extremist leanings. A history instructor in a small Eastern liberal arts college said:

When I lecture on Marxism I probably am led to spend greater time giving my disagreements with it than previously.

And then he added:

I'm embarrassed to say so.

It is surprising how similarly these experiences were worded by men who taught under quite different circumstances. An anthropologist at a New England college (neither of the two previously mentioned) described the matter as follows:

If you say something critical of the American government, for instance, you feel obliged to say something equally critical of Russia. You go out of your way in this respect to make your position clear. That's one of the bad effects of this whole current climate.

This sense of feeling obliged to show that one is on the right side is rather subtle, and probably not many of our respondents were aware of it or able to articulate it for the interviewer. It is therefore possible that our indicators of apprehension may underrate its statistical frequency. The teacher just quoted would be entirely justified in saying that he did not refrain from expressing his opinions; yet in some way his teaching has been distorted. One professor stated in so many words how difficult it is to describe such an ambivalent position. Discussing the general effects of the difficult years, he illustrated from his own case:

These trends have the effect of making people more concerned to conform to acceptable views. I find myself tending to be more cautious in presenting new ideas. My conscious attitude is "Go to Hell!"; but subconsciously I am influenced.

The complicated mixture of caution and activism appeared particularly in the answers to the following item:

Have you recently wanted to express publicly a political point of view on something, and despite your worry that you might be criticized for saying what you did, you said it just the same?

A third of the respondents reported such an experience, and surprisingly, there was a very sharp increase of this claim as we compare respondents with increasing caution scores.[4] The figures are given in Figure 4-5.

The question conjured up what undoubtedly was a big problem for many respondents during the difficult years: whether it is nobler in the mind to exercise judicious restraint or to take arms against a sea of troubles. One might expect that the particularly cautious teachers would not be the ones to express controversial opinions. However, Figure 4-5 shows that the contrary is true. The question inquires into two things: worry, and action in spite of it. The more cautious professor was, we know, more worried. Yet more often he spoke out—a Hamlet on the campus, with all his hesitations. But why did the resolution tend to be on the side of courage?

---

4. The word "recently" in this question is important. We were only interested in such activities which occurred at a time when the respondent presumably was already apprehensive. We had intended to ask a similar question regarding recent joining of organizations. By a typographical mishap, however, the word "recently" was omitted, making the question (No. 6/5) useless.

Figure 4-5
The More Cautious Professors More Often Report
Defiant Expressions of Opinion

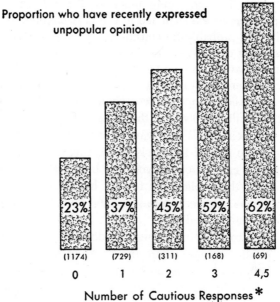

Proportion who have recently expressed
unpopular opinion

23% (1174) 0
37% (729) 1
45% (311) 2
52% (168) 3
62% (69) 4,5

Number of Cautious Responses *

* A cautious response is a "Yes" answer to one of the five items of Table 3-2.

Public and Private Courage

LET US VISUALIZE a college in which an academic freedom case has arisen. A series of incidents has made a teacher controversial and the administration is inclined to dismiss him. They would like to get faculty approval for this, however, and so they call a meeting to put forward their case for the dismissal. This presents no problem for many of the teacher's conservative colleagues: they approve the contemplated action. Other faculty members, who feel strongly about academic freedom, welcome an opportunity to take a stand and even prepare a joint statement.

The middle-of-the-road professor, however, may find himself under cross-pressures. On the one hand he does not want to put himself in jeopardy; signing the statement opposing the administration may some day bring him under attack. He is also threatened if he does not sign. The prevailing mood of the college fraternity is not conservative, as we shall see in the next chapter. If he refuses to sign, he will probably be considered "yellow" by the colleagues he meets every day. While outside forces such as legislative committees may have harsh and definite means to do him damage, he cannot underestimate the subtle deprivations to which his immediate professional environment could subject him. Most members of the faculty involved in this imaginary situation would have to make up their minds one way or another. But some might be "lucky": on the day of the decisive meeting they may be sick or away from the campus on unavoidable business. Then they cannot be blamed by their colleagues for not having signed the petition in favor of the accused colleague; nor will they later have to suffer for having signed it.[5]

This leads to a useful, though crude, distinction between private and public courage, where the frame of reference is the professional community. The professor decides that if a situation develops where he must take a visible stand he may have to chance it and join his peers. But when he thinks he can escape unnoticed, he prefers to be more cautious. If we look more closely at the items which were indicators of caution and those which were indicators of activism, the former appear to refer more to private and the latter more to public situations. Activism was indicated by willingness to protest if the president interfered with the academic freedom of students, and by remaining with an organi-

---

5. It is fortunate that priority disputes between playwrights and university professors are rare. Several months after this paragraph was written, the following lines from a famous musical comedy came to our attention:

> The Lord above made man to help his neighbor,
> No matter where, on land or sea or foam,
> But with a little bit of luck,
> *When he comes around you won't be home.*

We consider the similarity of idea and wording a valuable confirmation.

zation or continuing to read a magazine which could become embarrassing. These items have a strong element of visibility. Friends would notice if one were not to sign a protest or if one were suddenly to drop one's membership or, to a lesser degree, cancel a subscription. In addition, these are reactions to situations requiring a decision one way or another. A colleague is likely to request that one join a protest; an officer of an organization is sure to urge continuation of membership.

The items indicating caution are quite different. Being careful not to bring up certain political topics with one's colleagues is not visible because it means simply not doing something when there is no specific occasion for doing it; the same is true for the tendency to make occasional remarks showing directly or indirectly that one has no extremist leanings. Toning down one's writings or being more circumspect with one's reading lists can easily go unnoticed by colleagues, especially if the change is slow and not attached to specific challenge situations. Thus caution can be exercised without being noticed. Perhaps instead of public and private courage we might speak of its expected and spontaneous versions. Whatever the terms, our material points to an important distinction.

We mentioned earlier that speaking one's mind seemed safer on the campus than on the outside. Now this can be added: not speaking one's mind on the campus, not sharing the general mood of resistance, would also be inadvisable. Left to their own devices many teachers might have considered caution the better part of wisdom. But when the need arose to stand up and be counted, it was safer to do so. In a way, this is an unusual situation. For the most part we think of people's private thoughts as being more "dangerous" than those they express in public. In matters of academic freedom, however, the teacher seems inclined to be courageous in public and cautious in private. This is so because he really deals with two publics. What at times appears dangerous to the larger community is proper in the eyes of one's peers, and they are the ones who matter more.

Thus the community of teachers seems to have made its individual members better men than they would have been if left to their own devices. In intellectual matters we are inclined to think that a man thinks best if he works alone; the derision attached to "committee work" is well known. In matters of morale, the situation is different, at least as long as no panic situation is involved.[6] This last qualification deserves stress. Our study characterizes a specific state of affairs where the dangers threatening from the larger community are not as great as the consequences which would ensue from disapproval on the part of one's professional group. There is no doubt that a changed historical situation would make a considerable difference. If matters grew worse, then private caution and diminution of campus courage would undoubtedly begin to go hand in hand. Still, for those concerned with the integrity of the professoriate, ours is an important result. A professional group such as a college faculty is characterized by frequent and continuous face-to-face contact. If, in such a group, there is a tradition of freedom, this climate of opinion can hold in line many who would otherwise break down under attacks from the broader community. From a policy point of view, then, any strengthening of such local traditions of academic freedom may have disproportionate influence on individual attitudes.

Let us see how far this analysis has progressed. We are attempting a composite picture of the state of mind which is indicated by a sizeable apprehension score. We found a strong element of defiance intertwined with fear for one's job or for one's reputation. However, this defiance was tempered by a variety of precautionary moves. To continue a previous figure of speech: middle level courage and middle level fear are in a somewhat unstable equilibrium. Apprehension seems, indeed, to be a good term to describe this sentiment. But our picture of it would be incomplete without still another dimension: a general sensitivity to problems of freedom of expression and individual liberty, regardless of whether one is himself a potential victim. We shall call it alertness to academic freedom.

---

6. Similar observations have been made by students of the Army in several countries. See S. A. Stouffer, et al., The American Soldier, Vol. II. (Princeton: University Press, 1949), especially Chapters iii and iv, and the paper by Shils and Janowitz, Public Opinion Quarterly, Vol. XII, No. 2, 1948. In the preceding discussion we have used this notion of "support by the primary group" in a rather conjectural way. More specific evidence will be found in the sixth and the tenth chapters.

Apprehension and Alertness
to Academic Freedom

WE KNOW from Figure 3-7 of the preceding chapter that increased vulnerability means increased apprehension. The respondents can also be described according to their general concern with matters of civil liberties. Two items were included in our questionnaire for this purpose.

How closely do you follow civil liberties problems and issues in the news?

Do you find yourself discussing civil liberties issues and problems with your friends, colleagues, or family members?

The checklist answers and the distribution of replies are shown in Table 4-6.

Table 4-6
Distribution of Answers to Two Questions Regarding General Interest in Civil Liberties

Follows Civil Liberties News		Discusses Civil Liberties Issues	
More than most other news	34%	Fairly often	42%
As much as any other news	55	Just occasionally	44
Not as much as other news	11	Hardly ever	14
Total	100%	Total	100%

On the basis of these two questions we can form a crude index by dividing people according to whether they gave two, one, or no affirmative answers. (Affirmative here means "more than most other news" for the first item in Table 4-6 and "fairly often" for the second.) It is not surprising, of course, that personal vulnerability is related to concern with civil liberties. A person who has been involved in an incident, or thinks he might be one day because he has belonged to a controversial group in the past, is likely to follow pertinent news more carefully and to discuss such matters more often. This can be seen in Figure 4-7.

Beyond this we want to show that, regardless of a teacher's own vulnerability, he will be more concerned with civil liberties if he is more apprehensive. This would indicate that apprehension does

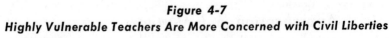

Figure 4-7
Highly Vulnerable Teachers Are More Concerned with Civil Liberties

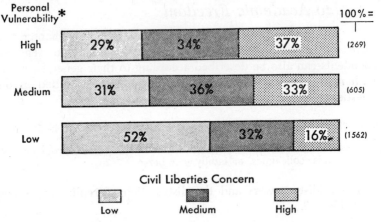

* For this classification, see Figure 3-7 and Footnote 7 in Chapter III. Three cases for whom no information concerning controversial organization affiliations was available, but who had been subjected to personal attack, are now included as ''High'' on personal vulnerability.

not just imply fear for one's own position, but also signifies alertness to the general state of academic freedom and the threats to which it is exposed. Confirmation for this general statement is provided in Figure 4-8. As in Figure 4-7, the whole sample is classified according to vulnerability and concern with civil liberties. Only now each point shows the percentage of respondents who have an apprehension score of 2 or more.[7]

This Figure confirms what we already know: the more vulnerable a teacher the more likely he is to be apprehensive. The new information appears in each of the three lines for teachers having a particular degree of vulnerability. If only fear for personal security contributed to apprehension, within each vulnerability

---

7. The proportions for each point in Figure 4-8 are computed against the "base figures" given in Figure 4-7. There, for instance, the reader can easily see that 52 per cent (815 professors) of the 1,562 having low vulnerability also have a low concern with civil liberties. Now from Figure 4-8 we learn that 29 per cent (237 cases) of the 815 have, nevertheless, an apprehension score of 2 or more. This would be the residual group (about 10 per cent of the whole sample) whose apprehension is probably accounted for by personality characteristics only.

level the proportions of apprehensive teachers should remain constant. A glance at the three lines shows, however, that apprehension is noticeably affected by the respondent's intellectual concern with civil liberties. We conclude, then, that this alertness is one more element involved in the general complex of apprehension.

Figure 4-8
On Every Level of Vulnerability, the More Teachers Are Concerned with Civil Liberties, the More Often They Are Apprehensive

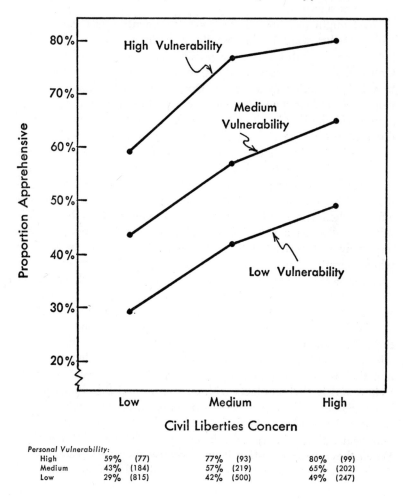

Personal Vulnerability:						
High	59%	(77)	77%	(93)	80%	(99)
Medium	43%	(184)	57%	(219)	65%	(202)
Low	29%	(815)	42%	(500)	49%	(247)

Additional Observations

WE HAVE SINGLED OUT the elements which, in combination, make up the mental set of apprehension: fear (or anxiety, if one prefers the term) not strong enough to paralyze resistance and defiance; activism ambivalent enough not to be tantamount to undaunted courage; alertness to the general problems of academic and civil liberties which goes well beyond mere concern with one's own security.

One might ask how these several elements affect each other. Do professors want to do something about a state of affairs and then become fearful about the possible consequences of their act? Or when they are worried about their own security do they turn to collective action as a result? Does alertness to danger lead to worry about their own situations, or does this work the other way around? Undoubtedly all of these interconnections exist. Moreover, different people go through different processes and there can be mutual interaction between these various elements within the same person over a period of time. Were we to observe individuals for long periods, we would undoubtedly find each of the elements we distinguish sometimes playing the role of cause and sometimes of effect; whenever studies with repeated observations have been carried out, such a network of mutual effects has appeared. But our study was restricted to a cross-section at one point in time, which permitted us occasional glimpses into the past of our respondents. While we can analyze the nature of apprehension and its various components as it existed in the spring of 1955, we can only surmise the dynamics of its development.

Two additional observations deserve mention. One relates to the 125 respondents who were singled out in Table 3-3: the teachers who expressed very little worry but who reported that they had nonetheless become much more cautious in their professional activities and in their contacts with colleagues and the community at large. To begin with, prudence is probably a natural state of mind for these respondents. As they watched the scene during the difficult years, they did not feel in any way threatened themselves. When they favored caution it was because they had become more firmly convinced of certain beliefs: a faculty should not embarrass its administration, nor subject its students to controversial reading materials. If a professor had a sizeable apprehension score, this did not necessarily mean that the difficult years had made him fearful for his job or more sensitive to civil liberties; it might only mean that the pertinent items in our questionnaire gave him an opportunity to reaffirm his basic attitude of caution.[8] (A keen observer of the contemporary college scene who heard about our study expected that this kind of anxiety would be quite widespread among the professoriate: according to his expectations, they would not have become professors if they had not been scared to begin with. Although we did not explore this matter directly, our general findings fail to support this interpretation.)

Our second observation pertains to a surprising negative result in our data. We had expected many professors to view the incidents of the difficult years as an indignity to their profession. To study this possibility we provided a question which would single out teachers who felt a threat to the status of the professor on the American scene. In the beginning of the interview, as described earlier, respondents were asked if the greater public concern with the political opinions of college teachers they had noticed had proved harmful. Anticipating that the answers volunteered to this question might be phrased only in the most general terms, we provided a checklist on which the professors were asked to choose one of four designated consequences of the difficult years. Two of these—"impairing the intellectual role of the college" and "discouraging constructive public discussion"—offered a choice between repercussions felt by the college itself or by the democratic process in general. Almost three-fourths of the respondents chose one of these two alternatives. A third category was political in nature ("It prepares the ground for totalitarianism"); this was checked by 7 per cent. But what about the view in which we were most interested: "It degrades the academic profession"? Only sixty individuals selected this alternative! Although the first two broadly stated choices may have detracted from the two more specific ones, if the connection between the incidents of the difficult years and

---

8. A different pattern seems to prevail in a few of these cases: some teachers previously had deviant leanings, then became converted to the conservative point of view, and no longer worry *because* they feel that their newly-acquired caution has made them secure.

the status of the academic man had been an urgent concern for respondents, certainly more than sixty of them would have chosen the degradation of the academic profession as the most harmful effect of public concern with the politics of professors. We cannot tell whether more indignation of this kind might have been elicited if a more detailed and clinical probing had been attempted. But we have scrutinized the approximately 3,000 free answers which referred to "harmful effects." Even including all comments which by any stretch of the imagination would be relevant, at most 100 contained references to indignities of some sort affecting the professorial role.

Indignation, then, is apparently not an important element in the complex of apprehension we have analyzed in this chapter. Perhaps one reason lies in the occupational inferiority feelings which we described in Chapter I. If so many teachers feel that laymen have little respect for professors, then it is understandable that degradation of the academic profession would not be seen as a major consequence of attacks and investigations. Recently Professor Arthur Schlesinger, Jr., stated as a matter of fact what for us was a hypothesis. In a review of a number of books on academic freedom, he said: "What is really at issue has not been so much 'academic freedom' itself as it is the self-respect and reputation of the academic profession."[9] Our data seem to indicate that Dr. Schlesinger and the authors of the present volume are too small a sample to permit general conclusions based on their own feelings.

---

9. In *The Journal of Higher Education,* June, 1956, pp. 341-42.

Chapter V

PERMISSIVE AND
CONSERVATIVE PROFESSORS

The REACTION of our respondents to the difficult years
depended on the schools in which they taught and on what kind
of people they themselves were. In the next three chapters we
shall take up two key factors which not only play a pivotal role
in relation to apprehension, but are of central importance to
academic life in other ways as well. One of these is a characteristic
of colleges—their quality; it will be discussed in Chapter VII. The
other is an attribute of individual teachers which we shall call
permissiveness. This chapter and the next are devoted to elucidat-
ing its meaning, its intrinsic importance to higher education, and
its intimate relation to apprehension.

A central problem in academic freedom is the right of teachers
to explore new and possibly unpopular ideas. Men professionally
engaged in intellectual inquiry are likely to get involved in controversial issues because their scrutiny is often aimed at the interests
and widely-accepted attitudes of the larger community. If the
ensuing distrust were to eliminate nonconformists from the professoriate, the chances for the emergence of new thinking in the
younger generation would be slim.

Our respondents' stand in this dilemma was bound to be a
crucial element in our findings. But how could it be established?
We needed to know whether these teachers were interested in new
ideas themselves and tolerant toward people who held unorthodox
views. To describe this characteristic we resurrected the word

permissive, in its original double sense. For in Latin "permittere" means to allow, as well as to reach and extend.[1]

Gauging Permissiveness

WHAT IS CONSIDERED an unorthodox idea varies from one period to the next. At one time an interest in radical scientific thought, for instance an early examination of the merits of Darwinism, made many persons controversial. Later an intense concern with women's suffrage or with the beginnings of social legislation would have been considered unorthodox. At other times the study of alien political systems, such an anarchism and Nazism, might have made a good test case for tolerance as well as intellectual curiosity. But these issues do not provide us with appropriate indicators of permissiveness today. There can be little doubt that at the time of this study the problem of Communism offered the only possible choice. Substantively this was not an issue for our project. People's attitudes toward Communism had been amply studied in another investigation also sponsored by the Fund for the Republic, under the direction of Samuel Stouffer.[2] However, we did ask in identical form a few of Stouffer's questions, to be able to compare college professors with the community at large and especially with the community leaders whom Stouffer had investigated.

Two of our items reveal how the respondents felt about people who wish to discuss or express Communist ideas. They provide the basis for a simple classification with which to identify highly permissive professors. Should students who wanted to form a Young Communist League be allowed to do so? Of our total sample 38 per cent said "yes," 53 per cent "no," and 9 per cent could not make up their minds. Second, should an admitted Communist teaching in a college be permitted to remain on the campus? Thirty-five per cent would let him continue to teach, 45 per cent would not, and 20 per cent could not make up their minds. Combining the two sets of replies, 598 teachers (24 per cent) would allow both the League and the teacher, while another 593 (24 per cent) would

---

1. Charlton Lewis and Charles Short, A Latin Dictionary (Oxford: Clarendon Press, 1955), p. 1348.

2. S. A. Stouffer, Communism, Conformity and Civil Liberties (Garden City: Doubleday, 1955), hereafter referred to as the Stouffer survey.

accept one or the other but not both. In the next chapter we shall elaborate considerably on the meaning of the permissiveness thus ascertained. One point, however, should be cleared up at once. While 48 per cent of the teachers were willing under certain conditions to accept the presence of Communists on campus, this does not imply in any way that they were Communist sympathizers. Such an assertion should neither be needed nor expected; but in an era of loyalty investigations and accusations of un-Americanism, it must, unfortunately, be documented.

One of the most interesting findings in the Stouffer survey concerns the aspects of Communism that Americans distrust most. Participants in his study distinguished between the elements of conspiracy in the movement on the one hand, and its incompatibility with American ways of thinking, and especially with religious feelings, on the other. Stouffer offers strong evidence that the average American is much more hostile to Communism on the latter ground: it is experienced as a heresy, a threat to the traditional values of family and country.

Our social science professors made the same distinction and made it even more explicitly. But they were likely to draw a different conclusion. They considered the conspiratorial aspect of Communism more dangerous. Heresy they did not take as seriously, and they wanted to fight it by free discussion. At the time of the Stouffer survey (1954), as well as of our investigation (1955), most experts were in agreement that the danger of acute infiltration of conspiratorial Communists into defense work or government planning agencies had been reduced to a minimum. That the general public nevertheless believed Communism in America a much greater danger than it was considered to be by social scientists is largely due to a difference in attitudes toward unorthodox ideas.

The disagreement in general assessment is quite marked: forty-three per cent of Stouffer's national sample considered Communism a great or a very great danger, compared to 14 per cent of our respondents. But the social scientists made finer distinctions. Six per cent of the general population would not fire a Communist in a defense plant and 26 per cent would allow one to continue as a clerk in a store, a difference of 20 per cent. With professors the same difference is 65 per cent: 82 per cent would not fire a Communist from a store, while only 17 per cent would not eliminate him from a defense plant. Thus in situations where sabotage can actually occur, the professor and the average American are in fair agreement; but when suppression of undesirable opinions rather than security is involved, the professors are considerably more tolerant.[3]

Frequently our respondents testified directly about this distinction. We can single out those who, in checklist answers, considered Communism a very great danger but would not oppose a Communist student organization or the retaining of a Communist colleague. Quite a number volunteered remarks to explain their response pattern. One professor of economics at a Methodist college put it this way:

A Communist is a very great danger—a potential saboteur. But communism is no danger to mass political thought.

In spite of his denominational affiliation, this teacher felt that the chances of an ideological influence on Americans are small. A professor of history at an Eastern private college used almost the same words:

Communists are a very great danger as an espionage group, but their ability to influence public opinion is nil.

Some strongly anti-Communist professors felt that a temporary attraction to Communist ideas would not harm students in the long run. A professor of psychology at a Midwestern private university stated that an admitted Communist is a dangerous person to have students exposed to, yet added:

But I would still be willing to have them exposed. Students handle rabbits with syphilis.

And a young historian at a private Southern university provided, so to speak, the theory for this position when he explained why he would allow a Young Communist League on campus in spite of the fact that he considered Communism a great danger:

It's good for them to get it out of their system.

_____
3. For details of this comparison, see Appendix 6.

It is worthwhile to dwell a moment longer on this distinction between Communism as a conspiracy and as an ideology. In Table 5-1 the two items in our permissiveness index are cross-tabulated.

Table 5-1
The Relation between Two Permissive Responses, One Pertaining to Teachers, the Other to Students*

YOUNG COMMUNIST LEAGUE	COMMUNIST PROFESSORS	
	Should Be Fired	Should Not Be Fired
Should not be allowed	888	198
Should be allowed	145	598

* The remaining teachers gave indefinite answers on one or both issues (250 teachers would allow either the student group or the teacher but were undecided on the other). We report in passing that our respondents were more undecided in regard to a colleague than in regard to students. In part, this was undoubtedly due to a greater empathy with fellow teachers. But the problem of handling Communist professors has also received more discussion; the ferreting out of all the divergent implications of the various alternatives probably contributed to a greater hesitancy in making a final judgment.

Most professors are permissive either on both counts or on neither of them. But there are 145 who would allow a Young Communist League though they would fire a Communist teacher, while another 198 take the opposite position. The divergence of opinion is by no means paradoxical; it can be explained in the light of our preceding analysis.

Both these groups are, as a matter of course, opposed to Communism as a conspiracy, and in most cases even as a political movement. Both belong to the sizeable minority who are willing to respect the expression of heretic opinions even when they disagree with them. They differ, however, in their assessment of what to expect from a student and a professor.

Some think that students' ideas need not be taken too seriously, whereas professors have a certain power which makes the transition from an idea to an act a more clear and present danger. Thus, among the 145 respondents who gave this combination of answers, comments of the following kind were volunteered:

My objection to a Communist teacher is that he has already committed himself to rigid ideas and he is not a free intellectual agent.

If they were not under orders from the Communist Party, they could teach, but they are under discipline and therefore unfit to teach.

The idea of conspiracy is implied here in two forms. One refers to party discipline, with the obvious implication that a Communist teacher might engage in dangerous action if an opportunity should offer itself. The second aspect is somewhat more attenuated: even though it be only a matter of intellectual judgment, the Communist is not free and therefore is not to be trusted. At the same time these respondents say they would not forbid Communist student organizations because they regard them mainly as debating clubs.[4]

In contrast, those who would forbid a Young Communist League but not fire a Communist teacher regarded professors as abstract thinkers who were harmless, but felt that young people might not have enough judgment to understand the line between heretic thought and conspiracy. They felt that a Communist student group might manage to do harm to the society, and would certainly hurt themselves.

By definition a Young Communist League wouldn't be a political party in the usual sense, but would be dedicated to the overthrow of the existing government.

They should study now, and they will have time later to take part in political activities. It will only instill prejudice.

We should protect students from the harm it will do them in the future if they have joined a Communist League.

These respondents said they would not fire a Communist colleague because they did not take him too seriously.

As a matter of policy every college ought to have a resident Communist. More people would know why they are against it. But I don't mean an underground one, or all the benefits would be lost.

There could be a Communist who subscribes to the economic system and not the political; a person who subscribes to the overthrow of the government shouldn't be left in a position to do damage, but profession of social and economic beliefs should not be grounds for dismissal.

Common to all of these comments was the clear implication

---

4. Occasionally there were additional points of view represented in this group. A few teachers approved of Communist student organizations because through them it is easier to keep student activities under surveillance. A few other cases involved the public relations aspect: a Communist teacher is more conspicuous than a Communist student.

that these professors had no Communistic sympathies themselves and were permissive *in spite* of their disagreement with the Communist position.

In addition to these individual declarations, a statistical result suggests rather cogently that permissive teachers were far removed from any subversive activities. We know which respondents had served as consultants to industry and other organizations. It turns out that the probability of such employment was slightly higher among the permissive respondents: 33 per cent of the social scientists who disapproved of having any Communists on the campus were outside consultants, while the figure is 40 per cent for those who would permit both the colleague and the student group. This, of course, is partly explained by the fact that, as we shall soon see, the more permissive professors were also the more expert professionally. In addition, it is probably partly due to their greater flexibility; men and women who have more understanding for other people's convictions may also be more successful at bridging the gap between the academic and business world. Certainly no one will argue that businessmen seek out subversives to hire as advisors.

This concludes our digression into a subject which under normal circumstances would not have deserved so much attention. To return to our classification, we remember that more than half of our sample did not agree with the two permissive items; to subdivide them further, additional information is needed. We can select a few situations in which most academic people would take a permissive stand. Those who nevertheless favor prohibitive measures will be classified as conservatives. Before explaining the choice of term the procedure itself needs to be described.

Gauging Conservatism

IN TABLE 4-1 of the previous chapter we showed that a large majority of the social scientists was in favor of allowing students to invite a controversial speaker to address them. A "don't allow" answer to this item, given by 14 per cent of the respondents, is one good indicator of a conservative position.[5] We also

---

5. There was also a very similar question regarding the China debate but

asked whether a Young Socialist League should be allowed on the campus if students wanted to organize one. Seventy-eight per cent of the social scientists were in favor of such action, 8 per cent were undecided, and 14 per cent disapproved; the latter answer provides a second indication of conservatism. A third item approaches the issue of unorthodoxy more directly. Since the wording of the issue provides, as we shall see, some rather instructive difficulties, it is reproduced in full; respondents who chose the first alternative were considered conservative.

Table 5-2
A Question on the Merits of a Controversial Teacher

"Do you think there is a definite advantage in having a teacher with radical or nonconformist views on the social science faculty here, or do you think that is a luxury at best, which this faculty cannot afford?"		
	Luxury cannot afford	22%
	Can't decide, or No answer	15
	Definite advantage	63
	Total	100%

Knowing that the conservatives are in a minority we wanted to give them every opportunity to go on record, and so we included a fourth item in our set of indicators. Taken from the Stouffer questions mentioned above, it asked whether a clerk in a store who admits he is a Communist should be fired; altogether, 9 per cent said that he should. We felt that this answer could hardly be related to problems of loyalty and security. One who wants to fire a Communist clerk in a store indicates his belief that certain types of opinions should be stamped out as a matter of principle.

Answers to the four questions are tabulated in Table 5-3. We

Table 5-3
The Distribution of Conservative Answers

Number of Conservative Answers	Number of Respondents	Per Cent
4	41	2%
3	127	5
2	213	9
1	494	20
0	1576	64
	2451	100%

the number of restrictive answers was so small that it could not be used for the present purpose.

see that close to two-thirds of the professors did not take any of the four possible conservative positions; only 16 per cent chose as many as two.

Now that we know how conservative and permissive respondents were identified, the choice of terminology needs explanation. We have used the term permissive when often the reader, quite correctly, might prefer that we speak of liberal or progressive teachers. We have avoided these two words because they have changed their meaning too often in the great debate of the last decades. Inversely one might ask why we speak of conservative teachers when our indicators are essentially restricted to campus matters. Now it so happens that the term conservative has not been blurred in recent years, but rather, in some respects, has become crystallized. Various spokesmen have chosen it, whether they take the rather extreme stand of W. K. Buckley or the urbane view of Russell Kirk. What behooves us, however, is to show that social scientists who gave a considerable number of conservative replies to our test questions did, indeed, share the tenets of today's "program for conservatives."[6] In the process of our analysis a detailed compilation of all relevant interview comments concerning the value system of the conservative teacher was made.[7] We present a few examples from it here to illustrate two major themes: disapproval of what Russell Kirk calls "excessive self-expression," and belief in the social function of authority. The former takes its most thoughtful form in Catholic schools where one frequently finds emphasis on the ecclesiastic virtue of *prudence*. The term itself appears quite often. Thus, a professor who would not let students invite a controversial public figure to give a speech on the campus explained his position in the following words:

It doesn't fit in with the pattern of our university. It would be outside the confines of Catholic doctrine; it would be socially imprudent; it would be civil liberties beyond proportion. Just not prudent in the light of his views.

In another college a respondent used similar language to describe

---

6. This is the title of Russell Kirk's book (see Chapter II, footnote 15) which helped us better to understand the conservative position even when we happen not to share it. Words like reactionary or fascist will not be found in our report.

7. It is on file at Columbia's Bureau of Applied Social Research.

the stand his administration had taken on issues of academic freedom:

You are allowed academic freedom within the bounds of the exercise of right, reason, and prudence.

Where all concerned agree on these principles, there is little danger of conflict. Much the same position can be attributed to many who did not explicitly use the term "prudence." A Catholic professor in a secular teachers college voiced his stand as follows:

Never be extreme—suspend judgment. But investigate. Then take a middle course.

The last part of this comment is especially interesting. The respondent recognized the need to investigate the facts of any situation; but, at the same time, he was confident that the truth of the matter would lie somewhere in the middle and that the indicated course of action would be the moderate one. In more detailed and articulate comments this position of moderation often focused on the distinction between liberty and license.[8] The following statement, made by an ordained priest who also has administrative duties, might be considered the text from which dozens of other respondents selected particular elements:

Academic liberty is restricted by the good of the individual and the community; and when a teaching or expressed opinion clearly runs

---

8. It is our impression that over-all disapproval of ideas of academic freedom is rare even in the group which scores high on the conservatism index. Just for the record a few such reactions should be mentioned. A professor in a Middle-Western state college viewed the "civil libertarian" in the following terms.

Civil liberties is looked upon by some as freedom of speech out of all reason. "Civil liberties" to me means, "Trample the constitution of the U.S.A."

For a few, the whole issue of academic freedom was a positive nuisance. As put, rather unanalytically, by one man:

I'm bored with academic freedom talk. . . . I dropped out of the A.A.U.P.—too much talk about academic freedom.

The desire not to be bothered with problems of academic freedom may very well represent an escape from a situation of conflict.

counter to the social good or the individual good, as such, that becomes, not academic liberty, but academic license. Academic license is lawless freedom, freedom which recognizes no restraint of any kind. Academic freedom is liberty under law, and here law is social or individual good.

Self-imposed restraint was not always based on such systematic considerations, nor, of course, was it limited to Catholic professors. In a second form, greater emphasis was placed on the importance of submitting to *authority,* regardless of one's personal opinion. In some cases these concessions were based on a belief that the president of the college, or other authority, has superior competence. A professor in a Protestant-affiliated college would not object to having students debate the admission of Red China to the United Nations; but, if the college administration were to forbid it, he would accept this decision without further question.

I would feel that the president had his reasons and knew something that was good for the college about this.

The implication is that if the respondent himself were as well-informed as his president, he would hold the same opinion regarding the debate on Red China. But in other cases the acceptance of authority was based on a broader principle.

The president has the right to run the school since he is the legitimate head.

In the eyes of this teacher, one does not argue with the president, not because he is better informed or wiser than his faculty members, but just because he is the president, and therefore the "legitimate head" of the institution. Sometimes the same position was presented as simply an expression of personality.

It is my nature to accept the president: I respect local authority along with my own personal choices.

A man in a Midwestern state university, asked whether he ever expressed his own views in class, described a general policy:

I seldom express my own opinion. I express the recognized and acknowledged point of view.

Belief in a hierarchy of responsibilities can also affect what the teacher in turn is willing to permit his students to do; in the following case, it is linked with the notion that, even on the college level, young people cannot yet be trusted to form mature judgments of their own:

My philosophy is that young people are subject to radical ideas. You should present all sides, but prevent them from joining organizations that might be questioned as to loyalty to our type of government.

The Permissiveness Index

IN THE PRECEDING PAGES permissive and conservative professors were identified; their ideas and experiences were given a preliminary review. However, all this does not yet prove that they can be considered to be at opposite poles of a meaningful dimension. It could well be that teachers might be permissive in terms of, say, wanting a Communist teacher protected from dismissal, but still disapprove of students forming a Socialist League. And this indeed happened occasionally, but so rarely that we shall feel justified to combine our two measures into one. If such irregularities never occurred what we should find is this: professors who gave a permissive response did not approve of any restrictive measures; those who scored on a conservative item would not favor freedom of Communistic expression either for teacher or for students. This was indeed the case most of the time, as can be seen from Figure 5-4, which shows how respondents answered both the permissive and the conservative questions.

The great majority of teachers did give answers of a consistent either-or character; 92 per cent of all respondents fall into the right-hand column or the top row of Figure 5-4. What, though, about the remaining 194 teachers in the four cells in the lower left corner of the table?

From the remarks recorded by interviewers we can understand the considerations which went into these apparently somewhat paradoxical answers. For in many cases the respondents seem to have seen all these questions as something of a unit (although they were asked at different points in the interview) and felt impelled

Figure 5-4
Number of Permissive and Conservative Answers
Given by Our Respondents

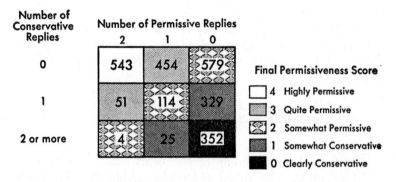

Number of Conservative Replies	Number of Permissive Replies		
	2	1	0
0	543	454	579
1	51	114	329
2 or more	4	25	352

Final Permissiveness Score
- 4 Highly Permissive
- 3 Quite Permissive
- 2 Somewhat Permissive
- 1 Somewhat Conservative
- 0 Clearly Conservative

to explain why they diverged at some point from a consistent pattern. The largest number of deviations were due to the conservatism item which inquired whether a nonconformist colleague is an advantage or "a luxury at best." Otherwise-permissive respondents in tax-supported universities sometimes took the question more literally than we intended; they were worried about the budgetary consequences of having a campus radical. This statement from a sociologist in a Midwestern college is typical:

Because of the trouble we would have with the legislature. Intellectually it's something we can use.

Here the conservative answer is explicitly given with regret. Sometimes it is qualified as a temporary position, as in this reply from a historian in a smaller Eastern college:

These days it is. In general, it is a definite advantage but in these times not so.

In other cases, respondents were reminded of the small size of their college. They approved of unorthodox positions as long as they could be balanced by other points of view. A historian in a Protestant college explained:

In a college of this size with one-man departments, the student would get only one viewpoint. Now in a large department where others would offset him that's different. Outside radical speakers would be a good thing and what a school our size could handle. I think radical ideas must be offset.

Finally, there are a few very specific ways in which an otherwise permissive respondent arrived at a conservative reply. In an Eastern state university with notorious academic freedom difficulties we were told:

This is no place for such a man—nothing to protect him—we would all let him die without a gesture. The university has been dead for many years.

The second largest group of comments came from permissive social scientists, who raised objections against the Far Eastern expert used as an example in one of our questions. Some disagreed with him on substantive matters of policy. (Their decision that he should therefore not be invited sheds doubt, of course, on the civil liberties position of these respondents.) That the expert was then under indictment raised legal doubts in the minds of some more teachers who otherwise gave consistently permissive and non-conservative replies.

A third group of ambivalent response patterns was due to the two questions on student organizations. If a social scientist had reason to disapprove of such groups in general, he would disapprove of the Socialist League, but might well give no other conservative answers. If he was also in favor of accepting a Communist teacher at his college, he would fall into the center 1-1 cell of Figure 5-4. Two typical answers of this kind came from a small private college in the East and a larger one in the Middle West:

It is not that I am against such groups. Rather, it is that I am against such groups being stamped with the name of the college.

No political clubs are allowed here. They should be allowed to exist but not use facilities of the university or be recognized as a university organization.

Most of the 194 answers which fall out of line can thus be accounted for either on the basis of special circumstances in a college or a special interpretation a respondent gives to a question. (Of course some are undoubtedly due to checkmarks misplaced by an interviewer.)

We have dwelt in some detail on these special cases to make three points:

a) Classification in social research always leaves a residue of ambiguous cases which have to be assigned arbitrarily to one class.

b) In the present case the proportion of such deviate cases is unusually small—only 8 per cent.

c) A study of these cases throws additional light on the meaning of the dimension under study.

To assign these deviate cases, the best procedure is to combine the cells so that deviations in both directions cancel each other. This has been done in Figure 5-4. For example, let us consider the teachers called "quite permissive." This group includes two cells. By far the larger of these is the "consistent" one in the top row, where 454 people give one permissive and no conservative answers. To this we have added the fifty-one cases where two permissive replies are attenuated by one conservative reply. Proceeding in this way we arrive at the following five groups.

Table 5-5
Distribution of Our Sample along the Dimension of Permissiveness and Conservatism

Permissiveness Score	Number of Cases	Per Cent of Total
4 (Highly permissive)	543	22%
3 (Quite permissive)	505	21
2 (Somewhat permissive)	697	29
1 (Somewhat conservative)	354	14
0 (Clearly conservative)	352	14
	2451	100%

The reader will notice that we do not call the middle group (score 2) "neutral." In comparison with the broader community, these teachers were still permissive. While they were opposed to any concession to Communists on the campus, they were unwilling to take a restrictive position on any other issue we raised. They would let students form socialist clubs, considered nonconformist colleagues an advantage for a college, and so on.

To avoid the cumbersome term "the permissive-conservative dimension," hereafter we shall simply talk of permissiveness. It will be understood that the terms "conservative" and "a low level of permissiveness" are used interchangeably.

Now that our classification is established, we can be somewhat more precise about the statement made earlier that in most social science faculties conservative teachers were in the minority. It would seem a fair estimate to say that the over-all size of this sector of the professoriate lies somewhere between the 14 per cent whom our index classifies as clearly conservative and the 28 per cent whom it designates as at least somewhat conservative. In

Figure 5-6

There Are Great Variations in the Permissiveness of Social Science Faculties at Different Types of Colleges

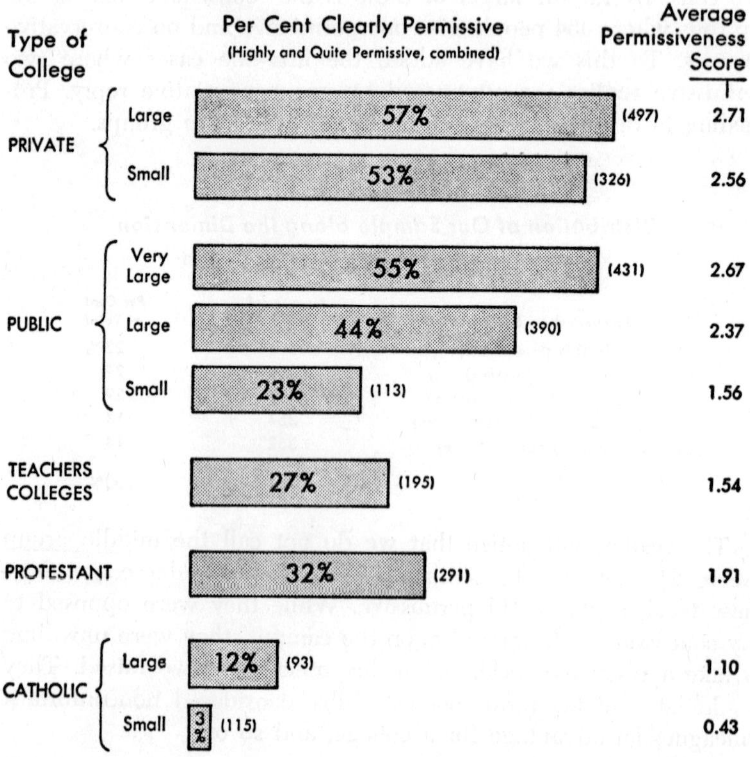

Type of College		Per Cent Clearly Permissive (Highly and Quite Permissive, combined)	Average Permissiveness Score
PRIVATE	Large	57% (497)	2.71
	Small	53% (326)	2.56
PUBLIC	Very Large	55% (431)	2.67
	Large	44% (390)	2.37
	Small	23% (113)	1.56
TEACHERS COLLEGES		27% (195)	1.54
PROTESTANT		32% (291)	1.91
CATHOLIC	Large	12% (93)	1.10
	Small	3% (115)	0.43

addition, the number of conservatives varies greatly between colleges. Or, to express the same facts differently, the proportion of clearly permissive professors, comprising the two top levels in the classification of Table 5-5, shows marked variation from one school to the next. Because the size of the permissive sector will have special significance, some more detailed information is appropriate.

Permissiveness and Type of College

WE TURN once more to our nine basic school types; Figure 5-6 reports for each the proportion of clearly permissive social scientists and their average level of permissiveness, using the scoring system of Table 5-5.

Most noticeable is the sharp difference between secular and traditional schools. (The small tax-supported schools are, as sometimes before, quite similar to the teachers colleges.) Furthermore, size now makes a consistent difference; the larger the school, the more permissive the social science faculty. Finally, the privately endowed colleges of a given size show a consistently higher proportion of permissive professors than the tax-supported colleges. This pattern stands strongly in contrast with the last Figure of Chapter III, where the differences in apprehension between the nine school types were much smaller. This is a strong indication of the pivotal importance of permissiveness. Its role deserves to be traced in considerable detail.

Chapter VI

THE ROLE OF PERMISSIVENESS

Our next goal is to elucidate the connection between permissiveness and apprehension. To this end we need to know more about the role of permissiveness in the world of the social scientist. This means putting the flesh of additional data on the bare bones of the index just developed. We shall, in the following pages, show how permissiveness is related to three characteristics of our respondents: their political leanings, their educational philosophy, and what we will call their professional orientation. Then, having broadened our store of information, as well as the meaning of the permissiveness index, we shall return, better equipped, to the topic of apprehension.

Political Leanings

A rough but useful direction finder in contemporary politics is the colloquial distinction between left and right of center. True, in some respects these terms have no clear-cut meaning: a militant Communist and a member of the Silver Shirts might have more in common with each other than the former shares with a New Dealer and the latter with a New Republican. Still, in the range of the more moderate positions within which our respondents move, the conventional left-right distinction has considerable validity.

Had our study been concerned mainly with such matters, we would have inquired into teachers' views on economic issues, prob-

lems of international relations, and other topics which make up
one's political position. We had space for only a few simple indicators, but they turn out to be sufficient for the present purpose.
We know how our respondents vote: in the first chapter their
over-all preference for the Democratic Party was interpreted as
a sign of occupational protest. But, and probably more importantly,
this vote also has more specific political meaning. In recent decades
the Democratic Party has been the proponent of major economic
and social innovations, and in this sense stood left of center. The
top part of Figure 6-1 shows that permissive professors overwhelmingly voted Democratic in 1952, with the proportion of Democrats diminishing sharply as one moves to the more conservative
groups. The objection could still be raised that we impute to a
Democratic vote an element of social dissent which for many
voters it does not have. So we add information on reading habits,
which were first mentioned in Chapter IV. Everyone will agree
that politically *The Reporter, The New Republic,* and *The Nation*
are moderately left-of-center in just the sense we are discussing
here. The middle part of Figure 6-1 shows that readership of
these journals is strongly related to our permissiveness index.[1]

The last information given in Figure 6-1 points in the same
direction. In Chapter III we discussed the proportion of professors who had joined controversial political organizations. Since
the great majority of controversies during the time of our study
involved groups which were to the left of center, this set of figures
reveals once more that permissive teachers tend to share that
position.[2] For full measure we have the testimony of our respond-

---

1. While studying the reading patterns of our respondents we came across
an interesting finding about *Time* Magazine. Clearly conservative respondents
were considerably more likely (70 per cent) to list *Time* among the "periodicals dealing with politics or public affairs" they read than were highly permissive professors (38 per cent); the other groups as usual fell progressively
in between. Whether permissive professors actually read *Time* less, or simply
less often thought of it as a periodical dealing with public affairs, we cannot
say. Both *Newsweek* and *U.S. News and World Report,* incidentally, follow a
pattern similar to that of *Time.*

2. Since respondents might vary in deciding what constitutes a "controversial" organization, and since a few of these were clearly not left-of-center,
a check on this result is desirable. We therefore classified the following organizations as "left-of-center": Americans for Democratic Action, American
Civil Liberties Union, American Veterans Committee, League of Women

Figure 6-1
Indications that Permissiveness Is Related to the Conventional
Left-Right Distinction

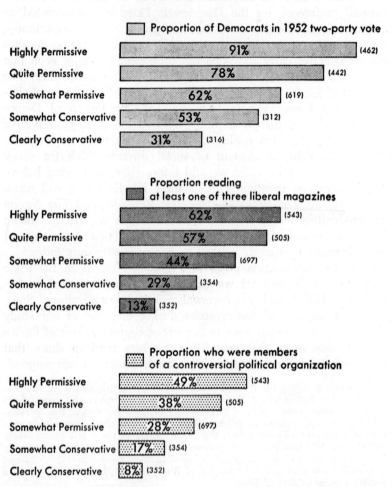

☐ Proportion of Democrats in 1952 two-party vote

Highly Permissive   91%   (462)

Quite Permissive   78%   (442)

Somewhat Permissive   62%   (619)

Somewhat Conservative   53%   (312)

Clearly Conservative   31%   (316)

Proportion reading
at least one of three liberal magazines

Highly Permissive   62%   (543)

Quite Permissive   57%   (505)

Somewhat Permissive   44%   (697)

Somewhat Conservative   29%   (354)

Clearly Conservative   13%   (352)

Proportion who were members
of a controversial political organization

Highly Permissive   49%   (543)

Quite Permissive   38%   (505)

Somewhat Permissive   28%   (697)

Somewhat Conservative   17%   (354)

Clearly Conservative   8%   (352)

Voters, cooperative and consumer groups, and miscellaneous similar organizations. It turns out that 30 per cent of the highly permissive teachers belonged
to or contributed to at least one of these organizations at the time of the
study; the percentage declines regularly to 2 per cent of the clearly conservative respondents. This independent check therefore verifies our interpretation
of the bottom part of Figure 6-1.

ents themselves. One of our questions read as follows:

Table 6-2
A Political Question

On political matters, do you feel that you are more liberal or more conservative than most of the faculty here?	More liberal	39%
	Same	39
	More conservative	12
	Don't know, or No answer	10
	Total	100%

Here the words liberal and conservative were used, which in general speech have much the same connotations as left and right. Very few professors had difficulty in classifying themselves in these terms. The distribution of replies, incidentally, is interesting in itself. One would logically expect that on the average an equal number of teachers would consider themselves more liberal and more conservative. Yet the self-designation of "more liberal" occurs over three times more often. Obviously, being politically progressive is at a premium in this sector of the professoriate. And this tendency becomes stronger, the higher a respondent ranks on our index. Among the highly permissive respondents, 57 per cent consider themselves politically more liberal and 6 per cent more conservative; among the clearly conservative professors, the corresponding figures are 20 per cent and 14 per cent.[3]

---

3. The question was also asked in regard to other groups connected with the college. The answers were distributed as follows:

Table 6-3
Respondents' Comparisons of Their Political Ideas with Those of Other Groups

			COMPARED WITH		
Respondent is	Trustees	Community	Alumni	Administration	Faculty
More liberal	67%	67%	56%	51%	39%
Same	11	16	14	32	39
More conservative	2	5	3	4	12
Doesn't know	20	12	27	13	10
Total	100%	100%	100%	100%	100%

Table 6-3 permits a kind of ranking of four groups as they are seen through the eyes of our respondents. Taking themselves as yardsticks, they consider the trustees and the community as most conservative. The alumni come next, although a large number feel that they really don't know enough about the alumni to make a comparison. The administration, interestingly enough, is perceived as most akin to the norms of the teachers themselves.

The figures given in the preceding pages do, of course, leave room for exceptions. A number of respondents in large universities who themselves say their economic and international views are to the right of center, opposing "the welfare state" and "international entanglements," nevertheless score high on our permissiveness index. They believe that everyone has to look for his own salvation and that it would not help to restrict students or colleagues in what they think or do. Inversely, there are examples of professors, especially in small schools, who hold what would customarily be called progressive points of view, except that they feel that politics in any form should be kept away from the campus; consequently, they answer the conservative items affirmatively. Statistically speaking, however, there remains a marked correlation between the permissiveness index and our information on respondents' political location to the left and right of center.

Why, then, don't we make the latter, a conventional and easily understandable distinction, the pivot of our further analysis? The answer is that the whole story has not yet been told. Permissive teachers also have a different educational philosophy and professional orientation. What we try to reach by our index is a rather basic characteristic which underlies a considerable variety of beliefs and attitudes.

Educational Philosophy

THE HANDLING of controversial subjects in the classroom is an almost stereotyped issue in discussions of academic freedom. We were, understandably, interested in learning whether a dangerously large number of teachers shied away from such discussions during the difficult years. One of our questions, given in Table 6-4, broached the problem head on.

At first sight, the replies are reassuring from a conventional civil liberties point of view. The results indicate a near unanimity among our respondents, in that very few said they avoided opportunities for the discussion of controversial matters. More than two-thirds of these social scientists, in fact, would seek them out. But in what spirit is this done? A teacher truly believing in the value of free discussion should probably become genuinely in-

Table 6-4
A Question on Classroom Discussion

Some claim there hardly exists an area in the social sciences which does not lend itself to value judgments—that is, subject to difference of opinion. Now, in general, for the courses you teach, which emphasis would you lean to?

1. Such controversial matters should be discussed frequently in undergraduate teaching because of the educational value of such discussion.   **68%**

2. One should answer such questions honestly when they come up but not seek out such discussion.   **27**

3. In times like these, it is better to avoid the discussion of such controversial issues as much as possible.   **1**

    Don't know, or No answer   **4**

                                Total   **100%**

volved in this interchange of ideas. If he does not, there remains an uneasy suspicion that he looks upon the discussion of controversial matters more as an educational device than as a serious effort toward intellectual enlightenment. This possibility was strongly suggested by a second question which, together with the distribution of answers, is given in Table 6-5.

Table 6-5
A Question on Revealing One's Views

In teaching subjects which might require questioning of traditional values, which of these two approaches do you personally feel is a better educational policy for teachers to follow:

1. After proper discussion, to argue in a measured way for his own point of view,   **38%**

                    or

2. To give all sides of the question impartially without revealing his own views?   **44**

    Don't know, or No answer   **18**

                             Total   **100%**

The picture is greatly changed. Barely more than a third chose to stand up for their own point of view, and the proportion who hesitated to express an opinion is quite high. Can controversial issues really be discussed if the teacher himself is not willing to present his own opinions? In order to assess the significance of the discrepancy between the two questions, several things would have to be known.

On what grounds are student discussions so highly approved? Three major positions can be taken in this connection. One is the nineteenth century belief that discussion leads automatically to truth, a belief best represented by John Stuart Mill's essay on freedom. The second position is almost the opposite one. There are certain topics on which there is no ultimate truth, and so we all have to adjust to each other's beliefs. Since controversial discussions will stay with all of us all our lives, we should learn in school how to handle them. This was Edward L. Thorndike's view; and, to our knowledge, he is the only writer who ever dealt seriously with how such discussions should be handled by teachers.[4] The third position is that of the educational technician: discussion of controversial issues, like Latin grammar or mathematical logic, sharpens the mind. In the first two cases it would seem helpful, perhaps indispensable, for the teacher to contribute an expression of his own point of view. Only in the last can his own neutrality be maintained without potential loss to the educational objective. Although further research would be needed to confirm this conclusion, we are inclined to feel that the high approval of student discussion is often equivalent simply to applauding an educational trick.[5]

To be sure of this, it would be important to know on what grounds 44 per cent of our sample feel they should not stand up

4. *The Teaching of Controversial Subjects* (Cambridge: Harvard University Press, 1937).

5. There are two attenuating circumstances which might make the discrepancy between the statistical findings of Tables 6-4 and 6-5 somewhat less drastic. From qualitative remarks we know that the wording of the question reported in Table 6-5 created difficulties. We used the phrase "argue in a measured way." Quite a number of the respondents listened mainly to the word "argue" and refused an affirmative answer, stating that they would express their point of view but would not argue for it. With different wording the discrepancy might have been somewhat smaller. It is also interesting that in Table 6-5 we find 18 per cent of the respondents undecided; accompanying remarks volunteered by respondents show that something more than difficulties with the word "argue" is involved here. In Table 6-4 the number of "Don't knows" is negligible. We are inclined to suggest that this difference is an indicator of the atmosphere created during the difficult years. It is still all right to let students have their say; but a teacher has to be careful, not only in what he does, but even in what he says proper educational policy should be.

for their own opinions. One possibility should be frankly faced. It is difficult to discuss controversial matters like religion or sex in the classroom, even if the teacher is free to proceed without any outside interference. One reason for this is the lack of both a consistent educational theory and recorded cumulative experience in the conduct of such discussions. It would be highly instructive to carry out an inquiry into such problems: How do social scientists actually handle controversial issues? Are they guided by the observed reactions of their students or their own inhibitions? What difficulties have they encountered in the classroom and what consequent adjustment have they made? To our knowledge, no such study exists.

Some of the many professors who preferred not to state their own value positions in class might have felt that the social sciences, succeeding an earlier emphasis on amelioration, have reached a stage where emphasis on careful description and scientific dispassion has high priority. By taking a position on issues only when they are substantiated by evidence, they would impress upon their students the scientific soundness of their profession. But the results of a third question hardly support such a view.

We wanted to find out how many social scientists would like to encourage in their students an enthusiasm for a better society. Fearing that in the threatening climate of the difficult years only a small proportion of social scientists would openly subscribe to such a philosophy if the question were put directly, we suggested a parallel with the less embattled and indeed almost universally accepted ideal of American society, the notion of technical progress. The rather elaborately worded question is given in Table 6-6.

Three-quarters of the professors say that they consider a better society an urgent or quite important goal of their teaching. It is possible that the parallel with technical progress induced many respondents to overstate their belief in the amelioratory duties or chances of the social sciences. However that may be, withholding one's own views on problems of values is not likely to instill in students the zeal for a better society.

Thus, while the educational philosophy of our respondents was only a marginal object of our inquiry, our data and its interpretation lead us to three impressions: there was considerable uncertainty on the matter of controversial issues among the rank and

Table 6-6
A Question on Social Betterment

In engineering school education, it is said to be important for students to understand the prevailing state of the mechanical arts. In addition, their education should prepare them to make their own original contribution and to accelerate new developments.

Some say this is directly comparable to the *intellectual* training of students in the social sciences. It is argued that these students should be prepared to make their own original contribution to help society better meet the needs of its people.

How important do you see this element of creative preparation in the teaching of the social sciences to undergraduates?

Urgent part of undergraduate teaching	36%
Quite important part of undergraduate teaching	40
Minor part of undergraduate teaching	11
Not proper function of undergraduate teaching	2
Honestly have never given it much thought	7
Don't know, or No answer	4
Total	100%

file of the professoriate; technical literature on the subject is almost completely lacking; and there is an insufficient formulation of the problem by those who consider such discussions a self-evident part of a civil liberties program. In one respect, however, we have a positive finding. Insofar as there is a consistent thread in our respondents' attitudes, it too is related to their level of permissiveness. This can be seen in Figure 6-7.

The more permissive a social scientist, the more likely he is to approve classroom discussions, and the more frequent is his belief that he should try to prepare students for participation in future social improvement. When it came to presenting one's own point of view, there is a reversal of trend in the figure for clearly conservative teachers. Special tabulations show that this rise was accounted for by teachers in denominational schools. At many of these colleges, the existence of a revealed truth was taken for granted; consequently, the exposition of this truth was considered a duty of the teacher.

Perhaps the most revealing result emerges from a fourth question in this educational sequence which dealt with a familiar, even stereotyped, issue: Should social scientists try to sensitize

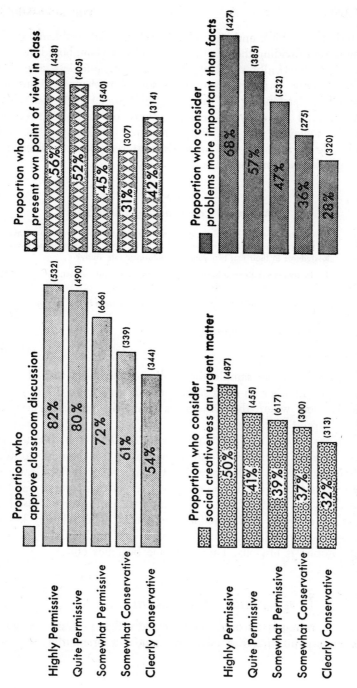

Figure 6-7*
Permissive and Conservative Teachers Differ in Their Educational Philosophy

Proportion who
approve classroom discussion

Highly Permissive 82% (532)
Quite Permissive 80% (490)
Somewhat Permissive 72% (666)
Somewhat Conservative 61% (339)
Clearly Conservative 54% (344)

Proportion who
present own point of view in class

Highly Permissive 56% (438)
Quite Permissive 52% (405)
Somewhat Permissive 45% (540)
Somewhat Conservative 31% (307)
Clearly Conservative 42% (314)

Proportion who consider
social creativeness an urgent matter

Highly Permissive 50% (487)
Quite Permissive 41% (455)
Somewhat Permissive 39% (617)
Somewhat Conservative 37% (300)
Clearly Conservative 32% (313)

Proportion who consider
problems more important than facts

Highly Permissive 68% (427)
Quite Permissive 57% (385)
Somewhat Permissive 47% (532)
Somewhat Conservative 36% (275)
Clearly Conservative 28% (320)

* The percentage figures reported here were computed after the elimination of those who declined to choose an answer. The size of this undecided group can be seen in Tables 6-4 to 6-6 and presently in Table 6-8. By and large, the proportions who could not make up their minds were the same on all levels of permissiveness.

students to think and care about major social problems, or focus
more on providing them with factual information about how society
works? Practically speaking, these are meaningless alternatives.
One cannot seriously attempt to solve problems without a detailed understanding of the facts, and social facts can only be
understood as outward manifestations of underlying concepts.
It is, however, well-established research experience that such a
vaguely formulated and unrealistic stereotype can often tap a
respondent's more basic beliefs.

Table 6-8
A Question on Teaching Stereotypes

If you *had* to make a choice, in general, which of these two approaches
do you think ought to be emphasized more in teaching the social sciences
to students in their first two years of undergraduate study?

1. To give the students a basic grounding of facts in the subject,	40%
or	
2. To get the students thinking about the problem areas in the subject?	39
Don't know, or No answer	21
Total	100%

For the whole sample the replies came like a toss of a coin:
an equal number on each side. And yet, as Figure 6-7 shows, this
is the item where the differences along the permissiveness score
were largest.

Considering all four questions together, the picture adds
up to this: permissive and conservative teachers do differ in
their educational philosophy; but the difference is not clearly conceived and articulated. The conservative position is more traditional
in the sense that it places less value on controversial discussion,
critical analysis, and ameliorative efforts. The relation between
left-of-center political leanings and a less traditional educational
philosophy is obvious. The syndrome becomes enriched if a third
element is added.

Professional Orientation

IT HAS BEEN OBSERVED repeatedly that professional workers
in an organization can have two kinds of orientation. Engineers

and natural scientists who work for commercial companies, for instance, may either place emphasis upon the approval of their business superiors or upon recognition by their professional peers.[6] The college professor, often without knowing it, faces a similar choice: should his reference group be his colleagues on the campus and all over the country, or his superiors in the college administration, and maybe the local community? Of course, such orientations are not mutually exclusive: local recognition is, for example, often achieved as the result of national reputation. But during the difficult years the two loyalties could potentially clash. Laymen at large were in a conservative mood, a mood which the social science professoriate, as we have seen, did not share. Did permissive and conservative professors, as a result, make different choices when faced with significant alternatives?

One of our questions approached the matter by raising a problem of public relations, a topic much commented upon by students of the American college scene. Robert M. Hutchins, for instance, in *Some Observations on American Education*,[7] calls concern with public relations the main motive driving trustees toward conformity. Our question dealt with the proper handling of a controversial colleague.

Table 6-9
A Question on Faculty Rights

If you had to make a choice, in a case in which a member of the faculty is accused of being subversive or of engaging in un-American activities, which do you think it *most* important for the college administration to protect—the reputation of the college or the rights of the faculty members?		
The reputation of the college		11%
Depends		15
The rights of the faculty members		65
Don't know, or No answer		9
Total		100%

As might be expected, the large majority of our sample considered professional prerogatives paramount. But there are still sharp differences among our respondents. As Figure 6-10 shows, 80 per cent of the highly permissive professors would give priority

6. See, for instance, Leonard Reissman, "A Study of Role Conceptions in Bureaucracy," *Social Forces*, Vol. 27, pp. 305-10. We are indebted to Professor William Evan for having brought to our attention the relevance of the notion of professional orientation to our materials.

7. Cambridge (England) University Press, 1956, p. 56.

to faculty rights, compared to but 46 per cent of the clearly conservative. Somewhat more inferential evidence comes from an interview question regarding a special teacher's loyalty oath. In colleges where such an oath was required, professors were asked whether they had welcomed signing it. In other schools the question was put on a hypothetical basis: If an oath were required, would our respondents refuse, sign with reluctance, or welcome the opportunity? Altogether, 18 per cent welcomed an oath. The lower part of Figure 6-10 shows how sharply our five classes of social scientists differed on this point. Only 3 per cent of the highly permissive approved of the oath, but 52 per cent of the clearly conservative professors did so.

Figure 6-10
Permissive Teachers Are More Concerned with
Their Professional Rights

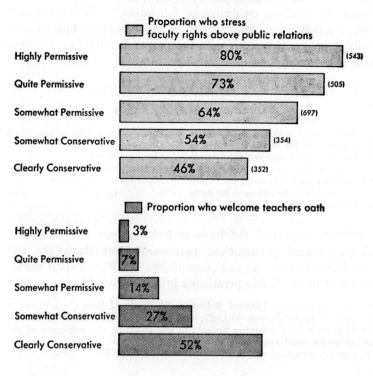

From these results, one could call the permissive professor union-minded, because he considered loyalty to his professional group more important. Actually, this is a more than metaphorical use of the term. Permissive teachers tended more often to be members of the American Association of University Professors, as can be seen in Figure 6-11. Finally, interest in problems of the academic profession was shown by a teacher's concern with civil liberties. Our questions on this matter, discussed in Chapter IV, dealt with the respondents' interest in discussing and reading about civil liberties topics. The answers made it clear that academic freedom issues were prominent among these. Figure 6-11, then, by reveal-

Figure 6-11
A.A.U.P. Membership and Interest in Civil Liberties again Show Permissive Teachers' Professional Orientation

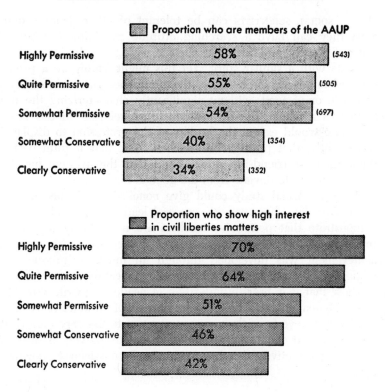

ing permissive teachers' strong interest, attests again to their predominant professional orientation.

The notion of permissiveness has now been broadened considerably. It is closely related to—and may be the basis of—the respondents' political leanings, educational philosophy, and professional orientation. It promises to be pivotal indeed for the further study of apprehension. But before turning to the final evidence, one more question needs to be raised: Is this characteristic a widespread but purely personal attribute, or a matter of relevance to the whole professional life of a social scientist?

The Occupational Relevance of Permissiveness

SOCIAL SCIENTISTS can be tolerant of other people's opinions; they can have a searching attitude regarding the current state of society and feel that their teaching should imbue their students with a similar spirit. Yet this might simply be a private state of mind—as, for instance, the preference for a certain type of music or of food—without significantly characterizing the profession as a whole. For an attitude to be relevant in this larger sense, we would expect the leaders of the profession to display it prominently, that prestige be attached to it, that it form part of the cement of friendship groups, and that the average member should hesitate to deviate from the general norm.

Only a special study could give conclusive evidence on this point. Our data, however, give several leads. First of all, we can demonstrate that permissive teachers are more likely to achieve professional distinction. In Chapter I a measure of professional achievement was developed through an index of productivity; while this measure is mainly based on publications, we were able to show that it is broadly indicative of academic merit. Now Figure 6-13 demonstrates that the proportion of productive scholars rises as we move from the very conservative to the very permissive respondents. It should be remembered that by its very nature our index of productivity increases with age. Permissiveness, however, has the opposite tendency;[8] younger people are much more likely to be permissive. It is therefore necessary to study the relation between permissiveness and productivity separately for different age groups. This is done in Figure 6-13. Within each age group, the proportion of productive social scientists is highest in the highly permissive group and declines continuously to the clearly conservative.

It is not essential to unravel the causal pattern implied in Figure 6-13. In part, permissive social scientists are more fully integrated in their profession and can therefore devote themselves more successfully to their academic work. At the same time, expressing permissive viewpoints might facilitate gaining a reputation, having, therefore, easier access to publishers, and so on. By a relevant characteristic we mean such an over-all effect resulting from several contributing factors.

A similar outcome can be sensed in another finding. It will be remembered that we asked our respondents how they felt about personal relations within the faculty. If permissiveness is a relevant characteristic on the campus, then we should find that where a group of colleagues have similar attitudes—either permissive or conservative—the cohesion between the members should be greater than in a faculty which is split on the matter. This would not hold true for an irrelevant characteristic: the good relations between social scientists are probably relatively unaffected by their feelings about baseball or food. To make an appropriate test, we restricted ourselves to seventy-seven schools at which we had sufficient interviews for the computing of rates to make sense.[9] By determining the proportion of permissive professors at each of these, we may

---

8. The relation between permissiveness and age is as follows:

Table 6-12

| | CLASSIFICATION OF RESPONDENT | | | | |
	Highly Permissive	Quite Permissive	Somewhat Permissive	Somewhat Conservative	Clearly Conservative
40 years or younger	328	258	299	127	126
41 to 50	125	132	188	86	101
51 years or older	90	115	201	140	121

The way in which increasing age makes for a decline in permissiveness will be discussed in Chapter X.

9. At each of these seventy-seven schools at least thirteen teachers were interviewed. They include twenty-eight privately-endowed, thirty-one tax-supported, seven Catholic, nine Protestant, and two teachers colleges.

Figure 6-13*
The Proportion of Productive Professors on
Various Levels of Permissiveness

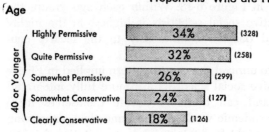

Proportions Who are Productive

Age

40 or Younger

Highly Permissive	34%	(328)
Quite Permissive	32%	(258)
Somewhat Permissive	26%	(299)
Somewhat Conservative	24%	(127)
Clearly Conservative	18%	(126)

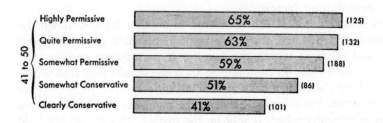

41 to 50

Highly Permissive	65%	(125)
Quite Permissive	63%	(132)
Somewhat Permissive	59%	(188)
Somewhat Conservative	51%	(86)
Clearly Conservative	41%	(101)

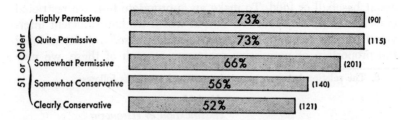

51 or Older

Highly Permissive	73%	(90)
Quite Permissive	73%	(115)
Somewhat Permissive	66%	(201)
Somewhat Conservative	56%	(140)
Clearly Conservative	52%	(121)

* A reminder to the reader of how a figure like this operates: Table 6-12 showed that there are 328 highly permissive young teachers (this number is also found in parentheses beside the top bar in Figure 6-13). Now we learn that 34 per cent of the 328 have a high productivity score; the remaining 66 per cent of them, of course, have a lower productivity.

classify the colleges themselves according to the spread of permissiveness on the faculty. In somewhat loose language, we can then speak of permissive institutions and conservative ones, as distinguished from those where the faculty is divided. Figure 6-14 corroborates our expectation. In permissive as well as in conservative colleges the proportion of respondents who consider their relations with colleagues unusually good is higher than in the two middle groups which are more divided.

Figure 6-14
Homogeneous Faculties Have Better Social Relations than Faculties Divided on Permissiveness

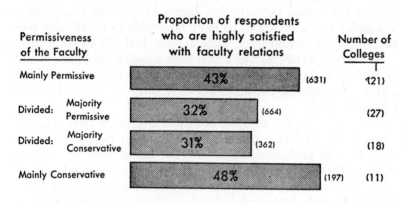

Several studies have shown that the sharing of beliefs which are relevant to a group facilitates friendships among that group and that, inversely, close personal contacts lead to a similarity of relevant attitudes. If this general finding is accepted, then Figure 6-14, with its intimation that faculties divided on permissiveness are likely to be socially less satisfied as well, supports the relevance of this characteristic for social scientists. This raises a question which requires some speculation: Why is permissiveness, in its broad meaning, so frequent among, and so relevant for, these teachers?

The Professorial Mind

THERE ARE SEVERAL REASONS for a natural selection of permissive persons among entrants to academic life. For a young man coming from a business background, a teaching career involves a break in tradition. The business community has an understandable affinity with the conservative credo, with its belief in the value of tradition and authority, its corresponding distrust of people who critically scrutinize institutions like religion and the family, and its belief in the social advantages of private property and the disadvantages of state interference in economic affairs. A son or daughter who for some reason—be it rebellion from parents or intellectual curiosity—has begun to question these values will look for new ones, and be more hospitable to unorthodox possibilities. In our terminology, such an individual will be permissive.

If the prospective teacher comes from a professional background he is likely to have grown up in an atmosphere of permissive ideas and—barring special circumstances—will carry them into his own academic work.

Once he is on the campus, economic and social circumstances also militate against a conservative affirmation by the academic man. College professors are among the lowest paid of all professions. This might not be decisive if the lack of economic advantages were counterbalanced by considerable prestige, as is true for certain ecclesiastic and judicial positions in America and for the university professor in Europe. But such is not the case with college teachers in this country. We know that our respondents believe their occupation is not highly esteemed in the community; the higher the professional status of a professor, in fact, the more strongly he feels that his prestige is low in the outside world. Some of the reasons are not difficult to trace. One important factor is the organization of education in America. The American college is a strange combination of an extended high school and the beginning of a true academic training center. One hundred fifty thousand college professors staff these schools. Although many of them may not deserve special prestige, the elite among them, who properly compare themselves with the small number of university professors in other countries, find that they have in no way comparable prestige and influence, because, to the general public, they are indistinguishable from the large mass of all other college teachers.[10] One might answer that the American professor could derive his self-respect from the prestige he has within his own profession and could forget about what the community thinks of him. Apart from the psychological unrealism of such an idea, the very size of the American professoriate makes it improbable. In a small professional group there can be a high degree of social acoustics. What one man says will be quickly appraised by the others, and their appraisal may matter a great deal. In a large profession it takes a long time before a single voice is heard, and the lack of an echo deprives the individual of another means of psychological support. Small economic return, little prestige on the outside, and scarce means of mutual prestige reinforcement— little wonder that the very position of the professor in the American social structure is not likely to make him approve of it unequivocally.

What has been said so far is true in general for the academic world. The social scientist faces an additional situation deriving from the nature of his work, which is likely to strengthen a basically permissive attitude. A great discovery of anthropology was that there are social systems completely different from ours and yet viable. A major contribution of historians is the idea that in other periods the modes of thinking and the forms of social relations were different than ours, and require reconstruction for contemporary understanding. The intellectual task involved in these and many similar endeavors of the social scientist are contingent on his ability to visualize a state of human affairs radically different from that of today. It is true that as a scientist he is subject to the same laws of evidence as are his colleagues in all other realms of knowledge. Yet for him ultimate scholarly accomplishment must depend upon a kind of imagination which has initially to be akin to criticism and is not, therefore, consonant with the intellectual mood of the conservative.

---

10. At least one other comparison with Europe is worth mentioning. In the United States the teacher in the grade school, the one with whom every American has contact, is usually a woman. Especially in small towns, she does not have nearly the prestige of her male counterparts in European villages and towns.

Occupational self-selection, then, certain features of the American social structure, and the very task of the social scientist, make permissive tendencies probable to begin with. Once these conditions have come into play, an additional process sets in. Any group which inclines to a professional ethos—doctors or businessmen or civil servants—will tend to reinforce it by mutual interaction. There is no conspiracy by which faculties exclude candidates with a conservative bent from appointment. The mere balance of power, which in most colleges is on the side of the trustees and the administration, would in the long run preclude such a possibility. What actually is likely to happen is this: When people drift into occupational pursuits without any clear ideological commitment, as many do, they can develop either conservative or permissive tendencies in their thinking. But two factors crystallize and reinforce the nonconservative component. For one, young teachers see that professional success is attained more often by permissive seniors. Furthermore, once permissive colleagues are in the majority, even a slight numerical differential may build up to a considerable effect on the uncommitted man. By mere chance he is likely to find friendships among the less conservative; the result will be a slow atrophy of conservative potentialities unless they were very strong to begin with. This is a process to which we have referred before: the development of norms by mutual interaction. And it applies to faculties as well as it does to any other group.[11]

Irrespective then of one's personal predilections, it must be accepted as a "fact of nature" that permissiveness characterizes the prevailing climate of opinion among social scientists in twentieth-century America. Our speculative digression has tried to explain this in terms of the experience of the typical academician. But we undoubtedly also face here a trend which considerably overreaches individual experience. The historian Carl Becker would doubtless see corroboration of a much broader development in our data:

Until recently the chief function of the sophisticated, the priests and

---

11. The disagreements among the armed services provide an interesting parallel. Self-interest and selective perception would explain that the majority in the Army and the Navy are on different sides of current controversies. But the *extent* of in-group agreement on both sides can only be explained by a process of mutual reinforcement.

scribes, has been to stabilize custom and validate social authority by perpetuating the tradition and interpreting it in a manner conformable to the understanding of common man. During the last three hundred years . . . there has emerged a new class of learned men, successors to the priests and scribes, whose function is to increase rather than to preserve knowledge, to undermine rather than to stabilize custom and social authority.[12]

This is to say that a permissive professoriate, or an equivalent in some other part of the social fabric, is needed now to help society adjust to novel conditions while discarding outmoded patterns. It is thus the *function* of the social scientist to be sensitive to innovation, to be permissive in the full sense of our analysis.

As usual when such a situation is met, one question deserves to be raised. Why doesn't the system veer into extremes? Why aren't all social scientists violent radicals? At least part of the answer is obvious. Personality types inclined toward radical action would not, in general, be prone to choose classroom teaching as an occupation; and men disciplined by intellectual training would also be less susceptible to unreasoning criticism. A cross-sectional study like ours does not permit the tracing out of this kind of ramification. It happens, however, that a few of our data shed light on some additional restraining factors.

We have seen that the permissive teachers are more oriented toward the profession at large, and the conservative social scientist more toward the local college institution. It seems that an inverse relationship also holds true: the local institution, including the faculty, is less likely to reward the permissive professor than is the profession at large. We asked each respondent whether he had been a member of a college committee which was entrusted with some administrative function and whether he was or had been a department head. It is not the most permissive group which has most often had these local honors. This is true in spite of the fact that, as we know, the most permissive social scientists furnish the largest proportion of highly productive scholars and the most men and women called in as consultants to business. We are inclined to interpret this finding in the following way: When a faculty wants to see its interests represented on a committee, it is not inclined to pick the man with the greatest professional

---

12. *Progress and Power* (Stanford: Stanford University Press, 1936), p. 93.

prestige, but the one who is likely to be most successful in negotiations with the constituted authority. The natural choice is a
middle-of-the-roader, and it is indeed among this group that we
find the highest proportion of such representatives.[13] In the case
of the departmental chairman, this tendency is even stronger, because very often he is not selected by the teachers, but appointed
by the administration. It is often claimed that academicians re-
coil from administrative duties. Still, the position carries a certain
prestige which is undoubtedly attractive to many persons. When
local honors go to somewhat more conservative professors, then
we have another countervailing force setting limits on the rewards
of permissiveness in the academic community.[14]

A second restricting factor is age. In a more or less conservative community people tend to grow more conservative with age.
We have already seen that among social scientists, too, permissiveness is most frequent in the youngest age group. There are several
indications that this is not the result of temporary political circumstances. The depression generation, now well past the age of forty,
is more conservative than the most recent recruits to the profession are. What actually seems to happen is that age exercises a
dampening effect on the innovating spirit with which younger
people enter the social sciences. The equilibrium is maintained
because each generation brings its own momentum into the system,
replacing an older generation which has become less permissive.

Despite these qualifications our data leave no doubt that
permissiveness is a prevailing norm in the social science profession.
As such, we can now use it to present some of our major findings.

Permissiveness and Apprehension

FROM ALL that has been said so far one result is almost
a foregone conclusion: the more permissive a social scientist, the

---

13. The somewhat complicated evidence supporting the statements in this
paragraph is given in Appendix 8E.

14. An additional set of data seems to indicate that the respondents of
highest permissiveness are less favored by salary increases, but our information on this point is imprecise. The indications are strong enough to deserve
further explorations using more exact data on salaries wherever available.

more apprehensive he will be. The relation is strong, as can be seen from Figure 6-15.

Figure 6-15
Permissive Teachers Are Much More Apprehensive than Conservative Teachers

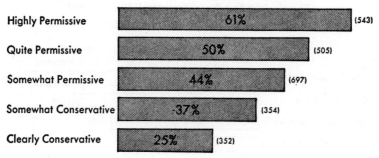

Per Cent Apprehensive
(Score 2 or more)

Highly Permissive	61% (543)
Quite Permissive	50% (505)
Somewhat Permissive	44% (697)
Somewhat Conservative	37% (354)
Clearly Conservative	25% (352)

Inversely, of course, there are many more permissive professors in the apprehensive group.[15]

In some respects this table corroborates previous findings. If apprehensive people are more permissive, this means that many teachers are not subdued by their apprehension. They are willing to go on record that unorthodox colleagues and students should not be interfered with. Also, the interrelation reminds us of a common element in both attitudes: being permissive means looking at the contemporary scene with more critical eyes, and apprehension, it will be remembered, has a marked component of alertness to civil liberties. A third link between the two positions deserves more careful documentation.

---

15. The percentages of clearly permissive teachers (highly and quite permissive combined) among respondents with different apprehension scores are:

Apprehension Score	Per Cent Clearly Permissive
0	33%
1	38%
2	48%
3	53%
4	56%
5, 6	60%

The full cross-tabulation of the two indices will be found in Appendix 8F.

Our data show that it was the permissive teacher who bore
the brunt of the attacks on colleges during the difficult years. At
three points in our questionnaire respondents had opportunities to
tell whether they themselves had come under fire. They were
asked whether their own academic freedom had been threatened,
whether they had ever been reported unfavorably to higher au-

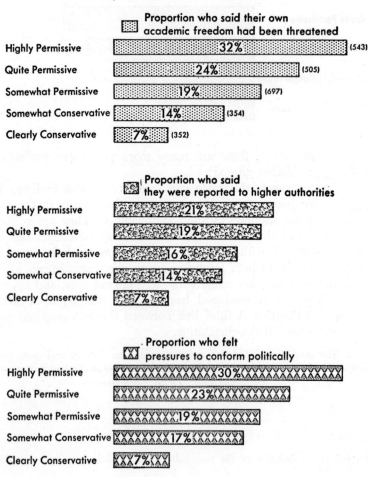

Figure 6-16
Permissive Teachers Reported Unpleasant
Experiences More Frequently

Proportion who said their own
academic freedom had been threatened

Highly Permissive	32% (543)
Quite Permissive	24% (505)
Somewhat Permissive	19% (697)
Somewhat Conservative	14% (354)
Clearly Conservative	7% (352)

Proportion who said
they were reported to higher authorities

Highly Permissive	21%
Quite Permissive	19%
Somewhat Permissive	16%
Somewhat Conservative	14%
Clearly Conservative	7%

Proportion who felt
pressures to conform politically

Highly Permissive	30%
Quite Permissive	23%
Somewhat Permissive	19%
Somewhat Conservative	17%
Clearly Conservative	7%

thorities, and whether they had felt pressures to conform politically to the prevailing climate of opinion. Figure 6-16 shows that on each of the three matters permissive teachers reported unpleasant episodes much more frequently.

This result cannot be taken lightly. We have seen that the permissive social scientist is most representative of his profession. He furnishes much of the academic leadership; his way of thinking is in harmony with the intellectual tasks entrusted to him. It is not surprising that being under attack makes him more apprehensive. But the attacks themselves now appear in a new light. They are not only directed against single individuals: they might endanger the very nature and quality of social science teaching. This point decidedly requires our further attention. But first, two other aspects of the situation need to be discussed. One is the role of party politics.

Figure 6-17 reports the relation between permissiveness and apprehension separately for Republicans and Democrats. Comparing the proportion of apprehensive respondents among the two groups of voters, we find that Democrats are considerably more apprehensive than Republicans on each level of permissiveness. It seems likely that professors in both political camps regarded the attacks during the difficult years as to some degree party inspired. Irrespective of their own attitudes, and the extent to which they might therefore be subject to attack, the Democrats felt considerably more endangered than the Republicans.

To the extent that our interpretation of this finding is correct, it harks back to a problem serious for any popular government. An important function of political parties is to crystallize issues and thus to mediate between the interests of various sectors of the nation. Sometimes, however, the process gets reversed. There are issues of national concern on which no genuine disagreement among the general population is possible. And still, such issues may be seized upon by parties and become sources of spurious division. Foreign policy has most often provided pertinent examples in the United States as well as in other Western democracies. We seem to have a similar case here. Basically all Americans will agree on both the need for national security and for civil liberties. Nevertheless, even as sophisticated a group as the teachers in our study ends up by experiencing the problems involved as party issues. It might very well be that men of good will are not fully aware of this fact, and that a finding like Figure 6-17, if better known, could have a salutary effect.

One final question needs to be raised and answered. Conservative professors were likely to be spectators rather than objects of the scrutiny undergone by American colleges during the last decade. Since they were in a minority in most faculties, it might have been that they were attacked and restricted in their freedom of expression by the majority on their own campuses, just as the majority was attacked or considered suspect by a number of

Figure 6-17
Apprehension among Respondents Classified by 1952 Vote and Level of Permissiveness

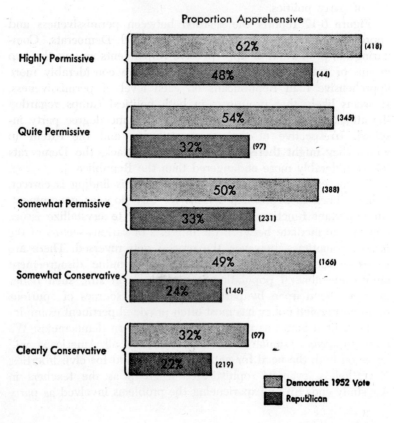

Proportion Apprehensive

Highly Permissive
62% (418)
48% (44)

Quite Permissive
54% (345)
32% (97)

Somewhat Permissive
50% (388)
33% (231)

Somewhat Conservative
49% (166)
24% (146)

Clearly Conservative
32% (97)
22% (219)

Democratic 1952 Vote
Republican

groups in the larger community. But this has hardly happened. We get a first lead if we return to Figure 6-16: attacks from the left would most likely be directed against the clearly conservative respondents, but (as it happens) in each case only 7 per cent mention any difficulty to begin with. A more detailed study of all the incidents in which conservatives were involved clarifies the picture further. About thirty conservative respondents complained that their academic freedom was threatened or that they were under pressure to conform. Some of these incidents were of a special kind. In denominational schools, particularly, conservative respondents sometimes talked of doctrinal differences which got them in trouble with their administration. When these cases are eliminated there are not more than a dozen concrete incidents in which a conservative teacher was attacked or embarrassed "from the left." Two of these occurred in schools where teachers who had belonged to Nazi organizations were refused promotion. A few other teachers complained that they were under pressure to give money to a cause of which they disapproved, or had been ridiculed for their views. We have cited in Chapter II one case where a conservative teacher was let go.

An important qualification must be added to this finding. Our questionnaire directed attention to the post-war period, and especially to the years following the onset of the cold war, with its repercussions on the domestic scene. It is quite possible that the situation was different at the height of the New Deal, say around 1935, or at the beginning of World War II, when the issue of anti-fascism was paramount. A strong stand in favor of academic freedom usually goes with a politically nonconservative position —this is implied in the findings of the present chapter. Will the proponents of these liberties respect the rights of the conservative minority in times when permissive beliefs are dominant in the larger community? This is a serious question indeed and will require further study when the occasion arises. Our survey, by the nature of the events, provides no such information.[16]

16. The questionnaire did, however, make careful provision for the expression of any conservative complaints. One of our problems was to overcome the permissives' reluctance to talk to a stranger. We used the technique of approaching the same topic—say apprehension—in a variety of ways. This gave some conservatives the feeling that the questionnaire was biased in favor of "leftist" attitudes. Actually, the same questions would have elicited reports of

The fact remains that attacks are mainly directed toward permissive teachers, the more distinguished and representative sector of the professoriate. Many readers might feel that this is not serious. Even if a few good social scientists were endangered, there were undoubtedly many equally good ones who remained safe because they were less permissive. Besides, the argument might run, the conservative sector of the professoriate should be strengthened anyhow. Thus the whole problem would be reduced to a matter of individual human rights, serious enough in itself but not affecting American colleges at large. As the next chapter will show, the matter is not this simple.

attacks upon the conservatives if these had occurred with any frequency during the difficult years. There was nothing in the wording of the questions which made them less appropriate vehicles for conservatives' experiences. It was only the actual trend of events in the difficult years that made many of the questions seem superfluous to these respondents.

Chapter VII

THE VULNERABILITY
AND STRENGTH
OF THE SUPERIOR COLLEGE

LET US TAKE TIME for a brief review. In Chapter III an
index of apprehension was developed, permitting the characteriza-
tion of each social science teacher in our sample according to the
level of apprehension he felt at the time of the study. The items
in the index were originally chosen, on common-sense grounds, as
typical expressions among teachers of what might ordinarily be
meant by this term. Then, to determine more precisely the meaning of the classification, in Chapter IV we cross-tabulated the
apprehension index against other characteristics of our respondents, including their interest in matters of civil liberties and
their experiences in the realm of academic freedom. We concluded that the apprehension we measured was a combination
of fear for one's own professional security and an objective concern with the state of academic freedom in general. For most
professors it was not a paralyzing apprehension, since it left room
for a considerable readiness to defend their rights and to express
their own opinions, especially in the confines of the campus. We
postponed for later chapters an analysis of the more subtle ways
in which academic morale and freedom had been corroded during
the difficult years.

Keeping still to the over-all statistical picture, the causes of
teachers' apprehension were then considered. To organize our
material we followed the well-established idea that all human

(159)

experiences are determined by two broad groups of elements: the characteristics of the people themselves and those of the environment in which they live and work. In the two preceding chapters, the pivotal attribute of the social science teacher turned out to be his permissiveness. We discussed the professional significance of this trait. And the data showed that permissive respondents were more likely once to have engaged in activities which, during the difficult years, became controversial in the larger community. They were also more interested in the free flow of new ideas on social matters. These were the two main personal reasons for the apprehension of permissive teachers.

We shall now take up the college, and attempt to find out whether its characteristics affect faculty apprehension. When we look again for a pivotal variable, the quality of schools moves to the fore. Discussed in the first chapter, it now appears as a basic characteristic around which many of our findings about colleges can be fruitfully organized. It is also something more. The quality of education is surely in itself a vitally important matter. Its preservation, in fact, may provide the main reason for caring about academic freedom. Thus the findings of the present chapter acquire heightened significance.

A great philosopher once made an observation which describes very well the way in which college quality came to hold a central position in our study:

Not until we have unsystematically collected observations for a long time to serve as building materials, and indeed only after we have spent much time in the technical disposition of these materials, do we first become capable of viewing our idea in a clearer light and of outlining it architectonically as one whole.[1]

Our building materials were various characteristics of college organization, some of them already reported, others to be added now. The technical disposition shows that they are in various ways statistically related to the quality rating we have presented in Chapter I. Its architectonic importance begins to appear when we discover the closeness of its link with the pivotal variable on

---

1. Kant, *Critique of Pure Reason*, quoted from Michael Polanyi, *The Logic of Liberty* (Chicago: University of Chicago Press, 1951), Preface, p. v.

the personal level, professors' permissiveness. The social significance of the whole, we hope, will become evident.

We shall proceed in four steps. First, from our preceding data
it appears probable that there are more permissive social scientists
in the colleges of higher quality. We shall document that this
is indeed the case.

Second, knowing that permissive teachers were more likely to
be under attack, we shall then want to know whether this was
only an individual experience, or whether it was the superior college as an entity which came under pressure during the difficult
years.

Third, if this too is the case, then a third question becomes
crucial: How did the administrations in the more distinguished
institutions handle this situation? They were under obvious cross-
pressures: Precisely because they had a more distinguished social
science faculty, the community at large might be expected to
attack their institutions more vigorously. Which way did the administrations side?

Finally, having given what evidence we have on this crucial
point, we shall then try to explain our findings. And we shall
show how all this affects the level of apprehension among social
scientists.

College Quality and
Individual Permissiveness

THE FIRST POINT in our outline is easily settled. In Chapter
I, an index was set up to distinguish colleges according to their
quality, using objective data obtained from independent sources
not connected with our survey. It now turns out that the quality
of a college is highly related to the permissiveness of its social
science faculty. This can be clearly seen in Figure 7-1.

The better a college, the larger the proportion of permissive
social scientists included in its faculty. The reasons for this are
apparent from the data given in the previous chapter. Colleges
which have larger resources and more desirable working conditions attract more distinguished social scientists. These teachers
in turn are more likely to be permissive. The original and creative

Figure 7-1
The Better a College, the More of Its Social Scientists Are Permissive

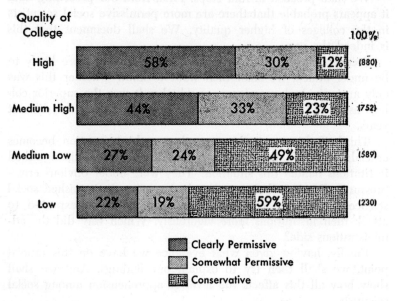

Quality of
College   100%

High	58%	30%	12%	(880)
Medium High	44%	33%	23%	(752)
Medium Low	27%	24%	49%	(589)
Low	22%	19%	59%	(230)

▊ Clearly Permissive
☐ Somewhat Permissive
▦ Conservative

minority among them will often have analytical minds which do not automatically accept current beliefs, minds willing to entertain unorthodox ideas as to how a modern society can best function.[2] Next to the creative leader comes the competent teacher and productive research scholar. Even if he might be by nature more amenable to the general currents of public opinion, he is more directly in communication with the leaders of his profession, and his thinking is shaped by the process of mutual interaction among primary groups which we have described above. Thus he

---

2. On page 157 the question was raised as to whether teachers who are permissive in terms of this report would protect conservative colleagues when the latter were under attack. A similar issue comes up here: does the analytical training of the more qualified social scientists enable them to scrutinize leftist stereotypes more closely? It is possible that a general hospitality for social improvements might make one less critical toward programs of political reform, regardless of their real merit. This too is a question our study can only raise, not answer.

too will add to a permissive climate when appointed to a distinguished institution.

Next we want to gauge the pressures which the larger community brings to bear on colleges of differing quality.

Clouds over the Campus

WAS THE STREAM of accusations during the difficult years heavily directed toward the more distinguished colleges? We turn first to one of the questionnaire items which furnished material for the description of incidents in Chapter II:

Has any group or person accused anyone on this faculty here of being subversive or of engaging in any un-American activities in the past few years?

To guard against bias, the answers need to be tabulated separately for more and less apprehensive respondents. For there is the danger that the apprehension of our respondents distorted the descriptions of events in their colleges; the more apprehensive teachers were likely to paint a darker picture, partly because they were more attuned to potential difficulties and partly because they were simply more observant. And in this special case another point must be considered. There are, of course, more professors in larger colleges, and therefore the numerical chance that at least one teacher on the campus was accused is greater. So in Figure 7-2 the findings are reported separately for larger and smaller institutions.

Irrespective of the size of the school or the respondents' state of mind, we find that the frequency of accusation reports rises with the quality of the school. For the remaining Figures in this chapter, we shall not separate the judgment of apprehensive and non-apprehensive professors, because the picture is always the same: apprehensive professors are more pessimistic when they describe the situation at their college, but when it comes to comparing schools—whether for attacks, pressures, or the other factors we will consider—the result is the same regardless of which segment of the faculty we listen to.

Figure 7-2
Accusations against Teachers Occur More Frequently
in Superior Colleges

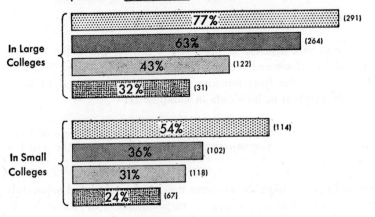

Proportion of <u>apprehensive</u> respondents who report accusations

In Large Colleges
- 77% (291)
- 63% (264)
- 43% (122)
- 32% (31)

In Small Colleges
- 54% (114)
- 36% (102)
- 31% (118)
- 24% (67)

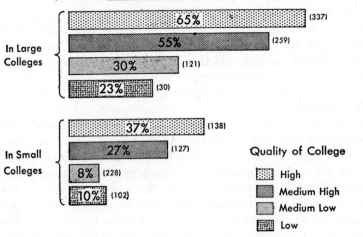

Proportion of <u>non-apprehensive</u> respondents who report accusations

In Large Colleges
- 65% (337)
- 55% (259)
- 30% (121)
- 23% (30)

In Small Colleges
- 37% (138)
- 27% (127)
- 8% (228)
- 10% (102)

Quality of College
- High
- Medium High
- Medium Low
- Low

In a similar vein, what do the teachers say about the pressures which were directed against their administration during the difficult years? At the beginning of Chapter II, we reported a widespread feeling that these pressures had increased. Now our interest focuses on quality differences. Figure 7-3 reports for each of the four quality groups the proportion of respondents who thought that their administration has been under increased pressure in the last six or seven years from at least one of the four sources—politicians, alumni, trustees, or the community at large.

Figure 7-3
Proportion of Respondents Reporting Increased Pressure on the Administration

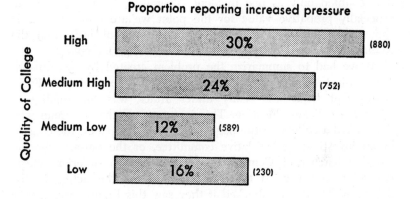

Proportion reporting increased pressure

In general, as with accusations, the pressure reports increase markedly as we move up the quality rating of institutions. There is, however, a small but interesting break in this trend. The lowest quality level does not have quite the lowest frequency of pressure accounts. A more detailed study shows that this irregularity can be traced to the five secular institutions in this group. Two of these are tax-supported Negro colleges in the South, where the integration issue has recently become acute. The other three are relatively large private schools, each of which serves a big industrial city and is completely dependent for support on local money, either from industry or some other interest group. With no tax support and little private endowment, they appear to have been especially at the mercy of their local sponsorship.[3]

Having its administration under pressure and its faculty under attack necessarily makes for a definite strain on a college. Probably our best concrete measure of this strain is the prevalence of the incidents described in Chapter II: episodes ranging from long-drawn-out Congressional investigations to an attack by a student group on an individual professor. A count of these incidents has an important advantage over the data given in Figure 7-2. There our percentages pertained to the proportion of professors who, reported an accusation against a faculty member. If many respondents in a school referred to the same case, the figures would be inflated. In the incident count, however, such overlapping stories are pooled; however many teachers referred to the same episode, it is counted only as one incident. Therefore, Figure 7-4 has an especially probative value for the point we are now making. It shows that, without exception, in every type of institution the frequency of incidents was greater in the superior colleges.

If we had to summarize the problem created by the difficult years in just one Figure, we would probably choose this one. For it shows that what was really under attack was the quality of American college education. This is not to say that the man who denounced a college in the pages of a local newspaper, the counsel of an investigating legislative committee, or the parent who accused a teacher of Communism, was hostile to superior college education and wanted to lower it. Many of the actors in the drama might well be shocked if they saw this Figure, and would, with much right, stress the purity of their motives. Such is often the difference between individual acts and their collective implications. Their unanticipated social consequences can be very different from what the individual actor had in mind. To bring into visibility the full aggregate picture which is usually inaccessible to the individual observer is one of the main functions of a study like the present one.[4]

---

3. According to impressions reported by Professor Riesman, direct pressure by parents also occurred more frequently in these "streetcar colleges."

4. Sometimes the attack on the distinguished colleges is actually spelled out. In his speech in Wheeling, West Virginia, on February 9, 1950, Senator McCarthy began his crusade against domestic Communism by locating the enemy in the high quality schools:

Figure 7-4*
The Difference Which Quality Makes in the Average Number
of Incidents in Nine Groups of Colleges

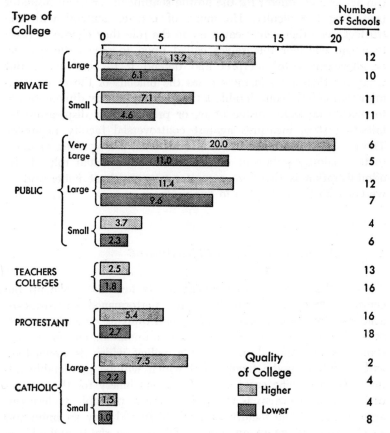

Average Number of Incidents

Type of College			Number of Schools

PRIVATE — Large: 13.2 (12), 6.1 (10); Small: 7.1 (11), 4.6 (11)

PUBLIC — Very Large: 20.0 (6), 11.0 (5); Large: 11.4 (12), 9.6 (7); Small: 3.7 (4), 2.3 (6)

TEACHERS COLLEGES — 2.5 (13), 1.8 (16)

PROTESTANT — 5.4 (16), 2.7 (18)

CATHOLIC — Large: 7.5 (2), 2.2 (4); Small: 1.5 (4), 1.0 (8)

Quality of College
▦ Higher
■ Lower

* For this figure each of the nine types of colleges is divided as evenly as possible into two groups of higher and lower quality schools. The dividing line, of course, varies from one type to the next.

It has not been the less fortunate, or members of minority groups, who have been selling this Nation out, but rather those who have had all the benefits the wealthiest nation on earth has had to offer—the finest homes, *the finest college educations,* and the finest jobs in the Government we can give. (Italics supplied.)

This quotation, from *The Congressional Record,* Vol. 96, Part 2, p. 1954, 1950, was brought to our attention by Professor Hans Zetterberg.

The college professor is in a peculiar situation. When attacks and accusations are made against a teacher, before they can have an ultimate effect upon him they must be refracted by an intervening medium: the administration. The president of the school can act as a conductor for the hostile sentiments, or as an insulator protecting the faculty. He must, of course, contend with the trustees, who themselves can vary in the role they choose to play; they can consider themselves called upon to police the college, or alternatively to interpret and defend it to challengers. But whatever their role, in most cases the officials of the college administration have considerable latitude. They can try diplomatically to placate an irate trustee body, or prevent their displeasure by initiating stern measures against controversial faculty members. The president can make full use of his legal prerogatives, or defer to the majority judgment of the faculty. The actual role of the administration is therefore a matter very much at issue; and so we come to the third step in our program.

Administrative Performance

IT IS NOT EASY to pinpoint the factors that make up the central ingredients of administrative performance on issues of academic freedom. According to general thinking on such matters, at least three aspects are important. As a minimum, clearly defined standards are needed, providing a policy which is understood and accepted by the faculty and which will be predictably adhered to in specific cases. Secondly, a machinery for the making of individual decisions is required. There is probably widespread agreement that the faculty as a whole should play an important role at some stage of an issue involving the rights and obligations of teachers, even though the final decision will, according to American tradition, generally remain with an administrative authority. Finally, in any organization a good administration must be willing to protect its staff. This means more than just fair procedure in handling accusations. Every occupational group develops certain norms for which an outsider will have little understanding. A capable college administrator must be alert to the traditions of the professoriate; if they come into conflict with the oscillating moods of the larger community, he will, if at all possible, give the edge to the enduring needs of the academic man.[5]

There was insufficient time in our interviews to ask teachers for a detailed picture of the philosophy and behavior of their administrative officials. And even at best the pooled judgments of professors could not give a really complete picture; for this, interviews with administrators and trustees, investigation of documentary evidence, and so on, would be necessary. Nevertheless, we did obtain at least some information on each of the three aspects of administrative performance just sketched: clarity of policy, adequacy of procedural machinery, and protective orientation.

On the first point two simple and direct questions seemed appropriate. One read:

Do you feel the administration of the college has taken a clear stand on matters of academic freedom, or not?

In the whole sample 59 per cent reported a clear stand, and 29 per cent the absence of one; the remaining 12 per cent could not make up their minds. The other item required a report rather than a judgment:

Has the faculty and the administration discussed questions of academic freedom in joint meetings within the last year or not?

Thirty-six per cent of the respondents reported such meetings, 53 per cent said they had not occurred, and 11 per cent could not remember. On both items, Figure 7-5 shows, the administrations in high quality schools get a better verdict from their social scientists.[6]

---

5. An understanding for some of the nuances of this situation has been put very succinctly by a former A.A.U.P. President, Helen C. White. In an essay on "Freedom in the University" (*The Phi Beta Kappa Key Reporter*, July, 1956) she describes the difficulties of a professor who dislikes to atone publicly for former activities, even if he regrets them by now himself:

"But if you were a fool, why not stand up and say so," some will ask. . . . If only you could be sure that people would understand precisely what *kind* of fool you have been.

6. In this particular matter, probably because it does not call for an evaluation, apprehensive respondents do not follow their usual pattern of passing more severe judgments.

A detailed picture of procedural adequacy would have required questions about the school's formal regulations for the handling of cases involving academic freedom, as well as concrete examples of how they were carried out. But there was time during the interview for only one question. We therefore started with a double assumption: it is desirable that the faculty play a considerable role in educational matters; trustees, since they are relatively most remote from the academic scene, should exercise great restraint in this connection. Against this background we asked the following question:

If you had to choose one, who would you say has the most powerful voice here on this campus, in determining the degree of academic freedom that exists here—the trustees, the president, the deans, the heads of departments, the faculty, the students, or who?

Figure 7-5
The Better the College, the More Articulate
the Administration's Policy

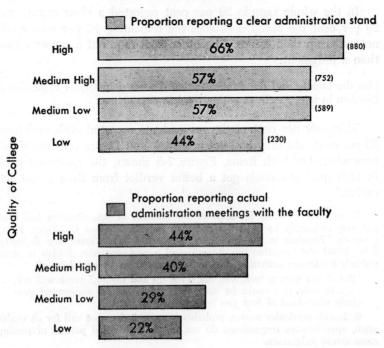

Each school was separately characterized by summarizing the answers of all interviewed teachers. A value of 2 was given to each response giving the faculty the most important voice, of 1 if the administration (president and deans) was considered paramount, and of 0 to a choice of the trustees. For each college the scores were then added together and averaged. Values for the resulting school index vary from about 0.5, indicating a dominance of the trustees in the handling of academic freedom matters, to about 1.5, attributing a considerable role to the faculty.

Dividing the schools as nearly as possible into two equal groups according to this index, we can compare procedural adequacy in colleges of different objective quality ratings. Results are reported, in Figure 7-6, only for the seventy-seven schools with more than thirteen interviews.[7]

Under the assumption that faculty participation is the most desirable and trustee dominance the most inadequate administrative device, on the whole the superior colleges have a much more desirable record.

The third element of administrative performance, protectiveness, should in many ways be most important of all. General standards and procedural rules so often don't quite fit a concrete case. It is then that the motivation and understanding of the administration comes to the fore. But how may the situation be gauged through the eyes of the faculty? One set of data, while inferential, has a rather convincing ring. It will be remembered that respondents were asked at one point if any of their colleagues had been accused of subversive activities. A second item in the questionnaire read:

Have there been any cases here in this college where you feel the academic freedom of any member of the faculty has been threatened?

In answering the two questions, 46 per cent of the respondents reported accusations, but only 28 per cent stated that someone's academic freedom was threatened. In a rough way the difference between these two figures can be used as an indicator of the

---

7. Among these seventy-seven schools only five were on the lowest quality level; they were combined with the "Medium Low" group. (See also footnote 9 of Chapter VI)

Figure 7-6
Superior Colleges Give the Faculty a Greater Voice
in Academic Freedom Matters

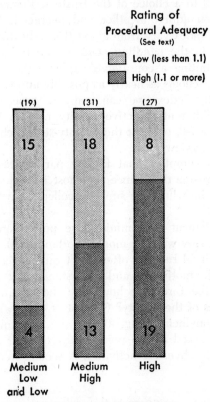

Rating of
Procedural Adequacy
(See text)

Low (less than 1.1)

High (1.1 or more)

Quality of College

readiness of an administration to absorb attacks without passing
them on to the teacher—to build, so to speak, a security wall for
him behind which he can do his professional work. (We are, of
course, aware of other factors which could enter into this difference
of 18 per cent; we want to use this figure only for comparative
purposes.) It turns out that the protective element in good administration is indeed the more frequent, the higher the quality of a
college. The inferential evidence is offered in Figure 7-7.

Figure 7-7*
School Quality as Related to Accusations of Subversion, Threats to Academic Freedom, and the Administration's Treatment of Accused Professors

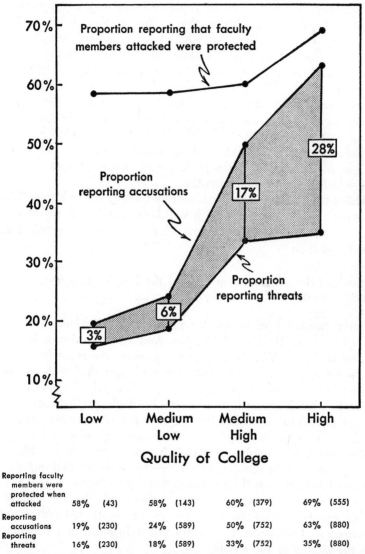

Reporting faculty members were protected when attacked	58%	(43)	58%	(143)	60%	(379)	69%	(555)
Reporting accusations	19%	(230)	24%	(589)	50%	(752)	63%	(880)
Reporting threats	16%	(230)	18%	(589)	33%	(752)	35%	(880)

* The results given in this Table are duplicated, separating answers given by apprehensive and unapprehensive teachers, in Appendix 5. The last two parts of this Appendix deal with the question of how much teachers' own characteristics affect results which make use of their perceptions of their surroundings.

The line representing the proportion reporting accusations is only a summary of Figure 7-2 in this chapter. The figures for threats provide new, but by now not unexpected information: Threats to academic freedom are reported by an ever larger proportion of respondents, the higher the quality of their college. Our main interest at this point is with the four enclosed percentages inside the shaded area. Representing the difference between accusations and threats, they provide a rough index of administrative absorption. In the low quality colleges there are few accusations, but they seem to be readily converted into actual difficulties for a faculty member; the difference is only 3 per cent. In the best colleges both accusations and difficulties are more frequent, but the difference is 28 per cent; at these schools the administration is much more likely to shield the professor and not to pass on accusations which come to their attention.

This interpretation is strengthened by the top line of Figure 7-7. About half of our respondents, it will be remembered, report accusations against faculty members. Those who did were asked a second question:

Do you feel the administration handled the incident in a way which protected the rights of the faculty?

In almost two-thirds of the cases reported the respondents testified to the fairness of their administration. And again, as shown in the top line of Figure 7-7, the affirmative answers are more frequent in colleges of higher quality. Here we no longer deal with an inference, but with the direct reports of teachers who had occasion to watch what happened in concrete incidents at their schools. Another consideration makes this increase from 58 per cent to 69 per cent all the more impressive. The superior colleges have a considerably larger number of permissive professors who are likely to apply rather strict standards to the performance of their administration; inversely, it will be remembered from Chapter V that the conservative teachers, who are more numerous in the low quality schools, are in general likely to approve of constituted authority. Nevertheless, testimonies to fair treatment increase in frequency with the quality of the school.

One more approach to the topic of protection by the administration remains. The following questionnaire item was intended to meet the issue head-on.

If someone accused you of leftist leanings, do you think the administration of the college would support you wholeheartedly, with reservations, or hardly at all?

At first sight this approach would seem the most direct one, but interestingly enough, the resulting figures are more complex than anticipated. The matter deserves some discussion, since it throws light simultaneously on variations in the atmosphere of different types of colleges and on the kind of decision we had to make in designing this study. We should first explain why this question was restricted to leftist leanings. It will be remembered that another question asked whether respondents went out of their way to show they had no extremist opinions either of the "left" or the "right." There, both possibilities had to be considered, since a professor might be concerned about giving offense to either the liberal atmosphere prevailing on campus, or the conservative mood of the larger community. But at the time of the study it would have been absurd for all but a tiny minority of respondents to ask whether the administration would lend support against an accusation of rightist leanings. As common sense would anticipate, and as the data have shown (see Chapters II and VI), accusations of being too much to the right were very rare during the difficult years. The issue of the day was leftist leanings, and we could safely limit an investigation to how administrations met such accusations. Respondents not only understood the question, they answered it in a confident mood. Sixty-two per cent said that the administration would support them "wholeheartedly," the top term on our checklist; 20 per cent said "with reservations," and only 7 per cent said "hardly at all." Eleven per cent felt unable to say what the administration would do. If we remember that 40 per cent indicated that pressures on the college had increased, it is impressive to see that only 7 per cent considered themselves without any protection from the administration in matters of this kind.[8]

---

8. A similar question asked whether the respondent would expect his colleagues to support him if someone accused him of leftist leanings. Sixty-six per cent felt that most colleagues would support them, 24 per cent that some or only a few would do so, and 4 per cent said hardly any; 6 per cent didn't

What about the relation between protection by the administration and quality of the school? From our data so far one could expect that the professors in the better colleges would testify to greater protection by the administration. This is indeed the case, and markedly so, in the secular colleges (the private and public institutions). For these, the administrative performance of the superior college is confirmed in Figure 7-8.

In the traditional schools (teachers colleges, Protestant, and Catholic schools) the trend is just the opposite. This might possibly be due to a special interpretation of this questionnaire item by conservative teachers in a conservative school. There the reaction is likely to be as follows: "Of course the administration would support me if someone accused me of leftist leanings, because they would consider him crazy; who in his right mind could ever call me such a thing?" However, there are more significant implications in Figure 7-8, to which we shall return presently. For the moment, because the secular schools furnish the large majority of social scientists, we add their feelings of protection to the other findings in this chapter, which now permit a clear-cut summary:

The higher the quality of a college, the larger its proportion of permissive social scientists.

The higher the quality, the stronger the pressures and attacks from the off-campus community.

The higher the quality of a school, the better the performance of the administration in defending the academic freedom of its social scientists.[9]

___

know. The number of respondents who anticipate wholehearted support by the administration is almost as great as the number of those who count on most of their colleagues for support in a controversial emergency. There are some colleges where the trust in the administration is considerably greater than the expectation of help from one's peers; in other colleges, the reverse is true.

9. If an administration takes a clear stand on academic freedom, it usually is also protective in its attitude and gives the faculty a reasonable voice in the handling of individual cases. How such correlations come about cannot be told from one survey. Sometimes a powerful faculty will enforce high standards of administrative performance; in other situations granting faculty rights is part of the administration's own policy. There are in our sample clearly deviate cases, where, for instance, apparent faculty power is the result of a president's indecisiveness and does not lead to security for the individual professor. Future study of the interplay between the three dimensions of administrative performance will, it is hoped, throw light on this whole little-understood subject.

Figure 7-8
Proportion of Respondents Who Would Expect Wholehearted
Administrative Support if Accused of Leftist Leanings

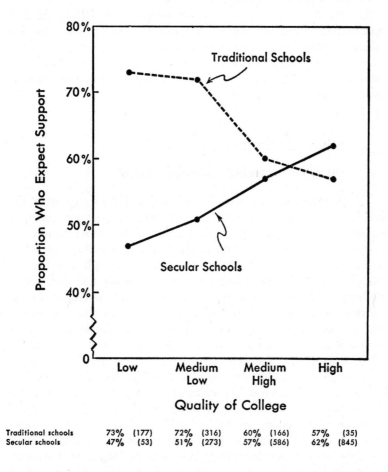

	Low	Medium Low	Medium High	High
Traditional schools	73% (177)	72% (316)	60% (166)	57% (35)
Secular schools	47% (53)	51% (273)	57% (586)	62% (845)

The first of these three findings reinforces the discussion of the preceding chapter. If permissiveness is a pivotal characteristic of the social science profession at large, then it is not surprising that it is also a prevailing property of the superior college.

The second finding is the one which calls most for contemplation. The fact that the difficult years put the superior college under especially heavy strain shows that the problem goes considerably beyond the realm of the rights of individual teachers. It was the very quality of social science teaching and of inquiry as a whole which was put into jeopardy.

The third finding requires some further speculation. At first glance we have here a paradoxical result. If the more distinguished colleges are more subject to pressure and more frequently the scene of controversial incidents, how is it, nevertheless, that their administrations perform better by all of our criteria, including the protection given to social scientists?

Some Speculations
on the Superior Administrator

IN AMERICAN COLLEGES the trustees and their appointee, the president, have great power. If it is true that power corrupts, one would expect that when the temper of the times brings the permissive social scientist into distrust, a strong college president would be tempted to exercise his power and curb the faculty. Actually, the better the college, the less frequently does this occur. We have here another example of a rather curious feature in the American scene to which Harold Laski has drawn attention in discussing the American system of mass communications. He considered it a rather bad one, because it was not conducted in the public interest but for private profit. Still, he wondered why it wasn't even worse. By mere economic mechanics there should be no limit to how much a low cultural level of broadcasting and a sensational handling of printed news could be made ever more marked and ever more profitable. Laski concluded that there must be a self-corrective in the American system which makes for a tolerable level of performance.[10] We seem to face such a self-corrective device in the management of colleges. Offhand, one might expect that college administrations in America should behave very badly in academic freedom matters. They are appointed by the

---

10. A similar observation is made regarding the power of business management by Clark Kerr, "Industrial Relations and the Liberal Pluralist," Proceedings of the Seventh Annual Meeting, Industrial Relations Research Association, Detroit, Michigan, Dec. 22-30, 1954, Publication No. 14.

board of trustees and are responsible to them rather than to the faculty. The trustees and regents themselves are representatives of the community, and in most cases of its wealthy and conservative sector. It is probably here that the unexpected safety device comes in. For the most part the individuals chosen as trustees are selected because they are successful in their own enterprises. Many of these men have undoubtedly acquired respect for efficiency and intrinsic success. If they are responsible for a college, they want it to have prestige, so they appoint presidents whom they hope will make their regime "successful," without going too deeply into the existing academic implications of the idea. The president, in turn, will build up a staff whose men and women command the respect of their peers and live up to the prevailing norms of the teaching profession. We have shown that a permissive atmosphere is a part of these norms. In quiet times, undoubtedly, this system works without much friction, because the external prestige and success of the institution is paramount for everyone concerned: the trustees, administration, and professors. Ideological differences seldom come to the fore.

But suppose a crisis develops, in which the trustees, together with other agencies in the community, become very conscious of and desirous of a conservative temper. How easily can they enforce this mood upon their school? As we have seen, the answer depends partly upon the control system, which in turn is already related to the type of president the trustees will have appointed. But to a certain degree the matter is not in their hands. Even if they themselves have conservative attitudes, it will be exactly those administrators who have built up successful colleges who will have the strongest personal and professional involvement in the prestige of their institutions, and be least willing to sacrifice good teachers in the interests of possibly temporary cycles in ideological mood. At such a moment the professional pride of the college administrator can take on an autonomy of its own. The more successful he has been in building up the prestige of his college, the more likely he will be to protect it now against the pressures upon it. In such a crisis, the better colleges, even if under more attack, will be better protected by their administration.

This interpretation is limited in one respect. It assumes that trustees and administrators were not originally inclined to protect permissive teachers. Actually this whole social mechanism often places men in important positions who defend a permissive faculty because they genuinely believe in its worth. Many institutions, especially those which are privately endowed, draw trustees from families greatly concerned with the intellectual inheritance of the nation. These, in turn, are likely to appoint as administrators distinguished professors who belong to the permissive tradition we have described. A cursory review of recent appointments shows how many university presidents indeed come from the ranks of the social scientists nowadays. Our speculations thus suggest that a more careful analysis of the recruitment of trustees and university administrators would be important for the study of academic freedom.[11] Meanwhile, we can make one contribution, by giving some findings which compare the reports of teachers in tax-supported and privately-endowed schools.

Some Differences
Between Types of Schools

IN CHAPTER II various pressures on schools, as judged by their faculties, were described. We return briefly to these data, concentrating on the public and private schools among the seventy-seven which have enough interviews to provide usable rates. A college is classified according to the proportion of teachers who say that in their impression, "the administration of this college is under more pressure to avoid controversy than it was six or seven years ago." A number of sources for these pressures were mentioned in the question. We focus here on two of these: politicians and trustees. Three observations are provided by the figures, which are shown in Figure 7-9. Both of these pressure sources impinge more often upon tax-supported than on privately endowed schools. This

---

11. A beginning was made in Hubert Park Beck, *Men Who Control Our Universities* (New York: King's Crown Press, 1947). In the early 1930s he studied the trustees of thirty leading universities, stressing their wealth and their general conservative outlook. But Beck did not inquire how these men looked at their role in university affairs and where they stood in relations between the campus and the larger community.

simply confirms for the seventy-seven colleges what was shown in Chapter II, Figure 2-2b, to be true of all. (It is also worth recalling from that table that not all pressures were felt more widely in public than in private schools; the reverse is true of those from alumni.) Secondly, in both types of schools politicians appear more often than trustees. And, finally, the prominence of politicians as sources of high pressures is noticeably more pronounced in the public schools.

Figure 7-9
The Privately-Endowed Schools Are Less Subject to Pressures from Politicians and Trustees than Tax-Supported Institutions

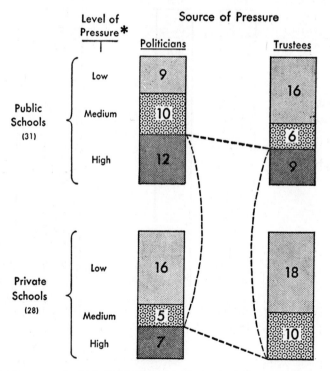

* A low pressure level is indicated if less than 20 per cent of the respondents report increased pressures, a high level if 40 per cent or more do.

The interplay between politicians and trustees in public institutions can be suggestively traced if the thirty-one larger schools are tabulated according to whether each source appears to create a high or a low pressure level. In Figure 7-10(a) we find a clear tendency for trustees (often called regents) and politicians to take the same position. From a survey taken at one time only, one cannot

Figure 7-10
Pressures Follow Different Patterns in Public and Private Schools

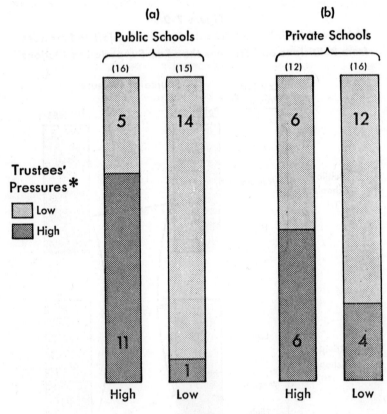

tell whether the trustees follow the policies of legislators and governors or whether they take the lead themselves. Common observation, however, strongly suggests that their general tendency is to be guided by the initiative of political forces.

In private schools (Figure 7-10b) the trustees appear to act more independently. In half the schools they remain aloof even if the level of political pressure is high. And in a few colleges the trustees independently initiate pressure—perhaps to forestall the politicians' interference.

From the faculty point of view the position of the administration matters most, and here the difference between the two types of schools is also the most marked. We know from previous tables that about two-thirds of all social scientists feel the administration would support them wholeheartedly in case of attack. Thus a rate of 40 per cent or less indicates a relatively low, and 70 per cent or more a high, level of protection. In these terms the difference between tax-supported and privately endowed schools looms high indeed. Figure 7-11 gives the evidence.

Political pressures, to begin with, are lighter on the private schools. The trustees are then less inclined to pass them on. And the administration is often prepared to follow a policy of interposition. This last step can be inferred from Figure 7-12, which relates political pressures to the level of protection attributed to the administration.

The situation actually reverses in the two types of schools. In tax-supported schools, the higher the political pressures, the lower the administrative protection. But in privately endowed schools our figures indicate an impressive example of countervailing powers: the higher the political pressures, the more ready the administration to protect its faculty.

One could say that in a private school a more pluralistic system of power prevails. Our data suggest that all three elements considered here, political authorities, trustees, and administration officials, are likely to make decisions independently of each other. Under such circumstances there are checks and balances which serve to give the faculties more breathing room in times of crisis. The tax-supported institutions are more monolithic. All components of the system move together and the full brunt of pressure is likely to fall directly on the teacher.

The findings also throw some light on the role of the private trustee as compared to the politically-appointed regent. Both are often chosen from the conservative sector of the community. But when a man becomes a trustee of a private institution he is more free to absorb the atmosphere of the academic tradition. Though he represents the business community, he isn't directly accountable to it, and can change his beliefs in the light of his experiences on the campus. The regent, if he wants to keep his position, must in most cases be reappointed by some political body. He cannot, therefore, deviate too much from the spirit in which he was initially

Figure 7-11
In Private Schools Faculties Had Much Better Administrative
Protection than in Public Schools

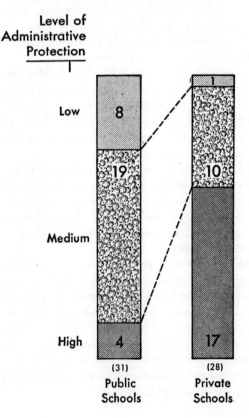

Level of
Administrative
Protection

Low

Medium

High

(31)   (28)
Public   Private
Schools   Schools

chosen. This need not be a conscious process; it is quite possible that his perception of academic life will be limited and colored from the start by this commitment. Thus in times of crisis the private trustee is more likely to become a mediator between the

Figure 7-12
The Relation between Pressures from Politicians and Administrative Protection

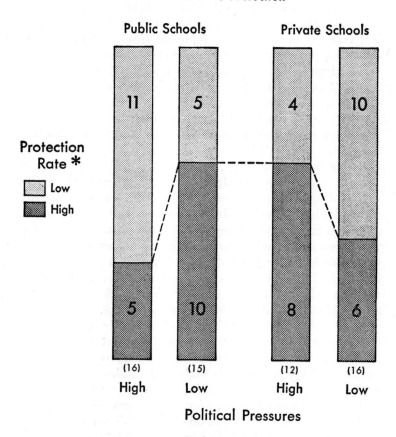

* Here the pressure levels are again separated by a rate of 30 per cent in public and 20 per cent in private schools. The protection rate division is at 50 per cent and 65 per cent respectively, because it is generally lower in tax-supported colleges (Figure 7-11). It will be remembered that in low quality traditional schools, the question on administrative protection seemed differently interpreted. But these Figures deal only with the secular public and private schools.

community and the college than is the regent of a tax-supported institution. Some data from the study by Beck (cited in footnote 11) corroborate our findings. There are more public officeholders and twice as many lawyers—potential officeholders—among the trustees of state universities. And while they have somewhat less conservative views on economic affairs, being also less wealthy, they have less respect for academic freedom. What was a casual observation in the 1930's emerges from our study as a major issue today. How can trustees of tax-supported institutions be made more independent in their decisions? Several possible ideas come to mind: broader representation of other professions besides lawyers; limits on the number of trustees who hold or have held public office; preference for men and women who participate in other cultural or philanthropic activities. Only a more detailed study of present-day trustees could determine whether these or any other solutions are promising.

Finally, one more word about the traditional schools. All through the analysis of our data we realized how little has been written about these colleges. Authors who deal with higher education in this country are almost always concerned only with the larger and superior institutions. Even those who are alarmed about the standards of these schools seem to feel that they are the places where the intellectual destiny of the country is forged. The prevailing concern is with the frontiers of higher education, and cognizance is hardly taken of what happens in those institutions where social analysts are rare, either as students or professors. Our data call attention especially to the traditional schools with higher objective quality ratings. In Figure 7-8 it was shown that social scientists at these schools feel relatively unprotected by their administrations. Other signs of discomfort can be added: relations among faculty members are reported as less good, turnover in teaching personnel is high, and incidents involving academic freedom are relatively frequent. Thus while in secular schools objective quality makes for a better atmosphere all around, this is less or sometimes not at all so in traditional schools, where the administration presumably wants to maintain a specific ideological climate. The institution has the material means to attract productive and correspondingly permissive professors. But their permissiveness, when it is brought into the limelight by an accusation or a climate of suspicion, may come almost as a shock to the administration. Giving priority to considerations apart from formal academic standards, its officials will have little impulse to protect them. Between the professional orientation of the faculty and the traditional norms of the administration an imbalance of mutual expectations develops which leads to the kind of anomalies we have mentioned.

One might also see the picture in an historical context. Not too many decades ago most American colleges were of the traditional type. Many of them have evolved into the fully secular type. They appoint teachers distinguished for their research, and see their main task as the training of students who later will perform specific intellectual functions either in the professions or in specialized managerial roles throughout the community. Many smaller schools remained wedded to the earlier function of improving the educational level of the population at large. The traditional colleges of high quality rating are, so to speak, in a transition stage. They are beginning to have resources and teaching personnel like those of the larger secular institutions. But in many cases their administrators, to all appearances, do not yet favor the newer and more specialized academic functions. Objective quality, therefore, is not paralleled by a greater acceptance of the concepts of academic freedom.

Apprehension and College Quality

THE ESSENTIAL POINTS of the last two chapters can be pulled together into a schematic presentation.[12] Figure 7-13 indicates that the proportion of permissive professors (1) at a college, and the amount of pressures (2) impinging on it, increase as we move from less to more distinguished institutions. A third line refers to the performance of the college administration regarding the management of academic freedom issues. In order to emphasize a specific point, this line does not indicate positive performance of the administration, but rather the inverse: its shortcomings (3). We found that such shortcomings are less frequent in the superior colleges.

---

12. This was suggested by Professor S. A. Stouffer during a discussion of our findings.

Figure 7-13

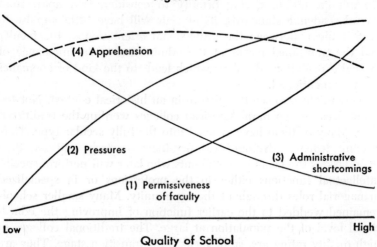

(4) Apprehension

(2) Pressures

(3) Administrative
shortcomings

(1) Permissiveness
of faculty

Low   High
Quality of School

To these three lines in Figure 7-13 we have added a fourth, indicating approximately what we should expect the results concerning apprehension to be like on the basis of what we know so far. In superior colleges (to the right in the Figure) the pressures are great and so is the vulnerability of the faculty; but at the same time the administration has fewer shortcomings and is more likely to protect its social scientists. On the left side of the graph the professors are less vulnerable and, as a result, the outside community has less of an inclination to create difficulties for the college; but at the same time the administration is less likely to help the faculty if trouble does arise. In both these situations, then, we have compensating factors, and this should make for approximately the same level of apprehension (4). Somewhere in the middle range, we expect to find a relative maximum of apprehension, because the two contributing factors—permissiveness of the faculty and pressures from the outside—outweigh the factor which protects against it—excellence of administrative performance. All in all, the scheme suggests that variations in apprehension are not too great. College quality is closely related to all three basic variables. But in two instances the relation is negative while in the third it is positive. The resulting apprehension should, therefore, be about the same on all levels of quality.

The actual figures of Figure 7-14 corroborate this schematic analysis quite well. The top line reports the proportion of professors who have a score of 2 or more on the apprehension index. Below are shown the two component elements of the apprehension index, discussed earlier in Chapter III: the proportions of respondents who are worried and who are cautious.[13] This is done partly to show that all these measures lead to approximately the same general result. But the two auxiliary indices of worry and caution give us an additional piece of information: the difference between the two, shown by the percentages inside the shaded area of Figure 7-14.

As we expected, there is a peak of apprehension—although the differences are not large—on the third quality level. This group, as was shown in Table 1-9 of Chapter I, is composed mainly of large (but not very large) tax-supported schools, and of Protestant colleges which are atypically high in their socio-academic resources. The more distinguished Protestant colleges experience conflict between their orthodox traditions and the more secular-minded faculty they can afford. The tax-supported schools in this group can afford a more distinguished faculty, but are not large enough to impress the legislatures, and therefore are subject to greater political pressures.

In addition to this general trend, Figure 7-14 reveals a somewhat unexpected finding: apprehension does not trail off on the lowest quality level. The schools in this group are mainly teachers colleges and very small denominational institutions. Careful reading of the interviews suggests a psychological interpretation. The teachers in these institutions seem to be especially timid, and it is likely that they feel apprehensive under circumstances in which the average social scientist would still be relatively at ease.

The differences between worry and caution in Figure 7-14 lead us back to the complexity of apprehension. As we move toward higher quality schools the component of worry in the appre-

13. A teacher is considered "worried," for purposes of the present discussion, if he answered "yes" to two or more of the six worry items in Table 3-1; he is "cautious" if he answered "yes" to two or more of the five caution items in Table 3-2.

Figure 7-14
The Relation between Quality of College and Apprehension

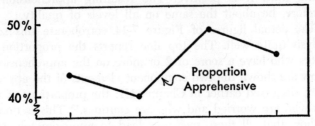

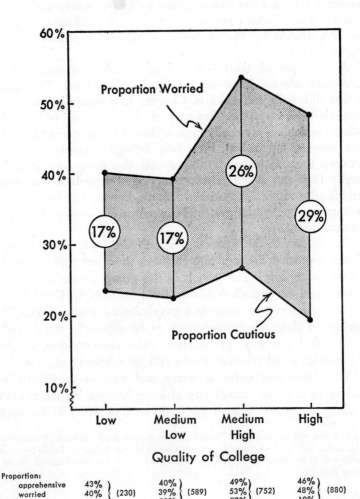

Quality of College

Proportion:								
apprehensive	43%		40%		49%		46%	
worried	40%	(230)	39%	(589)	53%	(752)	48%	(880)
cautious	23%		22%		27%		19%	

hension index increases as compared to the caution element. In view of all the preceding evidence, we are inclined to make the following interpretation. In the more distinguished colleges apprehension is relatively less determined by fear about one's own job, and more by general concern with the status of academic freedom. Precautionary moves in particular are less necessary, but the whole matter is more on professors' minds and so the expressions of worry are relatively more frequent.

Our two pivotal variables have given us a general view of the whole situation. Permissiveness of the individual professor makes for high apprehension in a variety of ways. The quality of his college is a redeeming factor, because the better schools have a more protective administration. With this basic structure in mind, we can now explore in greater detail significant aspects of the way some teachers in our sample experienced the impact of the difficult years.

Chapter VIII

PATTERNS OF CAUTION

THE APPREHENSION FELT by teachers at the time of our study consisted of a rather complex mixture of reactions. Experienced inwardly as a sense of worry and uneasiness, it sometimes found outward expression in acts of caution and withdrawal. In the greater part of our analysis up to this point the inward and outward aspects of apprehension have not been separated. But changes in overt behavior among college teachers, no matter how slight, merit especially close attention, for they may reflect or portend changes in our whole system of higher education. They deserve to be examined in some detail, for while we have shown that, as a group, even our most apprehensive respondents cannot be described as paralyzed with fear, the evidence indicates that the difficult years did place a noticeable damper on the activities and opinions of a sizeable minority.

A certain amount of information concerning teachers' reactions of caution has already been given. On two of the six questionnaire items in our apprehension index a small group of teachers conceded precautionary moves in connection with their professional work: 9 per cent of our respondents said they had toned down their recent writings, and 12 per cent told of increased care in assigning potentially controversial works to their classes. While these two matters were picked for inclusion in the apprehension index because of their professional relevance, other aspects of precautionary behavior were also investigated. Substantial minorities of teachers reported exercising more care in recent years to prevent embarrassing colleagues in political discussions (18 per cent), to avoid expressing opinions or joining organizations which might in some way reflect adversely on the school (22 per cent), and to make it clear to others that they had no extreme leftist or rightist leanings (27 per cent).

The five questions, useful as they were to the development of our statistical measure of apprehension, necessarily dealt with only a few of the many specific manifestations of caution and withdrawal possible among teachers. This chapter and the next one will develop a more complete picture of the constraints reported by our respondents. First, we shall make use of a group of questions that have not yet been explored to provide an abbreviated statistical sketch of the extent of precautionary behavior in different areas of conduct. Then, for a more detailed examination, we shall turn to the rich supply of description and comment recorded by our interviewers.

Patterns of Caution among Colleagues

NEAR THE MIDDLE of the interview respondents were given a series of questions asking them to compare the attitudes now prevailing among their colleagues with those which existed six or seven years earlier. One of them read:

Do you feel that in the selection of reference materials they recommend to students, your social science colleagues here have become more careful today, as compared to six or seven years ago, or less careful to keep out materials that might prove too controversial, or don't you think this has generally happened?

A second question referred to the publications and speeches of professors: Did colleagues, in our respondents' observation, more often avoid "subjects which might have political repercussions?" A third asked whether colleagues were less "willing to express unpopular views in the classroom."

Table 8-1 gives the answers to the three questions. In each case somewhat more than half the respondents noted little if any change. And the number who had no impressions on these matters was almost as great as those who noticed a difference in their colleagues' behavior. However, practically all the change reported was in the direction of withdrawal; on all three matters, approximately 20 per cent reported more avoidance or care, while only a very small fraction found less.

Table 8-1
Report on Changes in Colleagues' Precautionary Behavior in Professional Activities

In Publications and Speeches		In Assigning Reference Material		In Classroom Expression of Unpopular Political Views	
Colleagues avoid controversial subjects more	17%	Colleagues more careful	19%	Colleagues less willing	20%
Avoid subjects less	2	Less careful or bolder	4	More willing	3
No change	64	Has not happened	54	Not much change	58
Undecided, or Don't know	17	Undecided, or Don't know	23	Respondent undecided	19
Total	100%	Total	100%	Total	100%

Just as we have shown that about 10 per cent of our respondents conceded greater personal caution in toning down their recent writings and avoiding controversial authors in their class reading lists, we find again here a minority, of somewhat larger size, who noted a similar pulling back among their colleagues.[1]

_____

1. A comparison of the questions about personal curbs with those about constraints observed among fellow teachers is presented in Appendix 5. This appendix provides a general discussion of questions, like those reported here, eliciting teachers' descriptions of events and prevalent attitudes on their campuses.

The reader may notice that these results appear to be in flat contradiction to a passage in Chapter IV, in which we suggested some of the reasons why both activism and caution may characterize an individual. Our activism items dealt with situations in which a teacher's behavior is relatively public: protesting an act of the school president, or joining a controversial organization. But our indicators of caution, we said, involve behavior which is considerably less visible to others: not bringing up certain political topics which might embarrass a colleague, or quietly toning down one's writings. Table 8-1 clearly shows, however, that toning down writings, or changing reference materials, is indeed noticed by one's colleagues. This data, actually, permits us to speculate that interesting psychological and social mechanisms may intervene in such a situation. Professor X has quietly toned down his more recent articles, but _thinks_ his colleagues haven't noticed. His colleagues _have_ noticed, but have politely said nothing, so Professor X doesn't know they've noticed. Just as the unofficial norms of a colleague group may in some situations press individuals to take a public stand, there may be others in which widely shared knowledge is not made the subject of "public" inspection in the same sense:

A clue to the path which repressive forces may take is provided by further data. In the questionnaire the last item of Table 8-1 was repeated in two other contexts. Respondents were asked to reflect on their colleagues' behavior outside the classroom, and to report whether they were at the present time less willing to express unpopular views "in the community" and "privately among friends." The distribution of answers is given in Figure 8-2 (the middle bar is the item included in Table 8-1).

The comparison of the three questions again reveals that, whatever the area of conduct, only a minority of respondents reported increased constraint in colleagues' behavior. Figure 8-2 also traces a clear trend: the decline in discussion of controversial political matters was most marked in teachers' contacts with the

Figure 8-2
Report on Changes in Colleagues' Willingness to Express
Unpopular Political Views

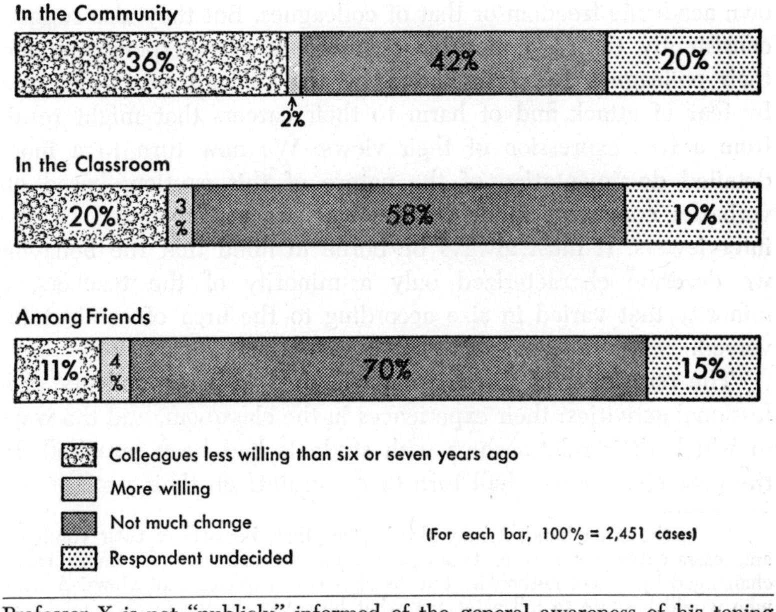

In the Community

36% | 2% | 42% | 20%

In the Classroom

20% | 3% | 58% | 19%

Among Friends

11% | 4% | 70% | 15%

Colleagues less willing than six or seven years ago
More willing
Not much change
Respondent undecided

(For each bar, 100% = 2,451 cases)

Professor X is not "publicly" informed of the general awareness of his toning down. Further study of such patterns would be necessary to confirm these speculations.

community at large, became less widespread in the classroom, and occurred least when teachers talked over issues among their friends. It is traditional to distinguish two aspects of academic freedom for teachers: their right to unhampered expression on the campus, and their right to act like any other citizen within the larger community. Figure 8-2 shows quite clearly that the latter aspect seemed to our informants to be more constricted by the events of the difficult years. In one respect this could be viewed as a reassuring result: encroachments in the classroom were still relatively infrequent. But from another point of view this table indicates the path which a dangerous trend might follow. It suggests that the pressures begin in the larger community, are transmitted from there to the academic sphere, and end up by corroding even private and intimate human relations.[2] The first line of defense for academic freedom might very well turn out to be the public forum outside the campus.

Taken together with those given earlier, these figures again indicate that the majority of teachers felt no curtailment of their own academic freedom or that of colleagues. But they also suggest consistently that a noticeable segment of our respondents and their colleagues felt intimidated by the difficult years—deterred by fear of attack and of harm to their careers that might result from a free expression of their views. We now turn to a more detailed documentation of the nature of this caution, based on verbatim comments made by the teachers and recorded by the interviewers. It must always be borne in mind that the behavior we describe characterized only a minority of the teachers, a minority that varied in size according to the area of conduct involved.

The remainder of this chapter will deal with respondents' professional activities: their experiences in the classroom, and the ways in which their relationships with students had been impaired. In the next chapter we shall turn to constraints on their professional

---

2. On the other hand, it may also be true that, because of their voluntary, and extra-curricular nature, teachers' community activities are more easily challenged by school authorities than is classroom expression of views. A dean who would hesitate to tell a teacher what he could discuss in class might be less reluctant to make suggestions about appropriate topics for a speech to a businessmen's club downtown.

writing and research, and to aspects of their lives less centrally connected with professional activities: their relationships with other professors on the campus and with the community outside.

Constraints in the Classroom

AS ONE ATTEMPTS to get a composite picture of the limitations these teachers felt in approaching their classes, five themes stand out. First, some teachers omitted certain topics which they believed, on professional grounds, ought to be discussed. Other respondents slanted their presentation away from their professional convictions, or balanced an intellectually preferred but controversial position with discussion of a more popular opposing viewpoint. All three ended up by giving students an altered version of what in their best judgment was the truth. Other teachers, while they did not modify presentations as directly, nevertheless detached themselves from personal responsibility for the views they discussed. Finally, some respondents took rather elaborate precautions to avoid getting into difficulty over controversial issues.

The omission of controversial matters. It is hardly surprising that specific omissions occurred in connection with the classroom study of Communism, Soviet Russia, and Red China. During the difficult years the suspicion of subversion could be based on sins far less grievous in an accuser's eye than open and impartial discussion of these topics in the classroom. One historian gave a reading assignment on the constitution of the Soviet Union, only to find that "the mere fact that I said they had a constitution made the students think that I was a Commie." Another professor, assigning works by Karl Marx to his students, sent them to the public library of a neighboring city when he found that the college library did not have sufficient copies; he later learned that the names of all those asking for the books were written down. It was in such a climate that the omissions occurred. A West Coast geographer, aware that as an ex-Wallaceite he was already open to criticism, reported his decision that a lecture on the geography of the U.S.S.R. might be too risky. Other respondents said they no longer assigned "The Communist Manifesto" or bulletins sent out by the Soviet Embassy. Less frequently, the omission was on a larger scale: there were a few college administrations which completely dropped certain courses on these topics.

The reader will notice that the examples used in this chapter often deal with Communism. It is not our task to say how matters involving Russia and Communism should be presented in the classroom. Different schools and different departments will disagree over the proper handling of these topics. But the problem, it seems clear, is the contemporary instance of a much older dilemma: how should institutions of higher learning deal with matters on which the larger community has, perhaps only temporarily, taken an uncompromising stand? We are attempting here simply to point out the constraints adopted by some teachers and schools when they faced this problem.

While it was mentioned most frequently, Communism was not the only specific topic teachers withheld from students. Novels of protest from the 1930's were also sometimes found too dangerous for classroom use; a West Coast sociologist, accustomed to assigning James T. Farrell and *What Makes Sammy Run*, had to be "more careful now." More than one Southern professor, under orders from the school president or by his own reluctant decision, completely avoided the subject of race in class. Social security was still a bad word in some quarters. Religious matters were sometimes considered too hot to handle; Darwinism was discussed in only the most guarded terms at a small New England school with a predominance of Catholic students, and at a major West Coast university plans to conduct a seminar on religion were dropped because the topic was "too controversial."

Teachers avoided not only particular subjects, but also discussion of considerably broader areas, such as "political and economic problems," "any criticism of the status quo," and "explorations of the merits of dissent." Sometimes the topic itself was not the cause of the omission. One respondent did not assign a textbook he considered ideal because the author had been involved in a controversial investigation. An objection from a powerful source to one chapter of a book, or in unusual cases even a single word, was sometimes enough to cause it to be discarded.

It should be added that a few professors, rather than baldly concede that they omitted certain topics and areas in their classrooms, preferred to rationalize the procedure. One said he refused to deal at all with such issues unless conclusive scientific evidence could be brought to bear on them. Another postponed discussion of a controversial issue until, as he put it, "the thing was cleared up." And a third respondent said, "I'm less willing to discuss controversial issues; I don't eliminate them, but if there's a choice between a controversial or a noncontroversial issue, I take the noncontroversial." Whatever the merits of these different approaches, they share in common a reluctance to air many unresolved but important issues.

Slanting the presentation. Rather than shun a subject completely—and sometimes total avoidance is impossible—teachers often chose to slant their presentation of it. This is particularly true, again, of respondents who had to deal with Communism and Soviet Russia in their courses. In typical instances, an economist became critical of Russian economic forms, a political scientist underplayed his approval of certain administrative devices developed by the Russians, a historian concealed his support of the recognition of Red China and stressed the opposing view instead. Replacing textbooks may have the same effect; an economist at a private New England school reported a "trend toward conformity . . . Five years ago they picked John Maynard on Russia, now they pick Rostow."

In a few cases, interestingly enough, teachers slanted their approach to a controversial subject in the direction, not of the popular, but of the unpopular viewpoint. A Midwestern teacher, for example, suspected that in an effort to compensate for his students' prejudices against the Soviet Union, he may have neglected to point out the defects of the Russian system sufficiently. When a subject is highly controversial, an impartial presentation may indeed be difficult.

"Balancing" the presentation. The wish to forestall attack, which prompted some teachers to omit or slant material, led others to "balance" remarks they expected to be received unfavorably with statements of more conventional opinion. A respondent, already quoted in an earlier chapter, made it a practice to follow any criticism of the United States with one of Russia. And if a favorable reference to Communism was made, it was often carefully surrounded with distinctions and disclaimers. One teacher said:

In discussing communism, I sometimes say that communism (small "c") is probably the most ideal form of economic organization yet devised, yet I carefully differentiate communism with a little "c" from Russian Communism. I point out that communism would work only in a society of angels, because it fails to take into consideration the imperfections—laziness, etc.—inherent in human nature.

This comment permits us to return to an earlier point. Let us forget for a moment that it deals with communism, with all its present connotations. Suppose that the teacher had simply been describing a vision of a good society. *Any* such vision, whatever it might be, would conflict with the beliefs of some sector of the community. The offended group might feel strongly that their beliefs should not be challenged. How should a teacher communicate to his students such a vision, or indeed any view at sharp variance with prevailing opinions? Is he entitled to describe it as graphically as he can, so his students will understand it clearly? The teacher just quoted had come to the theoretical conclusion that a true communist society would have a high economic efficiency. He would certainly reduce the impact of his point by hastily making a balancing observation that imperfect human beings could never establish a true communist society. An abstract idea of this sort often requires a forceful and vigorous presentation to be understood by students. This would be more difficult to accomplish if the teacher were also anxious to make sure that no one thought he was talking about Russian Communism. The teacher's timing of his remarks would be dictated, not by his judgment of how best to put across his points, but by prudence. He probably would not dare, for example, to postpone discussion of the inherent flaws of communism to the next lecture so students could consider its advantages at leisure.

Many teachers, of course, tried to maintain a balanced presentation as an obligation to their students. One stated, "I try to guard against presenting a better argument for my view than for the other side." Another said, "I usually express my point of view, but also sincerely try to express the opposing view with equal force." Here, however, the impetus comes not from an external pressure but from an inner sense of obligation, and the "balance" sought is a true rather than a slanted one.

Detachment from personal responsibility. Social science teachers who neither omitted topics nor biased presentations often found it necessary to detach themselves conspicuously from personal agreement or association with the views and ideas they presented. Some, of course, were unwilling to disclose their own convictions because they wanted students to form an independent opinion of an issue, and feared they might be swayed more by the teacher's position of authority than by the merits of his case. But others decided against revealing their views on different grounds.

Some were unwilling to express personal opinions because students might misunderstand what they said and spread distorted versions of it. "I have frequently worried about this possibility," one teacher said, "and I habitually keep all my classes as confused as possible as to my own views." In another approach, a teacher appeared to disassociate himself from views he actually shared, by quoting an authority and letting whatever discussion or controversy developed center around him. One respondent said, "Every time I have to talk about Red China, I always preface it with the fact that this is the opinion of Tingling; she wrote a prize novel about Red China and as she gives it, Red China is doing a wonderful thing and really going in for reform." The approach of such a teacher is the exact opposite of that taken when views are concealed to facilitate independent student judgments. Here, for instance, the teacher actually seemed anxious to have students adopt his own view, but hid behind Tingling. He let the weight of authority have full force, while remaining personally unaccountable.

Perhaps a more subtle device by which a teacher can avoid responsibility for views he wants students to learn about is to acquaint them with the politics of authors they read. Respondents often said that the incidents of the difficult years sometimes alerted teachers to the desirability of making sure that students took into consideration the ideological positions of writers they studied. Be that as it may, a number of teachers were more cautious in this regard than they once felt necessary. And it seems clear that at least in some cases such remarks were intended to imply to students, "Those are the author's views, not mine."

Special precautions to avoid misunderstanding. Apart from this effort to disassociate themselves from the views of others, teachers took additional precautions to forestall trouble. Some of them commented on the care with which they chose their words in discussing a controversial issue. One reported, for instance, that he was "prone to look behind and in front of my statements to be sure they can in no way convey a wrong impression." But as other teachers pointed out, the man who adopts such practices may pay a price: "It becomes impossible to give the true picture as to what is going on when you have to be concerned with the exact phraseology you use in class." Just as the need to quickly balance an argument with a counterargument may diminish the impact of the whole discussion, so it seems inevitable that an over-concern for language may impair the clarity and vigor of a presentation.

Sometimes the problem of avoiding misunderstandings is handled more directly. One teacher, for instance, habitually told his students, "Now don't go out and say I said 'so-and-so,' because what I actually said was 'such-and-such.'" Perhaps the ultimate insurance against garbling was achieved at an Ivy League school, which, having carefully described one of its courses as "A *Critical* Study of the Philosophy of Marxism," (emphasis added) systematically wire-recorded every session of the class. How much the presence of the machine inhibited the group from speaking out is another matter.

One possible consequence of these precautionary activities should not be overlooked. A teacher who must give time and thought to elaborate precautions in class will often put considerable energy into the effort. In extreme cases, he may feel forced to expend his major energies in near-compulsive protective gestures. When this happens, of course, his work is bound to suffer.

The difficulty of pinning down slow and subtle changes. It seems evident that some teachers, while aware of pressure against taking controversial positions, at the same time found it difficult to say whether they had actually shifted their class presentations. The economist who described the change of textbooks in his department, for instance, went on to add, "It's happened very slightly and unconsciously." We have shown, too, in connection with reference materials, that teachers apparently noticed changes in their colleagues more often than in themselves. Apart from the perhaps greater difficulty of admitting one's own yielding of position, it may also be easier to notice changes when observations are intermittent, as is usual with one's colleagues, than when they are continuous, as is likely with oneself.

Among the teachers who most clearly sensed new constraints on their classroom work were several who had experienced an extensive change in their environment. Teachers who had recently moved from a Northern school to a Southern school where race topics were not discussed, or from a nondenominational school to a denominational one, were often sharply conscious of the more restrictive character of their new colleges. Also, a few teachers who had been away on leave from their campuses for a year or two said they had immediately noticed a different atmosphere on their return.

But those who simply suspected that a change had occurred, without being able to pin it down exactly, were likely to be troubled; they sensed that they might have in some way retreated, but they were not quite sure. A typical comment came from an introspectively-inclined Southern economist:

I feel a rather tenuous connection between a changing intellectual environment and my own teaching practices. It's not so much an avoidance of controversial issues, as a feeling of hesitancy or uncertainty in pursuing a discussion of these issues in the classroom. I don't have any idea how that feeling has affected my teaching. I am aware of it as a subjective thing.

Such a comment suggests that if a pressure is sufficiently subtle and continuous, a teacher may respond to it without realizing he has changed his behavior. In such a situation, too, the impulse to exercise caution may seem almost a reflex, unpremeditated and somewhat disconcerting. Witness the remark of a California teacher: "I recently made some pretty obvious comments about Governor Knight's tax program without mentioning any names; I wondered why I just hadn't come out with it." Clearly a less self-perceptive teacher might easily overlook this kind of change. All in all, it appears likely that for every teacher who was actually conscious of shifting his classroom stand, there were more who had unwittingly either drifted along with the times completely, or partially reoriented their positions.

Some consequences. When constraints occur in the classroom, certain consequences are inevitable. A student cannot react to an idea unless he hears it stated; if a teacher chooses to avoid discussion of controversial issues of the day, some students will remain unaware that they exist. A slanted classroom presentation denies to the student the privilege of hearing the other side. Furthermore, as many teachers pointed out, a vicious circle of increasing constraint can develop; a teacher who surrenders today his right to discuss what he considers peripheral may find tomorrow that he cannot discuss the central. In any case, whenever teachers do not speak out, but go along uncomplainingly with the dominant forces of the day, colleges and universities as strongholds of reform and progress are weakened.

Other consequences, if less sweeping, may nevertheless substantially alter established academic custom. It has long been the practice of many teachers to try out their new ideas, their new formulations and interpretations, upon their students; innumerable textbooks and journal articles contain tributes to the students who have tested them in preliminary versions. And yet if the ideas in such works are somehow unconventional by today's standards, many teachers are no longer willing to risk them on students. As one teacher put it, "How far may I speculate and come out with outrageous opinions, which may turn out in the future to be conventional ones?" If today's conjectural extravagance can become tomorrow's truth, to inhibit it is costly.

Impaired Relationships
with Students

A MAJOR REASON for teachers' constraint in their classes was a lack of trust in their students. Respondents complained that some students were rigidly conservative in their approach to classroom problems, that it was extremely easy for such a student to misunderstand a teacher, and that student misrepresentations could have serious consequences. We shall now elaborate upon these matters, and show that there were strains on the rapport between professor and student in other ways as well.

Fear of the conservative student. A major problem for many teachers, and a source of considerable fear, was the inflexible and ultraconservative student. Numerous respondents reported that some of their students approached topics with such unshakeable conviction that classroom activity was impaired. Certain subjects and opinions were labeled "bad" in advance by these students. They might, for example, refuse to consider the possibility that a socialist form of government could have positive features. We have already quoted the teacher who gave a reading assignment on the constitution of the Soviet Union only to find that "the mere fact I said they had one made the students think I was a Commie." A New England teacher was fearful about recommending that his classes work with *The New York Times* because of such student remarks as "Well, obviously *The New York Times* is Communistic," and *"The New York Times* is not allowed in my house because it is Communistic."

Teachers were particularly wary of these students because they seemed both prone to make snap judgments and easy to take offense. To them, an exposition of Keynesian economics quickly became Communism, an expression of religious tolerance the revelation of atheistic views. To a few students, the mere fact that a man taught Russian history was cause for suspicion. The ease with which some students can jump to the conclusion of subversion, and the extraneous nature of the evidence on which the judgment may be based, are well illustrated in the following incident.

Recently, I received a pamphlet from the Fund for the Republic, "The Fifth Amendment Today," by Griswold. It had a shiny black cover with big yellow glaring block letters. I held it up before my class and said, "Does this look like something you'd carry in the streetcar?" They roared with laughter and said, "No, that sure looks like something subversive." Then when I told them what it was they were very much surprised and laughed to think they had supposed it was a subversive publication.

These students were also feared by teachers because they sometimes did not hesitate to make open accusations in the classroom against a teacher. As several respondents pointed out, it was one thing for a student to take offense at a professor's classroom remarks, and quite another for him to say, in front of the other students, "That sounds Communistic to me." Such an episode can be most humiliating to a teacher, particularly when, as in the following incident described by a Midwestern sociologist, a contemptuous attitude on the part of the student is apparent.

One incident stands out in my mind. I was describing economic systems, and mentioned communism. As I was discussing it, someone threw a penny, meaning to say, "You're cheap"—it's a stage symbol. I felt sick that someone could misinterpret my remarks. From then on I have made sure that students understand what I am doing. I don't avoid the topic, but I put it differently now.

Garbling and quoting out of context. Apart from the unpleasantness of possible classroom episodes, many teachers expressed great concern that rigid or irresponsible students who misunderstood their views would pass garbled versions on to others and quickly land them in trouble. Some 989 respondents, in answering one of the apprehension index questions, said they had worried about such a possibility. Part of the problem appears to be that the same students who are most likely to misinterpret a teacher's remarks are also most certain to believe in the accuracy of their own version and to pass it on to others without qualms. It is true that many charges made by students on the basis of a misunderstanding were laughed off. But we have considerable evidence that others were sometimes taken very seriously by parents, school administrators, or state legislators. Sometimes, as in the following incident, the matter was cleared up without detriment to anyone.

A student who had failed here—flunked out—was a reporter for a local paper. He dreamed up a story that there were Communist pamphlets being distributed in the Christian Center building. This story was carried by papers all over the state. The local paper ran editorials criticizing the college for permitting this to happen and for denying the validity of the report. Retractions and apologies were printed several days later in small stories on inside pages.

Many respondents were convinced, however, that such an incident could rapidly balloon into real trouble. A respondent at a Southern public college, for instance, believed that if a view of his, warped by a student, "should ever become a question of public or administrative concern," he would receive no protection.

For as he saw it, a public institution is unable to withstand any really strong pressures.

Underlying such views, we should note, are two implicit assumptions. First, these teachers expected that charges made against them were likely to be believed immediately by the authorities without further investigation. And second, they felt that an accusation might lead automatically to punishment regardless of the merits of the case. We shall say more about these themes later on.

Surveillance in the classroom. If a misunderstanding, with all its consequences, can arise so easily, teachers are naturally often more watchful of their students and more careful about their classroom remarks. In much the same way, classroom rapport is seriously disturbed when teachers believe they are under surveillance.

In some cases, teachers were sure that a student had been asked to report on them. Respondents described instances where students reported to a colleague, a dean of the school, a local American Legion post, a politician, or a state legislator. Some students were members of formally constituted organizations, such as Students for America, which take it upon themselves to seek out subversive attitudes among teachers. Several teachers, too, were convinced that the F.B.I. had an agent in their classes.

On the other side of the coin, a teacher often learned that he was under surveillance from a friendly student. Sometimes a pupil came to the professor with a warning that others were reporting his activities and statements. More often, the student who had been asked to keep an eye on the teacher indignantly refused and himself reported the suggestion. We might add, parenthetically, that students are, of course, a frequent channel for many kinds of information. When a professor learned that a "super-patriotic group circulated a file of information to all of my students that because I used the *Reporter* Magazine I am a pro- Communist," or that "my outspoken remarks about the security program led to criticism from some of my colleagues," as often as not the information came from a student.

Even though tangible indications were lacking, a considerable number of other teachers suspected classroom surveillance. At one school respondents wondered if their own classes were audited because at a nearby college formal charges of subversion were placed against a professor on the basis of such evidence. Sometimes questionable strangers appeared in classes:

In my outline for a class in American Intellectual History I put a lecture on Marxism in the 1930's in the United States. It was arranged in advance. Two older people were present that I had never seen before. Whether they were parents, or just who they were, I don't know.

For others it might be nothing more palpable than a sense of antagonism in the air: "I had the feeling that there was somebody unfriendly in the room." Nor was this uneasiness allayed by the thought that students, whatever else their talents, might indeed make good spies. "The best Gestapo," said one respondent, "is the student."

With or without evidence, many teachers were responsive to the idea that they were under surveillance. This is revealed again in their willingness to lend credence to a rumor: "Once a rumor went around that there were watchers in the class; although I never actually knew if there was one or not, once the rumor was voiced, the feeling of being watched persisted." A teacher who had once been the subject of attention by the Communist Party ("they sent me some propaganda to my house to try to correct an impression I had given in class") now found it natural to wonder if there were F.B.I. agents among his students.

In any case, it seems clear that a teacher who believes he may be under scrutiny will tend to be guarded in conducting his classes, and that, as we have seen, this caution will often take the form of the constraints and withdrawal described above.

Reporting on students. If students are sometimes asked to report on teachers, it is equally true that teachers may be asked to report on students. Frequently, government agencies request an evaluation of students who are applying for a federal position or for a commission in the armed forces. Also, inquiries are received from potential academic or industrial employers about students' political "safety." In such situations teachers, if they happen to know anything about a student which might be considered detrimental, may find themselves faced with unpleasant alternatives. One of our questionnaire items set up a hypothetical situation of this nature: "If a student had told you about some political indiscretion in his youth, but now you were convinced of his loyalty, and if the F.B.I. came to you to check on that student, would you report this incident to the F.B.I.?" The distribution of the answers reflects the dilemma of respondents; 46 per cent said they would reluctantly give the information; 35 per cent would equally reluctantly withhold it, and the remaining 19 per cent refused to attempt a choice. The conflict in which such a situation can place a teacher, and an indication of some of the issues involved, is expressed in a typical answer to this question.

Oh boy! My first feeling is that I *wouldn't* like to report the incident to the F.B.I. All of us as we grow up and all during our lives have the right to be wrong. I voted for Wallace in '48, but I was wrong. I am glad now he didn't get in, but I would hate to think I couldn't be wrong. If a student during his student days was a member of some left-wing or right-wing political organization, and later on dropped out of that organization in the present climate of fear, I wouldn't like to report that knowledge to the F.B.I. But if the F.B.I. came to me and asked me point-blank, I would tell the truth because I respect the job the F.B.I. has to do in order to safeguard our security.

A number of respondents said they might feel compelled to speak up for fear they would get into trouble, or perhaps even lose their jobs, unless they reported the student. On the other hand, some expressed great concern about the manner in which the F.B.I. would handle such information: "The way the reports are often used is absolutely atrocious; they put them in a file with no evaluation, and the F.B.I. treats them as sound and revealing." Furthermore, as another teacher pointed out, such a practice can have wider negative consequences.

I would like to go on record as objecting to questions about students' opinions that have been given in the classroom. It limits discussion and destroys trust. I told the last agent that. I think they go beyond what their organization expects of them.

The implication is that inquiries from the F.B.I. were so frequent and so commonly known as to bring on a noticeable over-all change in the classroom behavior of students at the school.

Some of the respondents who said they would not reveal the information added, "unless the F.B.I. man asked point blank about

the specific situation." To a few, the unwritten code which forbids
us to inform on our fellows had even greater force.

I am listed as a reference by every student who gets a master's degree
here. I have been interviewed by representatives of every security agency
in the U.S. government and I follow the practice of telling them no
details on the students I supervise except those that have occurred during their studies here. This follows from my unalterable opposition to
the security program as it now exists. My own little private veto.

In a small way, this respondent felt compelled to take the law into
his own hands to protect his standards of conduct.

Furthermore, as may always be true when the only choice is
between obnoxious alternatives, being in effect forced to reveal
information about a student is often humiliating to teachers. A
Southern professor described a situation in which he felt great
pressure to make a derogatory report to military authorities about
a student.

I teach a class in an off-campus military base. A student, neurotic and
about to be discharged—honorably, I believe—made statements that
looked like the Communist *Pravda* line. I hinted and hinted and warned
him in this one class session to be careful. His rejoinder was, "In the
university anything goes, any idea—just so it's within the bounds of
propriety and decency." At the end of the session he announced that
he knew the incident would be reported since there were unknown
intelligence men in the class. I felt that I ought to report this incident,
but I felt like a rat. A friend who is also teaching in the military told
me to cover myself. I phoned the next day to the civilian security man,
and explained the situation to him. I later learned that the F.B.I. had
already heard most of the conversation. I didn't have to repeat the
story to them. They had already received reports of the incident.

This incident has a number of interesting implications. It is somewhat chilling to note the race between the teacher and the invisible
"spy" to be the first informant. Quite apparently the teacher felt
that if he spoke out openly to warn the student that his statements sounded Communistic, he himself might be suspected of
subversive tendencies. To go to the aid of someone else who is under
suspicion is often to come under suspicion oneself. We also note
that the teacher did not contradict the student's assumption that
within the bounds of decency all ideas are appropriate grist for

the classroom, and yet by turning in the report the teacher himself
demonstrated that the student was wrong. It is perhaps a sardonic
sidelight on the current state of academic affairs that a strong
affirmation of classroom freedom should come from a neurotic
with an evident overdose of self-damaging tendencies. And it is
worth noting that, in good soap-opera thriller style, the intelligence
man in the class is not only unidentified, but undeniably efficient.

Clandestine elements in the teacher-student relationship. Much
of the foregoing might be described as having elements of the
clandestine: students covertly reported on teachers and teachers
covertly reported on students. Sometimes an overtone of conspiracy
entered into the relationship *between* teacher and student. Occasionally, a teacher will encounter a student whose turn of mind
is less fixed and more inquisitive than that of the community or
the home from which he comes. Wishing to encourage such a
student while not exposing himself to trouble, the teacher contrives
a solution which permits the student to continue his inquiries in
secret. One teacher told how, a few minutes before the interview,
a student had come to him and asked permission to have the *Daily
Worker* sent to her at the college in his name; if it was mailed to
her home she feared that political repercussions would ruin her
father's business. Here, perhaps, only a student's idle curiosity may
have been at stake, but sometimes materials of importance to class
work are involved. Such was the case in an episode related by an
instructor at a small New England teachers college.

I have a student who is comparing the economic systems of capitalism,
socialism, and communism. I recommended a book that was biased to
the U.S.S.R., but I warned her not to spread it around the community
that we had recommended it—that we knew what we were doing, but
the community might not understand. I wanted her to know what such
a book said—she has got to know to be able to compare the three systems.

It is a tenet of the American system of legal procedure that the
merits of a dispute are best settled in the courtroom through the
vigorous partisan arguments of opposing counsel; similarly, this
teacher apparently felt that an unfamiliar economic system can be
better understood when the arguments of its vigorous proponents
are inspected. He clearly believed that the community could not
understand or accept such an argument, and so advised the stu-

dent to pursue her work in discreet silence. As a result, if only in a small way, the gap between university and community was widened, and the student was invited to join a sort of academic underground.

An element of the clandestine may also enter in when a teacher discloses to his students some of his methods for keeping out of trouble. One respondent said that "in private talks with a student I try to help him understand the social processes and functions involved in voicing unpopular views, and I try to assist him to master the technique of raising such issues for discussion so they can be considered as far as possible on the merits of the issue, without involving the student necessarily in the attitude about the issue." It is easy enough to picture this teacher also explaining to his students how to make sure that nobody thinks they are leftists.

One teacher, in a more unusual gesture, confessed the use of one of his students as a vehicle for the expression of opinions which he was unwilling to make public in his own name. Far from urging this student to conform, he said, "I encourage him in unpopular views; I write vicariously through him—I criticize almost every word he writes." This too, is an ancient device of the underground and the underdog—to put an idea into circulation by insinuating it into the minds of people who do not appear connected with the underground. Here it seems little more than the evasive gesture of a scared and timid teacher.

Outside the classroom. Caution and constraint may also characterize contacts between teacher and students outside the classroom. Students of course frequently approach their teachers for advice. In such situations, some teachers suggest the complete avoidance of certain controversial career specialties; as one teacher put it, "some areas are critical and no longer open to the student." A few, mindful that in recent years individuals have come under suspicion for innocently joining student organizations which later became controversial, might even advise the student to join nothing at all (although there is no guarantee, of course, that a future shift in public opinion will not bring the nonjoiners under suspicion). One teacher, noting that past association with currently suspect figures can also bring difficulties, advised his students to avoid any contact with presently controversial figures: "I wouldn't want the students to become involved in bringing either Lattimore or Senator McCarthy here; they're both key figures in this big dispute and close association with either one would bode no good for a student." A more typical respondent advised his students "not to take an extreme position either right or left." Many teachers considered it wise for a student to conform to the approach of the majority. The prevalence of such thinking is indicated by the fact that out of the 2,451 respondents, 264 said in a checklist question that when they talked privately to students with unpopular ideas, they encouraged them to adopt the prevailing campus views. Many respondents, themselves adhering to this principle, were reluctant to become faculty advisers to student political organizations which advocate unpopular views; another checklist question revealed that a total of 467 respondents were "more hesitant today" about sponsoring such a group. Comments volunteered by teachers indicated they were by no means thinking here only of Communist, Socialist, or Progressive Party groups. At one school, a group of students attempted to organize a club to study civil liberties issues, but was unable to find a faculty sponsor. The result is again to deprive students of experience in dealing with controversial problems and extreme ideologies.

Some Further Observations
on the Student's Role

ALTHOUGH it is difficult to show directly, it seems likely that teachers' sense of caution was reinforced considerably by the widespread caution and constraint they found among their students. Certainly, it was the opinion of many respondents that their present students, compared to those of a few years earlier, were more conservative, less willing to experiment with novel or radical views, and more cautious in their activities generally.

To show this we turn once more to statistics. To parallel information about their colleagues, our informants were asked in another group of questionnaire items about the students on their campuses. These questions inquired whether, compared to six or seven years ago, respondents' students were "less willing to express unpopular political views" in the classroom and in private talks with faculty members outside the classroom. Were they also less willing "to form and to join student political organizations advocating what might be unpopular political beliefs?" Figure 8-3 summarizes the answers.

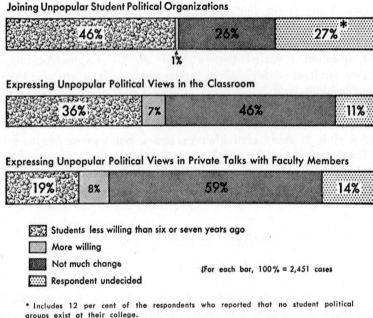

Figure 8-3
Report on Changes in Students' Attitudes

Joining Unpopular Student Political Organizations

| 46% | 26% | 27%* |

1%

Expressing Unpopular Political Views in the Classroom

| 36% | 7% | 46% | 11% |

Expressing Unpopular Political Views in Private Talks with Faculty Members

| 19% | 8% | 59% | 14% |

Students less willing than six or seven years ago
More willing
Not much change   (For each bar, 100% = 2,451 cases
Respondent undecided

* Includes 12 per cent of the respondents who reported that no student political groups exist at their college.

The middle part of Figure 8-3, concerning classroom behavior, permits a direct comparison with the corresponding part of Figure 8-2. Our respondents reported even more intimidation among students than among their own colleagues[3] (interestingly

---

3. Judging from the frequency with which he reported caution in his own activities and among his colleagues and students, the typical reply of a social science teacher ran about as follows: "Even if I am apprehensive, by and large, I am not giving in; about my colleagues I am much less sure; about our students I am quite pessimistic indeed."

enough, they also claimed to know more about the students, as can be seen from the right-hand series of percentages in both Figures). While the other two questions in the two Figures are less directly comparable, more respondents saw students as shying away from organizations than noticed colleagues avoiding public expression of opinions. And the private contacts between students and professors seem more adversely affected than the free expression of opinion among the teachers themselves.

From the point of view of those who favor the free flow of ideas, the picture which professors gave of what happened to students during the difficult years is more pessimistic than their view of their colleagues. Apart from this, in one interesting respect Figure 8-3 corroborates the general trend revealed in Figure 8-2. It is again the participation in general public affairs which appears to have been most affected; the classroom comes next, with personal relations, here between students and professors, relatively least impaired. Thus once more a possible chain of events suggests itself, beginning in the outside world, then affecting the campus, and finally impinging on the private world of teachers and students. While a survey made at one point in time cannot prove such a process, it militates against the belief that an atmosphere of freedom within the academic community could long be maintained once its members grew hesitant to take their place in the larger society.

That students today are much less interested in public affairs than they were prior to World War II will be agreed upon by even casual observers of the college scene. An interpretation of this trend is more difficult. Partly we are undoubtedly faced here with the same type of intimidation that is reported among teachers. But additional causes may play a role. The large number of job opportunities which have opened up in recent years focused students' attention upon their personal careers. Another factor might be a change in the social scene at large. During the depression unemployment called for improvements in social legislation. Solutions were not difficult to discover, and small groups of students could work toward them with some hope of making an impact. The problems which we face today are certainly no less serious, but they are much more complex and clearly less amenable to personal effort. Thus the lack of a program in which a student's efforts can count might help to explain his withdrawal from public discussion. In any case, comparison of the depression years and the recent period is appropriate. Then, from all accounts, students were more radical than their professors. Today the depression generation have become teachers, and they complain that the post-war student lacks social fervor. Whether such an oscillation in the positions of faculty and students is a long-standing historical phenomenon is of course difficult even to guess without longer periods of observation.

In answering the three questions about students, teachers often provided illuminating details. Several respondents described the disappearance of the outspoken Marxist from their classes.

You no longer get the Marxist view brought up in class. In 1946 to 1949 they made this place hum. I don't know whether they believe differently today or if they are unwilling—they may have changed position. Vigor and extremeness of position are gone.

One teacher added that advocacy of a Marxist position today would almost be like breaking the laws of nature: "I can just as well imagine the sun coming up in the west as students even wanting to form a Young Communist League." Nowadays students believe that far less grievous sins can permanently stigmatize them. A professor of geography reported a rumor widely circulated and accepted among his students that a graduate could not get a job if he had taken a course in Soviet geography. Another teacher described how undergraduates at his college had refused to join a student committee called "Books for Free Minds," to send textbooks to anti-Communist students and trade centers abroad, because the title sounded subversive to them. And the following incident, fresh in the mind of a respondent as he spoke to the interviewer, is a far cry indeed from the time when a classroom might "hum with Marxists."

Today in a seminar a student was making a report on slave labor in Soviet Russia and gave some preposterous figures overestimating the number of slave laborers in the Soviet Union. None of the other students questioned his statistical error. I had to. I know one student was afraid to speak up even though he knew that the figures were wrong. I had to step in, even at the risk of being considered pro-Soviet, to bring the report back to credibility. Seven years ago my students weren't afraid to speak up or question ridiculous reports about Soviet Russia.

Again we see the preference for a gross distortion of fact over the risk of being considered controversial. Since the knowledgeable student remained completely silent in this incident, and the teacher himself spoke up only reluctantly, one wonders how frequently "preposterous figures" remain unchallenged in such a situation. But the central point lies in the suggestion that the teacher's reluctance was increased by the silence of the well-informed student; his own sense of caution appears to have been freshly sharpened by the caution of the student. And, of course, it seems clearly possible that the students in turn were infected by the hesitancy of the teacher.

Chapter IX

PATTERNS OF CAUTION
(Continued)

In this chapter we continue our description of the corrosions and restrictions marking the lives of the minority of teachers in our sample who were more highly apprehensive.

Constraints on Professional Work
Outside the Classroom

The professional work of many respondents extended beyond the classroom to writing and research, and to community activities. As in the classroom, teachers reported a variety of constraints in these areas.

Toning down on controversial issues. Interview after interview indicated that an attempt to write impartially about certain social problems might bring anything from annoyed letters to the loss of a job. In such circumstances, it is not surprising that 218 respondents conceded they had "toned down something I have written lately because I was worried that it might cause too much controversy," an item in the apprehension index. Sometimes this involved little more than changing language which might appear immoderate; the respondent who altered a passage in an article in which he said that "TV is 97 per cent trash" to read "97 per cent tinsel" may have done so more to be fair and judicious than for fear of reprisal. Others, however, conceded that they tried to be more clever in their phrasing to avoid repercussions.

Toning down is such a delicate and important matter that

(218)

teachers do not always trust themselves to do it alone. One professor described his role as a cooperating editor:

A fellow will write an article to be published in the *New Republic,* and bring it around for comment—do I think it will get him into trouble? I suggest he change some ideas so that they are implicit rather than openly stated. Another case, a colleague brought me an article he had written for a local newspaper, not for intellectual criticism, but for political "safeness."

This teacher is evidently something of an informal security officer for his colleagues. His qualifications for this task may stem from his being a specialist on the Far East, who had doubtless become conversant with the ins and outs of handling a controversial topic. In any case, it is noteworthy that he seemed neither indignant nor morally troubled over being called on in such a way. In fact, like another respondent who said, "I am at a point where I know what words to say and what to avoid so I do not get into trouble," he sounds rather proud of his editorial skill.

The complete avoidance of controversial topics. Sometimes a professor decided against writing at all on a topic. Consider the instance of a Midwestern teacher who said, "If you're in a college where the administration policies are designed to play up to certain economic interests, then criticism of those interests, even if just, may place the individual professor in a bad light with his superiors, which may be reflected in his personal advancement." And so, he continued, he had written nothing which might be controversial, concentrating only on technical articles. A historian who was completing a book decided to play it safe by "stopping with 1945 when the cold war began." Another chose not to start work after all on a history of China. A somewhat cynical economist had developed a simple formula for avoiding trouble: "I just limit my writings to things that Congressmen can't understand." And there were a few respondents who, feeling that writing on the topics in which they were interested would be risky, preferred simply not to publish at all.

Limitations on research materials. Teachers often complained of problems in obtaining and using materials needed for their writing and research. Leading the list, of course, are books and pamphlets dealing with Russia and Communism which cannot be obtained or are considered too risky to use. But *Pravda* and *Izvestia*, the *Daily Worker*, and other outright Communist literature by no means completed the inventory, for many "leftist" and "liberal" books and periodicals were also mentioned. A respondent at a Mississippi Valley A. & M. college noticed that the *New Republic* no longer appeared on the table in the library reading room. At a New England state teachers college, books by Howard Fast and others had been stolen from the library: "Somebody crept in and purified us." A political scientist, engaged in research on the Netherlands, came across a brilliant speech on his topic by a member of the Dutch parliament, yet upon discovering that the speaker was a Communist, decided to quote another man who had said approximately the same thing in less effective language.

A few teachers had been denied access to their subjects of study. Some had been refused passports to go into the area of their specialization, and others were worried about passport clearance, like the respondent who, shortly after the war, had joined "a group to improve opportunities for housing for veterans and equal rights for minority groups." First-hand observation of certain social groups and movements had also become dangerous. A student of Communist front organizations, who had once thought nothing of joining such a group in order to study it more closely, would now avoid such a move, and was in fact anxiously trying to hide his previous experiment.

The extra effort to keep a clean record. Respondents who had not restricted their writing and research might nevertheless go out of their way to preserve their uncontroversial status. They felt impelled to make their position crystal clear in their writings, to avoid any possibility of a misunderstanding. One respondent, even, told us that he was "supersensitive" about requesting the school library to purchase books he needed, some of which are critical of American society; he felt that his own more moderate position had to be stressed.

A revealing story was told in this connection by a professor of political science at a large tax-supported university west of the Mississippi, who at the time of the interviews was just completing an analysis of the power structure of a nearby metropolitan community. Although he claimed considerable friendship with businessmen in the city he was studying, he expected that his findings would be unacceptable to them. Anticipating that his theories might even be labeled "un-American" by his business friends, he had devoted great effort to preventing the slightest doubt about his objectivity. In his classes, for instance, he avoided any discussion of weaknesses in the American political system or advantages in Russia's. Although not overly interested in politics, he had in any case declined to join any kind of organization which might conceivably be labeled subversive. Before expressing a political opinion to anyone, he told us, he was "extremely careful to make a reconnaissance of the person's potential effect on my security or promotion." He was even unwilling to reveal the magazines he reads that deal with political affairs in the confidence of the interview. All this, apparently, so that in the coming clash with business interests his record would not offer the slightest ground for charges of political bias.

The curbing of peripheral professional activities. Professors do many other things which to some extent make use of their professional skills—they give lectures, write newspaper columns, participate in discussion groups, and so on. As we have shown in Chapter VIII, these activities are subjected to more criticism than campus duties.

The changed climate of opinion in such matters is illustrated by the following ironic episode at a large Midwestern state university. According to the respondent who described the incident, a colleague in the same department had recently given a speech off campus on "George Washington as a Man." A furore resulted; editorials appeared in newspapers and the board of trustees rose up in arms. As it happens, the speaker had given the identical speech twenty years before to the Elks Club, and had stirred up no reaction at all; he had just taken the speech from his files and repeated it word for word. Not surprisingly, at a time when it was difficult to know what might turn out to be controversial, we find that other respondents refused invitations to speak or lecture. Sometimes such an invitation was rejected because the teacher suspected that it concealed a hook; one respondent felt that he had been invited to address a businessmen's club on "The Welfare State" so evidence could be gathered to support a charge of un-Americanism against him.

Letters written to the columns of a newspaper by professors

have also become a sore spot on a number of campuses. Like speeches, these are often considered public statements which may be detrimental to the interests of the school. A Western respondent explained that his small college, a private one, must draw support from groups that "might not like open discussion," and so felt that out of loyalty to the college he had to "use somewhat more restraint in such things as writing letters to the newspapers." While this respondent seemed relatively undisturbed, a Southern geographer appeared to be quite embarrassed in admitting his acquiescence to a similar arrangement.

I have felt an urge to write to the editors on segregation, but I have refrained. I more or less have instructions from the department head not to go out of my way to discuss segregation, not to make public statements, or write letters to editors. I guess I agreed to do this in a moment of weakness, without discussing it with others in the department. But there's a kind of gentlemen's agreement in the department with which I don't completely agree, that nobody will make public statements which might reflect on the department as a whole and might endanger its position.

In like fashion, some professors found that other uses and outlets for their professional skills had been curtailed. The radio Sceptic's Hour conducted by one respondent was stopped, the newspaper column written by another discontinued, participation by a third in local discussions of conservation discouraged, and so on. As a result, many talents possessed by college teachers have to some extent been lost to the community.

Constraints on Teachers' Nonprofessional Activities

WHILE THE CONSTRAINTS on teachers which occur within the classroom and in other professional activities are perhaps of paramount concern to the student of academic freedom, noteworthy difficulties arose elsewhere in the lives of our respondents simply because they happened to be teachers. Important among these were problems involving the interplay between their role as teachers and as citizens, for at many universities the political activities of teachers are subject to scrutiny, constraint, and censure. But the fact that they are college teachers also colors other aspects of our respondents' lives—their social relationships, their participation as private citizens in civic activities, and their general standing in the community.

Difficulties over political activity. A number of respondents who might like to take part in community politics reported that the school or the city considers such activity inappropriate for a teacher. Although a teacher's right to vote was not challenged, any more active participation, particularly when conspicuous, was censured. In a typical instance, two teachers at a Southern university decided to run on the local Democratic ticket for the precinct committee; the board of trustees thereupon passed a resolution barring any faculty member from such activity. It is often argued that the teacher's role requires impartial and disinterested pursuit of knowledge for its own sake, while politics are necessarily partisan and oriented toward social action. Frequently, also, the objection results from the fear of offending those upon whom the school is financially dependent. In one case at a small Midwestern school, a teacher's contract was not renewed when his political activities happened to bring him into direct opposition to a benefactor of the school. Teachers also spoke of promotions withheld, tenure delayed, and other sanctions imposed for being politically active.

Other teachers, not challenged in their right to partisanship, were nevertheless dubious about joining local political groups, for fear that some future shift in general opinion might find their organization on the Attorney General's list, or stigmatized in some other way. The comment of a California respondent is representative:

In the present state of affairs, I won't join any political group. Almost any group that is trying to protect what it thinks is civil liberties, I think could end up on the Attorney General's list. I know for a fact that in the past contributions by check to certain organizations were photostated, and it goes on now. I send no checks to such things.

This respondent was by no means the only one to express belief that any past connection with an organization on the Attorney General's list would be efficiently ferreted out. Such teachers often concluded that the only safe course is simply to shun all political participation. One respondent whose political activity, from the evidence of his interview, had gone no further than a vote for Stevenson in 1952, nevertheless now felt that "complete with- drawal from involvement in politics" was called for. In explaining his avoidance of political organizations, a respondent who grew up in Nazi Germany saw a parallel between the current scene and the experiences of his youth.

I don't belong to any and I would be very hesitant to join any. I learned this in Germany in high school. Never join any group at all. This isn't a case of lack of interest, but experience that something might turn against you, because in ten years if you join any organization someone might say this was subversive.

These respondents, then, recited recent history to explain their shunning of political activity.

The principle of avoiding partisan behavior may get generalized beyond the realm of politics. One respondent told us that his job "depends on not getting embroiled in any controversy," citing as evidence the case of a fellow sociologist at his university who had been passed over for promotion recently as a result of his political campaigning. The propriety of participation in politics by teachers is an issue of long standing in this country; such activity has been barred or frowned upon for many years at some institutions. But if the newly developed caution of respondents in this regard is any criterion, its prohibition is a more recent development at many schools.

Whatever the explanation of the avoidance of politics, one consequence seems evident. Just as students may be denied under- standing of political matters, if unconventional political philoso- phies are shunned in the classroom and barred on the campus outside, so these teachers will be deprived of potentially valuable training and experience in the practical working of a democratic system of government.

Tensions within the community. Apart from differences over political partisanship, there was widespread agreement among the respondents in this study that the relationship between a college and the public it serves contains other troublesome ele- ments. For instance, some 67 per cent believed that they are politically "more liberal" than most people in their community, and a number went on to add that to be "more liberal" is today often to be more suspect. In the eyes of the public, they said, social scientists in particular are, if not radicals and "pinks," at the least a group which questions and denigrates established beliefs. Such suspicions were often highlighted by incidents in the daily contacts of respondents. One teacher told how "after dinner at a neighbor's house we were practically thrown out when a discussion led to our host's condemning the university as being Communist." In this case distrust spoiled a neighborly relationship, though perhaps an unimportant one, for a teacher. An episode at a small Midwestern private college illustrates how a broader rupture can occur. It began when a member of the faculty made unorthodox remarks in a speech, and to quote one respondent, "was accused by a local patriot of being pro-Communist." In short order the speaker was asked to resign from several local clubs and organizations. There was no newspaper publicity, and many on the faculty heard nothing of the incident. But among those who knew of it, several became disturbed and decided that they too had better resign from the organizations; some even withdrew all their memberships in the community. As one respondent explained, "I was one of those who dropped out of these organizations, because I figured that if he got in trouble there was a chance that I would also, sooner or later." Since he taught, among other topics, a course in comparative economic systems, he might indeed eventually have encountered difficulties. Such incidents as these, it need hardly be added, by decreasing contact between teacher and community, serve to promote distrust and suspicion on both sides.

Even when there was no open clash, respondents who sensed potentially disruptive differences in orientation from the community sometimes tried to avoid behavior which might seem controversial. They stayed out of organizations like the American Civil Liberties Union and the Consumers Cooperative, or gave up subscriptions to magazines like the *Nation* and the *New Republic*. Some discarded mannerisms which they felt might be annoying: "When I talk to others these days, I solicit their views instead of selling my own." A few simply took extra precautions to avoid being misunderstood. One respondent, a self-styled "conscientious objector and pacifist," told how the local Junior Chamber of Commerce had conducted a drive to have every house display an American flag; although the flags were rather expensive, he and his wife bought and displayed one to forestall any doubts about their patriotism.

Other respondents concealed their views from the community in which they lived. A West Coast professor had "made an effort not to exhibit any outward evidence of nonconformity while at this school," going out of his way to develop a speaking acquaintance with "the most conservative people in the community." A New England teacher said that, when he mowed the lawn around his home and got to chatting with a neighbor, he was always careful to "moderate my dissent . . . so he will think I am a pleasant guy and be more inclined to testify to my over-all character in the event I would be checked by the security people." For, as another respondent expressed it, many teachers feel that "the picture we give the outside world is a more popular one when it is a conformist picture." A dissenting political opinion expressed over the lawnmower means that a teacher is not "a pleasant guy" or a man of good character.

For some teachers, inevitably, fitting into the community became something of a game. A New England professor, for example, wryly told of displaying different reading matter in different settings.

At my farm in Vermont I wouldn't dare to leave Stouffer's book on civil liberties on the table in the living room. But I could have it around my home in the city. At my home, on the other hand, I wouldn't dare have the McCarthy book by those two Yale men around, but I would have it around in Vermont.

Whether the concealment was a serious matter to the teacher or something of a joke, it was always a special method of adjusting to the climate of the community. For such teachers, the community can be a potent arbiter of right and wrong. In particular, they often granted special importance to local businessmen, who were seen as conservative in outlook, powerful in the community, and quick to challenge a professor whose views they disapproved of. As Chapter I has shown, the opinion was widespread among respondents that businessmen are inclined to look down on them. This view, according to some respondents, is reflected in the confidence with which some of these men instruct professors on matters actually well within the bounds of professorial competence. As one respondent put it, "If I take issue with a businessman on these views, I get the feeling sometimes that my views are distinctly out of place with the *right* way to think about political problems." Another teacher described the certainty with which a local stockbroker, invited by students to address a social science class, stated his position on various issues—sometimes, according to the respondent, directly contradicting himself with the greatest assurance. Most of these professors, however, while annoyed by the businessman's posture of superiority, seldom seized an opportunity to assert themselves. Only after the broker had gone back to his office did the teacher just described point out to his class the contradictions in the speech. This timidity is typified by the Midwestern economist who, though a man in his sixties and a full professor at a large state university, said, "When I go into a men's club, I intend to act like a sheep; the healthy thing for a professor to do is to let the businessman talk."

The Endangered Self-Respect of the Professor

THE READER has just seen that many people in the community grew suspicious and hostile in the difficult years toward the faculties of local colleges and universities. When this feeling was shared by the presidents and deans of the colleges, teachers often found themselves placed in an anomalous and disconcerting position.

The situation is perhaps best indicated by the increased seriousness attached by administrative officials to the views and complaints of students' parents, and especially of students themselves. A number of professors maintained they had concrete evidence that certain students reported regularly to their deans, and a larger number were suspicious of such a possibility. According to a respondent, one dean had established a smoothly working system in which scholarship students were used to supply information about the entire faculty of the college. Other officials, we would assume, found no need to recruit students, since volunteers provided them generously with reports and accusations. True, in many cases the complaint was laughed off, or dismissed after a quick investigation. At the other extreme, however, some officials appear to have accepted a charge made by a student against a teacher without further inquiry.

The debasing assumption that the teacher is in the wrong. Although no teacher enjoys a reprimand, being confronted by an administrator who has apparently accepted an accusation against him without hearing his side of the story is likely to be particularly galling. A revealing incident was described by a sociologist at one of the nation's most prominent state universities.

I used a questionnaire one time which contained a question on the U.N. and another on government ownership of defense industries. There were complaints to the president. The president wrote me a letter that I should not have used them, and no attempt was made on his part to find out why I had used them.

Elsewhere in his interview this teacher said he felt under considerable pressure to avoid having further charges made against him, "for my job depends on not getting embroiled in a controversy." And so, when asked whether controversial matters deserved classroom discussion, he answered, "although they have educational value, a teacher might avoid bringing them up as such." Obviously, since his administration seemed predisposed to assume him in the wrong, this respondent was unwilling to take any chances.

The sense of powerlessness. Teachers who found their administration ready to distrust and quick to censure them often evinced a sense of powerlessness in their dealings with school authorities. It was revealed, for instance, in a teacher's complete dependence upon his administration to clear all decisions. One respondent was even reluctant to take his students on a trip to dig up Indian arrowheads without an official's consent. Again, such a feeling was disclosed in the alacrity with which some teachers acceded to the wishes of an administrator: "Although I'm opposed to that, if the president wanted it, I'd say, 'Yes, sir!'." This sense of weakness was apparent, too, when teachers told us that their only weapon against the school president was resignation from the faculty. And it was demonstrated when a respondent said he was "too old to start fighting these losing battles," for the suggestion is clear that the majority of battles are lost before they are started—and that the professor had yet to enter such a fight.

Sometimes the feeling of powerlessness was manifested in a teacher's sense of being completely manipulable by school authorities. A professor of economics at a Midwestern state university was convinced that his administration was able to hire and fire teachers at will: "The administration of the university so arranges it that the faculty doesn't know the answers to these questions— we never know why a man isn't hired, never know why a man left."

Feelings of guilt over compromises of principle. Finding themselves essentially powerless in dealings with the school, many respondents indicated that a compromise of principle may be required to prevent a clash with administrators. As they pointed out, a powerful administration need pay no attention to the convictions of its faculty. Thus numerous professors indicated both their strong belief that a presidential ban on the Red China debate would violate campus freedom of speech, and their certainty that a vigorous protest to the president over the issue would endanger their jobs. They often added that they would anticipate considerable difficulty in getting a position elsewhere, particularly if blacklisted or publicly criticized by the president. Many respondents mentioned family responsibilities as a deterrent to speaking their mind. These teachers, when they openly admitted the necessity for compromise, sometimes expressed feelings of guilt and deep embarrassment: "I would be mad as hell, and I'm sure I would like to protest, but I'm the type of person to make compromises— I'm afraid."

Strains in Colleague Relations

ANYONE FAMILIAR WITH the college scene knows that factionalism, back-biting, jealousy, and maneuvering for advantage are frequent enough to be an accepted, if not inevitable, part of academic life. Yet our interviews detected an atmosphere of tension among campus colleagues which went beyond such normal manifestations, as it were, of human failings. In this section we shall describe some of the constraints and hidden animosities noticed by respondents in their relationships with fellow teachers.

The divisive influence of incidents. We suggested in Chapter II that reactions to attacks and charges against colleagues varied considerably from respondent to respondent. When an incident was widely known at a school, individual differences of opinion might burgeon into divided faculty camps. An articulate professor of political science described a dispute among his colleagues that followed when the school's board of trustees summoned two teachers to explain statements they had made and then fired one of them.

The reaction was that it divided the faculty, with a few members outraged by the trustees' actions, others who felt one ought to be more careful in what one said, others who felt that it was the duty of the faculty members to be sure that what was printed or published was what he had actually said. Others felt that you were a damned fool to get involved in such controversy, and others felt that the views allegedy expressed were so outrageous that the university should make no efforts to retain such members on the faculty. The over-all effect was that everyone ought to be more cautious.

By bringing previously latent and unrecognized differences to the fore, such an incident can seriously disrupt the cohesion of a college faculty. What may have been a philosophy of "live and let live" is replaced by pressures to conformity and a general sense of caution.

Distrust and suspicion. There was additional evidence in our interviews of the recent growth of distrust and suspicion between respondents and their colleagues. On rare occasions it was described directly by a respondent: "In faculty discussion, in our department at least, there is fear of one another and a consequent hesitating to speak out on issues." Far more often it was revealed only indirectly. One respondent said he discussed civil liberties matters "fairly often with my friends and my family, but not so often with my colleagues." Others remarked that they are more discreet today than in former years about discussing personal political beliefs with colleagues. Again, a checklist question shows that 356 respondents have been offered advice by colleagues on how to avoid getting into political trouble on the campus. And when 445 have "noticed more of a tendency lately in social gatherings on the campus to avoid controversial political topics," an atmosphere of restraint and distrust is again suggested.

A number of factors contribute to such a climate. It can obviously result when one faculty member attacks another; but oblique challenges, as when colleagues implicitly question a teacher's motivations and integrity, are more frequent. One Russian-born teacher at a small private college told of showing a class income-distribution figures from the 1950 census, only to learn shortly after that another professor had characterized this to a student as "propaganda." Teachers reported they were not sure that their colleagues respected confidences: "When I talk with individuals I don't always trust their social integrity, and I sometimes wonder whether I have exposed myself to the authorities." Furthermore, a colleague can easily get a teacher into trouble without criticizing him in any way. A West Coast respondent told how a colleague, apparently knowingly, exposed him to possible embarrassment.

A colleague who does a lot of public speaking and was not free on a certain evening to accept a speech urged me to accept the speech if I were interested. I did speak for him that evening, and found out later that the organization at which I spoke, the Clover Hills Forum, apparently had a reputation of being extremely left-wing. Without wanting to accuse my colleague, I felt afterwards he probably declined because of the political color there.

The great majority of respondents describing friction among a faculty were targets and not initiators of hostilities. But on rare occasions the aggressor himself comes through the pages of a questionnaire. Such is the case of a teacher of geography at a small state teachers college in the West. In his forties, he is a Democrat who voted for Eisenhower in 1952 and, according to him, is politically more conservative than most of the faculty. He is at evident odds with his colleagues, for despite his conservatism he says that were he accused of leftist leanings, only some of them would come to his support. In discussing the possible effect of such an incident on the school, he returned the compliment. "Protecting the reputation of the college would be the best protection for those particular members of the college who deserve protection; all should be protected to some extent, but some should be dropped at the earliest possible moment." It may be significant that he seemed to feel unusually close to the school administration. He told us that his politics were much the same as those of school officials, and indicated his close agreement with them in the important matter of the state loyalty oath for teachers. An interesting note of expediency appeared in his answer, already quoted, to a question concerning the advisability of encouraging class discussion of controversial issues. "I don't eliminate them," he said, "but I'm less willing; if there's a choice between a controversial and a noncontroversial issue, I take the noncontroversial." It may be that the same expediency and unawareness of ethical issues implicit in this remark contributed both to his alienation from his colleagues and his manifest resentment of them. It is not difficult to imagine that such a man could bring charges of leftism or subversion against his colleagues.

Hesitancy about supporting colleagues under fire. If some of the teachers in our study believed their colleagues were not above getting them in trouble, many also felt that colleagues would do little to support them if trouble did arise. The statistics show that 66 per cent of our respondents believed that most of their colleagues would back them up if they were accused of being leftist. But we cannot dismiss the 28 per cent who would expect less complete support, nor the 6 per cent who were uncertain. As one respondent put it, when asked if his faculty would rally to his support, "One would hope, but the record nationally is not good and I can't see *this* faculty leading the vanguard." It is true of course that many professors had been vigorously backed by their colleagues. But other respondents, recounting the reactions of their colleagues to such attacks, described feelings of fear, of indignation, or even of indifference, but not one gesture of support. The following story is typical in this connection.

A friend of mine was under indictment in Washington for lying before a Security Board. I agreed to raise money in this area for his defense. When I approached a senior member of the faculty, I was advised not to continue the solicitation for funds on the grounds that this man was probably guilty and that therefore I would be discrediting, or using up the good will, of the academic community for a lost cause. So I stopped soliciting. The ironic part of it was that later on my friend was cleared completely.

The respondent's impulse was to help his friend. Yet he was somewhat reluctant in his venture, for he readily took the advice of the senior colleague, either ignoring the agreement of other professors to whom he had already spoken, or at least failing to consult anyone else before abandoning his solicitation. Here again an accusation was considered tantamount to conviction, the more remarkable in this instance because the respondent seems to have easily acquiesced in a judgment on a friend the senior colleague had apparently never met. We note further that the respondent was impressed by the argument that his attempts to raise money could discredit the school or at least "use up its good will"; he seems to believe with his colleague that the credit and good will were in short supply. As was shown in Chapter VI, 11 per cent of our respondents shared this opinion, that it is not worth risking a blot on the reputation of the school to try to protect individual members of the faculty. And finally, we see again in this episode the extent to which even remote association with suspected persons is thought to bring stigmatization; there must be an anticipatory withdrawal to avoid a possible future taint.

In one respect, it might be added, the case of the respondent who so readily stopped raising money for his friend is atypical, because there is a suggestion in his words that he was ashamed of himself. In the great majority of incidents there is little evidence of self-recrimination for not having supported a colleague under fire. Exceptions do occur, however. A professor at a Southern school, after describing an incident in which a young instructor had been fired without explanation for something he said, indicated that he and some of his friends had felt "remorse for not having fought for the young man." Perhaps one reason that colleagues are infrequently backed is that many teachers are willing to join a support movement, but few to initiate it. Such an attitude was evident in many areas of behavior touched upon in the questionnaire. It was revealed when respondents were asked what they would do if the school president arbitrarily banned a debate on Red China or a speech by Owen Lattimore which they had favored. While it is true that more than half the respondents, in the language of our checklist category, would "protest vigorously" to the president, they often added such qualifications as, "If two or three people got together, I'd certainly protest." The clear, if unconscious, implication is that the initiative would have to come from someone else. It may be that many a ground swell of support dies for lack of leadership.

Underlying this reluctance to lead a support movement may be the sense that heading such a protest renders an individual particularly vulnerable, for it is the conspicuous leadership which is often singled out for punishment. And the opinion was widespread that punishments can be severe: firing, difficulty in getting another job, a promotion permanently denied, a pay rise long delayed. This was reflected in the resigned statements of a few respondents who felt it would be beyond the call of duty for colleagues to come to their defense against an accusation of subversion: "If it were a difficult situation I would not want them to." As one respondent put it, "I would expect my close friends to support me, but if they did not, I would understand."

Following the middle of the road. The caution manifest in reluctance to back accused colleagues appears in other contexts. In particular, there is an inclination to disapprove of unconventionality, not only in political opinions but in appearance and mannerisms as well. Respondents frequently found it safer, and perhaps more considerate, to be careful in their choice of topics for political conversation with colleagues; 432 respondents, on a checklist item, said they were "more careful now" about such matters. Although in many cases this involved nothing more than a discreet effort to avoid embarrassing fellow teachers, a certain withdrawal of sympathies was also often evident. One respondent explained, "Here at the university I've been careful with one or two people because they've been in difficulty and I'm afraid it will hurt them to talk about their experiences," but went on in the same breath to add, "Certain colleagues I just avoid seeing." Teachers faced with the familiar stereotyped choice between the unconventional-but-brilliant and conventional-but-less-brilliant colleague lean nowadays toward the man who fits in. In the interviews we can see this situation from both sides of the fence. One respondent who described his recent success in faculty circles was proud of his ability to "swing with the tide." But an unregenerate, outspoken "liberal" complained of his exclusion.

I am an expert on labor matters. I am advisor to labor arbitrations quite often, and employers think I am too liberal. I have not been elected to a [school] Senate committee because my colleagues are afraid that I would make trouble for it. I know I have been put up for that committee, but they always elect some timid fellow who will go along with the crowd.

It does not necessarily require an overt exclusion to convince a man that he is considered unconventional by his colleagues. A Western professor said his colleagues simply registered their "amazement when I speak out freely at meetings before the Rotary and the Lions." Another teacher described the subtle feeling that "emanates" when he expressed certain ideas:

Shock, incredulity, a mocking kind of disapproval. Watch yourself, or they'll get you. Or being described as a character, an eccentric—which of course is true!

As several respondents remarked, there was a time when colleges were proud of their eccentrics and their outspoken "characters." Such appears to be less often the case today. The wistful respondent who can still say, "Some of us would like to be leftists," is evidently out in the cold; the teacher who says, "We all want to be known as innocuous members of the horde," seems to speak for many.

For Whom the Bell Tolls

REGARDLESS of whether or not they personally attempted to develop middle-of-the-road attitudes, teachers were often deeply disturbed when a colleague came under what they considered unjustified attack. A typical example was described by a respondent at a small private college: The librarian, at the school for many years, had long been known to associate with left-wing groups. He freely admitted it, and no one paid him much attention. Then when the cold war commenced, he began to be severely criticized, especially after he circulated a petition asking clemency for the Rosenbergs. In 1954 he was named as a Communist by a witness before a Congressional committee. The president of the college ordered the librarian to go to Washington, or at least to deny the accusation. The librarian thereupon resigned his position. Following this description, the respondent continued:

I thought it was shocking! He was given no chance to give his side of it. They just took the other man's word for it and that was that. I thought, "There but for the grace of God go I."

For other teachers, the sense of disturbance arose over more distant events, often stemming from the feeling that "any threat to the academic community is a threat to me." As one respondent expressed it, "When one university is threatened, all are." Such an attitude is suggested when respondents, asked for "specific civil liberties problems and cases," replied at once by describing eight or ten instances in which professors and schools throughout the nation had come under attack. Many professors, it seems clear, would agree with the teacher who put it perhaps best of all:

No one has put any pressure on me. And yet, I feel "the bell tolls for thee."

Chapter X

THE SOCIAL CONTEXT OF APPREHENSION

Now THAT we have presented a detailed exploration of teachers' caution, the main outlines of our report are complete. In order to give coherence to the discussion of our principal results, however, it has been necessary at points to pass over some intricacies and bypaths in our data. In this last chapter we would like to return to a few of these matters, by examining more fully some of the determinants and consequences of apprehension. The full complexity of the situation we set out to study is still bound to elude us in one single inquiry. And yet, we can indicate some lines for future work by discussing two sets of data in more detail.

To begin with, there is a marked difference in apprehension between younger and older teachers. This finding, if not a particularly surprising one, nevertheless turns out not to be simply explained. Quite an array of data will be introduced in order to interpret it. Our conclusion from this discussion will be a renewed and more precise emphasis on an element to which we have alluded repeatedly in earlier chapters: the mutual support which creates a common climate of opinion and morale among social scientists. This emphasis will be further justified by returning once more to age differences, this time in terms of permissiveness.

Next, we shall use an important illustration to elaborate on the description of incidents and pressures on teachers first outlined in Chapter II. This will provide a background for some data on the interplay between the incidents occurring on a campus, the extent to which they are perceived by various kinds of teachers, and their resultant bearing on the spread of apprehension.

In short, this chapter directs special attention to the social context of apprehension.

Age and Apprehension

IT WAS SHOWN in a footnote in Chapter VI that younger teachers are likely to be more permissive than older ones. We would expect, because of this, that they are also more apprehensive. This is indeed the case: 53 per cent of the teachers aged forty or younger are apprehensive, compared to 46 per cent of those between forty-one and fifty, and 31 per cent of those over fifty. However, even when the factor of permissiveness is eliminated, age continues to play a role. The three parts of Figure 10-1 show this, for they reveal that among the professors on each level of permissiveness, the younger respondents are more often apprehensive.

Why do younger teachers show more apprehension? Because they lack the security of tenure, will be the first answer which comes to mind. But surprisingly enough, this is not the correct explanation. Figure 10-2 compares the proportions of apprehensive respondents for those who have and who do not have tenure. Within each age group the differences are small and inconsistent. Among both those with and without tenure, however, the younger teachers remain more apprehensive than the older ones.

Thus the role of tenure should not be overrated. It is true that ousting a teacher is legally more difficult for a school if he has tenure. But on the one hand, life can be made unpleasant for a professor even though he does not lose his job; on the other, flagrant discrimination, if brought to light, is not easily defended even when directed against a person without tenure.

Another possibility deserves exploration. As a professor grows older he is likely to have published more, he becomes better known, and so might feel more secure because he can count on the support of his academic public. Also, his publications sometimes provide him with independent income, and thus perhaps with a cushion against temporary unemployment.

Our productivity index suitably represents a professor's publications. The questionnaire also asks: "Do you have any outside sources of income besides your salary?" Since outside income can, of course, come from other sources, such as consultations or investments, this more general formulation of the question permits an additional test of whether economic security affected professorial apprehension during the difficult years. The results of Figure 10-3 are quite surprising in one respect.

Looking first along the two lines, in each case the most appre-

Figure 10-1
On Each Level of Permissiveness, Older Teachers Are Less Apprehensive than Younger Ones

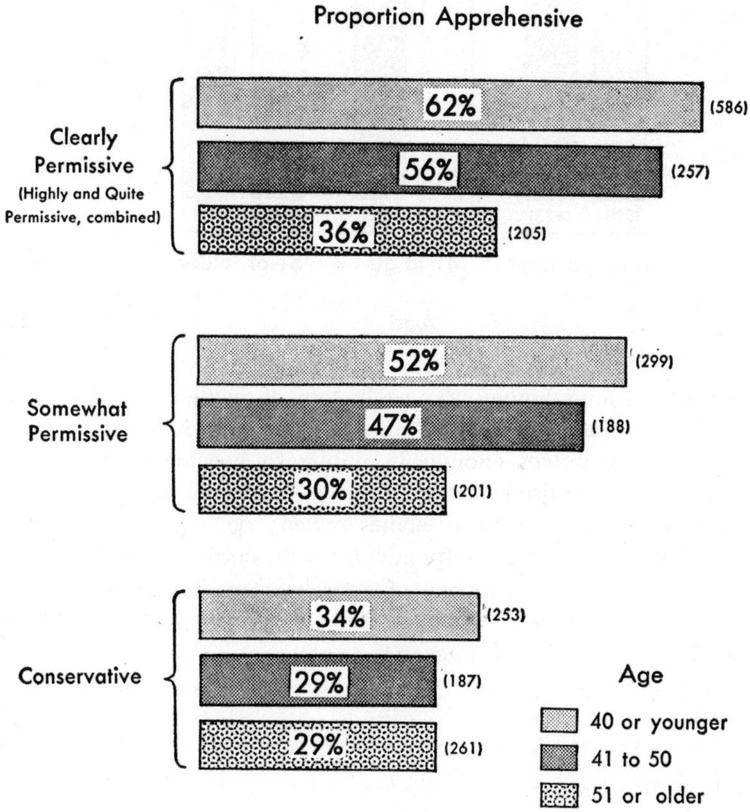

Proportion Apprehensive

| Age |
| ☐ 40 or younger |
| ▨ 41 to 50 |
| ▩ 51 or older |

Figure 10-2
Tenure Does Not Account for the Lower Frequency
of Apprehension among Older Professors

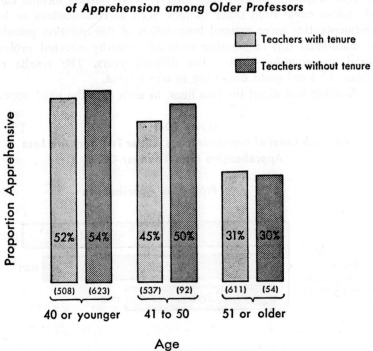

Teachers with tenure

Teachers without tenure

Proportion Apprehensive

| 52% | 54% | 45% | 50% | 31% | 30% |

| (508) | (623) | (537) | (92) | (611) | (54) |

40 or younger   41 to 50   51 or older

Age

hension is found among the professors of medium productivity. This makes intuitive sense: quite likely these individuals have expressed themselves enough in public to become controversial, but have not acquired enough status to take attacks with relative equanimity.[1] The surprise comes when, on each productivity level, it develops that respondents with outside income in no way show a lower frequency of apprehension, but in most cases a slightly higher one. Outside income is often derived from consultations. We have noticed before that men and women who do such outside work are likely to be more permissive. We took

1. Since productivity is of course cumulative with age, Figure 10-3 had to be set up separately for the different age groups. Since the pattern remains the same, the figures need not be shown here.

Figure 10-3
Apprehension as Related to Productivity and the Availability
of Outside Income

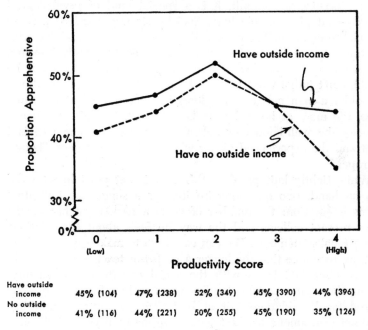

	0 (Low)	1	2	3	4 (High)
Have outside income	45% (104)	47% (238)	52% (349)	45% (390)	44% (396)
No outside income	41% (116)	44% (221)	50% (255)	45% (190)	35% (126)

this as a sign of their greater sensitivity to a diversity of demands; it would also make them more alert to civil liberties problems, overbalancing whatever security they might derive from their additional income. In their net effect, then, none of the elements of objective security—tenure, professional status, outside income—which come with higher age are noticeably related to apprehension.[2] These factors, therefore, cannot explain why it declines so markedly with age.

2. One other indicator of objective security was investigated. Because an unmarried teacher has fewer responsibilities than his married colleagues, we thought that he might be less apprehensive. Not to confuse the problem, the analysis was restricted to men and excluded teachers at Catholic schools, who often were priests. When the factor of age is kept constant, there is only a 3 per cent average difference in the apprehension of married and unmarried men.

The Role of Integration

RATHER, we submit, it is a special kind of psychological security that plays a role here. Sociologists might call it a sense of social integration. The newcomer at a school, unacquainted with the traditions of his profession or of his college, feels insecure. He doesn't quite know what is expected of him, and even if he is told, can't judge what latitude he has for individual variations. The older a man gets and the longer he has taught at the same place, the more at home he is likely to feel. It is the difference between the well-known apprehension of the first-time weekend guest and the experienced visitor who, as the saying goes, "knows the ropes."

While tightly knit proof of this idea is not possible with the data on hand, two questionnaire items are suggestive indicators of this integration: the number of years a respondent has taught at his present college, and the way he feels about the relations among faculty members. We can use them to make several points. First, let us notice that the longer a professor teaches at a college, the more satisfied he is with the social climate in the faculty. Among those on a campus for five years or less, 20 per cent considered faculty relations fair at best; this proportion diminishes to 10 per cent among teachers with more than ten years' residence. Doubtless this is partly a question of self-selection; teachers who feel especially uneasy are likely to leave or to be forced out by conflict. And for those who remain on the campus, it is probably also a matter of personal adjustment.

In any case, apprehension is related to both of these integration factors. Figure 10-4 classifies all respondents by their length of residence at the present college and their judgment of faculty relationships, and reports the proportion of apprehensive teachers for the nine resulting combinations.

The separation of the three lines shows that apprehension is more frequent among respondents who consider relations among faculty members less satisfactory.[3] Undoubtedly, this works both

---

3. Turning to our seventy-seven largest samples, we can classify the colleges according to the proportion of social scientists who think that faculty relations are fair at best; formation of these rates helps to eliminate the biases

ways: A satisfying personal environment puts a man more at ease; this enables him to look at other people with more trust and he thus encourages their good will. And inversely, apprehension and interpersonal difficulties can reinforce each other.

Reading along the two lower lines of Figure 10-4, we find that the longer teachers have taught at a school, the less apprehensive they are. The top line is interesting: for the minority of 369 respondents in whose judgment faculty relations are not good at all, apprehension is about equally high, regardless of the length of time they have taught at their colleges.

This is, then, how we think the more widespread apprehension of younger teachers can be explained. They were newcomers at their schools, inexperienced in the rules of the game, and uncertain about the support they could count on, and so the events of the difficult years were bound to appear more threatening to them than to their older colleagues.

Since the uncertainties of a beginning career are in themselves something of a trial for young teachers, it can only be regrettable if these teachers are put under additional stress by outside forces. Under such circumstances it would seem important that the American Association of University Professors, as the major professional organization of college teachers, pay special attention to the newcomers. We found in Chapter VI that permissive social scientists are more likely to belong to the A.A.U.P.; because younger teachers are more permissive, one might expect that they are, therefore, more often A.A.U.P. members, and that this would help alleviate their apprehension. Actually, the opposite is true. Figure 10-5 indicates that membership is more frequent among older teachers; and it is especially rare exactly among the younger people who have not yet been able to achieve attention through professional activities. The question arises whether the A.A.U.P. has not missed out in attracting the very social scientists who need help most.

The importance to teachers of a sense of social belonging is reinforced by one more finding. We saw in Chapter I that our social scientists have what we called a feeling of occupational in-

---

of individuals and so to describe the actual state of affairs. In the most satisfied schools (rate below 10 per cent), 45 per cent of the respondents are apprehensive, while in the most dissatisfied ones (rate above 30 per cent), the proportion of apprehensives is 52 per cent; the increase in the intermediate groups is proportional.

Figure 10-4
**The Longer Social Scientists Have Taught at a College,
and the Better They Feel about Faculty Relations,
the Less Apprehension They Experience**

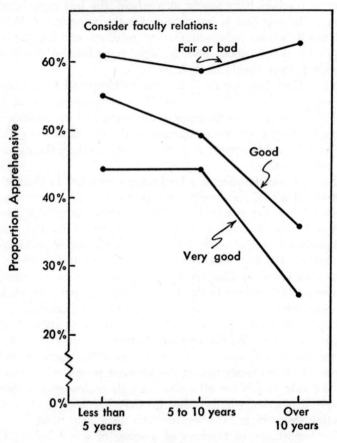

Consider faculty relations—					
fair or bad	61%	(159)	58%	(137)	62%	(73)
good	55%	(349)	49%	(409)	36%	(326)
very good	44%	(281)	44%	(322)	26%	(347)

Figure 10-5
**Membership in the A.A.U.P. Is Lower among Younger Social
Scientists and among the Less Productive Ones**

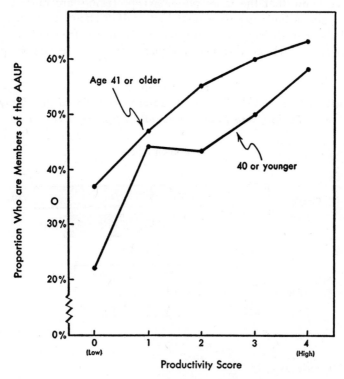

Age					
41 or older	37% (57)	47% (181)	55% (259)	60% (368)	63% (418)
40 or younger	22% (166)	44% (280)	43% (349)	50% (219)	58% (106)

feriority: they think that community leaders, especially businessmen and politicians, attribute little prestige to the professor when
he is put beside three comparable occupations.[4] Apprehension is the
greater, the more pronounced this feeling of low standing. Figure
10-6 selects as an example the image professors have of how busi-

_____

4. The prestige attribution, it will be remembered, was obtained in the
following way: The imaginary judges were to rank the college professor as
compared to a lawyer, a manager of a branch bank, and an account executive
in an advertising agency.

nessmen judge them. The respondents are divided according to the prestige they attribute to themselves: they may expect high esteem (first or second rank) or low (third or fourth).

We know that the more permissive professors are more pessimistic about their prestige; now Figure 10-6 shows that on each level of permissiveness apprehension is more frequent among teachers for whom this occupational inferiority feeling is pro-

Figure 10-6
Social Scientists Who Have a Greater Occupational Inferiority Feeling Are More Frequently Apprehensive

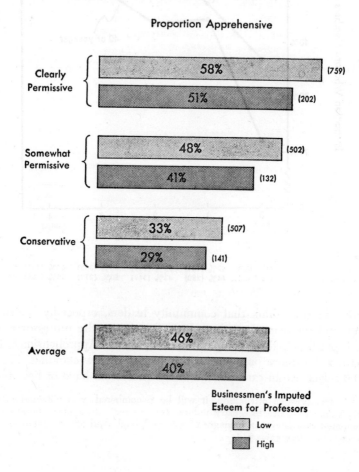

Proportion Apprehensive

Clearly Permissive
58% (759)
51% (202)

Somewhat Permissive
48% (502)
41% (132)

Conservative
33% (507)
29% (141)

Average
46%
40%

Businessmen's Imputed Esteem for Professors
☐ Low
■ High

nounced. Additional tables (given in Appendix 8G) show that the image of the Congressman's judgment, as we might expect in the difficult years, is more salient: the average difference in apprehension is 11 per cent, twice as large as that found for the businessman at the bottom of Figure 10-6. For the trustees, the figure is also 11 per cent. It is because of the current special importance of Congressmen, and the perennial significance of the trustee, that we choose the less obviously meaningful figure of the businessman to mirror the professor's sense of community integration.[5]

The meaning of integration, it is true, has now changed. Earlier, we talked about respondents' integration among their peers. Now we talk about the way they feel their profession is integrated in the larger community. Still, in this more general way, Figure 10-6 shows again the socio-psychological determination of apprehension. Mutual support within the college makes for less apprehension, just as lack of support by the larger community (or teachers' doubts to this effect) makes for more.

Age and Permissiveness

THE IMPORTANCE of one's social environment can be shown in still another way. We have so far treated as "obvious" our finding that permissiveness decreases with age. But is it? Actually, two competing explanations come to mind. Perhaps as we grow older our individual enthusiasm for and belief in innovation declines just like other elements of our vitality. Or it may be that growing up in a basically conservative society explains this trend; would a country where something like a permanent revolution prevailed not show a very different "effect" of aging?[6]

---

5. Several hundred respondents said they didn't know how outsiders would rank their profession. Invariably, these teachers were less apprehensive than those who expressed an opinion, even an optimistic one. They might be persons who "just don't give a damn" what other people think about them, and being less concerned about the opinion of others, are less apprehensive in terms of our index. Whatever the interpretation, the data are consistent.

6. We are reminded here of the study by Theodore Newcomb, *Personality and Social Change.* He showed that in Bennington College, where the prevailing environment established by the faculty was nonconservative, the students became *less* conservative from year to year. For a summary, see *Readings in Social Psychology*, Guy Swanson et al., editors (New York: Henry

A cross-sectional survey does not permit a definitive answer, but we have some evidence that the environment in which a man lives does, indeed, affect the role of age. While our respondents are all part of the same essentially conservative society, they work in colleges with quite different climates of opinion. We turn again to our seventy-seven schools with thirteen or more interviews, permitting us to develop characterizing rates. We can distinguish permissive colleges, where 60 per cent or more of the social scientists are clearly permissive; conservative schools where this rate is 39 per cent or less; and a middle group, where the permissive sector is from 40 to 59 per cent. Figure 10-7 reports the relation between age and permissiveness in these three groups of institutions.

In order to summarize the information in a compact way, the Figure presents, for each type of school, the average permissiveness score for each age level. At the end of Chapter V we saw that these averages may provide a more sensitive measure of differences than percentages.[7]

Let us begin by comparing the first two age groups. Between the youngest and the middle age categories we find the following decline of average individual permissiveness: 15 points (3.13 minus 2.98) in highly permissive colleges, 32 points in the medium school group, and 36 points in the most conservative schools. Thus the trend toward conservatism among older teachers is markedly smallest in the permissive colleges and highest in the conservative schools. Comparing next the middle and oldest age categories, we still find that the professors in the most permissive institutions show

---

Holt, 1952). Where Newcomb followed the same students over a period of four years, we compare social scientists of different ages today. It could be that thirty years ago colleges were more likely to favor the appointment of conservatives. However, a detailed analysis of our age figures shows a steady decline of permissiveness with age, and this makes it more probable that the age results in Figure 10-1 reflect a true biographical trend. This conclusion is also in harmony with what is known about the effect of age on the population at large. So we shall accept our data as evidence that the average novice starts out with a high degree of permissiveness and is likely to be more conservative toward the end of his career. We don't need to worry about another historical factor, the often-discussed role of the depression generation. They now would be in the age group 40-to-50, but we find the highest proportion of permissives in the youngest age group, who were adolescents just before the Second World War.

7. It will be remembered that highly permissive respondents were given a score of four, and the clearly conservative one of zero.

only a decline of 12 points after the age of fifty, while in the medium college group the decline is 36 points. The only place where the figures seem to run against the general trend is with the oldest teachers in the conservative schools, whose permissiveness score does not again drop sharply. Special tabulations suggest that this may be due to the fact that we do not have a larger number of "restrictive" items in our index. On two of these items (disapproval of a guest speech and of the formation of a Socialist League), the

Figure 10-7
The Average Level of Permissiveness According to Age, in Three Groups of Colleges

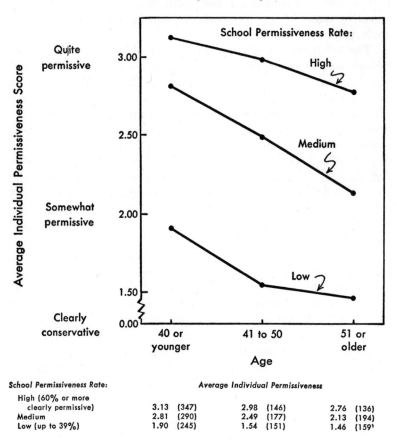

School Permissiveness Rate:	Average Individual Permissiveness		
High (60% or more clearly permissive)	3.13 (347)	2.98 (146)	2.76 (136)
Medium	2.81 (290)	2.49 (177)	2.13 (194)
Low (up to 39%)	1.90 (245)	1.54 (151)	1.46 (159¹

oldest professors in the conservative schools are not more prohibitive than the age group between forty and fifty. Probably a greater
variety of such items would be needed to bring out an extremely
low level of permissiveness. On the other hand, it is of course
possible that there is a limit below which the conservative attitude
of a social scientist cannot go in the contemporary American scene.
In this case, the bottom right percentage of Figure 10-7 might not
be a statistical artifact, but the measure of a cultural ceiling which
limits the degree to which age and social environment may induce
a conservative position. Only future studies can clarify this point.
However, apart from this one exception, Figure 10-7 shows again
that the social context in which these social scientists work has
a pronounced influence on their attitudes. The proverbial conservative trend of age is much smaller in a highly permissive
environment.

The relatively small conservative age shift in the most permissive and, as we know, most prominent colleges has a considerable bearing on an argument we made in Chapter VI. Discussing
the occupational relevance of permissiveness, it was pointed out
that the more prominent social scientists are likely to be highly
permissive. From this we deduced that for many of the less committed teachers, permissiveness is often tied up with the image
of professional success. This might seem to be contradicted by the
fact that on the whole the older and presumably more powerful
members of the profession are more conservative. It now turns out
that this tendency is weakest in the leading colleges, which are
surely the most visible to those younger teachers oriented toward
the profession at large.

So far the notion of social context has meant relationships with
other people: how long one has worked with them, the way one
gets along with them, and the influence of the prevailing climate
of opinion. But during the difficult years another element was
bound to be important and therefore deserves special attention:
the series of attacks and accusations against teachers which beset
a number of campuses. How were these episodes perceived and
what effect did they have on our respondents' apprehension?

The Experience of Pressure

PRECEDING our statistical evidence, some preliminary observations are called for. In Chapter II we surveyed the actual incidents on the campus. We wish now to describe more fully the way they reach the "ultimate consumer," the professor himself. Rather than review all types of incidents in this light, we can concentrate on cases of pressures from the school administration. The reports are essentially of two kinds. Some tell of crude interferences; a few examples will quickly give a picture of such cases. Second, and more interesting perhaps, are the descriptions of relatively gentle pressures.

Harsh pressures. Our interviews contain reports of abrupt dismissals for such things as taking the Fifth Amendment, for "speaking too freely in class on the subjects of race and sex," for "having too liberal politics," and so on.[8] Professors also described a number of instances in which they themselves had been directly threatened with firing. Still others were convinced that opposition to the wishes of the president of their school could readily result in their dismissal. Teachers who said they would like to protest strongly against a ban by the president of a debate on the admission of Red China to the United Nations or of an invitation to a controversial guest speaker, sometimes added that such a move would probably bring them instant dismissal. As a Southern respondent put it, "A vigorous protest is not worth much when you can't get an audience, you just get fired."

Promotions and tenure, too, are often arbitrarily withheld by administrations. In many cases, nothing is said to the bypassed teacher, leaving him to wonder how he has erred. In others, the administration frankly informs the individual that he has fallen short or been passed over because he is controversial, sometimes advising him to be more careful so that it will be possible to

---

8. An indication of the over-all extent of firings appears in the answers to a checklist question: "Do you know of anyone who is no longer teaching here as a result of his political views, or don't you know of any such cases?" The results show that at 102 out of the 165 schools included in our survey there has been at least one case where a teacher was either directly fired or in effect forced to leave the school. We cannot say, however, how many of these cases were considered arbitrary or unfair by respondents.

advance him in the future. A respondent at a small private college in the Midwest told the following story (corroborated by several colleagues).

I am considered somewhat radical in my thinking. This is a Republican community and I sponsor a Democratic Club in the school. I used to write articles for the newspapers—a political column. I have also been asked by the trustees to stop making radio speeches that are in any way related to politics. They feel it their duty to sit in on my classes to see just what nonsense I am teaching. Just last week I was questioned by the administration about being too liberal in my political views; nothing definite—they just think I'm too liberal in my teaching. The subject of my promotion came up, and I was plainly told that I could expect no promotion until I quit spelling out my political views so freely.

Classroom visits from trustees at this college, it appears, are rather frequent, for they are mentioned by other respondents in our sample. It might be added that the general level of apprehension at this school is one of the highest to be found in our entire sample.

At some schools, presidents and administrative officials take it upon themselves to monitor the research produced by their faculty. Our interviews contain instances in which research reports had been significantly delayed for publication; one Southern school president, for instance, postponed publication of a survey showing that the community predominantly opposed the local dual school system until after the election in which the issue was voted upon. Some school presidents do not hesitate to request that certain research topics be completely avoided, that important passages be deleted, etc. Sometimes, in fact, research reports are edited in advance by teachers, in anticipation of adverse administration reactions. One respondent recalls an instance in which a favorable quotation of one of Franklin D. Roosevelt's remarks was cut out so that a rabidly anti-Roosevelt dean (who impartially labeled Roosevelt, Truman, the *New York Times,* and *Time* Magazine as "Communist") would not be offended. Finally, as mentioned in earlier chapters, our records show that a few college administrations have dropped controversial courses, usually in a social science, from the curriculum. A biting description of such a withdrawal is provided by an economist now teaching at an Ivy League college (the episode took place at a school where he formerly taught).

I taught a course in Soviet economics. My opinions traveled widely through the college and were reported back to me from teachers and administrators, not always correctly. Members of the administration sat in on the course—a charming idea! Good course, they said afterwards. I was never actually criticized, never anything wrong with my teaching. There was something wrong with the course—it didn't damn Communism enough. The president suggested to me that it wasn't advisable to have the course just now. It didn't look nice in the catalogue. It was dropped.

We recognize here another occasion which was considered sufficient justification for a breach of the powerful if unwritten tradition at most American colleges that it is highly inappropriate for senior professors and administrative officials to audit a teacher's classes.

Gentle pressures. When a teacher is told that he can either cease his political activities or give up hope for promotion, the decision he faces is clear-cut. But in many cases the exercise of power by administrative officials is more complex. Students of organization have often observed that authority has many indirect ways to reach its goal. The subordinate believes that he has to obey certain rules. But the rules are often not made explicit. The teacher feels it is up to him to sense what is expected, and often expends a great deal of effort in looking for the right clues. Sometimes he may even misinterpret an unintentional remark by an administrator as a hint fraught with danger. In such situations a man in authority does not need to be explicit to influence a teacher. He can intervene so deftly as to give no appearance of interfering, and still get things his way. The yielding of teachers to these gentle pressures is a problem of academic freedom important enough to deserve detailed examples.

The "request" is a favorite device of many administrative officials. Teachers are requested to avoid controversial topics, to refrain from political activity, to make contributions to the "right" political activities, to avoid unfavorable references to school benefactors, to increase their contacts with students, to decrease their contacts with students, and so on. Typically, the request is accompanied by a disclaimer, to show it is not an order. An instructor of sociology described a characteristic instance in which administration pressure of this kind was applied, along with the rather typical circumstances leading up to the pressure, and his own more idiosyncratic subsequent actions.

A year ago somebody in the military forces objected to a chapter on war in Ogburn and Nimkoff, one of the outstanding textbooks in the field. The book was banned by the military people for overseas use, and an inferior textbook was substituted. I was told I could use any book, but the pressures were such that the safe thing to do was to knuckle under. In class, I announced what the official textbook was, but after a time, lectured from Ogburn and Nimkoff. The students saw through this, and I semantically confused them in a legalistic fashion by telling them that the banned book seemed to be unsuitable for their consumption but they could use it for outside reading.

We can almost hear this professor being told by the president, "Of course you're entitled to use any text that you please" (the disclaimer), "and I wouldn't think of interfering with you in such a matter, but you know, some of those military people have been offended by that chapter on war, and I'm just a little bit afraid that they might withdraw that R.O.T.C. unit we've been promised— so I'd appreciate it if you would consider using this other text."[9]

Sometimes the request is implicit. Teachers frequently describe how a matter was "called to their attention." In a typical instance, a Midwestern economist, to illustrate a general discussion of social class, cited fraternities and sororities as examples of social distinction. The story was carried to an official of the university, who phoned the teacher simply to "remind" him of it, going on to say that of course the professor had the right to say whatever he wanted. Nevertheless, the call was taken by the respondent as a veiled threat to his academic freedom. Another form of the implicit request might be called the "nudge." A respondent who has made frequent speeches in recent years says that whenever he talks on a noncontroversial subject, no comment at all is forthcoming from the administration, but when he deals with a topic like the admission of Communist China into the United Nations,

---

9. Since this teacher has the high score of 6 on the apprehension index, we should point out that a general relationship established in Chapter IV is illustrated here. An apprehensive teacher, who has prudently accepted the officially approved book and assigned it to his class, nevertheless in the end finds himself, on a note of defiance, returning to the approach of his favored text and finally announcing that students may use it. In addition, however, it also seems rather probable that as a result of the partial and vacillating nature of this man's defiance, his students experienced confusion, first when he lectured from the barred book without explaining what he was doing, and doubtless again when he asked them to use a book which was "unsuitable for their consumption."

the dean of the school invariably remarks casually to him, "Oh, I hear you've been urging Red China's admission to the UN."[10]

An interesting light is thrown on the underlying meaning of administrative "requests" by the manner in which two respondents reported an episode at a small private school. One, a recently hired young instructor, gave the following description:

My predecessor agreed to address the meeting of a political group here. The news was picked up by papers all over the state and the president of the school asked him not to make the speech. He didn't make it.

A dean at the college, also a respondent because he taught social science courses, described the episode rather differently:

Last year some of the constituents of the college objected to a faculty member's speaking to an N.A.A.C.P. group. They misunderstood entirely what he was going to do, incidentally. Their complaints were reported to him, and he decided not to make the speech. It was his own decision, I might add.

We note that the dean's report appears to be accurate as far as it goes, but when he says that the decision not to make the speech was the teacher's own, he neglects to mention that the president of the school had requested the teacher not to make it. The replacement for this would-be speaker recalls the president's request, and appears disturbed that he too is in a position where such requests must be obeyed. By contrast, the dean, somewhat embarrassed perhaps by the repressive nature of the request, conveniently forgets it, and prefers to imply that the speaker's decision was made without any pressure from him or the president.

Sometimes, finally, the pressures felt from the administration are completely indirect. A respondent at a Southern school tells how the man he was hired to replace had "lost his job here two years ago—no one knows quite why but there is a rumor that it was because he persisted in putting unacceptable reading matter on his reading list." Almost needless to say, this respondent is in-

10. David Riesman, in interviewing teachers for his follow-up study, encountered some professors who felt that slight pressure was being exerted on them, perhaps unconsciously, when the public relations office of their school clipped and sent them all published reports of their speeches and other activities.

deed cautious about his own reading lists. Here, then, a teacher feels definite pressure from an administration which may never have said a word to him.

From such more subtle influences goes a continuous line to the overt interference described previously. Somewhere in the middle, perhaps, we find instances such as those in which the president of a school is "consulted" before a contemplated faculty move is made. The following story, related by a respondent at a public college in the South, illustrates clearly the attitudes of faculty members to a powerful college president, particularly the cautious manner in which his approval is sought:

I am a member of our A.A.U.P. chapter. The speaker we wanted for our last meeting was unavailable, so several members suggested that we try to get Mr. D. (a publisher) to speak. I could have gone ahead and contacted him, but since I was aware of the fact that there was a recent directive from the board of trustees that speakers must be screened by the president, I consulted other people before going ahead, particularly since I knew that Mr. D. is *persona non grata* with the administration because of a recent article for a national magazine. I'm a stranger, a Northerner, and I felt constrained to protect myself or to dissociate myself in some way from the invitation. The upshot was that we decided to sound out the President. This was done, and it was made very clear to the chapter president that Mr. D. would certainly not pass. It was unfortunate that we did this informally, because the president can now say that Mr. D. was never turned down. It involved me personally. I wasn't quite proud of my behavior, but felt that I had to be cautious, I suppose, because of the atmosphere that prevails here and throughout the state.

It is apparent that this professor is somewhat ashamed of himself on several counts. As he looks back, he does not admire his own caution in feeling compelled to consult other colleagues before inviting Mr. D.; although there was considerable support for the invitation, he clearly felt that he would be held personally responsible by the administration if it were made. He therefore attempted to arrange the situation in such a way that the responsibility would pass on to others. He also appears embarrassed by the fact that as a direct outcome of his own caution, a situation developed in which the president was able to veto the invitation privately and so escape public revelation of his act of censorship.

The Impact of Incidents

WE KNOW from Chapter III that a teacher who had himself been the target of an incident was especially likely to be apprehensive. But how did his colleagues react to the episode? Did they know of it at all? And if so, did they too become more apprehensive?

The accounts of incidents reported in Chapter II were summaries of descriptions given by numerous respondents. Some teachers in the same college reported many of these episodes; others had noticed nothing. It is not surprising to learn that a respondent's general ideology affected his perception of the local situation: the more permissive respondents noticed more incidents.

To bring this selective perception clearly to the fore, Figure 10-8 introduces two precautions. Only those incidents are considered which are reported by at least two people—corroborated incidents, we will call them for short. And excluded as interested parties are the 269 respondents who were themselves the target of any kind of personal attack. By keeping the objective situation constant, each part of Figure 10-8 shows that permissive teachers noticed more incidents than conservative respondents. For instance, at all schools where there were from one to three corroborated incidents,[11] an average of .67 incidents was reported by clearly permissive respondents (two reports for every three teachers), compared to an average of .36 for conservative professors (about one for every three).

Does the number of incidents which come to a professor's attention increase his apprehension even if he is not himself involved? The matter is not easy to resolve. Even if apprehension and the number of perceived incidents turn out to be correlated, we can not be sure how this connection comes about; the apprehensive teacher is more sensitive to academic freedom problems and therefore undoubtedly is quicker to notice if a colleague encounters difficulties. But we can take account of this, at least to a considerable degree, by a separate study of professors on different

---

11. A detailed tabulation of colleges for each exact total number of corroborated incidents leaves the pattern of Figure 10-8 unchanged.

levels of permissiveness. This should help to discount their selective perception. If, then, the number of incidents is still related to increased apprehension, we can well argue that a threat to colleagues spreads apprehension among all social scientists. The facts are summarized in Figure 10-9, which is again restricted to corroborated incidents and excludes all respondents who were accused or attacked themselves.

Looking at the separation between the three lines, we see again our familiar finding that permissiveness is strongly associated with apprehension. The new information is to be found reading across each line. Regardless of teachers' own ideological position,

Figure 10-8
Within the Same Objective Situation, Permissive Teachers Noticed More Incidents

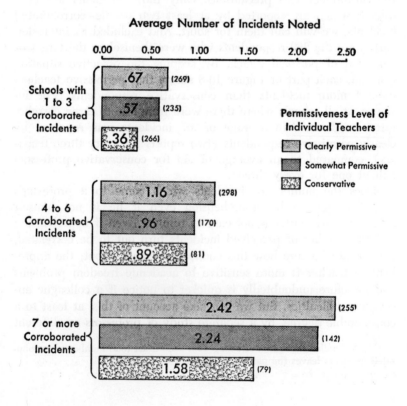

Average Number of Incidents Noted

```
         0.00      0.50      1.00      1.50      2.00      2.50
```

Schools with
1 to 3
Corroborated
Incidents
- .67 (269)
- .57 (235)
- .36 (266)

Permissiveness Level of Individual Teachers
- Clearly Permissive
- Somewhat Permissive
- Conservative

4 to 6
Corroborated
Incidents
- 1.16 (298)
- .96 (170)
- .89 (81)

7 or more
Corroborated
Incidents
- 2.42 (255)
- 2.24 (142)
- 1.58 (79)

and despite the fact that none of the individuals considered here has personally experienced difficulties, the more that incidents involving colleagues occur around them, the more apprehensive they are.

Figure 10-9
The More Incidents Professors Learn About,
the More Apprehensive They Are

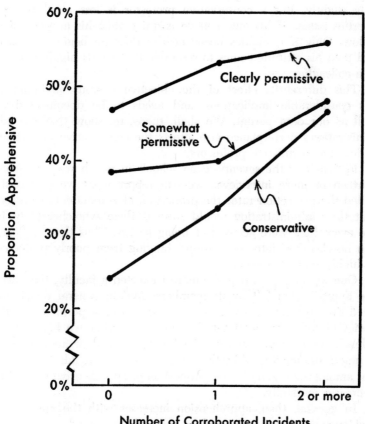

Number of Corroborated Incidents
Reported by Individuals

Clearly permissive	47%	(240)	53%	(279)	56%	(304)
Somewhat permissive	38%	(284)	40%	(210)	48%	(135)
Conservative	24%	(230)	33%	(140)	47%	(56)

But Figure 10-9 also tells an unexpected story. The effect of campus events is greatest, not upon the more permissive, but upon the more conservative professors. In the top line the figures increase by 9 per cent, in the bottom one by 23 per cent. The most probable explanation is as follows: A highly permissive teacher is concerned with civil liberties in general; he pays attention to events in other colleges and to discussion on the national level. His apprehension is considerable even if nothing especially dramatic happens on his own campus; local events increase his apprehension only slightly. But a conservative professor is less alert to civil liberties issues. If his own college is quiet, then his apprehension is low. Only if casualties occur nearby does he begin to worry, and then his attitude comes to resemble that of his highly permissive colleagues.

This differential effect of the objective campus environment has considerable implications, and needs to be documented as well as our data permit. We shall, therefore, show that the administration's performance also affects the conservative more than it does the permissive professors.

For each of the seventy-seven schools in which we conducted thirteen or more interviews, we can report what we previously called the protection rate: the proportion of respondents who feel that their administration would support them wholeheartedly in the event they were accused of being leftists. Thus these colleges can be classified into four groups, ranging from poorly protected to highly protected schools.

One would expect that the more protected a faculty, the lower the apprehension felt by its members. And in general this is indeed the case. But it is not true for our two most permissive categories of teachers (who together make up what we have called "clearly permissive" teachers). In Figure 10-10 their apprehension is practically unaffected by the protectiveness of the administration; but among the remainder the proportion of apprehensive professors decreases markedly.

In general, then, apprehension increases with the number of incidents on the campus and is relieved by an administration's protective performance. This result was already implied in the concluding scheme of Chapter VII. There the relatively similar amounts of apprehension on all levels of college quality were explained as the result of a balance between attack and defense. The new and important aspect of the last two tables is the differential reactions of professors with varying degrees of permissiveness. Conservative teachers are quite strongly affected by local events. Permissive social scientists, on the other hand, show a high apprehension which is little influenced by events on their own

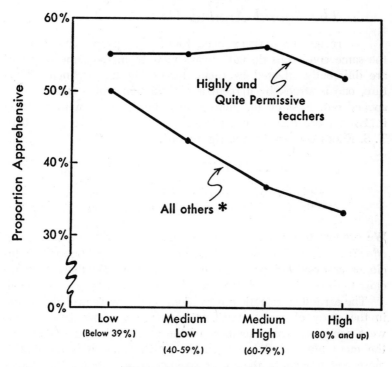

Figure 10-10
How Administrative Protectiveness Affects the Frequency of Apprehension

Protectiveness of Administration

	Low (Below 39%)	Medium Low (40-59%)	Medium High (60-79%)	High (80% and up)
Highly and quite permissive	55% (117)	55% (268)	56% (366)	52% (151)
All others	50% (143)	43% (315)	37% (336)	33% (158)

* In these seventy-seven larger schools, the number of conservative professors is rather small; to get reliable figures they were combined with the somewhat permissive group. Figure 10-10 is based on all respondents in these seventy-seven schools.

campuses. Several previous findings make highly plausible our surmise that the reaction of these men and women is more affected by what happens in their profession at large. Permissive social scientists are more interested in following civil liberties news; they put much more emphasis on general professional privileges than on the public relations problems of their own college; their publication record shows that they are more oriented toward a nationwide audience. All this fits in with a way of looking at the world which has been given considerable attention by social analysts.

The World Around Us

IT HAS REPEATEDLY been found that people living under the same conditions do not always view them the same way and are differently affected by them. Reviewing the pertinent literature, one is struck by a recurring distinction which is not easily spelled out. First of all, there is no established term to describe it. Even more than in other parts of this report, we share here T. S. Eliot's concern for the right word:

> the word neither diffident nor ostentatious,
> an easy commerce of the old and the new,
> the common word exact without vulgarity,
> the formal word precise but not pedantic.

We propose to say that people's meaningful worlds are of varying *effective scope*. For some this scope is relatively bounded—it includes as events of psychological importance only those that are close to them. Others' effective scope is considerably more extended.

The earliest systematic observations on this were probably made in the study of social stratification, when working-class persons were compared with members of the middle class. For example, the mere physical distance within which friendships develop is more compressed in the lower socio-economic strata. The topics about which such individuals talk and the items they read in newspapers are also centered more on local matters. But effective scope goes beyond literal distance. Social research has directed attention to variations in individuals' level of aspiration. The wishes and fantasies of working-class youths have repeatedly been found to be more restricted than those of their middle-class age-peers, even when realistic monetary considerations are excluded. Moreover, criticism of existing conditions, when it occurs at all, is more timid in these lower economic strata. This has been found in diversified fields—in criticism of radio programs as well as of one's commanding officer in the army. As a matter of fact, it has occasionally been said that the problem of the underdog is not so much that he does not get his share of the world's goods as that he has been kept from developing a strong enough drive to want them. The man with an environment of limited effective scope does not notice many things which are more distant; and even if they are pointed out to him, he thinks that they are quite out of his reach.[12]

Socio-economic position is by no means the only factor related to the effective scope of individuals' worlds. Differences in personality and in the public role one is expected to play make for similar variations. We have referred in Chapter VI to the studies which show that some professionals working for industry or for government agencies are oriented mainly toward their employer, while others are more concerned with the reactions of their profession. A corresponding observation has been made in studies of community leadership. Some leaders are primarily interested in helping to solve strictly local problems, while others feel called upon more to bring the larger world, say of art or music, to their community. The apt terminology of "local" and "cosmopolitan" leaders has been suggested for these two orientations.[13] Clearly, what is meant is a difference in the effective scope of the environment: the cosmopolitan type has a relatively extended scope; the local type is more limited—he knows less and cares less about what is going on in the world at large.

---

12. See, for instance, Genevieve Knupfer, "Portrait of the Underdog," *Public Opinion Quarterly*, Vol. XI, No. 1, 1947.

13. Robert K. Merton, "Patterns of Influence," in *Communications Research 1948-49*, P. F. Lazarsfeld and F. N. Stanton, eds. (New York: Harper and Bros., 1949). In a study of a Midwestern college, Alvin Gouldner has applied this distinction in classifying members of the faculty. Among other things he found that "locals" and "cosmopolitans" were more likely to associate with colleagues of their own kind. Following a suggestion by Everett Hughes, he used the expressive term "Home Guard" for the local type of teacher. Alvin W. Gouldner, "Cosmopolitans and Locals: Toward an Analysis of Latent Social Roles," *Administrative Science Quarterly*, 2 (Dec., 1957 and March, 1958), 281-306, 444-80.

External circumstances can restrict or widen an individual's effective scope. Studies carried out during the depression of the 1930's indicated that long-lasting unemployment made the effective scope of workers and their families even more limited than before. Paradoxically, the longer workers were unemployed, the less they kept track of employment opportunities outside of their communities; the unemployment of parents also led to an impoverishment of their children's fantasy world. Conversely, it has been found that if businessmen happen to travel abroad, not only do they develop more interest in international affairs, but they also become more hospitable to ideas of international solidarity, such as approval of the United Nations or a free-trade policy.

What we call the effective scope of a man's world characterizes, thus, what he perceives, what he has contact with, and what he reaches for through his interest or his expectations. Partly still a metaphor and partly a step toward a precise concept, the term is backed by a broad array of empirical data. It greatly facilitates the summary of our own findings regarding the permissive social scientist: on the average, his occupational world has a more extended effective scope than that of his conservative colleague. But the difficult years have threatened to restrict this scope. As a matter of fact, as we saw in the last two chapters, this has sometimes already happened: a number of social scientists, for instance, have withdrawn from participation in community activities, and some have confined themselves to a narrower sphere of teaching and research.[14] *In these respects, then, the effective scope of higher education in America was threatened.*

One must look at this in the light of the history of higher education in this country. A new and rapidly expanding country needed colleges in order to train ministers and school teachers. It was only at the turn of the century that a group of far-sighted men realized how provincial American college education had remained. Basic research, the teaching of world history, the social sciences—in short, most of the topics concerning the world at large—were neglected until the first graduate schools were created, barely sixty

---

14. Data on women teachers further strengthen our argument. As things are today, the effective scope of the woman's world is necessarily more bounded than that of men, even if she is a professional herself. And indeed, on each level of permissiveness, we find women less apprehensive than men.

years ago. In an amazingly rapid development, American universities became the equal of European institutions, and, since the end of World War II, have even passed them on many fronts.

It would be dangerous to have the effective scope of the American college campus restricted again. Experience in other fields suggests that this danger may not be easily visible to an outsider. For example, before World War I, people knew dimly about slum conditions in big cities and the ravages of child labor; and yet it took many surveys concretely describing these conditions before the demand for social legislation became articulate and strong. And so with questions of academic freedom. We are concerned here again with an issue raised once before. Many citizens who believed they were serving the security of their country by attacking college professors probably did not realize that, in doing so, they endangered an important development in American higher education.

A FIELD REPORT

David Riesman

SOME OBSERVATIONS ON THE INTERVIEWING IN THE TEACHER APPREHENSION STUDY*

Every competent study director takes precautions, when working with a national cross-section, to secure the most comparable and reliable interviews that he can. First of all, he conducts a pre-test of the questionnaire to iron out bugs in its administration and the wording of questions. Secondly, on matters of special importance, he goes after the same data through questions variously

* This chapter is the product of collective effort. It would not have been possible without the support (in addition to that received from the Fund for the Republic) of the Interview Project at the University of Chicago, which operates under a grant from the Foundations' Fund for Research in Psychiatry. Mark Benney, co-director of the Project, worked with me on the survey from the outset, and was principally responsible for the mail questionnaire we sent to respondents and for statistical analysis of the returns. We interviewed interviewers and respondents together in the summer of 1955, and many of the conceptions of our investigation came from him. Mrs. Elizabeth Drake analyzed the mail questionnaires, contributed to the classification of colleges, and made many helpful suggestions concerning this chapter. June Sachar worked on the IBM runs (done at N.O.R.C. with assistance from Shirley Star) of the mail questionnaires and analyzed their representativeness vis-à-vis the total sample of respondents; she contributed to the understanding of the influence of college climates upon respondent attitudes toward the survey. Laurence Kohlberg, Michael Maccoby, and Jacob Schoenfeld, graduate students at Chicago, aided in analysis of the interviews with interviewers and with respondents. My colleagues, James S. Coleman and Rolf Meyersohn, and Robert S. Weiss of the Survey Research Center, read an earlier version of this chapter and made helpful criticisms.

worded; thus one question can serve as backstop or cross-check on another. Thirdly, he will ask each interviewer to write a report on her field experiences, the so-called "job report." And then, fourthly, he may follow the lead of Professor Samuel Stouffer (cf. *Communism, Conformity, and Civil Liberties*) and employ two survey agencies of high standing, giving them comparable assignments, thus allowing comparisons of the results secured by field forces of different training and experience. All these precautions were taken on this study—and one additional, retroactive one: I was asked, after the survey had been completed, to make a check on the adequacy of communication, and to see what issues, important for the understanding of academic apprehension and freedom, had not been explored to the satisfaction of respondents. To this end, Messrs. Lazarsfeld and Thielens made available to me the original interviews, and all the codes and tabulations made from them; and the two survey agencies, Roper and National Opinion Research Center (N.O.R.C.), with candor and generosity, gave my colleagues and me access to the interviewers who had worked on the pre-test and the original survey. And a total of nearly 600 respondents cooperated directly with us, either in person or through correspondence and the answering of mail questionnaires, to help us get a picture of what had transpired in the original interviewing.

The respondents were in this case social scientists, often deeply concerned about academic freedom, and sometimes no less concerned about survey methodology. Many were outspoken in their criticism of the questionnaire, believing either that a nationwide survey was not the way to approach problems of academic freedom or that this particular survey had missed the boat. We shall report on some of these criticisms hereafter, but it should be borne in mind, in evaluating the Teacher Apprehension Study, that we have learned more about what went wrong than is known in most surveys of analogous complexity—and that the survey dealt with a clientele, namely professors, more apt to be critical, and to communicate their criticisms to each other, than is true of most Americans. I say this, not to exculpate this particular survey, but rather to permit surveys in general to be judged by the skeptical in terms of broader considerations.[1] In this report, I naturally con-

---

1. I have elsewhere set forth a few such considerations of my own: cf. "Orbits of Tolerance, Interviewers, and Elites," *Public Opinion Quarterly*,

centrate on the "pathology" of the survey—as, in many instances, did the respondents themselves who, when asked about their experience of the survey, could more readily sketch the details of what went awry than of what, since it went well, was not so easily remembered.[2]

However, my assignment was not only to study what might have gone wrong, in terms of the aims of the original questionnaire, but also to see what light the reaction to that questionnaire might shed on academic freedom, on apprehension, and on the sociology of higher education generally. In talking with the interviewers (and we talked with about a quarter of the 212 who worked on the survey), Mark Benney and I enlisted their often considerable knowledge of the climate of fear and freedom at the colleges where they had worked; when we talked with respondents, we asked them to speak of their preoccupations in the areas of academic freedom that the questionnaire had, in their judgment, omitted or touched but lightly. What we learned in this way, we made available to the study directors through a series of vignettes of the colleges we had visited; this material also informs the report that follows. Just as experts on the Rorschach test have made use of reactions to the test situation itself, as well as the substantive responses, as projective material,[3] so we have found that reactions to the interviewing were often, in combination with other material, diagnostic of the situation at a particular college; that is, the survey changed its meaning and import for respondents, depending on the climate within which they work.

Vol. 20, 1956, pp. 49-73; and (with Nathan Glazer), "The Meaning of Opinion," *ibid.*, Vol. 12, 1948-1949, pp. 633-48, reprinted in *Individualism Reconsidered and Other Essays* (Glencoe, Ill.: The Free Press, 1954).

2. Of course, memory can play tricks in either direction. A student of perception and its social and psychological structuring, or someone fascinated by Bartlett's studies in remembering, would find of interest the cases where nonexistent questions were "recalled." Thus, at a college where the faculty mistakenly believed an intrusive and unpopular president was insisting that they be interviewed, several professors objected, in talking with me, that they had been asked their salaries (whereas they had only been asked whether they had had an increase).

3. Cf., e.g., Ernest Schachtel, "Subjective Definitions of the Rorschach Test Situation and Their Effect on Test Performance," *Psychiatry*, 8, 1945, 419-48.

An Over-all Assessment

BEFORE TURNING to necessary qualifications that must be entered, both concerning the adequacy of communication in this survey and the adequacy of my own investigation of it, it is important to state my over-all judgment: namely, that deficiencies in the interviewing did not seriously impair the information gathered. Or, to put it another way, the interviewing was, in general, sufficiently skillful and conscientious to carry the somewhat unusual demands put upon it by this particular survey. A sample of the respondents themselves (at forty-five colleges), who returned 432 mail questionnaires (a 55 per cent return) giving their own appraisals of the encounter, were asked two interrelated questions: "Do you think that—in spite of any specific reservations you might have had about the study—a generally fair and true image of your attitudes to academic freedom was elicited by the questionnaire?"; and "Do you think that the interviewer got down a generally fair and true record of your attitudes?" In contrast with the impression left by a number of often vehement criticisms voiced concerning the survey, 85 per cent said "yes" to the first of these questions (5 per cent said "no"; 10 per cent, "don't know"), and 78 per cent checked "yes" to the second question (3 per cent said "no"; 19 per cent, "don't know"—the latter sometimes observing that they "didn't see what she wrote").

Many of the respondents who answered affirmatively did so grudgingly and with serious reservations. Moreover, the minority of the "no's" and "don't know's" are not to be slighted, for a study such as this (as the authors of the main report observe in another connection) is not a census where every respondent counts one and no more than one: it may well be that the dissatisfied minority includes many who have more of relevance to say than the average. Furthermore, the respondents' judgments as to adequacy, like my own, must rest on surmises, not only as to what the interviewer actually recorded, but also as to what levels of truth or of detail were intended to be tapped by the survey. Nevertheless, given the fact that at least 30 per cent of our mail questionnaire respondents were sharply critical of the original questionnaire, their frequent admission that it accomplished at least a substantial part of its aims is impressive.

I am in a somewhat better position than any single respondent to make an over-all assessment, for I interviewed and questioned not only respondents but also interviewers who had worked on the study; I read the latter's handiwork, and followed their procedures. As in so many human ventures, one can find in the field work much misunderstanding and some gross incompetence (we found no dishonest reporting on the side of the interviewers), but the safety factors built into the questionnaire itself, and into the operation of the agencies' field forces, generally carried the day, assisted by the good will and patience of most respondents and the concern for academic freedom of many of them.

Thus, while fully aware of how hard it is to make such a retro-active judgment, I conclude that the findings of the study are not, in the main, contaminated by the way in which the field work proceeded; on the contrary, it is my impression that the defects in communication probably diminished the sharpness of the differences of the cross-tabulations. For instance, the distinctions drawn elsewhere in this volume between colleges of high quality and others might be even more marked if the interviewing at the colleges of high quality had always been of comparably high quality, or if the questionnaire itself had found a greater receptivity at some of these colleges.

One example here will have to do duty for many possible ones. There are twenty-four colleges out of the 165 in the sample from which we have no reports of incidents or attacks. All but three of these twenty-four are either teachers colleges or small denominational schools where, for reasons developed elsewhere in this volume, we would not expect attacks. Two are small Southern publicly-controlled schools, one for women only, and there, too, there is nothing surprising in the lack of incidents. But there is one distinguished Ivy League college on the list. I visited it, and I am convinced that poor interviewing is responsible for the lack of mention of attacks: The interviewer who worked there was the most inadequate of any we saw, poorly educated, ethnocentric, and apathetic; and her respondents, quickly defining the survey in terms of her evident deficiencies, made plain to me that they were not such passionate devotees of academic freedom as to care to make the effort to get the record straight.[4] Yet in the cross-tabulations of

_____
4. At another Ivy League college where this same interviewer worked, her

this volume, the difference between twenty-three and twenty-four is not significant, and the findings would in fact only be more conclusive had this college been correctly classified.

In summary, then, if we look first at what respondents reported, in interviews with them and in mail questionnaires, we would estimate that roughly 10 per cent of the interviews misfired in some decisive fashion. This 10 per cent includes both those respondents who felt the questionnaire did not cover the topics they felt significant for academic freedom and those who got caught in the machinery and could not get their story across to the interviewer. In contrast, a third of the respondents had no fault to find (save perhaps a detail of question wording here or there). An additional half of all respondents had complaints of greater or lesser seriousness about the questionnaire, but were satisfied that their interviewer was competent to take account of these and make the proper qualifications. The remaining 10 per cent were unwilling to commit themselves to an over-all evaluation even though they had few specific complaints.

Actually, however, in many cases where respondents were dissatisfied or dubious, it is clear from examining all the material that the main outlines of their attitudes and experiences did get covered, on the pre-coded questions at least. As with parents who talk to children who pretend not to hear, the professors' subjective feelings of blocked communication exaggerated the ineffectiveness of the encounter. I would guess that no more than 6 or 7 per cent of the interviews contain serious errors of reportage—though a much larger proportion, of course, could have been fuller and given a richer sense of the semantics and the subtleties of individual minds.

The Nature of the Investigation

AN ENORMOUS VARIETY of factors may serve to structure the expectations of both respondents and interviewers about their

---

irritated respondents patiently managed to get some of the attacks on record. She also worked at one of the teachers colleges where we have no record either of attacks or of criticism of her—a syndrome of passivity we shall take up later.

encounter, and thus to influence what is deemed relevant—what is even conceived and thought—and what is said and what is heard and recorded. In a retroactive study of this sort, we can reconstruct only a few of these factors and seek to illustrate their interaction; and in this section we shall concentrate on the way in which the interviewers' expectations were set for them by their agencies' "house-style" in general and by this survey in particular, while the respondents' expectations were influenced in many cases by the discussion about the survey among their colleagues, as well as by images of the Fund, of Professor Lazarsfeld, or of survey research as such. But, in a continuous process, many of these influences reacted on each other. Thus, if the interviewer was relatively self-effacing, or if the respondent was deeply engrossed in problems of academic freedom, the questionnaire might, as it were, speak for itself in a Eugene O'Neill *Strange Interlude* type of dramaturgy, while the interviewer's personal qualities sank into the background. Correspondingly, if the respondent's expectations were highly structured in terms of an ideology about questionnaires, the interviewer again might make relatively little difference, and the questionnaire more of a difference. As in any human relation, so in that of interviewer and respondent, the kinds of "parataxis" that psychotherapists discuss can become decisive: each may "see" the other through a penumbra based on extrapolation (or "projection") of experiences with others of the "same" sort, as, for instance, in terms of collegiate or agency definition, or in terms of the ideology thought to be implicit in the questionnaire or in the sponsorship of the Fund for the Republic.

And all this says little enough about idiosyncratic variables such as the eminence of respondents vis-à-vis that of their department, their college, or their interviewer; or the ways in which, for a respondent of particular background, personality, and interest in the topics covered, the voice shadings of the interviewer affected his responsiveness, his aliveness, at various points in the questioning;[5]

---

5. We do have testimony by a number of respondents that their interviewers spoke monotonously—and by several interviewers that, given the length and lilt of some of the questions, they could hardly speak otherwise. But, on the whole, respondents indicated but little sensitivity to interviewers' voices and accents, apart from total impressions of educational or social-class background. It is perhaps a testimony to the forms democracy takes, and first impressions make, that many more respondents could recall or describe how the interviewer looked than how she spoke.

or the accidents of setting which, as in any "projective" encounter, may influence the range and freedom of response. We can touch here on but a few of these; for the most part, our methods lack the subtlety to catch the myriad ways in which (as in the novels of Henry Green) people can talk past each other, while believing themselves to be understood—or vice versa.

To save space, I have consigned to a later publication a more detailed account of the procedures we developed for this follow-up study, including detailed information on the mail questionnaire and the ways in which we satisfied ourselves that replies to it did not—despite the skepticism of many experts about the validity of mail replies[6]—underestimate the degree of disapproval or distrust of the questionnaire and/or the interviewer.

Among other things, it turned out that proportionately a great many more replies were received from professors at leading colleges where there was much criticism of the survey (as usual in life, the busier men seemed to have more time!). Indeed, at the most eminent institutions in our mail sample, nearly 80 per cent of the respondents told us that they criticized the questionnaire to the interviewer (yet three-quarters of these also felt satisfied that the questionnaire had, in the main, gotten their story).[7] Likewise, reading of the mail questionnaires indicates no softness of critical temper concerning the details of the survey (or of the mail questionnaire itself); and such criticism is concentrated among the younger, more sophisticated men at the more cosmopolitan schools. (As we shall see later, the nature of this criticism tends to vary in terms of the protectiveness of the college in question vis-à-vis the more exposed faculty members: where the latter feel safe, they often concentrate their fire on the survey's alleged methodological defects, whereas where they feel threatened they are more apt to emphasize substantive lacunae.)

Moreover, men at such schools were over-represented among those to whom mail questionnaires were sent, for time and cost limited our direct investigation to the East and Midwest (with a

---

6. Cf., e.g., David Wallace, "A Case For—and Against—Mail Questionnaires," *Public Opinion Quarterly*, Vol. 18, 1954, pp. 40-52.

7. While signing one's name to the mail questionnaire was made optional, most respondents, especially at the more distinguished and critical colleges, did sign their names; and only thirty-five returns in all could not be assigned to a college (and were hence discarded when comparisons between colleges were made, though not of course in the over-all assessment).

brief visit to the Upper South and Florida), and even within these regional limits we concentrated on the larger and more cosmopolitan schools. Furthermore, liberals were slightly more likely to return questionnaires than conservatives (as such matters could be assessed from internal evidence) and, as indicated elsewhere in this volume, liberalism, in terms of a concern for civil liberties, and cosmopolitanism tend to go together. For all these reasons, the testimony of the mail questionnaires, coupled with the interviews which we did with some 120 respondents at over thirty colleges,[8] gives me confidence that I have collected the major sorts of criticisms of the survey, and that I have gained a fair sense of what kinds of errors and distortions occurred.

Even so, my investigation was far from complete and only moderately systematic. I have a picture of what went on in the field, but not how often it happened, let alone of the implications of errors and distortions for the final analysis. While in the pages that follow I shall frequently draw on the mail questionnaire returns for illustrative material and, upon occasion, for statistics also, these data are not to be taken as irrefutable proof but as a preliminary mapping and a personal judgment on what lawyers call the weight of the evidence. And, as already indicated, whatever is said is intended to serve a dual purpose: at once to sketch the varieties of encounter that give concreteness to the over-all verdict, and at the same time to illustrate the substantive themes of academic freedom in terms of the experience with the survey itself.

One of the inevitable problems of my investigation of the interviewing was that it had to begin while the trail was fresh (though we did not reach some interviewers or respondents until six months or more after the original encounter), hence prior to analysis of the main survey data, and with no clear idea as to what was expected, or should be expected in the way of fullness of response—that is, as to the norms against which the actual communication should be judged. No doubt, not all respondents had told all they knew, at all levels of potential response, but, given the numerous cross-checks built into the questionnaire or developed in the course of analysis, how much was enough? Moreover, to

---

8. In addition, as many of my friends have discovered, I relentlessly interviewed them if they turned out to have been respondents in the Teacher Apprehension Study at institutions I could not otherwise reach.

the extent that the questionnaire itself grated on the sensibilities —political, cultural, or methodological—of respondents, was it reasonable to expect the interviewers to caulk the gaps in communication, and if so, to what degree? More specifically, could more have been done to compile detailed accounts of incidents of violation of academic freedom with fuller answers to relevant questions in the interview? Would it have changed the results substantially if a few more respondents had been kidded into completing the question which asked them how businessmen, congressmen, and trustees might rank professors in comparison with other professionals—a question some regarded as irrelevant to their definition of what the survey was after, or too "iffy" to make sense? In general, what difference would it have made to the statistical tables if each respondent had given to the questionnaire the optimum degree of thoughtfulness, of serious introspection, that led some professors to take three or four hours as against an average of an hour and a half?

These are not only the sorts of questions that confronted me in this investigation; they also, usually in less explicit form, confronted many of the thoughtful and self-critical interviewers and respondents in the original study. The former were sometimes perplexed as to the areas which, given pressure of time or respondents' impatience, should be most fully explored; the latter either relied on the interviewers for such definitions of salience or brought their own definitions in terms of their preoccupations or earlier colleaguial verdicts on the survey. When, in our mail questionnaire, we asked people whether they felt that "in terms of the aims of the study" they had been good, average, or poor respondents, many in free-answer comments said they had no yardstick by which to make a clear judgment.[9]

---

9. Forty-seven per cent thought they had been "good" respondents; 38 per cent "average"; 7 per cent "poor"; 8 per cent said "don't know." On the whole, the higher the quality of the college, the more the respondent expected of himself and the greater his tendency to deprecate himself—and, inferentially, the survey; however, many men strongly committed to academic freedom were inclined to feel they had been "good" respondents because they cared and had been conscientious. Indeed, at leading colleges some respondents managed in effect to re-tailor the questionnaire to fit their own conceptions as to what were the salient questions of academic freedom; to do so required flexibility both of them and of their interviewers, and where they succeeded, they regarded themselves as "good" respondents. (The interviewers were torn in such cases between their obligation to secure comparable

There is in fact no yardstick. Instead, there are various traditions of investigation: historical, anthropological, and sociological, and within these, various sub-varieties. Some would have preferred to examine a few colleges in great detail, for instance, by participant observation; others would have chosen a national survey, but not only of social scientists; still others would have asked different questions. I have not considered it part of my mission to comment on which course should have been chosen, but rather to see what, within the limits of the type of investigation made, could be added by a retroactive spot check, as well as to make a reasoned surmise as to the freedom and fullness of communication, again within those limits. For example, I felt that the original questionnaire had paid insufficient attention to pressures from students and the parents of students,[10] and in questioning respondents I stressed this issue. It is obvious, however, that any method of investigation involves choice: the present study was adapted to a set of particular concerns, necessarily time-bound, arising in what its designers term "the difficult years"; since neither studies nor books about them can go on forever (only nearly so!), this meant many decisions not to ask questions about other aspects of academic freedom which many respondents were eager to talk about. Free-answer questions permitted some of this excluded material to leak in, sometimes providing leads to interpretation or illustrations of respondents' attitudes. In general, I assumed in my work that the more free-answer material the interviewers got, the better, even though it became apparent that much of this was cumulative or superfluous.

This was the case because, given the main report's mode of analysis, with its reliance on the development of indices, "how true" is more important than "how much"—though of course these questions, as any short story writer knows, cannot be entirely separated. Only if respondents lied to interviewers or unconsciously deceived themselves, or if the interviewers did not write down the relevant portions of what they were told, or if respondents failed to understand the questions or could not be guided into choosing with reasonable verisimilitude among the precoded alternatives suggested to them, would the work of coders, tabulators,

responses from everyone, and their obligation to secure the idiosyncratic story of each particular one.)

10. Respondents had an opportunity at various points to comment on this, both in precoded and free-answer materials, but it was not a salient theme.

and analysts be threatened by serious error.[11] Much of what follows will be an effort to sort out these sources of potential error, although as to most of them I have been unable to arrive at a conclusive judgment which could be expressed, like sampling errors, in a series of percentages.

When we began our investigation, we assumed that differences in background between the interviewers and the respondents would be extremely important in qualifying the fullness of possible communication. We assumed, for example, that the fact that most respondents were men and most interviewers women would have marked effects,[12] although not uniform ones: for, on the one hand, politics is a "male" subject and one about which women are not supposed to know much, or at least not much that is low or disagreeable; and, on the other hand, emotion is a "female" theme and men might have felt freer to express fears and anxieties to "understanding" women than to their own peers. At the same time, an older man talking to a younger woman might have tended to treat her, depending on many circumstantial factors, as a student or a secretary—not expecting contradiction or probing; he might have wanted to pose as more intrepid than he felt or he might have found himself tempted toward candor by the very disparities and the need to communicate across them.

Accordingly, we gathered data on the age of interviewers as compared with that of their respondents, and we paid special attention to instances where interviewers and respondents were of the same sex (there were not more than half a dozen male interviewers, and 250 women respondents). But we found no systematic effects of the interviewer's age, in part because the younger interviewers were also those with more education and hence were more

---

11. One qualification to this generalization must be entered here. It sometimes happens that people, torn between "yes" and "no," will answer in one direction and then add qualifications in the other, showing for example that their "yes" doesn't quite mean "yes," and may even lean toward "no." Thus, fuller response may lead to recoding, or at least to great caution in interpreting certain answers. And if the encounter discourages such response, errors may lurk under apparent simplicities. The study directors were of course alert to this danger, and used the "tracers" of respondent qualification to point to possible ambiguities in precoded answers. They would be misled only if interviewers systematically (not necessarily consciously) discouraged or disregarded such qualifications—and this, in my judgment, did not occur.

12. Cf. Benney, Riesman, and Shirley A. Star, "Age and Sex in the Interview," *American Journal of Sociology*, Vol. 62, 1956, pp. 143-52.

at home even with older professors than were many of the older interviewers. We did discover, however, that younger men, and those in the junior ranks, tended to give longer interviews, even though some of the interviewers may have been less interested in them or patient with them than with the more amiable, more distinguished, and often less critical senior men.[13] The younger men appeared to have more to say, more dilemmas to resolve, and perhaps less certainty in stating their views; in some cases, where they were new to their institutions, they had fewer outlets for grievance and welcomed the chance to talk.

Women interviewers are, of course, accustomed to listening to men, to dealing with them, and to getting their story, irrespective of age disparities. Conversely, men expect to find women in the interviewer role, but in this study they sometimes did not expect a survey interviewer, but a colleague, a social scientist (of either sex). Such expectations, however, were not randomly distributed. Soon after embarking on our follow-up, we concluded that the most important variables affecting communication in the interview were the type of college at which the respondent taught and the type of interviewer, in terms of educational level, who had gone there. Disparities of collegiate culture proved to mean more than disparities of sex or age (or of status in terms of social class). And following up these disparities also told us more about the substantive problems of academic freedom at various levels of intellectual quality. Hence the material that follows (after a brief discussion of the problem of concealment and evasion in the interviewing) is organized in terms of four levels of college which I differentiate as the avant-garde, the upper-middle, the lower-middle, and the rear guard (within which there are a number of subcategories). I believe that in the course of describing the encounters characteristic for each of these levels I shall be able to pass in

---

13. From the evidence of our mail questionnaires, 45 per cent of full and associate professors got through their interviews, they reported, in an hour or less, compared with 33 per cent of assistant professors and instructors. Furthermore, when asked if the time given were adequate, 93 per cent of the former group answered "yes," while only 73 per cent of their junior colleagues found the greater time they took adequate. In conversation as well, the younger men were more apt to say they felt in some degree cut short, but I doubt if at major institutions many restricted themselves, or allowed the interviewer to restrict them, because of the modesty of their age and rank. We have already noted that the younger respondents were more critical both of the questionnaire and of the interviewer in our mail questionnaire; no doubt,

review the major problems of communication,[14] as well as to contribute something to the grasp of what these levels have experienced during the difficult years.

Thereafter I shall describe the two principal types of interviewers who worked at these different levels and indicate something of the effects their previous training had upon their interpretation of this assignment.

The Problem of Conscious Evasion or Deceit

NOT A SINGLE RESPONDENT in my own survey felt that his
interviewer had misrepresented him on purpose, however incompetent or mechanical she appeared to be. And none of the interviewers we saw "cheated" by filing invented ballots—a practice I
would not expect anyway from the staff of a leading agency, and
a practice virtually ruled out in this case by the complexity of the
survey.[15] Even, or sometimes especially, the poorest interviewers
were doggedly conscientious.

---

they were more likely than their elders to be familiar with survey methods and
aware of their deficiencies. By the same token, as we shall see more fully later,
in exploring reactions at different quality levels of college, young men at
some leading universities were quite complacent and went routinely and rapidly
through the questionnaire, while men of like age and intellectual background
at less protected institutions took the survey with great seriousness and gave
protracted replies. This latter group of younger men were also more likely
to feel the heavy hand of their seniors, whereas in the major colleges and universities young men were more apt to feel they were sitting pretty and in a
few such institutions it was the older faculty members, heirs of the ideologies
of the New Deal and World War II era, who were most critical of and concerned with the survey. Thus, it was not age itself which was a significant variable, but rather age as related to training, setting, and experience of life in
and out of academia.

14. This overstates the case somewhat, since in the light of our present
limited knowledge about communication, we cannot be dogmatic about what
facilitates or blocks it. Certainly, many personality variables of both participants are influential in any encounter which seeks to reveal subjective attitudes.
Some people talk more readily to those who they think resemble them, whereas
others talk more easily precisely where communication must occur across apparent barriers—these are, of course, matters psychoanalysts discuss under the
headings of "transference" and "resistance." Our own follow-up could go only
a short way into such questions, and had to remain largely on the level of
"sociological" rather than "psychological" variables, focusing on what was
general rather than on what was, no less relevantly, idiosyncratic.

15. The reader may wonder how I can be so sure of this. In the first

But of course not all respondents were conscientious. Had they been so, a mail questionnaire might have sufficed;[16] but interviewers were necessary in part because they could persuade uninvolved or forgetful professors into answering—and, in some cases, could get through the defenses of men who would have preferred to dodge the issue. A number of prominent respondents realized that, though nominally anonymous, they could readily be identified by their rank, the subjects they taught, and the experiences with or without academic freedom they had had. Some of these men expressed fear to me that their questionnaires might fall into the hands of a Congressional committee. At one leading college, much was made of this possibility, and some wanted the questionnaires returned so that they could be destroyed. One young assistant professor at a leading liberal college told me that, having left a leading university at a time of controversy over a loyalty oath, he was especially gun-shy in answering the questionnaire; he had no fear vis-à-vis his present institution, but didn't want his affiliations and opinions to fall into government hands. He is one of the handful of men who, in person or in the mail questionnaire, gave any sign of pulling his punches on this account; most who raised the question about a governmental investigation said they had answered honestly, though they were anxious about it at the time or afterward.

One man told us how, when he had gotten home and reported to his wife that he had said it would be all right to have a Young Communist League chapter on campus, his wife insisted that he hunt the interviewer up and change his answer, and he did so (though it was not clear to me whether he was more scared of the Velde Committee or of his wife). Several interviewers also told us of cases where, in the course of the interview, respondents had

---

place, before talking to the interviewers, I read over the questionnaires and job reports they had turned in; knowing the colleges from which these came, I was sensitized to implausibilities. In the second place, in talking for several hours with interviewers concerning their experience in general as well as on this particular assignment, I had an opportunity to gain a sense of their commitment to their agencies' strict standards of performance; moreover, since Mark Benney and I have been studying the "interviewing industry" for several years, we had some basis for comparative evaluation.

16. The 55 per cent return in our own mail questionnaire, considering the months that had elapsed since the date of the original survey, and considering the lack of follow-up, is very high; it is ordinarily expected that 15 to 30 per cent will respond by mail.

gotten worried about their responses and had asked to have "radical" answers changed.[17]

Apprehension about the interviewer herself as an audience for
"left" opinions, including distrust of her as a member of a local
community hostile to the college, scarcely existed at those leading
private colleges where respondents believed they enjoyed the support of their colleagues and the administration, and did not worry
about local repercussions. Even in the case of less protected faculties, however, men often found themselves talking more freely
than their "better judgment" might have dictated: during the
give-and-take of the interview, they were afraid to be afraid, and
only later in a kind of hangover effect did they allow themselves
to worry. What seems sometimes to have happened in some of
these cases is that the interview reminded the respondent how
widely his previously unarticulated or unsummarized opinions put
him at odds with the community in which he lived and taught. Yet,
by the same token, it is clear how American such anxious respondents were: in their willingness to trust strangers, in their unwillingness to "play it close to the chest," and in their consequent fear
(at times leading to later resentment of the survey) of having
talked too much.

I have spoken here of the relatively very small number of cases
in which men were conscious of their misgivings, and the even
smaller number in which they pretended to know less than they
did.[18] These included, I would assume, men who had been Communists or fellow-travelers, as well as liberals in a hostile milieu,
especially in "traditional" colleges. In contrast, the reactionaries,
though they frequently denounced the Fund for the Republic, and
attacked the survey as an attempt by liberals to prove that academic
freedom was in peril, talked in every instance known to me with
great freedom—a freedom to speak out which some attributed to at

17. Such cases, it is plain, presented the interviewers with difficult ethical
and practical dilemmas. In general, they pretended to make the change but
also to note the circumstances; some felt disingenuous about concealing this
course from the respondents. My already high regard for the scrupulousness of
interviewers for top agencies was buttressed by my discussion of such matters
with the interviewers on this study.

18. Such evasion was especially frequent in answer to the question about
belonging to controversial groups, to questions about reading matter and political associations, and to questions about knowledge of civil liberties incidents. In all probability, a number "forgot" they had voted for Henry Wallace.

last having the "liberals" and the "godless" on the run (other rightists still felt persecuted, but seemed quite uninhibited in saying so).

Much more problematic are the cases of those anxious liberals and ex-leftists who no longer knew what they thought and felt—men for whom evasion of politically-charged issues had become nearly second nature. In such cases, respondents were, so to speak, already dissociated from their own views and stood ready to produce from the file-drawers of memory those attitudes and even factual knowledge which would wear well in the light of social interaction. (I will speak later of cases where men were protecting, not themselves, but the public relations of their institutions.) A particularly skillful and intrepid interviewer might try, by probing, to get beyond easy answers, but there were limits of course to this in the guest status of the interviewer both vis-à-vis the particular respondent and vis-à-vis his colleagues. Ordinarily the questionnaire had to rely for its evocativeness on its own surprises, and on returning by a different route to items previously touched upon. Indeed, 35 per cent of the respondents to the mail questionnaire said that they felt during the interview that the questions were sometimes designed to trap or trick them into inconsistencies and self-contradictions—thus in all probability projecting onto the study directors even more guile than they actually mustered! But only two respondents said they became wary in their answers as a result, as against 102 who "thought this was standard procedure, and didn't mind," and fifty-one who checked "I take some inconsistencies in my attitudes for granted, and wasn't bothered."

It was a frequent experience, in talking with sophisticated respondents, to have them express doubts as to whether other people would answer the questionnaire honestly; often, these were men skeptical of surveys in general—and of people in general. Perhaps their skepticism did not go far enough: most respondents, in my observation, lacked the imagination and energy, as well as the motive, for consecutive cheating; like most professional people, if they lied, it was on a small scale, a question of emphasis, of shading. One interviewer commented: "They didn't lie to me—they lied to themselves."

Several respondents of above average political awareness voiced another misgiving—namely, that out of fear that the results of the survey would only serve to strengthen anti-intellectualism, men may possibly have held back unpopular opinions. As one man who had lived in Washington, D. C., said: "Wait till McCarthy sees how many professors voted for Stevenson or are willing to allow students to debate admission of China to the U. N.!" I sought, when such comments were made, to discover whether the respondent had himself tempered his views in order to help present a safer picture of academic opinion. While it would be foolhardy to be sure of such things, it is my impression that a tendency to present oneself as more conservative than in fact one was, on behalf of the public relations of the profession, was quite slight. One element leading to frankness among the more politically alert lay in the fact that many believed, at the time of the interviewing, that the worst excesses of McCarthyism were over—often enough, indeed, that the survey had come too late to be of very much use.

To present oneself as more liberal and more defiant than one was in fact was a tendency of which I was aware in my own inter- view (I was in the sample). But after carefully reading the in- terviews and in the light of discussions with respondents I am inclined to think that this was rare: self-deprecation seems to have been more frequent than preening. When asked how they might act in a hypothetical situation—involving, for example, a protest against a teachers' oath—it is striking how many highly self-conscious men qualified their answers, saying that they hoped they would have the courage of their convictions: not having faced fire, they had the misgivings of green troops. And, in a number of such cases, I gained the sense that the interviewer was simply the rapporteur of an internal dialogue in which the respondent was deeply engaged.

The psychological problems of candor I have been discussing so far arose among men who, seldom directly intimidated, might never- theless be inclined to do a bit of trimming or window-dressing on behalf of the eggheads. The nature of the problems shifts when we turn to the colleges of lesser quality—mainly those which are im- poverished and dependent for students, funds, and other support upon local powers-that-be; at such institutions, the administration which might like to serve as a buffer against the local car dealers, bankers, farm bureau officials, etc., is more likely to act as monitor against unconventional views. Accompanying such poverty and complaisance is likely to be a rarity of private offices, and the inter- viewer might have to choose between a cafeteria open to all (such colleges do not ordinarily possess faculty clubs) or the dean's office—in which she might be interrupted now and then by officials coming in to get files, or colleagues coming in to joke and to ask when their turn was, thus reminding any respondent overinclined to loquacity of his primary belongingness. My implication is not that there was any conscious effort to intimidate in most of these cases; quite the contrary, the survey was often considered a tiresome command performance of no conceivable relevance to local conditions. As one interviewer said, after describing her efforts to drag respondents at a sectarian college of less than 200 students through the schedule: "They had nothing to be not frank about."

The interviewers had, of course, been alerted in their instructions to the possibility of evasion; many of them, in any event, were sufficiently astute and familiar with problems of civil liberties to be on the lookout for it. Frequently, they showed great ingenuity in creating conditions of privacy—arranging, for instance, to interview respondents at their homes or, Baruch-style, on a park bench. Only rarely, in their observation or mine, did intimidation occur. As the study's data show, poverty, small size, and strong hierarchical controls tend to go together. At many schools of this "traditional" sort several overworked teachers may divide the social sciences among themselves: one teaching geography, business law, and European history; another, sociology, education, and government. In such a setting, an apprehension-prone respondent might worry lest his superiors could identify his comments. Not satisfied by the interviewer's initial assurances of anonymity, the faculty member might whisper to the interviewer (after saying something that would cause not a moment's hesitation in the upper reaches of academia): "How confidential is this, really, anyhow?" Occasionally, after such reassurance, there might be mention of an incident not known by or not forthcoming from other respondents, or a criticism of the administration's stand, or lack of it, on academic freedom. In a few cases, respondents who went blandly through the interview, having seen, heard, or thought no evil, caught up with the interviewer later and, over coffee in a restaurant, told quite a different tale. Understandably in such cases, an interviewer proceeding under the watchful eyes of a suspicious administration sought tactfully not to irritate possibly influential respondents by pressing them too hard, by probing into answers that might possibly have been evasive; for she was aware that any misstep could lead to her ejection, and she had to balance the potential gain of an item of information from a single respondent against the potential loss of the entire batch.

In visiting two colleges of this level, we found the president interposing himself between us and his faculty in no uncertain terms. In one instance, he gave us the "true" version of a case some years back where he had fired a professor for his "crazy" views, and sought to be sure also that we saw the "right" people on his faculty. We decided to see one he had not mentioned, and telephoned a woman teacher of sociology and anthropology to make an appointment to see her that afternoon at her home; when we called again several hours later to get directions, she told us that she felt too ill to see us; her voice gave the impression that she was frightened. We suspected—we could be wrong, of course—that she had telephoned the president to see if it was all right for her to talk with the visitors from the University of Chicago.

In the other instance of this sort we encountered, the enterprising president of a state-supported Negro teachers college in the South called professors over to his office to talk with us—pulling them from their dinners in such peremptory tones as to make clearer than any words could that he regarded them as hired hands in a business far more autocratic than most businesses are today. In fact, he set the interviews up in his own office, which he graciously vacated while leaving the door ajar—looking in every so often to see how we were doing! (To be sure, we reciprocated by closing the door and by arranging to see one or two faculty members in their homes.) The interviewer who worked at this particular college did not believe her respondents were frank with her in expressing the kind of 200 per cent Americanism they avowed—an Americanism so thoroughgoing that they never had heard of any civil liberties cases anywhere; nor could she believe that faculty-administration relations were as perfect as respondents said they were. But in my judgment, the gap between reality and appearance at this college is not so very wide. With the exception of one teacher, a part-time minister, who belonged to the N.A.A.C.P. and was critical of labor conditions in nearby plants, the faculty—notably the women—had worn the mask of spiritlessness for so long that it seemed almost second nature.[19]

19. It should be emphasized that we are discussing here a teachers college, not an institution like Fisk or Howard or Dillard. Even so, the interpreta-

At one teachers college in New England, the discerning interviewer described matters as follows:

I feel certain that the State Department of Education (i.e., "trustees" of the college) told the president to allow the survey to be conducted and that he, in turn, told the respondents that they were to be interviewed. I'm sure it never even occurred to any of the respondents to refuse. They had been told to appear in the office at a certain time and appear they did.

No wonder that at some of these colleges questions concerning attitudes in the local community found teachers unresponsive, for the president was their main channel of communication with the "outside"—an outside that might be located at the distant state capitol—and they left it to him to resist or to transmit pressures as in pre-union days a straw-boss might reflect economic conditions to the workers in his charge.

So far, I have been discussing the problem of evasion by individuals concerned with self-protection. I turn now to a different phenomenon, namely, the tendency of respondents in a number of the poorer and less critical colleges to voice only at best muted attacks on their administration and to gloss over what would be aired at leading institutions. In these colleges, the interviewers often encountered a kind of gentility and politeness which veiled any sharp and disturbing judgments, avoided "hearsay" and "rumor," and presented the institution in what respondents regarded as a favorable light. Whether we should speak of "evasion" here raises paradoxical questions, since the results reflect the institutional pattern and can be discounted accordingly.

In any event, sabotage of the questionnaire was seldom total, and the cross-checks built into the study design itself served to

---

tion ventured above may be mistaken, and quite possibly under current conditions in the South only Negro interviewers or whites who had proved themselves not merely sympathetic but worthy of trust could get through the layers of caution and even of self-deception. A white interviewer worked at this college. However, though there are too few cases for definitive conclusions, it is our impression that Negro interviewers were no more successful than white ones in piercing the screen of bland "Americanism"—possibly less so, being in this particular group we sampled less skillful and in any event motivated to show, in line with the respondents' own aims, that there is no "subversion" in the Negro colleges.

On the other hand, Negroes interviewed by whites in the North, in the course of interviewing a social science faculty, posed no special problems, and talked quite as freely—and, in one small sectarian college, much more so—as their white colleagues.

correct some of the consequences of deception for the analysis. For
instance, the design contained a congeries of questions aimed to
elicit knowledge of threats to academic freedom, and if the respondent shied away at the first question, he might not at a later
one, differently worded and received in a different context. Careful
reading of the questionnaires, college by college, provides some
illumination on this score, as do the job reports filed by the interviewers, or their occasional marginal comments on a questionnaire
concerning the circumstances which should be considered when
it is coded.

Summing all this up, I am inclined to conclude that evasion
was a problem primarily at two ends of the spectrum of colleges:
in the leading institutions where highly self-conscious men might
seek to disavow their past or present radicalism, and in the more
despotically-run institutions of poor academic quality where an
occasional professor, marooned by circumstance, had learned to
keep his liberal opinions to himself, and to be wary of knowing too
many unpleasant facts. (Indeed, too great knowledge in this area
might make him all too uncomfortable in the face of his own
passivity and powerlessness: better for his own morale to look on
the bright side of things.) In both cases, suspicion of the interviewer
or disapproval of the questionnaire might provide reasonably
scrupulous men with rationales for dissimulation—just as approval
of the survey and a sympathetic interviewer could lead in such
cases to release of long-pent-up opinions. Obviously, it is hard to
estimate the over-all weight of such countertendencies. But I
would guess that more than marginal intentional evasion occurred
in less than 5 per cent of the cases.

The Collegiate Setting
of the Interviews

On the Variety of Colleges. We began our investigation
with the prejudice that, in a great many cases, the interviewers
would be no match for their academic respondents: they would
lack the familiarity with academia, the quick intelligence, the social
science know-how, the ability to impress important men as worth
spending time with, to gain the confidence of a faculty and to give
respondents the sense that their interviewers were within range

of highly differentiated or oblique and complex communication.
This was frequently the case—though less frequently than many
respondents believed. The converse case, however, also appeared
frequently: academically oriented and capable interviewers, sensitive to issues of academic freedom, faced respondents of far less
alertness or concern with freedom—indeed, of far less familiarity
with the social sciences. Although in the last ten years I have visited several score colleges and, through colleagueship with Everett
C. Hughes, gained some familiarity with the academic rear guard,[20]
I was not fully prepared to realize that, at many institutions accredited as colleges, the faculty is by and large so little given to
reading, so unintellectual if not actively anti-intellectual, that survey
research would have been set back and academic instruction set
forward if respondents and interviewers had changed places.

Such an acidulous comment, to be sure, rests on the perhaps
ethnocentric assumption that avant-garde academic standards—and
preoccupations—should be universal; it disregards the possibility
that many of the rear-guard colleges serve important nonacademic
ends, as well as peripheral academic ones, and that a questionnaire
designed to fit the concerns of such colleges—such concerns as
raising the floor below lax entrance standards, or giving the faculty
fewer custodial duties—might have proved more evocative. However, I cannot enter directly into such matters; they arise tangen-
tially because they are relevant to the question of how well matched,
throughout the length of the academic procession, were interviewers and respondents, when the former came as emissaries for
the Fund for the Republic. In general, I would say that they were
very well matched in the large state universities and non-Ivy
League private colleges, for here the respondents in general were
sufficiently apprehensive to be concerned, and willing to put up
with a survey they regarded as far from perfect. The matching, as
just implied, was somewhat less adequate in the groups of colleges
the authors term "traditional," not because of objections to the
interviewer but because the questionnaire itself was often regarded

---

20. Professor Hughes has been studying for many years the "social mobility" of academic institutions, e.g., the teachers college (once a two-year
normal school) that becomes a liberal arts college and eventually a state
university, or the Protestant sectarian college whose constituencies slowly
become more secular. Cf. his forthcoming book on work and careers, to be
published by The Free Press.

as either irrelevant or the dubious work of liberals. As one respondent at an impecunious Midwest teachers college complained:

The questionnaire was designed by a do-gooder . . . designed for places like Columbia and Harvard. I'm a Columbia man myself, but Dr. Lazarsfeld certainly didn't know anything about small colleges like this one. It's all irrelevant to us: we don't have Communism here; we've never had a Communist or anybody who warranted the attention of the investigating committees.[21]

And yet the diversity within as well as among colleges is illustrated by the fact that this same professor was, after all, a Columbia graduate—perhaps the more resentful of the survey because it reminded him of the question: what was he doing *there*. At virtually all of the "traditional" colleges to which we sent mail questionnaires there was at least one person teaching who got his doctorate at a major institution. And, conversely, at many of the leading colleges one found respondents (not infrequently, among the geographers) with much less familiarity with controversies concerning academic freedom than the average of their colleagues —men who could not in any sense, technical or personal, be regarded as members of the intellectual avant-garde. We all know that departments and colleges change, often with astonishing rapidity, and a classification remains "good for this trip only." Despite such perplexities, as mentioned earlier, I classified the subsample of forty-five colleges to which we sent mail questionnaires into four groups: avant-garde, upper-middle, lower-middle, and rear guard. The categories were an attempt to measure socio-academic quality, and were arrived at by visits to most of the institutions in question, by perusal of their catalogues, student newspapers, and literary reviews, and by reading the interviews done there for evidences of intellectual quality.[22] Without naming names, it is hard to justify the rankings, but it should be said that, though arrived at independently and impressionistically, my judgments largely coincided

---

21. In our interviews with respondents, Mark Benney took as full notes as feasible and I, depending on the circumstances, sometimes took some; on returning to our hotel we would transcribe these immediately, through joint reconstruction retaining verbatim text as much as possible. Most interviews with interviewers were handled the same way; at a few, my wife took notes; a few were tape-recorded.

22. For fuller discussion of the problems in classifying colleges, and of the typology which served as my starting-point here, see *Constraint and Variety in American Education* (Lincoln, Nebraska: University of Nebraska Press, 1956. Also in Doubleday Anchor edition, 1958).

with those more systematic ones used by the authors of this volume.

Climates of Response in the Avant-Garde.

The colleges in this category are not all avant-garde in the same way, nor are they heading in the same direction. Some are experimenting with undergraduate education; still others emphasize the traditional humanistic disciplines; some have a "social" and a few a socially-conscious student body—or the nearest thing to such a student body to be found today. Moreover, with the exception of several eminent state universities, it was in the great private universities and well-endowed Ivy-League-type colleges that the survey met its most complex and critical reaction, and where inadequacies in question-design or in the interviewing were most sharply resented. The militancy many at these institutions exhibited on the substantive issues of academic freedom repeats itself in comments on the survey itself—comments that can be garnered under three headings: methodological objections to surveys as such, or to this one in particular; "activist" objections based upon a judgment that surveys, however meritorious in some instances, here served to delay coping directly with a political problem; and "conservative" objections to the alleged liberal bias of the questionnaire.

None of these objections was peculiar to avant-garde colleges (hence in reviewing them we will be canvassing the major criticisms of the survey altogether), but the differentiation, strength, and frequent consensus on these objections were far more marked in the avant-garde.[23]

1. *Problems of methodology:* The interviewers were not button-holing "the man in the street" to ask him about plans for purchasing

---

23. At avant-garde colleges, returns on the mail questionnaires came in from two-thirds of the respondents or more (if we include letters returned in lieu of mail questionnaires—often objecting to the latter), as against returns from less than a fifth at small Catholic colleges and some teachers colleges (on several occasions, where only a single return came in from a Catholic college, the respondent indicated his own atypicality among the group of respondents there). More striking still, men at avant-garde colleges were much more apt to add marginal comments to their check-marks on the precoded questions —even though their individual answers might not differ from those one could find also at less eminent institutions.

Since we visited more avant-garde colleges, it is arguable that the greater volume and intensity of commentary from them is due, less to an intrinsic critical temper and concern for academic freedom, than to the artifact of our own interviews and the discussion stirred up thereby. We have some evidence that this was not a factor—or, if it was, that it worked both ways. The "tra-

consumer durables, or methods of meeting medical expenses, or attitudes toward the U. N. (all issues of the sort asked about by some of the interviewers shortly before or after their work on this study). And at the same time respondents were not being visited as individuals and asked about problems concerning which they were considered specialized informants, although many of them at leading colleges were in fact authorities on academic freedom. Even as non-specialist respondents, however, many could be expected to have so deep an emotional investment in the issues as to make for difficulties when they were approached by interviewers with a standardized schedule—interviewers from agencies doing polling on a national scale. This collision of a sometimes "hot" subject with a cool methodology and an "outside" interviewer should be put in the context of the ambivalence with which many academic people regard the laity.

Furthermore, there has developed over the years in major intellectual circles an image of the fearless, activist professor—and here was a questionnaire which invited the respondent to expose contradictions between that image and his own apprehensions, his caution, his timidities. Indeed, one respondent wrote an angry letter to the study director criticizing the methodological ineptness of the survey—and later (being a man of unusual honesty and humility) admitted to him and to me that his ire had been aroused by the realization that, though he thought himself an intrepid liberal, his knowledge of academic freedom cases did not justify this self-image and that his liberal values had slowly been eroding; he displaced his antagonism onto the techniques of the survey, being himself highly qualified in this field.

Still other potentially sensitive areas were probed by the ques-

---

ditional" colleges we visited were not stimulated to return more questionnaires —or more expansive ones—than others in the same category we did not visit. And a number of the 35 anonymous returns which could not be assigned to a college came from those who said they didn't care to reveal themselves to me—an understandable hesitation that, as several people have told me, prevented others from returning questionnaires altogether. Moreover, since our mail questionnaire asked most of the questions we had also asked orally, a number of people felt no need for a second round, and these were largely people whom we had interviewed at length at leading schools.

My co-workers and I plan to publish later a group of papers on a number of matters which deserve more detailed discussion than can be given them in this report. These will include an elaboration of our observations about the avant-garde colleges, some further results from our mail questionnaire, and so forth.

tionnaire. How were faculty-faculty and faculty-administration relations? Had the respondent ever been a department head, published papers, or been a consultant?²⁴ Could he expect support from colleagues and from the institution if he were to be accused of leftism? A few men, though rarely in avant-garde institutions, found the survey so cathartic that they held the interviewer in tow, like the Ancient Mariner, for four, five, and in one case six hours. Others reacted in explosive antagonism, and in reverberant small and fairly homogeneous colleges helped to create a whole climate of disapproval and rejection. Given the emotional ingredients, I find it in some ways surprising that the explosions were not even more common—I suppose that psychiatrists, each time they tackle a new group of patients, worry about the possible traumas of interaction, only to discover that people's defenses are built for just such invasions, even from psychiatrists.

I intend no implication that technical objections to the survey were regularly defenses against deeper involvement, and of course an objection could be merited whatever its motivation. Indeed, we have some evidence that political conservatives, themselves relatively without apprehension, were more frequent than liberals among those who expressed a general distrust of polls. And understandably, at avant-garde colleges, since most research experts reside at such institutions, some respondents (especially, as already noted, among the sophisticated younger men) reacted as methodologists who would have done the study differently, rather than as liberals or conservatives.²⁵

---

24. Some interviewers reported that respondents were occasionally embarrassed to have to report their father's occupation or their own religious affiliation. A large proportion of respondents were, as social scientists, familiar enough with such "face sheet" questions to take them as routine. It may be that in some instances the interviewers' own hesitation in asking a question they regarded as intrusive communicated itself to their respondents. Understandably enough, in talking with me respondents seldom took objection to questions of this order, concentrating on those concerned with their attitudes rather than with who they were.

25. Likewise, since the Ivy League schools are those where sociology has sometimes been a low status discipline (which has also the bad grace to be rich enough to spend big money on projects!), a number of professors reacted in departmental terms: the political scientists, historians, and economists could look down on the crude and dubious methods of sociology—while members of the latter guild were sometimes embarrassed as the survey became an intra-academic counter in the snobbery and "guilt by association" of the several disciplines. Within political science, for example, the survey sometimes sparked

First of all, there were the respondents—including a handful who refused to respond—who were opposed to polls in general. Lindsay Rogers' critical volume, *The Pollsters,* was frequently mentioned, or its arguments cited, as ultimate verdicts. One political theorist declared:

I consider most such questionnaires to be a great waste of time. Indeed, the more questionnaires I see, and the more results I see tabulated, the higher I think of the opinion I formed of that method of acquiring misinformation over thirty years ago. . . .

This respondent refused to complete his interview. So did another leading political scientist who asked the hapless interviewer to convey his irritation with the method to Professor Lazarsfeld. Among historians and some economists, as well as among political scientists, there was frequent resentment against all that appears mechanical or stereotyped. In the two top groups of colleges, many respondents—at a guess, 15 per cent—emphasized their belief that the questionnaire method even at best is not adapted to the subtleties of the problem of academic freedom. One assistant professor wrote:

I'm inclined to discount the value and worth of the instrument. I engage in so much local politics . . . I've gotten the conviction that attitudes in politics are so infinitely complex that a poll can hardly get at them.

Another put matters this way:

I do not like questionnaires in general. I think anything as subtle as freedom, academic or otherwise, cannot be reduced to a questionnaire the answers to which can be tabulated and reduced to statistics. I was therefore very unhappy during the interview. The interviewer was fine and I have *no* complaint to make about her at all. But I felt when it was over that the total outcome was entirely false, although I did my level best to answer each question as truthfully as I possibly could. I believe the cause of this is not in any fault of the interviewer or the questions as such but in the basic conception.

---

arguments between the more traditional students of theory, constitutional law, or comparative government, and the Young Turks who felt their addiction to "behavioral science" to be on trial. (While it is primarily in the Ivy League that sociology has the status of a parvenu, there were of course other schools where its standing was low, either because of particular incumbents or because the campus was dominated by humanists, theologians, natural scientists, or other cadres with misgivings about the newer social sciences.)

One man who expressed himself as "truly amazed at the skill and ingenuity" of both the original and the mail questionnaires still felt it impossible "to get behind the other fellow's skull and see what makes him tick." Or again:

My strongest feeling is frustration at the questionnaire's either/or propositions most of the time. . . . I missed any give and take process. . . . The highest truths don't come out of machines.

Such generic objections shade over into those which found specific fault with this particular questionnaire: with its alleged crudities, its implications, its ambiguities. The comment of a young economist was of the first sort.

The questionnaire was so crude, it was necessary to rewrite questions in order to answer them. . . . I left the interview with little knowledge of what it was all about . . . , i.e., what order of answer was expected, or what sort of survey it was. I suppose it was trying to get at what one subjectively felt.

Likewise, a few men felt that in answering questions on academic freedom they were forced into postures that misrepresented them. One declared:

. . . all my answers tended to grant assumptions in the *questions* that I find unwarranted and misleading.

This fear is related to the belief, found in free-answer comments on many of the original interviews, that the questions were ambiguous, hence likely to entrap respondents. This complaint was voiced in our interviews with them by many professors at the distinguished college where most of the respondents signed a round-robin letter of protest to Mr. Hutchins, reading in part as follows:

Many of the questions were so ambiguous that our problem was not: what is the answer? but what does the question mean? Some of us simply said we did not know, a response which could be subject to various interpretations in this setting.[26] Others attempted to state the

___

26. Where interviewers were mechanical, and professors discriminating, this fear that a "don't know" response would be taken literally and coded in the "don't know" category, rather than spelled out as an objection to the ambiguity of such terms as "liberal" or "Communist" or an objection to hypothetical questions, was frequent and there were understandably hardly any avant-garde professors content to simply record themselves as "don't know's." A number of interviewers, unable to handle dialectical subtlety, tried to force respondents into one box of the trichotomy of "yes-no-don't know" and did end up with them in the "don't know" catchall, but many others took down what

limited conditions to which their answers applied. The pressure of time attendant upon answering so excessively long a questionnaire gave us little opportunity to consider the possibilities in the questions; we were allowed no means of checking whether the enumerator did, in fact, record our intent correctly.

These letter-signers went on record that the survey had not adequately gathered their views on academic freedom, and all four respondents previously quoted were among the twenty-two out of 410 who, in our mail questionnaire, answered "no" to the question whether the survey had in general added up to a satisfactory picture of their attitudes. They teach, as already indicated, at leading colleges. And, I suggest, they testify implicitly to the climate of freedom at their institutions by the very fact that they can afford preoccupation with the subtleties and "metalogicality" of questionnaires and of human beings; many of like eminence teaching in less protected places were led by their sympathy with the study's aims to focus less on its procedures.[27]

Repeated objection to the alleged ambiguity of questions and repeated requests for definitions occasionally rattled inexperienced interviewers; and in a few instances the latter in turn became irritated with what they regarded as "academic" quibbling. Even so, when I examined the interviews done at colleges where such mutual provocations were strong, including the one which sent the round-robin letter, I concluded that the interviewers got down more qualifications and red flags to coders and analysts to "stop, look and listen" than their painstaking respondents realized. The latter, preoccupied with what got left out or with what might be

---

was said and let the coders worry about what to make of it. We shall come back to this problem later.

27. Of course in the avant-garde, too, there were a number who expressed skepticism about surveys, or this survey, but were from Missouri, willing to be shown. Thus, one respondent indicated over-all satisfaction with the study, but in the mail questionnaire listed as his greatest "personal idiosyncrasy": "Doubt as to the scientific value of most questionnaires"! Others also gave over-all approval, yet described themselves as doubters or even antagonists of surveys.

Since this report was written, I have had a chance to see Daniel Lerner's article, "The 'Hard-Headed' Frenchman: On se défend, toujours," *Encounter*, March 1957, pp. 27-32. Professor Lerner describes the resentment of leading French officials, military men, and intellectuals to a questionnaire, designed in part by Americans, aimed to elicit French attitudes towards EDC. And he also indicates how these objections were often circumvented by asking the respondent for suggestions as to how questions like these could be put to others like himself, with their understandable reluctance as toughminded and seri-

misinterpreted, sometimes failed to realize how much actually did get said and recorded.

It follows that interviews which the respondents found subjectively unsatisfactory might nevertheless allow them to be correctly classified—much as (to use an analogy suggested by Professor Lazarsfeld) a physician might take a medical history which, in the patient's belief, omits the most important symptoms and events, and yet which allows the doctor, in combination with what else he knows and observes, to make a correct diagnosis. To be sure, if the patient's disease is psychosomatic—and what "social" disease is not—the doctor may miss important clues if he listens only to the patient's heart and not to all the details of how the patient feels, but the latter may also underestimate the doctor's skill in finding *multum in parvo*.

Related to the frequent avant-garde tendency to let criticism of the study's means submerge sympathy toward its aims is the feeling at many of these institutions that by the spring of 1955 academic freedom was no longer in critical danger—that, with McCarthy's censure and the 1954 elections, "the worst was over," and had in any event not been as bad as had been proclaimed. It was a sign of the inanity of the Fund, or of sociologists, that they should only now, too late, be getting around to the problem. Not infrequently, the men who voiced this position seemed, in their interviews with us, very involved in establishing their uninvolvement: theirs was the tone of the cool, the detached, the planetary.[28]

2. *The "activist" reaction:* A very different sort of objection to surveys came from many fighting liberals who objected to the questionnaire as they would to the appointment of a committee: as a delaying tactic in the battle for academic freedom. These activists (more characteristic, perhaps, of the upper-middle ranks to be described later, but also common in the avant-garde) were not hostile, for the most part, to surveys as such, but did not see

---

ous Frenchmen to have their privacy invaded. I was struck by the many similarities between the attitudes of Frenchmen, as Lerner met them, and the attitudes of many in the avant-garde towards the Teacher Apprehension Survey.

28. I am aware that my tone in the foregoing may convey some irritation with professors so secure as to be cavalier about continuing inroads on the freedom of less fortunately situated colleagues—an irritation which is partly the outgrowth of my work on the study. If I were as detached emotionally as I am intellectually, I might give more weight to the possibility that this attitude, in its variety, its subtlety, its security, and its avant-gardism, is a sign of health and progress!

how research, whatever its virtues, could advance the political struggle: more than enough was already known, and amply documented in the press, A.A.U.P. reports, and elsewhere; the search for further data could only imply fear and a lack of real concern for pressing evils. Understandably, moreover, such respondents were dubious of the survey even in its own terms: occasionally, they did not believe that professors, already intimidated, were likely to tell the truth, or they denied the relevance of many questions (for example, those on the respondent's philosophy of teaching, discussed in Chapter VI of this volume) to political intervention.

On the other hand, a number of those who reacted in this manner—especially teachers of history and of political science—felt that certain questions relevant to the political and institutional defense of academic freedom had not been asked, and probably could not, in any case, be ascertained through survey procedures. Believing that the study, with its sponsorship by the Fund, was aimed at collecting instances of violation of academic freedom (rather than primarily at attitudes and apprehensions), they stated that such "classified" information could only be obtained from insiders, if at all. They felt that the complex of pressures threatening—and protecting—freedom could be fully understood only by someone familiar with the history of the school, with the role of its alumni, and the personalities of its chief officials over decades. One historian emphasized this point by saying that one could not grasp the present situation at his university without awareness of faculty victories over the trustees going back to before the First World War. In this reaction, activism is combined with a particular view as to how contemporary attitudes can best be understood.[29]

It would be a mistake to conclude from these instances that resistance to the survey on the grounds that it came at the wrong

---

29. Many men who took the activist stand criticized the survey for not interviewing the right people. "You should interview the trustees or the president," they would say. And they were often critical (as were numerous respondents of quite different over-all orientation) of the decision to interview only social scientists. They pointed out that on their campuses the physics or math departments, art or English, had been under much greater pressure for harboring "leftists" than the social science departments. At one college, many respondents with whom we spoke were angry that geography, which they did not regard as a social science, had been included in the sample, while education, which they did regard as one, and one especially relevant for controversies over academic freedom, had been omitted. (They also felt in this a certain snobbery against "educationists" which they resented.)

time, asked the wrong questions of the wrong people, and was wrong to ask rather than to act, interfered seriously with the gathering of data. Thus, most of the respondents who did take the activist attitude were nevertheless cooperative with the questionnaire: almost in spite of themselves, they could not refuse doing a good turn for academic freedom even when they felt such a turn would amount to very little.[30] A number of them were torn between their belief in science, in factuality, and their worry lest research impede action, and this ambivalence sufficed to carry them through the questionnaire—having done this, they felt the freer to attack it afterwards.

3. *Problems of alleged bias in the questionnaire:* In Chapter V, Messrs. Lazarsfeld and Thielens discuss the minority of respondents who attacked the questions as "loaded" in a liberal or leftist direction. In the interesting way that extremes sometimes meet, this reaction occurred among a small group in the leading colleges, almost disappeared in the middle-level institutions, only to recur, much more vocal, in the rear guard, notably in the smaller Catholic institutions. But there is a great difference in tone and temper between the avant-garde "new conservatives" who criticized the survey's alleged liberal bias and the rear guard "old reactionaries" who assailed the Fund, the survey, Columbia, and Professor Lazarsfeld, all as part of the same "Red Network."

The former group sometimes had their teeth set on edge by the very first question, with its reference to "6 or 7 years ago"—a period plainly intended to embrace the Cold War and McCarthyism, but also one in which the views of some of these respondents, nothing if not timely, had become conservative. Such professors almost invariably felt themselves to be surrounded and outshouted by "liberals"—indeed, it is hard to imagine this type of "new conservative" arising in some of the apathetic and reactionary atmospheres of the more benighted colleges. The survey gave a number of such men a chance to react to what at times seemed a cherished

---

30. I should perhaps speak for myself here, since I have been critical at times of the Fund for the Republic for preferring investigations (e.g., into the roots of domestic Communism) to engagement directly in the political struggle over civil liberties: I would prefer to have the Fund leave such long-term matters to the more conventional foundations. As a respondent on the Teacher Apprehension Study, before my own connection with it, I was quite prepared to await Professor Lazarsfeld's analysis before passing judgment as to what use it might serve toward understanding or defending academic freedom.

feeling of isolation; they engaged the bewildered interviewer in a running dialectical battle over the "loaded" questions, asking her, for instance, to define what was meant by "liberal" and "conservative" in the question, "On political matters, do you feel that you are more liberal or more conservative than" . . . ("most of the trustees here," . . . "the faculty," etc.). At one university, much in the news as the result of the recent Congressional expeditions, one "new conservative" balked at the term "controversy" in one question, saying that to imply there is "lots more controversy" over academic freedom was an expression of liberal "loading."

The term "loaded question" came easily to people's tongues, was very often reported by interviewers, and turned up again in answers to our mail questionnaire (which was occasionally thought to be loaded in favor of the questionnaire and against the interviewer, or simply, along with the original questionnaire, loaded in favor of trouble). Criticism of such terms as "liberal" was, of course, not confined to conservatives old or new: a great many professors at many types of colleges objected to terms they thought clichés, and requested definitions.[31] They asked interviewers what was meant by "worry," by "academic freedom," by "Communist," by "radical," and so on. A fuller comment than most is the following, by an assistant professor at a distinguished college:

I . . . was disturbed by the ambiguities of the language of the questionnaire. The questions about liberal and conservative. . . . Then the questions involving the word "community"—which community did they mean, the department community, faculty community, town community, community of the neighbor college faculties? As a political scientist, I pride myself on the felicity of my references. . . .

As I have remarked, the more insistent semanticists tended to be conservatives who fought what they regarded as the liberal bias of the Fund and the survey from the outset. Some, as already indicated, resented the absence of enough questions allowing them to affirm that all was well with academic freedom, but only rarely —and then only at leading schools—did we run into the objection:

31. Of the respondents who answered the mail questionnaire—a group which, as already stated, I believe to be more vocal than the non-responders —70 per cent said they criticized one or another of the questions to their interviewers—this, of course, at the very least; many were, as already indicated, critical of the whole procedure.

"There were no questions enabling conservatives such as myself to report pressures against us by our overwhelmingly liberal colleagues."[31a] When I asked what pressures were felt, I was told they were evident in patronage from foundations, in promotions, in social slights, and peer disapproval. As an economist, a full professor at a leading college, complained:

. . . the survey seemed to lack objectivity. Although the survey was supposed to be concerned with academic freedom in general, the questionnaire concentrated on the position of a radical coerced by college administration, alumni, or public. No attention . . . was given to conservatives subjected to pressure from radical members of the faculty. . . .

So, too, an interviewer, working at a city college with a strong liberal tradition, encountered one conservative respondent who objected to the question as to whether the interviewee's colleagues and the administration would support him if he were accused of leftist leanings; he felt that the question was biased, since it didn't ask what would happen to someone accused of rightist leanings.

While these reactions shed light on the drift of thought among some intellectuals at pace-setter schools, it is another question whether they indicate that the interviewing of such men failed to collect any of the basic data desired. As we have seen, frankness is not the issue: the interviewers testify that these respondents were often argumentative but not evasive. I am sure that a few of these men had been harassed and made uncomfortable by their liberal colleagues, especially if they had actively cooperated with or perhaps merely defended Congressional investigating committees. Occasionally, such a man suspected that his interviewer was herself a liberal—a member of Americans for Democratic Action or at any rate the League of Women Voters. But I came across no instance where these experiences led the respondent to feel inhibited in the interview; indeed, several self-styled conserva-

_____

31a. A question which came late on the interview schedule did in fact ask all teachers who considered themselves politically "more conservative" than their colleagues on the faculty to give the details of any instances in which they had "felt pressures, direct or indirect, to conform to the prevailing political pattern." In all likelihood, conservatives who had from the very outset formed a judgment on the bias of the questionnaire did not "hear" this question or did not allow it to reorganize their over-all perceptions of the survey.

tives told me how they enjoyed ridiculing what they regarded as the interviewer's probable liberalism. These men sometimes shared with many liberals—often on the very same campus—the feeling of being more alone than in fact they were, but this tended to make them belligerent rather than apprehensive in the encounter.

We encountered several cases, however, where this orientation led to a refusal to be interviewed at all. One willfully crochety "character" told us that he felt he had to teach the interviewer—and along with her, his timid and conformist junior colleagues—that it was still possible in a free country to say "No!"[32] The interviewers in such cases, trained to "get their man," were extremely persistent, and it did take firmness (perhaps even a touch of ruthlessness) to maintain resistance. While William H. Whyte, Jr., in *The Organization Man,* wryly advises prospective employees to cheat on personality tests to preserve their individuality, I came across three or four cases at most where conservatives, old or new, gave signs of this sort of somewhat anarchistic evasion as a way of protesting against the Fund or the bias they felt in the questionnaire.[33]

Not all avant-garde schools on which we have data gave voice to this type of conservative complaint, but at a number which did, the opposite complaint—that the study would foster complacency

32. When a college president refused to let the interviewers in, that *prima facie* betokened a lack of even a modicum of freedom at "his" institution; but individual refusals are quite a different story. At an authoritarian college, if the president permitted the interviewing to proceed, the faculty for the most part dutifully complied. Contrariwise, it was at the more liberal institutions that faculty members felt free to refuse; in fact, in the case I am just speaking of, the professor believed himself to be striking a blow for liberty all the more because the president's influential assistant had telephoned him to arrange for the interview.

33. One observant interviewer, who worked both at a major avant-garde university and a Catholic college in the same vicinity, said she found one respondent at the former and many at the latter who criticized the "hysterical" or "nervous overtones" of the "loaded questions"; she thought this impression was given by a series of questions which asked if respondents were "more worried," "avoided subjects more," showed "greater concern," etc., and that if these had been handled by putting alternative answers on cards and letting respondents choose (as was done with two other questions) a greater appearance of objectivity would have been given to the questionnaire. At any rate, it would seem as if her public relations problems would have been eased by, as it were, inserting an impersonal card between her and her respondents who, at the Catholic college, repeatedly assailed the irrelevance and bias of the questions.

—was more frequent, if usually less vehement. We have already noted the dismay of the "activists" at one more fact-gathering expedition, but I speak here of a reaction specific to the questions themselves. One man wrote:

I am much more militant on the subject than the questionnaire allowed me to show.

And another spoke for many when he declared:

My answers to this questionnaire would mislead people to believe that there is much more academic freedom in the U.S. than there is, because I teach at a *very free* institution.

Still others were troubled because they felt impelled in the interview to give their university a clean bill of health since they could not put a finger on concrete violations of the most demanding norms, and yet they considered this record no true testimony to the actual views of the authorities—views never manifested in speech or other action. By the same token, their own apprehensions, as revealed in their answers, appeared not to rest on substantial grounds, and they tended to blame the survey for putting them in the position of alarmists, and not making it easy for them, from question to question, to reconcile lack of obvious external pressures with inner anxiety.

So long as respondents, of whatever political stripe, were convinced that the survey aimed chiefly at collecting incidents rather than attitudes, they were encouraged to fear, on the conservative side, that it would retroactively support Mr. Hutchins' thesis that "teachers are scared" and have reason to be,[34] and, on the liberal side, that the "realistic" reasons would not justify the circumambient fears.

4. *Criticism of the form and scope of questions:* Heretofore we have been discussing methodology in the largest sense: how one

---

34. Some reactionaries, as noted above, were glad their leftist colleagues were scared. Many respondents of quite different politics argued that teachers were more fearful than they ought to be. I found no evidence that any of these positions led respondents to willfully misleading answers on the questionnaire.

goes at a problem, whether by action or research and, if the latter, whether by surveys, by historical inquiry, by anthropological or journalistic field-trip, etc. But in addition respondents at avant-garde colleges and, to a lesser degree, throughout the sample took issue with particular questions in zealous detail. Virtually every criticism one can find of the polls in the twenty-year history of the *Public Opinion Quarterly,* and virtually every bit of advice to pollers that the experts have accumulated, reappear spontaneously in respondents' comments.

Thus there were complaints of ambiguity, forced choice among inadequate alternatives, vaguely-defined terms ("Do you mean by 'Communist' card-carrying Communist?" was often asked), or terms locally inapplicable ("We have regents here, not trustees"; "we don't have trustees; we are supervised by the diocese")[35]—these were frequently pointed out, first in many cases to the interviewers who did their best to make note of objections of this sort, and later to us. Many respondents objected to the hypothetical questions included in the study on a variety of grounds. They would say they weren't in the situation so how could they tell; in this connection, we have already referred to the self-critical liberals in major schools who said they weren't sure when actually on the spot that they would have the courage of their convictions—when it came, for instance, to protesting the president's ban on a visit to the campus by Owen Lattimore. Another question which met similar objections was the one which invited respondents to estimate how business-men, Congressmen, and trustees would rank four professional oc-cupations, including college teaching. A great many replied that it was idiotic to expect them to answer this—sometimes because they weren't in the judgers' shoes, or knew no judgers (many knew no trustees), or thought the proposed judgers to vary widely ("there isn't any typical trustee or typical businessman") either in

35. Perhaps in this category should also be included objections of the sort advanced at several Catholic colleges, namely that they were unsure what basis to use in judging the quality of teaching conditions and faculty-adminis-tration relations: they would answer one way if other schools in their "league" were the reference group, and another if they had to make a comparison with secular schools. It is evident that this is also an objection to a forced choice; indeed, the categories of objection plainly overlap and many complaints—e.g., "the wording of some of the questions made them very hard to answer"—are not easy to assign to a particular category.

general or with respect to the given institution. In our interviews with respondents, no question was singled out so frequently for attack as this one.[36]

In reflecting about this whole congeries of objections, I recognize that some are valid, and yet I am struck with the number of respondents who refused, whether intermittently or throughout, to play the game of the interview. In a sense, they took the matter too seriously, in believing, for instance, that it mattered whether they had been at their present institution for six or seven years. What was wanted of them—as it appeared to me as a respondent— was a general estimate of the climate of freedom as it felt to them, and not an annotated dissertation. At rear-guard colleges, professors were often proud that *their college* was "selected" for the distinction of being in a Fund-sponsored survey, but often did not consider that their own views mattered in the least; but in the less oppressed strata many who were too intelligent to think they had been selected as *individuals* nevertheless sought to answer as if the study was, or should have been, tailored to their idiosyncratic measure. Some never considered the possibility of answering the question asking for ranking of occupations as would *homo academicus*—a man with a certain mediated if not personal experience with businessmen, trustees, and congressmen; others, of course, resented the whole survey because they felt they were being reduced to *homo academicus* and objected to specific questions which seemed to press this definition home.

Moving in quite another direction were those respondents who concluded that the survey must be after facts and incidents of academic freedom, and thus could not grasp the purport of questions about their own teaching philosophy or their attitudes generally, let alone, in the face-sheet material, about their professional career. Such people appeared to stereotype the questionnaire at the outset, and then refused to allow any change in their picture of its intentions.

---

36. Another question which met similar resistance asked respondents, as a way of indicating something of their pedagogic philosophy, to comment on a parallel with engineering school training. Not only did some object to questions which departed from the main line of academic freedom, but they also balked at putting themselves into a hypothetical dilemma; a few, in fact, were so sure that the questionnaire wanted only "facts" that they resisted any question which seemed to call for "opinion."

The interviewers had some leeway in helping respondents define
what was expected of them in the role of respondent—partly by
cues as to the anticipated length of time (respondents were usually
asked to set aside from an hour to two hours) and partly by their
handling of specific questions (especially in probing). Still, many
social scientists—including sociologists—had grave difficulties in
knowing how to act as respondents; they often manifested this by
putting dialectical burdens on the interviewer herself (or simply
ones of reporting, in cases where interviews ran to four or more
hours[37]) that she was ordinarily not trained to carry—although in
many cases she rose to them.

5. *The impact of the interviewer:* The task of the interviewer, as
I see it, was to adapt the standard questionnaire to the unstandard-
ized respondents so that, without too greatly affecting the comparability of response, individuals were given the sense that the
occasion was meaningful, that their candor and responsiveness
were valued and important, and that they could, on the one hand,
qualify their answers to precoded questions and, on the other hand,
surrender to the alternatives given them without a loss of essential
truth. Where, as so often happened, the respondent had already
been briefed on the survey by his colleagues,[38] a notably capable

37. Some respondents in such cases complained: "She obviously couldn't
record *everything* I said"—thus shifting the issue from the interviewer's sense
of relevance (and their own) to her lack of stenographic skills. While Professor Lazarsfeld's letter to respondents asked them to regard the interviewer
as an amanuensis, the questions themselves made it evident to most that this
was not meant literally.

Some respondents asked why the survey wasn't done by mail (though one
who said this wryly admitted that he probably wouldn't have got around to
answering) and others said a tape-recorder should have been used. These suggestions were influenced both by the desire for greater accuracy and for more
time to think about the questions than the interview situation seemed to allow. At major institutions, respondents for the most part refused to worry
about anonymity and hence the oral interview as a personal safeguard was
not important to them.

38. The interviewers were of course instructed to impress on respondents
the need not to talk about the survey until it was concluded at their institution.
At the lower levels of academia, faculty members accustomed to obey instructions frequently obeyed this one; occasionally, however, some authority
gave a contrary lead, as at one teachers college where the Dean told the
faculty: "Here's a stinker of a survey" thought up by left-wingers.

In contrast, the sophisticated faculty at avant-garde institutions enjoy a
tradition of nonconformity; and they were not sufficiently impressed, in the
main, with the survey to take its mandates seriously or literally. Since at the

interviewer might go a long way to lessen stereotyping and to encourage a progressive redefinition of her competence and the survey's relevance. Thus, while over three-fourths of the respondents at avant-garde colleges, both in our interviews with them and in their responses on the mail questionnaire, stated that they felt in some degree "that the choice of answers provided for in the questions foreclosed [them] from expressing important shades of feeling and attitude," an interviewer at home in academia could nevertheless "level" with her respondents, encouraging them to feel that they were being understood as well as more or less adequately recorded.[39]

Conversely, where the interviewer at a high status college was quite plainly inadequate, a Gestaltist fusing in the opposite direction occurred; that is, a poor interviewer tended to lower the questionnaire to her level—and to force the respondent, if he wanted to get his views across, to come down to that level also. To be sure, not all respondents lumped interviewer and questionnaire together in this way; some, deeply involved in the topic and alert to the questionnaire's aims, sought to educate the interviewer to the point where she would be within range of his communication.[40] In West

---

same time they often took academic freedom very seriously (and, as we have just seen, survey methodology and its implications) the study was very apt to become a topic for discussion and consensual perception of its aims and emissary. Whether this in fact occurred depended, of course, on many things: the closeness of departmental and college-wide ties, the available alternatives for talk or indignation, the freshness of incidents affecting academic freedom, and the division of opinion concerning them. At several of the schools with close-knit faculties a kind of reinforcement effect operated to heighten criticism of the survey—in some cases a delayed reaction, analogous to l'esprit d'escalier, where people "remembered" greater annoyance with the survey than they had felt at the time.

39. In general, the greater the intellectual and social range of the interviewer, the greater was her ability to give life to the questionnaire in a variety of academic settings. Personality factors are of course relevant here, as well as status and education. Cf. a forthcoming paper, "Age and Authority in the Interview," by June Sachar and David Riesman, where evidence is presented that more rigid interviewers—age being equal—secured less frank answers from teen-age girls than more flexible ones, although beyond a certain age-gap personality ceased to count. As indicated above, we have no comparable data on the effect of great disparities of age in the Teacher Apprehension Study, particularly since a number of the older interviewers were also those of lesser education who struck even their younger respondents as "mechanical" rather than "motherly."

40. One such respondent, observing his interviewer's hapless efforts to

Africa, "I not hear you" is Pidgin English for "I do not understand you," and some interviewers, asked for a definition of terms, could think of nothing else than rereading the question, as if the respondent hadn't heard the first time.[41] College professors at leading institutions do not expect to have to contend with Pidgin in the representative of a foundation, and three of the interviewers whom we saw (none of whom had gone further than high school) were at a "Pidgin" level in their lack of grasp of the academic vocabulary.

The fog through which these interviewers worked is indicated by the comment of an infuriated professor at an avant-garde college who wrote:

Why couldn't you have sent a trained interviewer . . . ? This interviewer was wholly unfamiliar—the woman kept looking at her instruction sheets. At one point I said, "I'm contradicting myself," and she said, "I don't know"—and she really didn't know. . . . The interviewer tried hard to take things down, but I was not always sure she was taking down what I said—she gave me back what she'd put down and it wasn't at all what I'd said.

In fact, a great many interviewers made it a practice to read back certain answers to see whether they had gotten a correct paraphrase of the faculty member's meaning. The less competent ones—those less familiar with academic phraseology—did this primarily to reassure themselves, although as in the instance just given they may have succeeded only in unsettling their respondents.[42]

At avant-garde colleges, as already indicated, such interviewers, by implicitly defining the survey as crude and gauche, infuriated or irritated respondents, though differentially so; when they also worked, as they often did, at lower-level colleges, they were gen-

---

cope with the questionnaire, went over it with her for several hours, item by item; another commented to us that, with his naïve interlocutor, he was required "to do more explaining than as if talking to someone who knew more about it."

41. There were, of course, instances where to reread the question was more tactful than once more to remind the respondent that he was to use his own definitions, but the interviewers I am discussing here were anything but subtle.

42. The more competent ones, sensing a respondent's unstated uneasiness, usually anticipated him. However the initiative began, it was in general reassuring to both sides. We deal here, not only with the tact and conscientiousness of the interviewers, but with that of their interviewees, many of whom proved able repeatedly to correct an interviewer without coming to feel that they were taking unwarranted time or being "academic" in the pejorative sense, that is, mere quibblers and perfectionists.

erally considered entirely adequate. But our major effort here must be, not to examine the intriguing story of the survey's public relations, but to see what was actually lost in the way of data through the interviewer's lapses. This can best be illustrated by a case study which must stand for a number of similar ones which could be presented.

The case is that of a leading coeducational college, a pioneer in educational theory, which is located in a relatively small and decidedly bigoted community served by a reactionary press—a press which made much of a recent Congressional committee visit where several faculty members were questioned concerning alleged Communist affiliations. The interviewer who, by the luck of the draw, was sent there was a kindly woman in her sixties, of (at most) some teachers college training, lower-middle-class in mode of life, and resident (as a number of her respondents discovered) in a nearby town known for its conservatism. As one declared:

When I took a stand for freedom of expression, even for a Communist, she was taken aback. . . . I was a little surprised they would have someone from [Blanksville]. I wasn't conscious of this making a difference, but it might have, subconsciously.

At this college, the liberal faculty are, if somewhat apprehensive, also defiant, and no one indicated that he had explicitly tailored his replies to what he thought the local community could absorb.

But the intellectual limitations of the interviewer (probably not unrelated to her political naïveté) played a larger part in curtailing communication. One respondent spoke for a number in saying:

. . . a nice little housewife. . . . If she is representative of your interviewers . . . I would place little credence in your results. . . . She was a nice little woman and tried hard to avoid being exasperated with objections she probably didn't quite understand.

Another observed:

Her pace gave the impression that she did not need any details.

And yet another respondent stated that he gave in to her insistence that he answer certain questions yes or no, though in fact he had no position on them.

Although this college is one where sociology is not on the defensive and where, since the democratic ethos is strong, there was little resentment at the lower-middle-class style of the interviewer, there was still frustration at her lack of understanding. One respondent wrote that she

. . . did not seem to be either interested in the subject matter or in me as a person. She didn't impress me as being "too bright." . . . She knew nothing about social science.

And another indicated the consequence for him of these limitations:

After a while instead of trying to get my meaning across, I became interested in ending it. . . . I'd have spent more time had the interviewer been a social science person. Such a person would have eliminated some but not all of my objections to the questionnaire. On my own subjective position, the record was ample but not understanding . . . nor did the unique aspects of the college get down. . . .[43]

It is from this college that we have a tape-recording of an interview to compare with the hand-written questionnaire (as well as interviews with both the interviewer and the respondent concerning this encounter). In this case, the respondent was extremely patient; he spoke very slowly and plainly and continued to the very end to go into elaborate detail both in describing attitudes and incidents and in qualifying and explaining his answers. Some qualifications the respondent made to explain answers, or apparent contradictions among them, were unrecorded, and in one or two places the interviewer was confused (as where the respondent, discussing controversies over readings he assigned, compared problems in reading Marx to those in reading Ogburn, and she has it: "Marx and this conservative person like Ogburn and he's well received."[44] Nevertheless I must emphasize that on the precoded

43. He added, however, a countervailing observation: "But her professional attitude had its advantages. The results of the survey didn't concern her. When I'd get emotional, she'd be uninvolved."

44. My colleague, Mark Benney, had an interviewer who was far superior to the one whose handiwork we have just been examining, and comparing his tape recording with his interview turned up few significant distortions (these two instances are the only tape-recordings of which we have knowledge; one

questions the interviewer invariably got "the answer." Moreover, while as in any such case a tape-recording contains a great deal more wordage than an interview recorded in long-hand, it is possible from the written interview to reconstruct in large measure the salient issues of the original encounter (the interviewer used underlining to indicate respondent's emphases). Finally, if one reads the interviewer's handiwork in the order in which it was done, one can see that she improved with experience (one respondent observed that her task had been "very hard" for her but that she had been "educated" by it) and, taking all her work together, a good deal can be discovered concerning the college in question, despite the relative paucity of side-comment and the foreshortening of qualifications.[45]

In sum, I conclude that this interviewer was too intellectually alien and too preoccupied to give most of her respondents at this college the feeling that they were being understood; some felt, perhaps too hastily, that they would be grossly misrepresented. Had the study directors been in search of subtleties and shadings in individual protocols, they would, I believe, have lost things of value both through the interviewer's actual limitations and the respondents' perceptions of these. But in terms of the analytic procedures employed in this study, the most that I can say is that fear of the interviewer's surmised conservatism may have slightly tilted responses in the direction of safety. But I cannot be sure of this—I cannot, for instance, state that the guardedness which runs through the tape-recording is a tribute to the interviewer rather than to the "difficult years."

---

respondent wrote out his answers long-hand). However, when he referred to *Dissent* as run by a group of "nostalgic Marxists," his protocol had it as "nostalgic Communists"—a reflection, perhaps, of the interviewer's definition of the survey's aims as well as of the overwhelming confusion in the country at large to which many rightist publicists have contributed.

45. A number of respondents complained that pressures unique to their situation had not been specifically investigated in the survey—the influential role of students and of the press, for instance, in shaping the college's climate, or the venom of the local community toward inter-racial activities (and rumors of them among the undergraduates). A superior interviewer often did evoke considerable material on such themes, even though they were only peripherally asked about. (Actually, the interviewer disapproved of the college less than did her family and friends in Blanksville—a phenomenon generally true among even the least emancipated interviewers whose work helps them become more "permissive" and cosmopolitan.)

Indeed, there is some slight evidence, paradoxical and difficult to interpret, that in general the more conservative interviewers tended to get just slightly fewer conservative replies.[46] Let me venture a tentative explanation. If we look first at the reception of the liberal interviewer—the type we shall later describe as the "bluestocking"—at the liberal college, we find some of her respondents resenting her occasional effort to sympathize with them as victims of McCarthyism and the cold war—when in fact they might be consultants to the C.I.A. or complacent "new conservatives."[47] Skepticism of the Fund for the Republic, of surveys, and of the overeager interviewer might lead to a tendency to minimize the dangers one felt concerning one's own position or that of one's colleagues.[48]

The converse case is, I think, somewhat more difficult to understand. The unexcitable and apparently uninvolved interviewer may, where apprehension is at issue, get a somewhat franker response. Moreover, her very uninvolvement may help remind the professor at a liberal school that not everybody is a liberal. At most leading colleges, however, the very freedom respondents felt made them relatively unconcerned with clues that might indicate the interviewer's own outlook; apparently, they were not curious as to where the interviewer was from, or what her own political position was. At one college, where the interviewer's husband was the security officer at a defense plant,[49] as she amiably told any inquirer, only two out of her nine respondents apparently discovered the fact (judging by our interviews there and from mail returns). One—a Jew and a liberal in an area dominated by conservative Irish Catholics—told us he was slightly guarded as a

---

46. A good many studies (notably, those of Herbert Hyman and his co-workers) have shown that the political attitudes of trained interviewers influence respondents' answers rather less than the interviewers' own expectations as to how people "like" the respondent will in fact answer.

47. One such man told us that his interviewer had remarked to him: "How can you sit there and tell me you've full academic freedom here, when J. Edgar Hoover is on your Board of Trustees!" This interviewer was new to the field; others did not overtly tip their hand, and yet by their manner got something similar across.

48. At the same time, the heady dialectic created by this tension with the interviewer frequently resulted in much fuller interviews.

49. In general, the top agencies are alert to prevent such interviewers from handling surveys dealing with political opinions.

result, while the other—a Catholic and a liberal—said it didn't bother him.[50]

Summing up impressions on this potential source of bias and inhibition, I conclude that in most cases among the avant-garde, and well down through the middle range of academia, the respondent got involved eventually in his own dialectical processes, and that the interviewer had to be pretty obtrusive in her alienness to remind him that she was quite outside the ends of his political spectrum. Indeed, when liberal professors ventured a guess as to their interviewer's political orientation, they frequently perceived her as closer to their own than, in our own interview with her, we found her to be: far from being hypochondriacal about the interviewer, they gave her the benefit of the doubt.[51] Certainly at avant-garde colleges, most respondents were aware of the powerful convention of confidentiality in survey work, which puts the interviewer almost in the ethical position of a therapist or physician (it was usually at the lower levels of academia that respondents would stop themselves and suddenly ask the interviewer: "You're not going to report this to the authorities, are you?"). The interviewers were of course trained to neutrality— to acceptance of what the respondent said (on this or any other survey); indeed, as suggested above, the poorer interviewers were so characteristically overwhelmed by the sheer mechanics of the questionnaire and of recording an unfamiliar vocabulary that they had little freedom to emerge from their role as scribes. Moreover, they were for the most part women, accustomed to listening gra-

---

50. At one Protestant denominational college, a Polish Catholic interviewer wore a cross around her neck (as she said to us) without—so far as our information goes—arousing any misgivings or animadversions.

51. A small-group experiment by Scodel and Mussen sheds light on such processes. They brought together two students, strangers to each other, one high on "authoritarianism" and one low, and had them chat about movies, radio, and TV for twenty minutes; then they asked each how they thought their conversational partner would respond to the F-scale questions. Characteristically, the "high" assumed that the "low" must have opinions like his own. In contrast, the "low," more sensitive to differences, believed his "high" interlocutor to be more authoritarian than himself—but underestimated the degree of difference. It would seem as if the politeness of both parties masked the extent of their differences even from persons aware that not all people shared their "soft" or "tender-minded" outlook. See Alvin Scodel and Paul Mussen, "Social Perceptions of Authoritarians and Nonauthoritarians," *Journal of Abnormal and Social Psychology*, Vol. 48, 1953, pp. 181-84.

ciously while men hold forth on political questions—a trained neutrality of sex as well as of occupational role.[52] Furthermore, they came bearing a questionnaire on behalf of the Fund for the Republic and Paul F. Lazarsfeld—presumptively not written by reactionaries (to the annoyance of the latter, as we have seen).

One could argue, and I would be inclined to do so, that the survey lost more in volume if not in accuracy of data at the top quality colleges through the interviewer's trained neutrality than through her being seen as a "political animal" in her own right. At least with avant-garde professors, whose habit or duty it is to "think otherwise," bias seldom resulted from desire to please the interviewer, but constricted response may often have been due to resentment at a lack of empathy and the consequent routinization of the encounter.[53] Indeed, a respondent looking for excuses to avoid in the interview unpleasant confrontations with past or present views or behavior—or afraid of discovering that his complacency about the state of academic freedom was not wholly warranted—might use the inadequacies of the survey or the interviewer as a convenient out. How could he be expected to be reflective and self-critical in the face of so awkward or insipid an audience?

In my judgment, instances of such a reaction were infrequent even in the leading colleges. For one thing, most of the interviewers who worked there were much better educated than the one whose encounters have been detailed above. For another thing, by no means all professors in avant-garde schools have complicated or shifting views on academic freedom. When the interviewing was reasonably agile, most respondents even in such schools declared they had managed to get their story across, whatever constraints they had experienced en route. Nevertheless, while throughout academia there are men who feel themselves misunderstood by the laity,

---

52. There is a related factor which occurs in ordinary social interaction, namely that non-intimates tend to mute their differences—at least in this country, where the chairman's "Well, we're all in agreement, then," is standard closure for meetings.

53. Some sophisticated respondents objected that the survey started off "like a *Nation* editorial"; for them, the questionnaire did not come alive until the concrete queries of question no. 6, e.g., whether the respondent had ever told an anecdote to indicate that he was not an extremist of left or right. We cannot here explore the problem of the shifting bite of the questions for different levels of professorial expertise and experience.

and alternately fear and resent this, it is in the avant-garde that
sensitivity to such misunderstanding has the lowest threshold,
and it is from such men that we have the sharpest criticisms of
the wooden or platitudinous quality of the interview. At this level,
men have enough freedom to expect still more; enough appreciation from students, trustees, and other laymen to expect it from
an interviewer; enough individuation from their administrators
to expect it also from a study director. Elsewhere in academia, men
of similar objective outlook in terms of political position expect
less, hence complain less.

But I have no evidence, given the aims and the analytic mode of
this study, that there is much correlation between the frustration
respondents in the avant-garde often felt and the danger that they
have been misclassified elsewhere in this volume.

The "Fit" of the Survey in the Upper-Middle Ranks.

1. *Prescription for trouble:* In the course of surveying the avant-
garde experience with the survey, we have covered a number of the
reactions found in smaller proportion elsewhere in academia.
Yet, as has just been indicated, the whole climate of response
to the survey alters, even among men of national reputation,
as soon as one leaves the avant-garde, for one moves in the
upper-middle institutions into the group of universities where
pressures in the spring of 1955 were often quite intense and where,
since what might be called subsistence issues of freedom were at
stake, the luxury items that interested many at high status private
colleges played a smaller role.

We have defined as "upper-middle" in our mail-questionnaire
sample of colleges fourteen institutions, including some major state
universities, several academically distinguished urban "street-car"
universities, and some small private colleges which are not quite
avant-garde. The publicly-controlled universities which loom largest
in this category felt considerably less free (as more fully documented elsewhere in this volume) than did those Ivy League and
comparable private institutions whose trustees, as responsible conservatives of high social class, were not going to be pushed around
by demagogues and "public opinion." To be sure, a handful of
state university faculties, backed by a strong administration, had
managed to keep regents and state legislators under control—a

balancing act that depends on the distribution of power and prestige in the state, the role of the university's alumni in state politics, the university's own patronage powers, and so on. But outside this charmed circle, state and municipal university faculties felt themselves at the time of the survey—if they had any temptations toward liberalism or even political concern—presently or potentially threatened, or so recently and narrowly escaped from political coercion as to feel shaky still.

Thus, even when they criticized details of the questionnaire, their concentration on the relevance for them of the study's aims outweighed their critical eye on its means. Since they felt the questionnaire was addressed directly to their situation, they welcomed the interviewers, did not begrudge the time, or look too closely at the interviewers' limitations. Correspondingly, the interviewers, made to feel welcome, were less likely to be flustered even by the many critical objections they did meet, so that a "virtuous circle" helped interactions to go smoothly. At such colleges we find reactions of approval of the following sort:

I sympathized with the aims of the study and tried to give as meaningful and detailed replies as possible. . . . I wanted to cooperate.

Or, less completely affirmative:

I answered the questions to the best of my ability, was interested in the project and insofar as a questionnaire of that type is effective, the job was a good one.

At one such school, the interviewer reported that her sessions averaged two and one-half hours, and commented:

I believe that every respondent was perfectly honest and frank. The only time they seemed to hold back is when they did not understand the question fully or could not answer it the way it was worded. I didn't get the feeling they were hedging—I felt they just wanted so badly to be absolutely right in their answers. . . . I'm sure they were satisfied as to the intent of the survey and did their very best.

To be sure, as we would expect, given the lack of clear boundaries between our different quality-levels of institution, we find in the upper-middle universities many of the same objections and misgivings about the survey we have already noted for the avant-

garde:[54] attacks on the survey's "datedness," its claimed tenden-
tiousness or flat contemporaneity (as against a study in historical
perspective), or its lack of focus on unique aspects of the particular
institution; likewise, the many activists here as elsewhere were
pessimistic about any practical good emerging from gathering more
data about what was already all too well known. And, of course,
individual questions again met objections.[55] (It isn't until one
gets into the lowest range of academia that many respondents,
unable to imagine doing such a survey themselves, and unlikely
to have given any single topic outside their own field that much
attention, repeatedly complimented the interviewer for the survey's "remarkable thoroughness" or "unusual completeness," and
were as astonished by the "going over" to which they had been subjected as an ill farmer would be who, after experiencing nothing
more searching than his general practitioner's stethoscope, got a
complete work-up at a major teaching hospital.)

Our mail questionnaire provides some interesting evidence to
support these generalizations. Although the interviewers who went
to the "upper-middle" institutions were of about the same order
of competence as those who went to avant-garde colleges, when
we compare 106 respondents at private colleges with 106 at
publicly-controlled ones, we find that eight of the former, as against
one of the latter, believed their interviewer did not get down an
on-the-whole fair picture of their attitudes; similarly, 71 per cent
of the respondents at private schools felt the questionnaire had been
adequate over-all, as compared with 81 per cent at public insti-

---

54. Conversely, some of the same approbatory statements can also be
found, though less frequently, in the avant-garde. For instance, at the college
which, after extended discussion, sent Robert Hutchins a letter of protest,
one respondent declared: "I believe in the purposes of the study. If some
people are going to get information, others are going to have to give it."

55. As implied above, the questions which often met resistance in the
avant-garde as irrelevant or "iffy" were in many cases just what the doctor
ordered in the upper-middle ranks. This was true, for instance, of the questions concerning presidential bans on student-sponsored meetings, where
avant-gardists could seldom conceive of a quarrel with their own protective
administrations on the issue. Likewise, the first several questions, as one
interviewer at a big state university declared, "give the respondent a chance
to launch on his freedom of speech which heretofore he might have been
keeping to himself." But, by the same token, individual questions met detailed scrutiny by men earnest to see that they were getting their qualifications
across—a tribute to the salience of the themes for them.

tutions.[56] Moreover, while at none of the ten avant-garde schools in our mail questionnaire survey did every respondent give overall approval to the questionnaire, this was the case at six out of fourteen in the upper-middle category.

2. *Shadow of a doubt:* If the questionnaire met a better reception at the upper-middle institutions, due to the greater apprehensiveness of precisely the more critically-minded respondents, it is also true that this apprehensiveness made the issue of the confidentiality of the survey and the political trustworthiness of the interviewer of greater relevance.[57] At these institutions, interviewers were more frequently asked for their credentials, and at one state institution on the West Coast the interviewer reported:

Many respondents were concerned that the interviewer not be a local person and were complimentary to the survey in their choice of an outsider. I was asked in many different ways where I lived by nearly every respondent before we got into the interview.

(This was an interviewer of undoubted competence and liberal sympathies who at an avant-garde college even in a hostile community would not have been cross-examined this way save perhaps by a very small minority.) Accordingly, our respondents at upper-middle institutions referred to the problem of the trustworthiness of the interviewer in terms that we do not find employed at the avant-garde schools. Thus, one described his interviewer: "Neat, spoke well. Didn't entirely trust her, though." And another: "It is here [with regard to questions about personal experiences with problems of academic freedom] that one has to size up his interviewer for trustworthiness" (the respondent said he did trust her). Still another wrote concerning the questionnaire itself:

But I thought the question *re* respondent's own possible affiliation with so-called subversive movements was unwarranted—either exposing the individual if he were such a member and said so, or inviting him to falsify. It would be desirable from a scientific point of view to have such information, to be sure—but practically, under existing circumstances, you are not likely to secure reliable information. (Note to all legally-constituted agencies: I am not, and never have been!) But I do resent all the abuses of persons and abridgments of civil liberties!

56. There is not space here to examine the statistical justification for these comparisons: this is dealt with in an unpublished paper by Elizabeth Drake.

57. Likewise, a slightly higher percentage of unsigned mail returns came from the upper-middle institutions (the same is true at the teachers colleges which, in our "sample," are all state-controlled).

One leading state university, which stands at the border between avant-garde and upper-middle in our categories, provides an interesting example of the handling of this problem of trust. The interviewer was a somewhat parochial Old-Guard Republican of no more than high-school education; the resident of a medium-sized town in a neighboring state, she spent several weeks doing nearly forty interviews at the university. A large number of her respondents were critical of the survey; 30 per cent of those who returned mail questionnaires thought the survey failed to elicit, and she to record, a fair picture of their attitudes; many would have preferred an interviewer of more education, or a social scientist. Even so, her respondents gave her credit for more education and more sympathy with them than Mark Benney and I, who interviewed her in her home, believe she possesses.[58] This misperception, analogous to the same sort considered earlier, seemed to us to rest on these considerations: the eagerness of the respondents to talk about problems of academic freedom; the democratic ethos of the university, which would lead to minimizing demands for elite treatment; and the unusual degree of defiant freedom traditionally maintained by a faculty which would not want to feel itself overanxious about the interviewer. In this trust they were in fact correct, for the interviewers' code of neutrality and confidentiality is stronger than political party lines, and in this instance the interviewer, whatever her private head-shakings, gave no visible sign of disapproval and wrote everything down with animated good will.

We can contrast with this set of encounters the experience of the survey at a college we locate at the border between upper- and lower-middle. This is an old coeducational college in the Midwest controlled by a liberal Protestant denomination; it has quite good academic standing and some reputation for intellectual liveliness, but nowhere near the distinction or the atmosphere of freedom of the university discussed just above. The interviewer

---

58. One respondent who saw her exactly as we did, on the basis of a much briefer encounter, is an elderly professor of archaeology. He is relatively isolated from his colleagues and uninvolved in the storms over academic freedom that sweep many of them; a withdrawn and skeptical person, not many come to his door, and he was perhaps as interested in the interviewer as in the topic, and as detached. (Where it has seemed necessary to protect the identity of schools or of individual respondents, I have altered the data in inessentials.)

who worked there is the liberal wife of a liberal physician in a nearby city; she is college-educated and emancipated, with ample civic experience but new and just a bit shy as an interviewer. Thirteen per cent of her respondents doubted whether she got down a fair picture of their attitudes. One of her respondents made a comment concerning her which tells us a good deal about the climate at the college:

The only strong guard which acted in the background of my responses was the question of just how much understanding a non-intellectually dedicated person has. I might have been freer in my replies if I thought the interviewer understood the intellectual issues of the social scientist in society with some intimacy. . . . She was not "at home" with the whole material. This added to the "casualness" of the interview for me and might have meant freer "responsiveness" on my part. (But) I was still guarded in my replies. . . . I held back on some details for reasons of personal security—an evidence of the climate of intimidation which the study was attempting to assess.

The interviewer's shyness and lack of deftness seem to have been interpreted by this apprehensive respondent as a lack of at-homeness with the material itself—far from the case, for the dedication of the interviewer and her husband to civil liberties and academic freedom had actually cost them friends and patients.[59]

---

59. If we look further among our materials from this college, we can more readily understand the respondent's apparent misjudgment. For one thing, the local press is dominated by a reactionary industrialist (widely known for his anti-union views) who controls the largest plant in the area—a situation quite different from that of the freer state universities which are themselves often "the largest plant in the area." The controlling church body is the only "countervailing power" available to the college, but use of it depends on keeping a certain air of devoutness and traditions which some of the more secular and sophisticated faculty regard as restraints; that is, they tread warily in some fields as the price of freedom in others. In the second place, the faculty is far from being homogeneously liberal. Another respondent writes in our mail questionnaire as follows:

I am afraid that my experiences are of such a nature that I could not feel that my own academic freedom had ever been threatened. Furthermore, my own patriotism is so great that I have never been able to understand why any colleague would feel that a loyalty oath is in any way an interference with his right to teach as he pleases in his own classroom. I tried to be a good respondent but perhaps because of my personal feeling that this was an area of over-emotionalism I could not get excited.

In this connection, one respondent observed that a state-controlled engineering college in the same community had many reactionary men on its staff who

I do not want to leave the impression that all faculty members in the middle range of academic institutions were concerned with issues of freedom—far from it. There is not only the almost invariable complement of political conservatives (at one college to which I have just adverted, one man asked the interviewer to write down: "This is the very type of a survey that puts its blessing on the Pseudo-Liberals and is blank towards the Pseudo-Conservatives"), but also a number of men who are politically neutral or indifferent. Often it was the older men who had resigned themselves to their situation—and who made the less politically alert interviewers happy by going snappily and crisply through the questions—while younger men, perhaps those who had some hope of moving, had more to say and fewer ready-made formulae for saying it.

Still, the latter mostly managed to have their say. Men in big state institutions, when they possess "the liberal imagination," usually have gained experience in trying to communicate it; certainly they were on the whole, in comparison with men in the avant-garde, less impatient with the interviewers and more ready to try to help them rise to the level of the questions they were asking.[60] By the same token, they were less impatient with the questionnaire itself, insofar as they grasped its aims over and beyond the interviewers' inflections.

The Lower-Middle Ranks.

1. *A note on heterogeneity:* My categories are imposed on the

---

were unsympathetic to the liberalism of his own college. A final quotation is again indicative of the way in which apprehensiveness at this college may have affected some respondents' reaction to the survey:

> I'm sure my answers gave the impression that I'd be far more timid than I actually would. I should have changed my answers to make them stronger—e.g., "What would I do if there were a Communist on the campus?"—I should have asked, "Who the hell says he's a Communist!" etc.

60. No doubt, the enormous size of many of these state universities operated to prevent the development of an unfavorable faculty view of the survey, such as occurred at some of the leading but smaller private institutions. Talk about the survey in the state universities tended, so far as I could judge, to follow departmental lines, and seldom to cross them. And, as we would expect, humanistic hostility to surveys as such, on the part of the Humanities, although not absent among historians and political scientists in the Midwest and Far West, was usually less vehement than in the East (I know too little about the South to make comparisons).

data: they do not exist in nature, and they are crude. They may, I fear, encourage some readers, especially from the avant-garde, to underestimate the differences within the ranks "below" him—just as the rich tend to see the poor as more alike than they are (and vice versa). This warning requires emphasis because it is about as hard to draw a line in the world of academia between "upper-middle" and "lower-middle" as it is in the larger social world, where many social sets and status pyramids make unidimensional ranking manageable only in company towns and in parts of the South. Thus, while I have put several eminent institutions which their faculty sardonically term "street-car" or "subway" universities in the upper-middle range, most such schools in the sample are ranked low in my data, as in the ratings used elsewhere in this volume, because of small endowment, low tuition, limited library facilities, etc. Yet many of these institutions, like a large part of the rest of the academic procession, are very much on the move, as are the young men, often finishing graduate work at nearby avant-garde schools, who fill the lower instructional posts and bring the preoccupations but not the comforts of their training institutions with them.

We include at this level, also, the more impoverished state universities, including a number in the South, and some of the land grant schools in which social science, other than agricultural economics and perhaps rural sociology, is very much an adjunct (at one such school, the interviewer was struck by the fact that the social science departments were located in dingy surroundings —in one case in the basement of a girls' dorm).[61] We put in the same category the better denominational colleges, both Protestant and Catholic, although these differ widely according to order or denomination as well as region and clientele and tradition. There are several teachers colleges which we rank as lower-middle (we classify the others in the rear guard); I should add that no first-rate teachers college, such as Teachers College at Columbia, was included in our limited follow-up.

Here one begins to find, with some exceptions among urban and

---

61. At another such institution the dean, on whom the interviewer had called to make arrangements to proceed, remarked: "When you are interviewing some of these social science teachers ask them if they ever did a day's work in their lives."

Protestant-controlled colleges, not only that liberals are definitely in the minority, but that people who care one way or the other about academic freedom are in the minority. No president or chancellor of an avant-garde or upper-middle institution would dream— or would only dream—of saying that academic freedom was not a principal concern of his. But in the lower-middle ranks one does come upon institutions where the norm contains no commitment, either professorial or administrative, to academic freedom.

At this level, interviews begin to be short, sometimes lightly taken, with very few qualifications and side-comments. Respondents, far from quarreling with the yes-no or other forms of forced-choice questions, appear grateful for the saving of thought and time they allow, and make trouble for the interviewer only when (as happened, by a clerical error, with one question) there is no precoded category for "no change" or "not applicable here." Likewise, at this level our mail returns are relatively barren of side-comments. Interviewers reported that occasional professors welcomed a chance to reflect on topics they had obviously not discussed with each other.

Nevertheless, we have not classified as "lower-middle" any institutions which are monolithically uninterested in academic freedom, or, like many rear-guard colleges, convinced they have all they need. The expansion of academia, and especially of the social sciences (the more secular of which are just making their way into some denominational liberal arts colleges), have brought to these colleges, as have refugees from totalitarianism in Europe,[62] men of very different temper from the majority who teach there; this minority included men who were grateful for the questionnaire as the reminder of another world, from which they had come and to which they might some day return—or to the model of which their whole institution might hopefully assimilate itself.

Such heterogeneity is striking in some of the colleges described

---

62. At this level one finds an occasional refugee from a Soviet satellite or Communist China who either refuses to be interviewed or balks at certain questions "because I'm not a citizen" or "because I'll have trouble with my visa," etc. Most of the pre-World War II refugees from Hitler were uninhibited respondents—with possibly a few exceptions in denominational colleges; however, several to whom we talked violently objected to the survey and digressed from its forms because they regarded it as part of America's "Brave New World" they detested.

in this volume as "traditional," for instance, in those denominational schools where some of the faculty are oriented to professional and academic concerns while others see their constituency in terms of the ecclesiastical world and its lay adjuncts. One result is that, at this level, the survey met with more frequent objection to its presumed political aims than to its methodology. Even quite inadequate interviewers, in our own evaluation of them, met with little criticism.

2. *Problems of trust and politeness:* Indeed, at some of the least cosmopolitan institutions, interviewers had a red carpet reception. Professors took them to tea, lunch, or dinner. Sociologists, isolated from professional contact, discussed methodology with them. Many, too sophisticated to suppose they had been "personally" chosen as respondents, nevertheless enjoyed the opportunity for conversation-at-a-distance with Professor Lazarsfeld. Whereas in the upper ranks of academic life men have plenty of chance for intellectual games and have difficulty setting aside a couple of hours for an interview (or at least maintain a self-image of this sort), in the lower two ranks men are not constantly rushing off to Washington or London, and were more apt to appreciate what one respondent called "a sort of mirror, which I've needed."

In discussing problems of intimidation and evasion, I referred to the problem of privacy at the lower levels of academia—a problem mostly overcome by interviewers and respondents together (as in one case where a jittery administration of a city college controlled by the school board refused its facilities and the interviewer used her own car as a work-room). Far more troublesome was the fear of some respondents, not that the interview be overheard, but that their answers somehow get back to their administration, their conservative colleagues, or the locally powerful reactionaries. Anonymity, as already stated, was seldom at issue in leading institutions, even though respondents were often aware that they could be identified by virtue of their special courses, their position and honors, or in similar ways; even when, in our talks with respondents, some expressed concern lest the records fall into the hands of a Congressional committee, they were shamefaced about having this nightmare.

But the man of deviant outlook in many lower-middle institutions has often long since lost even the appearance of being san-

guine about free expression of his views. Many asked in the midst
of the interview what had been assured them at the beginning,
namely whether this was really confidential. We asked respondents
through our mail questionnaire whether they thought any harm
might befall them if their questionnaires should fall into the hands
of the administration of their school; most at leading institutions
thought it would have "no effect one way or the other," but in the
lower ranks a small minority (under 10 per cent) thought it might
have a harmful effect or didn't know. Occasionally, talking with
respondents from such schools, I had the feeling that they could
hardly believe that their despotic administration—Big Brother
style—would not somehow hear of any complaint they made, no
matter how many assurances the interviewer gave them that they
were just a number to her. Yet the over-all trustingness of Americans was demonstrated by the fact that they did not suspect the
interviewers themselves, but, in a phrase the latter often used,
"unburdened themselves" to the stranger.[63]

Let me illustrate these matters by quoting two interviewers who
worked at a Southwestern state university. One declared:

. . . One or two asked how sure I was that the comments would be kept
confidential. I told them that all I could say was that we were told that
the questionnaires would be held in strict confidence. They seemed to
take my word for it and didn't appear to be anything but frank. . . .
The ones that did ask were some of those who had the most comments
to make. . . .

The other interviewer said:

. . . many of the answers would have been more complete if they hadn't
been so darned polite. . . . The Regents seem to be phantoms who lurk
in the background. . . .

Politeness, indeed, becomes almost as much of a barrier as
fear as one moves down the academic procession. In the upper
ranks, as we saw, criticism is the norm, taken for granted, and few
feel they need protect their college's repute—this being high to

63. One interviewer at a state-controlled engineering school observed that
her respondents "would get in a position so they could see what I wrote (if
they had to do it upside down they could and did!)"—though some appeared
only to worry lest she not write down all their honors.

begin with—and identifications being in any case with worlds which transcend or overlap those of the collegiate parish. In the lower ranks, interviewers got used to hearing respondents say "have you stopped beating your wife?" as a criticism of questions which sought to pierce the mask of politeness—or which were regarded as politically loaded. To avoid passing judgment on their institution, while remaining "frank," they would refuse to repeat "gossip," "hearsay," or "rumor," unless it was already in the public domain through newspaper or committee report. They were more identified with their school than with a field or profession, although the public-relations orientation at institutions in the lower-middle range was seldom as strong as in rear-guard schools.[64]

We can grasp these matters better if we fully appreciate the fact that, at each academic level, the opinions that would be considered rude or impolite at one end of the continuum, and conventional or flaccid at the other, depend on local as well as nationwide reference groups. Views which, in the avant-garde, would mark a man as safe and sound, even stuffy, may ostracize him and threaten his job even in some of the colleges we classify as lower-middle, let alone in the rear guard.

The experience of the survey at a Midwestern teachers college

---

64. What appeared as politeness to the interviewer is not, I believe, the whole story, for professors who believed themselves stuck at a particular school often tended, for obvious reasons, to see it less bleakly than it might appear from elsewhere. It is interesting to see what occurred when on our mail questionnaire we asked respondents to rank their institution in the following categories:

It is among the top ten per cent of colleges in the country	210
It ranks just below the top ten per cent in the country	75
While a middling college in general, it's among the best of its own specialized kind	60
It's a run-of-the-mill kind of place	38
It's a pretty lowly kind of place	3
Other	14

We see that over half (53 per cent) located their school in the top 10 per cent (as compared with 42 per cent who said of their own department that "there are few better in the country" and 54 per cent that "there are many better, but many worse")—a considerably larger proportion than those we ourselves would generously put in the avant-garde, while hardly any of the respondents at colleges we would classify as rear guard would themselves have so categorized their school. Thus, when in the interview they described working conditions at their school as fair or good, or saw relations with colleagues in a rosy light, they were not necessarily sweeping the dust under the rug in the visitors' presence, for their own egos had become involved in creating a fairly wide zone of ignorance or equivocation which partly enveloped them also.

(whose superior tradition of learning led us to classify it with the lower-middle group despite its poverty) may illustrate these matters. The interviewer who worked there is the scrupulous and intelligent wife of a school superintendent in the nearest large city; to her, the liberals on the faculty felt free to expose views at odds with those of some colleagues and of the strongly isolationist rural area in which the school is located. She was described as a fine interviewer by four of the six respondents who returned mail questionnaires (there were nine interviews in all); one described her as "a very personable, *ethical* lady, some fifty years old; college training background" (italics mine); with these respondents, though they declared that they criticized the questionnaire to the interviewer and felt somewhat foreclosed by it from expressing their full meanings, the survey as a whole came off well. However, an angry rightist—one of the few at this level who bothered to return a mail questionnaire—expressed a very different judgment. Volunteering that he has had "25 years of college teaching experience," he wrote that the survey was "full of loaded questions" which raised "*unethical* semantic problems" (my italics); the time references, too, were "loaded," apparently because a comparison was made with the pre-McCarthy era. Observing that some questions were designed to trap or trick him, he added: "I'm used to a lot of silly and even loaded questionnaires." But he is one of the very few respondents to our mail questionnaire who thought that some of the survey's questions were intrusive or impertinent: "what I thought of the college administration, fellow teachers, etc." Since he is a reactionary among those he regards as liberals, what he thought can readily be imagined, and he appears to project onto the survey some of his own repressed aggression, for he is asked what he thinks of his colleagues and administration only in certain particulars and not as an over-all evaluation. Indeed, the constellation of his replies reminds me of the discussion in *The Authoritarian Personality* of the pseudo-conservative who, polite on the surface, seethes with resentment, cynicism, and suspicion.

This constellation raises a question: if the politeness of well-meaning respondents at lower-level colleges led them at times to refrain from criticism or from citing incidents they could dismiss as rumor or as trivialities, did the very different politeness of this irritable type of person also soften his replies? On the whole, it is my impression that this type did not hold back—certainly not in the infrequent cases where they returned mail questionnaires or talked with us in person. Their complex defenses must have found some way of reconciling—perhaps by projection of aggression onto the Fund for the Republic and the survey to start with —a nominal belief in correctness and politeness and keeping one's distance with often ferocious attacks on colleagues or liberals in general.

In coping with respondents of this sort, the interviewers often managed to draw on shared identities useful in bridging ideological chasms. The irascible man from whom we have just quoted, who saw the survey as "an effort of some eastern 'liberals' to carry on their stirring up of academic freedom storms," considered Elmo Roper trustworthy and told the interviewer he would not have cooperated had she been from the East or South.[65]

Let me conclude this section by turning to a Protestant denominational college. The experience there illustrates on the one hand the great variety of institutions under the single label of "Protestant-controlled" and on the other hand the somewhat similar problems faced by the interviewers at the "traditional" colleges. The college in question is in what has recently become a metropolitan suburb, a development which has led to growth of the school to an enrollment of nearly 800, including Catholics and Jews, and

---

65. This respondent rated the interviewer as "very competent" on his mail questionnaire, but stood alone among his colleagues in believing that the survey had failed to elicit, or the interviewer to record, a fair picture of his views. The contradiction would appear to be based on his fear of the questions as loaded and thus designed to trap him into saying what he did not mean. And yet such an explanation is too rationalistic, for in many cases, and not only with angry respondents, answers to the mail questionnaires express a whole series of ambivalences: one wants to be critical—yet not too much so; one wants to be a good fellow—but not at the cost of offending one's conscience; and one may want at the end either to rectify criticism by commendation or to resist a final verdict of approval at the "point of sale." Naturally, such inconsistencies made it only partially useful to code and quantify, item by item, the answers to the mail questionnaires; we also studied them as wholes, and of course by colleges. In assessing these answers, it would be helpful if we had a "sample" of general talk among social scientists coded in terms of criticism, affect, rejection, and other relevant categories. Lack of criticism is in many ways more problematic than criticism. Am I correct in supposing that a sample of book reviews by social scientists would show a high incidence of partial and highly critical disapproval coupled with over-all recommendation?

a doubling of the social science faculty. The newcomer instructors, the interviewer reported, were scared, and she felt they oversimplified their answers to avoid saying all they might. Indeed, one respondent to our mail questionnaire wrote:

Personally, I feel quite secure, being an ordained clergyman and having family roots in New England to 1632. But I am concerned for those who feel less secure.

On the other hand, several respondents were definitely hostile to the survey. They had heard neither of the Fund for the Republic nor of Professor Lazarsfeld, and both names made them uneasy. One respondent, breaking off her interview in the middle, declared:

This is becoming very boring to me. Questions repeat themselves. I could answer *no* to all questions on the last few pages. . . . I have been here fifteen years—there are no pressures whatsoever. We are free here. This is a different college than most. Those who made up the questionnaire must think a respondent is a moron or can't think if they repeat themselves so much.

After two attempts on subsequent days, a remarkably gentle and tactful interviewer managed to persuade this respondent, an assistant professor of psychology and sociology, to resume and complete her interview.[66]

It would be quite wrong to give the impression that, at all the

---

66. All of the five (out of ten) respondents at this college who returned mail questionnaires felt the survey had elicited a fair picture of their attitudes.

At this level, in our mail questionnaire, over-all approval of the questionnaire reaches 98 per cent (with an N of 56), as contrasted with 72 per cent among the avant-garde and 71 per cent among the rear-guard colleges, and it is only a very rare professor who wishes the interviewer had been someone of higher educational standing. Whereas in the avant-garde colleges the percentage believing their interviewer did a competent job of recording sinks to 68 per cent, the comparable figure for the upper-middle colleges is 84 per cent, while in the lower-middle group approval of the interviewer is unanimous, save in one college where 79 per cent call their interviewer competent. Nor are there overt or subdued "social" objections to the interviewer at these colleges of lesser distinction, although at one municipal college the single critic of a highly experienced interviewer wished that she had not been so "well groomed."

Some interviewers gave a good deal of thought to what they should wear on the survey, while others thought it would be wrong to care (just as some respondents wrote us that it was wrong even to ask, on our mail questionnaire, whether they would have preferred an interviewer of another race or social class), believing one should wear what came naturally, and dress no differently for academicians than for other people. But in fact dress is one signal by which the interviewer indicates the available range of communication, and most experienced interviewers, who are women of indeterminate age, seek

schools we have classified as lower-middle, the faculty are either in the main apathetic or angrily reactionary—this is a pattern we do not find to be at all general except in the traditional colleges (most of which, in my classification, are in the rear guard). At a number of schools ranked as lower-middle the social science faculty consists largely of liberals—often recruited within the past decade —and interviews were often as lengthy and serious as in the upper-middle ranks.

At some of these institutions, however, the interviewers occasionally met unanticipated obstacles from the side of the administration, which in almost every case had previously given formal permission to proceed. In such situations, the interviewers proved themselves models of persistence, and, sometimes, of ingenuity and tact. In one case, for example, where the interviewer was told that final approval would have to come from the Board of Education, she ingratiated herself with lesser officials, avoiding the suspicious and jittery president until she had them lined up, and finally wangled clearance. Another interviewer at a denominational college held long negotiations with the president; he finally told her she could stay on campus but a day; with the aid of a sympathetic professor, she managed to line up seven respondents for that day —a sixteen-hour day in all. In all such cases which came to my attention, the interviewers were themselves familiar with the local civil liberties scene, cared deeply about it, and brought personal as well as professional zeal to the enterprise.

The Rear Guard.

On the whole, as already indicated, the survey among the more depressed colleges we have referred to as the rear guard faced the problem of its felt or claimed irrelevance—how glad a few stranded respondents at such schools would have been could they have believed there might possibly arise an academic freedom case (in the survey's terms) among their ranks. Correspondingly, even more than was the case at many lower-middle rank colleges just described, the interviewing itself in the rear guard presented no technical problems comparable to those

---

to wear clothes of indeterminate quality—altered to suit the case, where need be, by earrings, high heels (as against flats), and a hat or stole. Of course, here was a case where those familiar with the academic subculture they were sent to fared better, and gained—or failed to lose—confidence thereby.

encountered at higher level institutions: the more primitive the school-culture, the less likely that its repertoire of available roles would include that of impartial research interviewer, and the visitor would sometimes be defined in some role more meaningful to the community. "On my final visit the publicity director interviewed me and had my picture taken with the president." "I was treated so cordially that the idea crossed my mind once or twice that the association of Ford and the Fund for the Republic with grants to scholars and to schools might have put respondents in a cooperative frame of mind." "One of my last respondents . . . had been warned that I might be from the F.B.I." To these comments from interviewers should be added those instances where an interviewer was asked to make a speech to the assembled social science faculty, or was spoken of as "the lady from the Fund," or taken to lunch by the president on the assumption his college had been selected by distant and inscrutable deities for a signal honor. (Indeed, in a small agricultural college in a mountain state, the administration was disabused of these glamorous interpretations when "the lady from the Fund" turned out to be a friend of the Dean's from a nearby small town; she had a very hard time persuading them that *she* could possibly be the intended expert from afar—a role she had no difficulty in playing at another small college where she was not known.) While at some small colleges there was no one who had ever heard of the Fund for the Republic before, at one teachers college in the East, where several respondents asked the interviewer how much she was paid and where they could get work like hers, there was excitement in feeling some connection with the distinguished names that were recognized on the Fund's letterhead.[67] At one small Negro teachers college in the South, at least one respondent seemed resentful that those who had been interviewed would not receive fellowships from the Fund (as one teacher well might have, because she suffered criticism for

---

67. At several such places, it was apparently assumed by some respondents that the expert interviewer would herself analyze the material—an assumption that may very well have heightened the concern for confidentiality voiced by those who had any critical or off-beat comments to make (the interviewer, of course, knew their names). So far were these respondents from imagining how a large sample survey is conducted, that this assumption seems not to have been punctured by the letter from Professor Lazarsfeld handed all respondents at the start of the interview.

volunteering to be interviewed before the study had been "cleared" by the administration).

At many rear-guard schools heterogeneity exists as it does in the lower-middle ranks—though there are other rear-guard schools which presented a nearly uniform picture of disinterest in the survey. To understand this somewhat better, we must subdivide this level and see the disparities in their full extent. We shall take up first the Southern colleges, then the denominational ones, and finally the teachers colleges.

1. *The South:* A good deal of the experience of the survey in the South cuts across the different levels I have been using to classify colleges—and "the South" is of course itself (compare such a book as V. O. Key's *Southern Politics*) heterogeneous; nevertheless, I shall attempt some generalizations (based, as indicated above, less on our own field investigation, which only skirted the South, than on reading the interviews done there and the corresponding job reports of the interviewers.)

We know from Stouffer's data that the college-educated Southerner approximates in "permissiveness" and concern for civil liberties the national average for the college graduate; the great differences between North and South are among those who have not completed college, a proportion of the total which is much larger in the still rural, still impoverished parts of the South. Hence there can often be a much more sharp gap between the cultural climate of the college and that of the surrounding community—a gap bridged partly by state and local pride, by denominational ties, by social-class prestige, and by professorial or presidential tact, but a gap which frequently requires of the Southern liberal a courage seldom demanded in the metropolitan North or West. At only one Southern college, however, in our mail questionnaire group, were the national concerns of the main survey, that is, the concerns brought on by McCarthyism and charges of Communism or fellow-traveling, salient. Elsewhere, with few exceptions outside the Border States, the issues that were salient—if any were—arose out of the fight over desegregation; and at these institutions the political focus of many of the survey's questions seemed beside the point. For not only had Communism and its offshoots been infrequently taken up in this more ethnically and patriotically united section, but the race question, always close to awareness, had become dominant in the minds of respondents with any claim to liberalism and social concern.

Such respondents, aware of the chasm separating their own views from those of the surrounding white community or the state legislature, were often apprehensive—not only for themselves but for their institutions.[68] In some instances, I believe that the "Southern charm" that got an interviewer by a college president who, in at least one case, confused the Fund for the Republic with the Sons of the Republic (a patrioteering group), inhibited an occasional respondent. "Southern charm" is, however, a two-way street. Interviewers who might, in old Southern fashion, emphasize their kin connections to gain entrée, might also evoke the gallantry of otherwise fearful administrators and respondents; this was perhaps especially likely where an apparently well-born interviewer could talk to the intellectual elite with freedom from demagogic clichés on the race question: class pride, in the South especially, can link Jeffersonian traditions of academic freedom to good manners in expressing such traditions. Obviously enough, such nuances of communication might well be lost on a City College graduate teaching his first year of anthropology at a state-controlled institution in the Deep South: it might take some amalgam of skill and courage for him to talk over the head of his interviewer (or his image of her) directly to the Fund for the Republic. And he might be discouraged from attempting this where, as was especially likely in the South, his interviewer lacked intellectual sophistication.

It should be noted, however, that some interviewers, and especially the supervisors, were from the Border States, and were relatively emancipated on segregation as on the other cultural and political issues involved in their day-to-day work. And even the lower-middle or middle-middle class interviewers—who might, had they not found this employment, have been running dress shops or tea shoppes—had chosen an occupation which, as I have previously pointed out, carries emancipating elements. Finally, the more inadequate the interviewer (and, in general, therefore the more likely to be crassly bigoted), the more the mechanics of the complex questionnaire preoccupied her.

Inhibition, as we know of course, is not a constant; it varies

68. Cf., for a sensitive comment, Iredell Jenkins, "Segregation and the Professor," *Yale Review*, 1957, pp. 311-20.

with the strength of that which is inhibited. We have seen in the upper ranks of the academic procession that respondents deeply apprehensive about and concerned with academic freedom usually paid less attention to the interviewer and more to what they themselves wanted to get across. So, too, in the South—and here I am speaking generally and without regard to academic ranking—many respondents saw in facets of the questionnaire enough leverage to unburden themselves concerning pressures to toe the line on the race front, and spoke their minds to the interviewers, as later to us, on that theme.

2. *The impoverished small Protestant colleges:* A number of the smaller Fundamentalist colleges in the "traditional" category are located in the South. I have little direct knowledge of these colleges, for the total number of respondents in any of them was seldom over five, and our mail questionnaires went to only three colleges in this group. From what little I do know, I am impressed by the diversity even within the South, let alone outside it, for of course denominations differ and orbits differ; thus, two Presbyterian colleges in the South present a very different picture vis-à-vis the survey, being in one case conservative and homogeneous and in the other riven by a clash of viewpoints between several older men of orthodox views and two young Ph.D.'s who felt stirred to take a Christian Social Action line on the desegregation controversy.

Likewise, the colleges, almost always small, run by the otherworldly sects such as the Seventh Day Adventists show up in our scant material as occasionally harboring deviants. At one such school, a respondent wrote on his mail questionnaire:

A man has a right to his beliefs. It doesn't mean he's going to blow the country up, just because he's a Communist.

This doesn't mean, of course, that a Communist, or indeed anyone who did not share the sect's tenets, could teach at this college, but the respondent did imply that such a man has a right to teach at a nondenominational college. At another such school, one man had refused, on grounds of conscience, to testify before a Congressional committee.

Such a comment as the one quoted above is most exceptional, yet it does help explain the greater interest in the survey (as measured by our mail questionnaire returns) at Protestant as against

Catholic colleges of otherwise equivalent academic rank. Fifty-nine per cent of respondents at the former, as against 29 per cent at the latter (including a number of Protestants teaching there) returned mail questionnaires. Moreover, the over-all response to the survey in the Protestant colleges was favorable. Three-quarters of our mail respondents felt it had elicited their attitudes and feelings, as compared with two-thirds of the men teaching at Catholic colleges; one-third felt at least somewhat foreclosed by the questionnaire (as against 53 per cent of the respondents at Catholic schools).

3. *The small Catholic college:* None of the major Catholic institutions were within our mail questionnaire subsample. Had they been, I believe they would have presented a picture not very different from that of some of the leading Protestant-controlled schools, where religion provides at once a ceiling—setting, if not bounds, then frames for controversy—and something of a shelter for politically and culturally liberal opinion. Likewise, the conflict within such a university between the aggressively orthodox and the apprehensively liberal—and, in the Catholic ones, between the clerical and lay staff—provides tensions quite similar to those found in many state-controlled universities. By the same token, such a university moves within the national orbit of debate and discussion, redefining even the limits of dogma, so that interviewers are not faced with the mask of politeness and assiduous public relations they so frequently found in the lower ranks and particularly in the smaller denominational schools.

It was characteristic of the small Catholic college to welcome the interviewer and to try to make it plain that, far from having anything to conceal, the institution possessed, subject to religious limitations, all the academic freedom of comparable secular schools. In fact, in the two or three instances in which I myself was able to talk about the study with a priest, the latter was curious to know how the Catholic colleges compared with the country at large—a concern not only for public relations but also for right conduct.

But this same understandable sensitivity about the reactions of the non-Catholic world—a sensitivity of course greater in the South, the Great Plains, and the Far West than in the areas of heavy Catholic concentration and power—posed problems for the more discerning interviewers. Protestant and Jewish interviewers, who had had no experience with priests and nuns, often reported how charmed they were, how surprised at the politeness and cultivation and spark of their respondents. Awed and impressed, they were diffident about probing, and even if they had not been, I wonder whether their casuistical skill could have been a match for that of many of their respondents. Some, in fact, found themselves hopelessly embroiled in dialectics over question-wordings, and how these applied or didn't apply to the special Catholic situation. Even Catholic interviewers often felt they had not been able to pierce the gracious reserve of their respondents, though they were sufficiently at home with priests and nuns to take them for granted. In talking with us, these interviewers wondered whether their respondents could possibly be as non-verbal as they appeared or whether they, the interviewers, had somehow failed to communicate the need for a fuller response. And it is possible that public-relations considerations did enter, given the closeness of colleaguial ties in many of the smaller schools.[69] Yet it is also quite conceivable that what the interviewers obtained at these colleges was a reasonably accurate picture—while the interviewers were themselves too sophisticated to wholly credit it. For the most part, however, the "ecology" of the survey which matched the less cosmopolitan interviewers with the less cosmopolitan schools meant that those who worked at the smaller Catholic colleges were not sophisticated, and not likely to question the words—or, more significant, the non-response—of a kindly Father or Mother Superior or lay brother.

Furthermore, as at other colleges on this level, there were occasional intimations of pressure. In one case, the interviewer at a small Catholic college for girls noted that "a door near me opened a trifle almost imperceptibly pretty consistently." Another, who worked at an urban Eastern men's college, stated:

One respondent, smiling, said several times he hoped no one was listening—altho' there was no possibility of this. I had the feeling that despite his laughter, he did mean it.

---

69. It is worth noting in this connection that a number of respondents at major institutions told us, both orally and through the mail questionnaire, that the university's public relations department was a subtle pressure for conformity—a reminder of the outside world that could give or withdraw largesse, prestige, or security.

However, such instances must be weighted against the much more general feeling of freedom that prevailed at the Catholic colleges. As one lay Catholic teacher pointed out to me, many Catholic colleges that recruit most of their students from parochial high schools feel much more secure than comparable Protestant colleges, not only because their diocese or teaching order protects them from many lay pressures under the aegis of the great historic spectrum of varieties of Catholicism, but also because the religious orthodoxy of the students coming from Catholic homes and schools can be taken for granted.[70] Indeed, I came across a number of cases where liberal teachers in Protestant-controlled colleges had come under attack from devout students and the latter's parents, but found in my limited survey no cases of this sort among Catholics teaching at Catholic colleges.

From our mail questionnaire returns, moreover, it is evident that many priests have thought long and seriously about the special problems of academic freedom at the Catholic college and had difficulty (as fully discussed in Chapter V) fitting their distinctions, for example, between "license" and "freedom," into the rhetoric of the questionnaire. This is one reason why, in contrast to men teaching in Protestant-controlled schools, they often felt that the survey had not done justice to their attitudes toward academic freedom.

Out of this semantic constraint and perhaps in some cases out of an uneasy feeling of not making, by secular standards, a good showing, there arose from some of the Catholic respondents at the smaller schools as much objection to specific questions and even fury at the survey as a whole as it encountered at a few avant-garde schools. To take one instance, the muted tone which is comme il faut in intramural dispute at a Catholic college led to objections to the phrase "protest vigorously" in the questions asking how respondents would react to a presidential ban on a debate or a controversial speaker; as one priest said, it would be "unprofessional" to protest vigorously. In a somewhat similar vein, the word "attacks," in a question about "possible attacks and accusations" on faculty political beliefs and activities, struck some re-

70. Such a comment is of course not meant to summarize differences which have a long history and great complexity, but rather to give some indication of why, in my opinion, most respondents (lay as well as clerical) at Catholic colleges felt free in the face of what, to non-Catholics, might appear as oppressive hierarchical controls.

spondents as too strong: a "dressing down" or "criticism," yes, but not "attacks." Moreover, so many of the Catholic respondents insisted—as did professors at all of the lower levels of the academic procession—that there had been *no change* in recent years, that interviewers almost grew gun-shy of asking the questions that assumed there might be change, for respondents found this, when not simply repetitive and routine, irksome and provoking. Whereas in the avant-garde such objections often signified "We are beyond that: these questions are elementary, my dear Watson," in the rear guard they implied anger at the implicit slight in the assumption that the shadow of McCarthyism should have been noticed, that there *should* be change, *should* be protest, or a nodding acquaintance with conflicts over academic freedom at other institutions.

In these last remarks I have stressed the objections, but it must again be remembered that these came from the more articulate and vocal—from that minority who returned mail questionnaires (a small number of whom we know, from talking with them, to be Protestants teaching at Catholic colleges, with all the marginality that implies). Two-thirds even of this minority felt the survey had accomplished its minimal mission as far as they were concerned. And for a large number of the rest it seems fair to assume that involvement in the survey was extremely low—something done graciously but as a chore.

4. *The teachers colleges:* We classified twelve of the forty-five colleges in our mail questionnaire "subsample" at the lowest level; these include five of the seven teachers colleges in our group, three Protestant schools, and four Catholic.[71] As we have already seen, the survey at this level sometimes spoke with alien tongue. The respondents could answer the face-sheet questions, although they sometimes asked the interviewer what was meant by "academic honors," and those having no honors, no papers, no professional associations to report, were occasionally close enough to the lower-middle orbits of academia to find this a bit embarrassing. However, many of the questions on apprehension and civil liber-

---

71. Out of this group, two teachers colleges, two Catholic colleges, and one Protestant college had rankings of 2.0-2.5 in the quality classification used elsewhere in this volume; the rest had ratings under 2.0. (We have here included in the lower-middle ranks one teachers college and one private "subway" college which have ratings under 2.0; as indicated above, this was done to take account of intellectual standards and aims not measurable in terms of social standing, endowment, or facilities.)

ties were regarded as virtually meaningless. Thus, asked what political groups or organizations interested in public affairs she belonged to, one teachers college respondent replied: "Home School Group and Red Cross." Indeed, the "don't know" response, which caused difficulty in the avant-garde where interviews forced respondents into it who refused to answer either "yes" or "no" and preferred to rewrite the question, here comes into its own, presenting the interviewers with serious problems of how much to probe and pursue matters. Some simply did keep probing mechanically —"can you think of anything else?" or "don't you lean a little more to one side than to the other?" and so on; this led to the mounting annoyance of respondents already weary of the questions and convinced of their irrelevance.

On the other hand, interviewers were in danger of concluding at all the lower-level colleges that one respondent was just like another in his brief, noncommittal and monosyllabic replies (this was perhaps especially a problem where the respondents wore the "uniform" of a clerical or teaching order). In a very interesting case, however, an interviewer's expectations led her to probe where many other interviewers accepted what respondents first told them. Working at a state teachers college, she was perplexed when her respondents stated, in answer to a question, that they had never signed a teachers' oath. She went to the state capitol to look the law up, concluded that it applied, and called her agency's home office to ask whether she should go back and re-interview those she had already seen. Instructed not to do so, she went on with her assignment, determined to see if she, without direct leading, could get more accurate answers. When respondents would say "no" to her question about having signed an oath, she would not contradict them but would stare out the window, not saying anything. As she reported to us, the professors would do a double take and say: "Well, come to think of it, I did sign an oath, but maybe not the kind you mean. . . ."

At this level, interviewers reported, it was sometimes hard to get respondents to talk about incidents they could scarcely help knowing about. At one municipally-run teachers college, the president had at first refused to permit the survey to proceed but, on being visited by a representative from the study, had relented. Thereupon some individual respondents said they were too busy, and the interviewer asked one if "he knew why I should be getting such a reaction"; her report continues:

He said they were not telling me the truth. That he had talked to them and they were afraid of the study. The chairman of the social science department is "way to the right of Col. McCormick" and thinks the study is a Red plot—he has them all scared for their jobs.

I then called on them in person (having failed by telephone) and was able to persuade three out of the four to do the survey with me. The fourth said he was "too busy"—but he did not attempt to persuade me of this. I did not press him beyond a reasonable amount because I felt they were all worried, already.

The interviews were conducted in empty classrooms and the faculty lunchroom.

The interviewer further commented that if she had not learned from her informant of "the real situation" she would have been taken in:

. . . I should have felt that they were very conservative—they had to be really encouraged to answer and made very few comments and responded negatively to direct probes ("anything else"), and out-sat me in the face of silent probing. . . . However—in one case—when the interview was over and we were just chatting one man said "I'm glad I teach geography—no politics in that." . . .

Another respondent took her to lunch after the interview and "let it slip out that two years ago there had been 'trouble' with a faculty member who had been dismissed—she indicated that the politics of the teacher involved had been at issue . . . directly opposite of her answers—and no one else mentioned this case to me."

Naturally, one wonders how many cases of this sort there were. After examining the job reports and talking with interviewers and respondents, I concluded that such possibilities of a run-around were most likely when the president was suspicious of the Fund and hostile to the survey's proceeding. At one teachers college in the western part of an Eastern state, the interviewer was received with great hostility, and felt that the president's attitude was responsible for respondents' lack of frankness in a situation where a professor with a Russian name was suspected by colleagues and the tiny local community of being a Communist (clip-

pings of his speeches the interviewer showed us made clear he
was a "White Russian," vehemently anti-Communist).

But there is more evidence in our material of modulated frankness than of rigid concealment. Take, for example, the following
comment by an interviewer with a possibly Irish name who worked
at a New England teachers college:

It was a small college and I think they were frank. However, several
Protestant professors spoke in very *guarded tones* when they indicated
that their replies would have to include a decided threat to academic
freedom by the dominance of an administration which was Roman
Catholic. (This was a state, not denominational, college.) That it has
become a really disturbing situation was really frankly and completely
discussed only by a Jewish professor. I think the others held back because
discussion of religious differences is always touchy.

Politeness perhaps again? Here, too, the president was suspicious
and hostile, and hence very likely put the interviewer on the
lookout for possible evasion.

At this level of college, moreover, there is a tendency for the
interviewer to be, in effect, "briefed" as to deviants by the dean
or her prior respondents. Thus, at one municipally-run college
(not classified as a teachers college), respondents, citing the case
of one of their number who had been a "Fifth Amendment" case
before a Congressional committee, warned the interviewer that
when she saw him she mustn't be taken in by his charm—not that
she took this to heart, though she was apprehensive when she
got to him lest he clam up (he didn't). At other small rear-guard
colleges, interviewers would be cued as to "neurotics" or "crack-
pots" who would tell them long tales of woe, and on one or two
occasions in the job reports from such institutions, I got the sense
that interviewers might have been a bit impatient with the one
respondent who did not, like the others, race through the questions, but made for "difficulty."

On the whole, however, it is my impression that the interviewers were alert to such matters, and kept the door open for
potential response until the end, even in the face of an apparently
routine act by respondents. Thus, one interviewer who worked
at a large state college in the lower ranks wrote:

I found the 2-3 questions with the most room for writing in a "Comment" drew no "Comment"—how come? When you apparently expected a straight "no" or "yes," they opened up all cylinders and gave me all they had.

This interviewer took down what she got, responding to the cue of the respondent rather than of the schedule, although a few others took the space between questions as indicative of where to probe more insistently despite the variations of terrain to which their assignments exposed them.

All the quotations here presented, however, must be read against a background, throughout the "traditional" colleges, of minimal concern with the survey. One respondent at a large Catholic men's college refused to be interviewed because, as he remarked to the interviewer, "It [the weather—not the survey!] was too hot to be bothered. . . . Do not think it is any problem"; another took a nap "on college time" by pretending he was being interviewed. These are extremes, of course, but indicative of the general conviction that, as one respondent at a teachers college put it, "very little happened on the campus and in general . . . there was nothing to hide." Similarly, at one Midwestern teachers college, professors bet each other as to who would get through the questionnaire the fastest (the record: forty-one minutes),[72] and, according to another respondent, the interviewer was given a hard time in part because she came from across the state line, that is, from a more prosperous and cosmopolitan part of a metropolitan area that straddles the line; he declared that "Some of the boys were a bit rough with her . . . and I sympathized with her" (though in fact, whether out of loyalty to "the boys" or fear of them, he didn't show it, as he somewhat sheepishly admitted).

Thus, the questionnaire at the teachers colleges caught in the main the absence of those apprehensions whose presence is a sign of academic freedom, but did not inquire about the issues, below even the "subsistence line" as it would be defined among the middle group of colleges, which arise from the close relations of the state teachers colleges with the world of secondary education. Yet when we turn to our seventeen respondents in seven

---

72. At many denominational and teachers colleges, without a conscious effort at speed, respondents loped through with like dispatch; 11 per cent of our mail questionnaire respondents said they took less than forty-five minutes (as against 29 per cent who took more than one and one-half hours).

teachers colleges who returned mail questionnaires, we discover that with one exception they had each taken graduate work at a major avant-garde university or a small private liberal arts college of high quality. Presumably, their involvement as students in the preoccupations that go together with a concern for academic freedom gave them that extra measure of interest evident in the return of a questionnaire.[73] All but two of this group of seventeen (out of a total of forty-nine interviewed at the seven colleges) gave over-all approval to the survey. This does not mean they were not critical of the questionnaire: many felt it did not fit their situation, though unlike avant-garde respondents of the same general opinion, they did not elaborate their criticisms. But, and here the difference with the avant-garde is clear, criticism of the interviewer is virtually absent, save among several political conservatives who rejected the survey as a whole.

In summary, then, the interviewer's task was in many respects heaviest at the two ends of the academic procession rather than in the middle ranks. Among the avant-garde, her flexibility or lack of it helped make the difference between a full record—potentially useful as historical data for other studies—and the bare completion of pre-coded answers: a difference which, I have contended, was often more important to her respondents' satisfaction than to the study directors'. Among the rear guard, her ability to gain rapport both got her by administrative obstacles and respondents' suspicions and oiled a transaction that might otherwise have come to an end through political friction or personal inertia. While different questions came to the fore in different academic climates, the questionnaire as a whole seemed to fit best those middle ranges where aspirations to freedom and high academic standards met frustration from the community or from denominational or administrative controls. Correspondingly,

---

73. Although those who failed to return questionnaires tended to be the more conservative and the less involved with the problems of academic freedom (and arguably the less eager to talk about academic matters in general), the small group of "activists" may be an exception: these were the respondents who, out of passionate involvement in the issues, regarded questionnaires as a delaying tactic; while some of them nevertheless responded to our mail questionnaire, others undoubtedly thought it simply piled survey on survey when what was needed was political action: they could not throw the interviewer in the wastebasket, but they could do this with our questionnaire. A few wrote me letters to this effect.

the interviewers bore the responsibility in the other reaches of the study of helping persuade respondents that they could adapt it to their situation. That is, the field force of a survey agency bears to the headquarters' desire for standardized administration something of the same relation that the field force of a government agency does—namely, it serves to mediate between centralized control and local apathy or resistance; likewise, the interviewer seeks to convince both her superiors in the metropolis and her clients in the field that she sympathizes with their sometimes not wholly compatible aims.

We turn now to see in somewhat more systematic fashion what this field force was like.

The Interviewers

MUCH HAS of course already been said, directly and by implication, concerning the interviewers, and especially about that minority of situations where they had or gave trouble. I have, however, said more about how the interviewers were received and perceived than about what they "were" in terms of training and tradition, and I want now to say something about this even though it must remain speculative to what extent differences among the interviewers influenced the data they got.

The Concept of "House-Style." Two traditions dominate the survey field. One emphasizes structured interviews, largely precoded, and drills its interviewers to assure the comparability of their work. The two types of surveys with which the general public is perhaps best acquainted are usually conducted within this tradition: election polls and "ratings" of TV and radio performers. The other tradition (given great emphasis during World War II by Rensis Likert in the Division of Program Surveys) emphasizes a more free-flowing or nondirective interview, largely free-answer rather than pre-coded, and drills its interviewers to assure their understanding of the substance of what is wanted. Roper and Gallup have in the past represented the best of the structured tradition (though not all their work is done within this framework); N.O.R.C. and the Survey Research Center at the University of Michigan have ably represented the more open-ended type.

Public opinion research, whether on behalf of foundations, government agencies, or private clients, is a highly competitive affair, but also in its leading representatives a reasonably research-minded one; the result is a tendency for the top agencies to learn from what is best in each other's work and hence to diminish "house-style" differences.

Nevertheless, in employing both Roper and N.O.R.C., the study directors provided something of a built-in check on the expertness of the interviewing. Their preliminary tables indicate that over-all differences between agencies are slight and do not operate in any one consistent fashion, although, as we would expect, the N.O.R.C. interviewers obtained somewhat larger volumes of free-answer commentary. But this finding needs to be qualified by noting that, as things turned out, the agencies did not have entirely comparable assignments. Since the Roper interviewers were older, more apt to be working at interviewing full-time, and freer to move about, they were given more assignments to colleges outside metropolitan areas where they had to stay for a week or more; while N.O.R.C. interviewers got comparably more metropolitan institutions, where the respondents were likely in any event to have more to say.

While it should be strongly emphasized that the best interviewers in each agency resemble each other more than they resemble the poorest interviewers in their own agency,[74] it seems fair to say that the N.O.R.C. interviewers tended to be what I shall term "bluestockings," while the Roper interviewers tended to be "market research" types.[75] The study itself was more in accord with the

---

74. And it also must be emphasized that "poorest" here must be taken relatively. If we leave aside the dozen interviewers who were plainly out of their depth on this study, the rest, even if unsatisfactory as interlocutors, got the gist of matters as we have seen—and even some of the hopelessly incompetent ones did passably enough at colleges in the rear guard.

75. I speak here primarily on the basis of the fifty interviewers we ourselves interviewed (of whom slightly more than half were from N.O.R.C.). On the study as a whole, I believe that the differences were less marked, for, especially in the South and the Mountain States, the agencies appear to have less choice and hence less differentiated staffs (on this survey there was also less difference on the West Coast). Cf. the study of the staffs of several agencies by Paul Sheatsley, done in 1948 and reported in Herbert Hyman, *et al., Interviewing in Social Research* (Chicago: University of Chicago Press, 1954), Table 28, p. 152. See, also, the comparison of the Gallup and N.O.R.C. interviewers who worked on the Stouffer study, done by Herbert Stember as a doctoral dissertation at Columbia.

"bluestocking" approach, although careful instructions (specifications) were given the interviewers at the outset in the hope of imposing the study's own "style" on both field staffs. Before turning to the question of the degree of the study's success in this effort, let me briefly delineate the two "ideal-typical" house-styles.

The "Market Research" Type and the "Bluestocking" Compared. We could divide the interviewers along a number of dimensions that would bear some relevance to their performance on the survey. There are the relative amateurs, who bring the enthusiasm and the risks of the beginner, and the seasoned professionals who grasped the survey's purport and no doubt got the story, but left some respondents with a feeling they had been handled too aseptically. There are the middle-aged clubwomen, a bit on the Helen Hokinson side, whose enormous energy and genteel aggression find a paying outlet in the unremitting contacts of steady interviewing. There are the lower-middle-class housewives who care more about the pay than about the quality and variety of interviewing and whom we termed the "battleaxes," insistent but insensitive, and the evocative men and women, the "empathizers," whom one finds in every good agency and who surprise their supervisors by getting the most reluctant or case-hardened respondents to spill over, flooding the page with side-comments.[76] But I want to concentrate on the market researcher and the bluestocking because the image many respondents had of the survey was influenced by the relative sociability of the one type of interviewer, the relative intellectuality of the other.

The bluestocking is characteristically a young, college-educated housewife with small children who wants a part-time job that continues her connection with the larger world and intellectual pursuits—a job that can be managed at her own pace and to suit her

---

76. One interviewer of this latter type, working at a big state university, had interviews which averaged over two hours, as compared with an hour and a half for her two very competent co-workers. She had been a singer and actress and possessed considerable presence; she told us that she got her schedules by heart and gazed steadily at the respondent, only glancing at her notes and editing them later (the actual record of her work showed a certain touch of carelessness: the interviews were of course extremely full, contained voluble and, for interpretative purposes, valuable side-comments, but occasional yes-no answers were not recorded). While one might wonder whether such interviewers get more than is "really" there, this was not our observation: they get more by "giving" more, and they get most of it down, their gift being evocativeness, not embroidery.

children's hours. She is eager to contribute to intercultural understanding, and to her own; she is interested in the opinions people
have concerning current affairs (and has become used to finding
them often unenlightened and widely variant from her own—or,
worse, finding them nonexistent). Her persistence and gradual
professionalization in the arduous and often anxiety-provoking task
of interviewing is sustained, less by her personal attachment to
her agency, than by her interest in and devotion to the subject
matter of the surveys she works on, be it mental health, civil liberties, or opinions on foreign affairs (the bluestockings invariably
jumped at the chance to work on the Teacher Apprehension Study).
Her alternative pursuits are likely to be social work or personnel
work or other occupations involving a combination of technical
and personal concern; and when her children are older, she is not
likely to continue interviewing, or she may become a supervisor.

In contrast, the "market research" interviewer has a less psychological orientation, and enjoys the exercise of her social as
much as of her intellectual skills. It would not be quite correct to
say that she likes to meet people, rather than to meet opinions
and ideas; indeed, many interviewers who had primarily done market research declared that they had enjoyed the Teacher Apprehension Study more than any they had ever worked on. But this,
I suspect, was at least as much because their respondents were, in
the better colleges, alive, idiosyncratic and even eccentric, while
the topic brought the interviewers (as election polls do also) into
the public spotlight, the glamorous area of the Cold War, of national affairs. Or, to put it in another way, just because the orientation of the market researchers is social rather than intellectual, they
were frequently able to appreciate the tone if not the content of
their novel contacts with academicians.

The market researcher is typically older and less well educated
(both formally and in terms of reading and adult education) than
the bluestocking. Vivacious and enjoying relations with people,
she finds interviewing a way of remaining active after the children
no longer need close attention, and of earning a modest addition
to the family income; if she were not interviewing, she might be
running an inn, or selling in a specialty store, or in the real estate
business.

While it would not be correct to say that N.O.R.C. had all the bluestockings and Roper all the market research types, the N.O.R.C. interviewers on this survey were, on the average, markedly younger[77] (81 per cent under 50, compared with 42 per cent for Roper) and newer at the job (42 per cent with less than one year's experience, compared with 9 per cent for Roper). And all of the N.O.R.C. interviewers in our sample had attended college, with a number working for advanced degrees; half of the Roper interviewers had a college education.[78]

Interviewing at its best is, of course, itself an education (the study was for as many as a third of the interviewers in both agencies the most illuminating and exciting one they had ever experienced); hence these differences should not be visualized too sharply. I am talking, as I hope I have made clear, about style, about the flavor of the two agencies; but the flavor is not so strong, even where most marked, as to prevent a competent interviewer in one "house" from working successfully for the other (as several of the interviewers we saw had in fact done). The flavor is illustrated by a look at the different sources of morale in the two houses, as reflected in their names: the impersonality and aura of science in National Opinion Research Center (whose field workers keep in touch in part through *The Sampler*, a mimeographed house organ), as against the more personal touch of Elmo Roper.[79] That the name

77. N.O.R.C. had recently changed its sample points—one reason for the fact that so many of its interviewers in our sample were relatively new to the game; this also led to N.O.R.C.'s getting more of the colleges in large cities where it could quickly recruit interviewers or already had them.

78. Patterns of recruitment were comparably different; the N.O.R.C. interviewers were recruited largely through advertisements in the local papers or through university and other research organizations, while Roper tended to recruit through voluntary associations such as the churches, women's civic groups, and sororities. Whereas more than half the Roper women we interviewed belonged to community organizations, such as garden clubs, the D.A.R., service club auxiliaries, and the like, only 27 per cent of the N.O.R.C. interviewers reported such affiliations—but 35 per cent belonged to the A.D.A. or the League of Women Voters as against 9 per cent of the Roper group.

79. It was a Roper "market researcher" who told us of her regret that the Elmo Roper firm had changed its name to "Roper and Associates," which struck her as a more bureaucratic term; and another said that she regretted that Mr. Roper no longer talked on the radio as she had always made a point of listening to him. In general, the Roper interviewer had a strong personal attachment to the agency and the home-office staff, with whom in the course of years of work she had become friendly. Indeed, by thus personalizing the work, the more thoughtful of the market research interviewers sustain their energies for filling quotas on the boring surveys—boring in terms of topic—

of Roper, like that of Gallup, is widely known and respected is
of course a contributing factor in the morale of the Roper interviewers—in fact, it turned out that our respondents were occasionally aware that their interviewer worked for Roper, while only a
few specialists discovered that their interviewer worked for N.O.R.C.

The relevance of the separately derived sources of morale depended on the problems that faced interviewers on the study: for
some, unexpectedly sharp and continuous criticism which they
sometimes termed "quibbles"; for others, having to ask questions
that might prove embarrassing, for example, of respondents whom
they knew had been before investigating committees; for still others,
the fear of possible political embarrassment for themselves.[80] Correspondingly, each type of interviewer succeeded in satisfying
respondents in certain situations and frustrated them in others.

At some colleges which were cohesive enough to frame a social
definition of the interviewer, and cared enough about the topic to
do so, the stereotype of the "market research interviewer" spread,

---

which keep the agency going between the more exciting undertakings. This
"family plan" morale of the market researcher is often enhanced by work on
"crew jobs," where interviewers are collected from different spots for a survey
in a single city, plant, government department, etc. A good deal of the extraordinarily high morale of the long-time Roper interviewers rests on their experience of such jobs, where they could become friends, trade tricks of the
trade, and succor each other in adversity. (The "bluestocking," tied closer to
home by young children, is much less apt to be available for such crew jobs,
and would in any case be less likely to develop close ties on the basis of
"front-fighter" emotions as against shared intellectual and political values.)

80. One such interviewer, a Southerner, seemed to fear guilt by association; she told us:

> Actually I was terrified. It wasn't that I was afraid to go out on the
> job, for they couldn't do anything to me! I wasn't a Communist, they
> couldn't think I was—I had enough to back me up. But I was afraid
> it was going to be on the nasty side!

It was, in our limited observation, primarily in certain pockets of the South
that an occasional interviewer thought that the aim of the survey was to find
out how much Communism there is in American colleges—interviewers who
expressed their gratification at being able to give their local college a clean
bill of health. Yet even such interviewers were apt to be far more enlightened
than their clubwomen friends, or their husbands who, as car dealers or insurance agents, espoused the easy bigotries of the semi-educated: three or
four spoke to us of the opposition their husbands put up to their interviewing "Nigras," or in lower-class districts, or on topics like those of this
survey. And here again we see how the decentralization of an interviewing
staff, however frustrating at times to the experts in the home office, allows
the latter's questions to reach the field through a buffer which strains out
some of the "noise" in both directions.

along with the implication that such an interviewer could not grasp
the subtleties of the academic mind, nor sympathize with the academic situation—would in fact be one of the ill-informed majority
against whom the academy needed to be defended. It was a picture of a woman trained to put simple questions about toothpastes
or detergents to simple people on doorsteps, who did so as a
regular paying job. Like most stereotypes, this one had some element of truth in it: the Roper interviewers, although they do political polls and a variety of opinion studies among elite groups,
do a great deal of market research as well; the N.O.R.C. interviewers
(who, unlike the Roper interviewers, are permitted to work for
other agencies) occasionally do some. But it was of course much
less true that interviewers equipped with this experience would
necessarily misunderstand the academic community or be ill-pre-
pared to elicit and record its reactions.

This becomes very clear in the case of a number of Roper interviewers who were unquestionably market-research oriented, but
who were nevertheless able to escape the derogation implicit in
that tag by their social éclat—they "related" to their respondents,
not as members of the consuming public, but as fellow-members
of the cultivated strata.[81] More effective still, in many relatively
unthreatened avant-garde institutions, was the market research
interviewer who found a rare stimulation, or, as one put it, "a
privilege to meet and work with the academic field." Several such
interviewers told us that they had gone to a distinguished college
with the notion—"What's wrong with those profs anyway; why do
they let Commies teach?"—and, after hearing the respondents out,
had become more appreciative of the academic position. As we
shall see in the final section of this report, such responsiveness to
their respondents may have brought about enhanced rapport—rapport all the more secure because of the initial handicaps to communication.

Conversely, the bluestocking who began by sharing, or more
than sharing, the respondents' own convictions might or might not

---

81. On the other hand, one well-educated N.O.R.C. interviewer of lower-
middle-class origins who had actually never done market research—and belonged to a local chapter of the A.C.L.U.—was described by a respondent at a
leading college as "a nice woman, could obviously check soap without any
trouble," and other respondents at the same college pictured her in analogous
deprecatory **terms**.

be an endearing interviewer as a result—some respondents, whose liberalism had ebbed away, might even fear they were being understood and seen through all too well. On the whole, however, in the middle ranges of academia where people felt somewhat apprehensive about their institutions' vulnerability, but not particularly defensive about their own attitudes, the bluestockings were well received. Likewise, at many metropolitan institutions bluestocking interviewers were accepted by liberal respondents as a proper tribute to the topic and as the appropriate representatives of the Fund for the Republic. Involved in this reaction was the liberal's principle of considering principles rather than personalities—not noticing, let alone resenting, for example, the bluestocking's flat-heeled garb (or that she was Jewish, as in a good many instances in our subsample she was). Only at an occasional college did undoubtedly liberal respondents comment negatively on the dress and manner of such an interviewer.[82]

Due to the differential distribution of interviewers already referred to, cosmopolitan bluestockings were unlikely to work at rear-guard colleges, but when they did it occasionally happened that their air of exigency grated on the uninvolved, or that their concern for the content of the study contributed to the irritation of respondents who were in any case politically hostile to the Fund and to its presumptive concerns. (That this did not occur more often is no doubt due to the bluestockings' experience in handling apathetic interviewees, coupled with the latter's own lack of criticalness toward a moderately accommodating stranger.) The matching of market-research-oriented interviewers with relatively uninvolved respondents raises more serious issues, because in such encounters the politeness common to both parties might permit too easy skipping over of themes on which criticism was called for. That is, whereas the bluestocking comes out of the academic and, on the whole, liberal culture where criticism is the norm both in formal and informal settings, the market research interviewer comes out of the general American "politeness culture": she is trained to ask the questions on the schedule, whether she believes them intrusive

---

82. It should be apparent that I am lumping respondents together with colleges here. When we break down such generalizations, however, and examine in detail the reaction of individual respondents at a college, we find a tendency for those who are politically or socially deviant in the college climate also to reject or not share the college's consensus concerning the interviewer.

or not, but she will of course try to ask them in such a way as to
minimize felt impertinence—or to get through them as hastily as
possible. Yet I cannot say, either a priori or after my investigation,
that one style was necessarily more effective than the other in
comparable rear-guard institutions: the bluestocking tended to
stick at it longer, to probe more insistently,[83] and to be more
critical of her respondents when she was through, but comparisons show that she did not uncover more apprehension or (beyond
fullness of detail) a greater number of incidents of attack.

A number of caveats, already implied, must be made explicit
in connection with these sketches of interviewer types, their relative effectiveness, and their reception. Thus, I must repeat that,
for most respondents, the survey was a total experience, of which
the interviewer's behavior was only one part. Perhaps a third of
our respondents, whether in person or through the mail questionnaire, had some, often marginal, criticism to make of their interviewer: a number would have preferred someone who was better
educated or a social scientist; but 88 per cent thought their interviewer either did a "very competent" job (54 per cent) or a "fairly
competent" one (34 per cent), and only 3 per cent out of 405 on
the mail questionnaire judged their interviewer as "very inadequate." Criticism of the questionnaire itself was twice as frequent
and intense—and this, I believe, reflects not merely the gallantry
of respondents but also, as many of their comments testify, their
awareness of the "A for effort" many of their interviewers deserved.[84]

_____

83. It was characteristically a bluestocking who told us: "It used to make
me uncomfortable when they'd say something, and then realize as they went
on that they were contradicting themselves. In one or two cases, when I felt
respondents could take it, I'd point out their inconsistencies to them."

84. It goes without saying that Mark Benney and I made every effort to
reassure respondents that their criticisms of the interviewer could not possibly
be identified or get back to her superiors. I would like to pay tribute to the
good will and generosity of the interviewers who allowed us to question them,
never for less than an hour and usually for two or three, concerning a survey
they thought they were through with. I am also greatly indebted to Elmo
Roper and to Clyde Hart and to their colleagues of Elmo Roper & Associates
and N.O.R.C. (Shirley Star of the latter agency provided helpful criticisms) for
facilitating a novel inquiry which not only probed their staffs' adequacy but
intervened between the field and the home office in a way which few institutions cheerfully encourage. Bernadette Mitchell and Mary Ellen Simon of
the Roper firm and Selma Monsky of N.O.R.C., the respective field supervisors,
were notably cooperative.

At the same time, as already observed, interviewers sometimes defined the qualities of the questionnaire in terms of their own ability to bring the respondent within range; it follows that some respondents might think the questionnaire rigid because of the interviewer's own behavior, and yet conclude that the interviewer, given the kind of survey her behavior helped define, was more than adequate. For example, a professor who concluded that he was not being asked for any subtleties might nonetheless find his interviewer, a market research type, charming and adept in recording his replies; his criticisms might then be deflected onto the questionnaire. Correspondingly, many respondents could remember the questionnaire better than the interviewer.[85] The latter made a distinct and memorable impression only in certain kinds of situations:[86] where her respondents were more interested in survey methods than in civil liberties; or where they were more interested in a pleasant encounter than in civil liberties (one reason for the frequent success of the market research type and the occasional discomfort with the bluestocking); or in the rare cases where professors had sufficient alertness and energy to concentrate both on the interviewer and the questions;[87] or of course in those cases where respondents found the interviewer getting between them and the topic.

I have already pointed out that there is evidence, not wholly satisfactory by virtue of non-comparable assignments, that the bluestockings got fuller communication, or at least wrote more down, than the interviewers who were defined as market researchers. Writing more down, however, was not only a mixed blessing at times for the coders, burying what was relevant in a mass of verbiage, but also for respondents with little time to spare—and

85. Several interviewers in fact wondered what kind of wives such "absent-minded professors" had, or concluded that the professors were treating the interviewer as a student to whom they could lecture without interruption.

86. Elizabeth Drake has made an elaborate study of these impressions in an unpublished memorandum on respondent perceptions of the interviewer.

87. I should like to emphasize here that some of the top interviewers in both agencies are genuine virtuosi who enjoy coping with taxing assignments and "difficult" respondents. Self-effacing when possible, their qualities might nonetheless impress themselves on respondents as part of the undifferentiated feeling of satisfaction in the encounter, but only another virtuoso would be likely to appreciate how skillful such an interviewer had been in dealing with him.

this was true of many who could only give an hour or so between classes or other appointments. Indeed, one very discerning interviewer described for us her predicament in this respect: she began taking literal notes; then realized that many professors thought out loud, repeating the question, looking at it this way and that, and only after a kind of warm-up came to an "answer"; if she took down every step in this process, she exhausted herself, wearied the patience of professors accustomed to dictating to machines or stenographers, and found that she had buried a codable answer among half-finished remarks. Thereafter, she relied on her sense of relevance, guided by her (unusually clear) surmises as to the study's aims, but realized that a significant side-comment might occasionally escape her.

Let me take another instance of the problems of relevance, this time from a question on which a few respondents commented. When asked what periodicals dealing with political affairs they read, those who read twenty or thirty faced the issue as to how full and detailed information on this was desired: were the study directors interested only in how many "radical" magazines were read, or also in how many were read altogether? Would they be interested—as I later was, in reading some of the interviews—in a carefully "balanced diet," like that of the man who said he read "*Life, The Nation, America, Foreign Affairs, U. S. News & World Report, The Reporter, Colliers. . . .*" and so on? Interviewers sometimes mechanically probed—"anything else?," "any others?"—thus irritating respondents, and one cultivated professor who read periodicals in five languages protested that he couldn't be expected to run through the whole list, which would run to a hundred! In such situations, of course, those interviewers who were familiar with academic and intellectual culture fared better, on the whole, however they handled specific dilemmas, while those who thought *The Commonweal* must be an auto club journal (they spelled it "Common Wheel") helped build up cumulative resentment and feelings of constraint in their respondents.

My own interviewer, like the best representatives of both agencies, was at once alert to the topic and sensitive to respondents' mood and feeling as these developed in the course of the encounter. In this connection, it is my impression that the blue-stockings were more inclined than the market researchers to take it for granted that professors might enjoy discussing even their fears, and they honored the topic of civil liberties by not regarding it as an imposition on a professor to take several hours of his time on behalf of the Fund for the Republic. Where these assumptions were mistaken, they might annoy respondents even to the point where the latter teased them by giving marginally more reactionary answers than they might have presented in a more neutral setting. In contrast, the market researchers at their best were slightly more attuned to their respondents' feelings than to the topic's urgency, "moved" with them, and kept the interview moving.[88]

The very poorest interviewers, of course, sensitive neither to feelings nor to content, dragged rather than guided their respondents through the questionnaire. One boasted to us that she always managed to do more interviews on a crew job than her colleagues. Almost entirely unaware of the resentment she aroused among her respondents at a leading college, she complained to us of the length of the schedule (though her interviews averaged an hour or less) and, when she worked at a teachers college, mechanically kept using the word "trustees" in questions although reminded by her respondents that they were under the aegis of the Board of Education.

Another interviewer of this type, who worked at a major university, wrote:

I did not encourage much talk about other than the questions, as some were so long-winded anyway and so slow in deliberating I thought the costs would mount up.

Still another, a woman in late middle age who had been interviewing in the Deep South for twelve years, exclaimed:

Well. It was the longest questionnaire I ever carried around. . . .

And another woman of the same age, who left a poor impression at an avant-garde college, found the "card question" (No. 6) gave the best response, explaining:

---

88. Correspondingly, market researchers were inclined out of tact not to interrupt respondents who appeared to digress, whereas bluestockings, on the qui vive for free associations, often permitted digression in the hope something of value would turn up.

That discouraged digression, and though there were some who complained, most went right along with it.

It was, in fact, as we learned from her respondents, she herself who discouraged digression by her evident impatience and lack of understanding (and more complained to us than to her).

Yet it would be all too simple to assume from such quotations that the interviewer's attitude toward time and toward topic always communicated itself to her respondents. On the one hand, there were many experienced market researchers, used to surveys lasting ten to thirty minutes, who adapted themselves to the new situation. Still others ran up against the inflexibility of their respondents, who held them spellbound for hours on end; some found no tactic to free them from these interminable sessions. Conversely, at a number of avant-garde colleges, interviewers in the bluestocking mode were felt by their respondents to be impatient of their "quibbles" and "hair-splitting"—self-deprecatory terms they often used.[89] At the same time, the bluestockings were on the whole better prepared, both in terms of vocabulary and of knowledge of academic culture, to respond to requests for definitions of terms. And they were, if at all experienced, used to "open-ended" interviews lasting two or three hours or more. The N.O.R.C. interviewers in our subsample had more than twice as many interviews which lasted over two hours as the Roper interviewers; and this difference remains substantial even when we control approximately for type of college.[90]

But before attempting any final judgment as to the possible consequences, for the data and for the respondents, of the two interviewing traditions, I want to describe the study's attempts to set its own norms.

---

89. A striking example was the case of a male interviewer at a women's college who managed to give a number of his respondents the feeling he was at once ill at ease and patronizing of them for the elaboration of their thought; himself interested in civil liberties, he seemed to be saying: "Please get to the point, and don't make me, a busy and harassed fellow, write down all these subtle qualifications." (Let the reader not assume that male interviewers were necessarily ill-received; at a nearby college another N.O.R.C. interviewer, also a man, evoked the most unqualified enthusiasm of any in our investigation; this interviewer was under less pressure, the college itself under greater.)

90. Of the ninety-four Roper interviewers for whom we have time data, 86 per cent got through in less than two hours, on the average. Their greater experience was no doubt a factor in their "high production."

The Interviewers' Preparation

I HAVE SPOKEN of "house-style" of the several agencies as
a sort of atmosphere which the interviewers in varying degrees
carried with them on the survey. I have made plain that the atmosphere was not wholly pervasive in either agency, any more
than the atmosphere of what, for instance, we refer to as an "Ivy
League" college actually influences all the faculty there—neither
survey agencies nor colleges are like the Marines or the old Foreign
Service, which implanted their outlook on nearly all who survived
membership. By the same token, it was possible for the study directors, in drawing up the specifications or instructions to interviewers ("spex" in survey argot), as well as in writing the questionnaire itself, to impose their own procedures in considerable
measure on both sets of interviewers. The spex took the form of an
elaborate—but, as one of the field directors felt, not elaborate
enough—thirty-five page document intended to anticipate the encounters of field work and to acquaint the interviewers with the
purpose of the study in general, and of specific questions in particular; indeed, in its effort to anticipate possible contingencies,
it resembled a legal document—and was for the uninitiated almost
as difficult to decipher.[91]

As envisaged in the specifications, the interview was to be a
meeting of an hour or an hour and a half between patient minds,
in which the interviewer's initial role was to allay doubts about
the inviolability of confidences given, to avoid setting any limits
to the answers beyond those established by the wording of the
questions themselves, to press gently but firmly for decisive answers where respondents seemed reluctant to give these, to make
sure by probing that the respondents' viewpoints were fully elicited,
and to record fully and accurately all that they said. The instructions anticipated that some respondents would tend to be evasive
or reticent at certain points, and assumed that interviewers would,
by a combination of sympathy, firmness, and detachment, be able
to overcome such tendencies.

---

91. The instructions were written after some field experience had been
gained in a pre-test of an earlier version of the questionnaire. Naturally, the
better and more experienced interviewers were used on the pre-test, since they
could work with a minimum of briefing.

Such a definition of the interviewer's role, with its overtones of psychological techniques, is perhaps more congenial to younger people educated in a climate of thought that stresses the subjective aspects of experience. One interviewer, who worked at a middle-sized technical college in the Southwest, wrote that she found the survey "demanding" and "at times, painful"; she continued:

Felt somewhat as a psychiatrist must feel in the presence of revealed emotions.

Another, whose assignment was at a leading and politically much harassed state university, wrote an unusually full report, saying *inter alia*:

Most seemed quite frank though I felt that they might have had more extensive descriptions and opinions if they had had a less formal and time-binding situation to develop them. About a fourth impressed me as being too formal and trying too hard to be objective because they were perhaps social scientists being rated (even if nameless) by social scientists. . . . Reminded one of a doctor himself being examined. . . . Holding back, if the kind of reserve I refer to here is holding back, was different with each person. With three or four it was a feeling, recorded in the schedule, that there was far too much to be said on the cases to take the time or energy to formulate it.

Elsewhere she recurred to an homologous theme:

"What do you think" or "what did you think" does not seem to me quite an adequate tool to pry open many of these people's opinions. They seem to grow formal and feel they must not make too much of their emotions.

It is not surprising that her shortest interview (one and a quarter hours) was longer than the longest interview of some who were less keen psychologically.

The younger, college-educated interviewers—the bluestockings especially—had no difficulty grasping the long and intricate "spex," with their resemblance to a multiple-choice exam. The less well-educated often spent hours puzzling out the instructions, paying especial attention to the procedural sections: whom to contact, how to make substitutions, how to space appointments, etc. At the same time, however, these were frequently the more experienced interviewers, who had had to follow complex schedules of other styles before this, and the spex served to warn them of the heavy burden of change from familiar patterns this particular study demanded. As one Roper interviewer put it to us:

As a rule you can take a Roper questionnaire, you don't need spex—you can go right through and see what it's all about. When I saw *this* questionnaire, I said, "This looks like Alfred Politz."

What she meant was that, as a trained interviewer, she could largely dispense with the specifications needed by neophytes—but here she was dealing with something out of the ordinary, something "deep."

Yet, as anyone knows who has tried to work from a "how-to-do-it" manual, it is often humiliatingly hard to learn an art by reading instructions, no matter how detailed: one has to try it out and then recur with sharpened understanding to the instructions. Indeed, perhaps the majority of the interviewers we talked to make it a practice on their usual surveys to do a pilot run on their own before playing for keeps. Here the need for this was greater than in less difficult assignments, but since only professors were to be interviewed—sometimes 200 miles away—and since confidentiality was to be strictly maintained, how was one to get practice? What many interviewers did was to try it out on a college graduate in the family: spouse, son, daughter—in rare cases, a friendly professor not in the sample. But of course, the less well-educated interviewers were less likely to have such guinea pigs around, and when, as sometimes happened, they tried it out on their husbands of limited education, their own misinterpretations —for instance, that the survey was aimed at ferreting out Communists—were confirmed; or perhaps only their worries about the schedule's complexity and (for them) meaninglessness was confirmed. Many, however, had to go cold into the field, having read it aloud to themselves, with a dictionary (some took this into the field, too)[92] and the spex at hand (many referred to them when

---

92. Some of the less well-educated interviewers found themselves spelling out every word laboriously; as one said:

Sometimes they talked above my head and I was afraid to abbreviate too much in case I forgot what they actually said.

Or another:

respondents raised semantic questions—the spex usually said to tell the respondent to use his own interpretation of terms such as "liberal" or "values").

It is understandable that in this situation many of the interviewers took to recording in a kind of personal but inadequate shorthand, and would spend much time later "editing" their questionnaires, erasing their illegible scrawls, expanding, and correcting spelling. Editing, whether done on the spot or thereafter, brings up the whole question of what the interviewers considered relevant. When a statement is condensed in an interviewer's notes, several kinds of distortion, substitution, or suppression may occur. When interviewers lacked verbal facility or experience, their difficulties in note-taking often appeared in the area of selection—a tendency to record what was familiar and appeared to make sense, and thus to minimize slightly unfamiliar qualifications and contradictions. A number of respondents, in their mail questionnaires, complained that their interviewers could not have been taking down all they were saying, since they were not writing furiously enough for this—these were often also the same interviewers they accused of wanting to force them into "yes-no-no opinion" responses.[93]

Mrs. X [another interviewer] and I would read answers to each other —they were such big words.

93. We see here, I suggest, one reason why the questionnaire itself used as many precoded questions as it did, sprinkled among those permitting free answers: it was no doubt hoped that these would both help focus respondents' expressions of opinion and help interviewers catch their breath (a large number of interviewers reported to us or to their home offices that they'd gotten blisters on the fingers and cramps from writing so much so fast). But many of the more critical (and sometimes more cagey) professors in effect rewrote every question before answering, while others reacted to specific questions by unloosing their free associations. As one interviewer wrote, "the most difficult part was to figure out if you *really* had an answer to the question after they finished." The interviewers were thus presented with dilemmas: they could take down what was said and hope that either they at home or the coders later could find an answer in what was recorded; or they could try to press for what they, in what might be only rubbing in their *bornée* horizons, could plainly see to be an answer. If they chose the former course, they might discover at the time of editing that they had missed essential data; if they chose the latter, they might further irritate already edgy respondents. This latter eventuality was especially likely in cases of the sort already adverted to where the interviewers probed mechanically—"anything else?"— as a coda to every answer they got. Some with little sense of relevance did

In giving the interviewers a sense of how long the interview ought to take, the combination of the spex with their prior experience was often all-important. The spex warned the interviewers that they should not space appointments too close together, since most interviews would take an hour or longer—it was only at the conclusion of his interview that a "bluestocking" interviewer working at an urban university notable for its highly articulate faculty "congratulated one man who took only an hour and a half!" Of the seventy respondents who indicated in our mail return that they had been under some time pressure, only four said this was the result of their impression of the time others took. The interviewer's own schedule was a source of pressure for twenty of our respondents, but what we do not know is the extent to which the interviewers subtly conveyed a sense of appropriateness.[94]

We see here one of the problems of a national survey, namely, that coverage and comparability mean that the same questions will be asked of those who are virtual "know-nothings" and those who could write a book on each theme. Thus, quite apart from the cues the interviewers might have given, the respondents were made aware by the forms of the questionnaire itself that they were expected neither to be monosyllabic nor to dictate their memoirs. Within this range, the briefer interviews of the older men testify not only to their slightly greater sense of security but also to their different judgment of proportion; perhaps, too, they shared with the older interviewers a lesser concern with psychological processes and attitudes.

Though systematic poll-type interviewing is not much more than twenty years old, with much of the lore gathered in this period still uncodified, every agency head and study director knows

this at virtually every free-answer question, like a housewife dusting in the wake of a sloppy maid. Sometimes the respondent would think of something else, only again to be faced with the probe, and yet again. In this situation, as the protocols imply (but cannot of course show conclusively), there was a slight tendency of the less involved respondents to answer "no" to such a free-answer question to avoid a further probe and to get through.

94. Cf. my discussion of "over-answering" on a questionnaire in the profile of Horace Weinstein, *Faces in the Crowd* (New Haven: Yale University Press, 1952), pp. 458 ff. It is interesting to note in this connection that, although the interviewers reported to us that their interviews averaged ninety-five minutes in length, our 432 mail questionnaire respondents reported an average of seventy-five minutes. We are inclined to think the interviewers more apt to be accurate on the point.

that briefing sessions with interviewers are advantageous, if feasible.[95] Such sessions encourage pooled foresight on field problems, reduce anxiety, and permit a greater variety of emphasis than printed spex alone. In the case of the Teacher Apprehension survey, it might have been possible in this way to get across to everyone that full response was genuinely desired, even if this meant that the interview took twice as long as the stated norm,[96] that costs were a secondary issue, and that there might be great variation in time among colleges and among individuals. Such sessions, moreover, might have given some interviewers a sense of the various departments which comprise the social sciences—one wrote that since she wasn't a social science major, she had been grateful for the liberal education she got as to the differences between historians, sociologists, psychologists, etc.

I am not sure what more might have been done to help the interviewers handle the barrage of objections to the survey and to specific questions they often ran up against at leading institutions (and, on the political side, at rear-guard institutions as well).[97]

95. Our *ex post facto* interviews with interviewers often gave the latter a welcome opportunity to discuss with people outside the field ethical and tactical problems that had come up on the study; the very fact that such people as ourselves were interested served to make their work seem still more interesting and challenging than before.

96. Underestimation of how long things will take is, of course, a characteristic American vice (one from which my colleagues and I have greatly suffered in preparing this report!); I have heard tell of a study which discovered that, when a wife tells her spouse she'll be down "in just a minute," her average time is five minutes.

97. A slight plurality of the interviewers, according both to them and their respondents, rolled with the punch to some degree—in the mail questionnaire two-thirds of the latter said they had expressed criticisms of the survey questionnaire to their interviewer, and of this two-thirds, 38 per cent said their interviewer had maintained neutrality, while 13 per cent said the interviewer had disagreed with them. In contrast, 32 per cent reported that their interviewer had agreed mildly with them, while another 10 per cent had been given the impression she had received many such criticisms and she had agreed strongly with the criticisms.

It would have been very difficult to anticipate a number of the objections the interviewers met. How was an interviewer at a small Protestant college in the South to have been prepared for a respondent who got angry at the question concerning Lattimore: "to think that a president would ask any man of questionable political opinion to appear without consulting the heads of the departments?" Or to be prepared for the insistence of the president at another Protestant college that religion was a social science and that she must interview the professor of Bible? At one university where the administration seemed

Frequently, the interviewers detached themselves from awkwardly worded questions, while seeking to jolly contentious professors along. Occasionally, but less often than had been anticipated, they redirected the respondents' annoyance against the outsider, the study director, while urging respondents to cooperate in completing the task; most, whatever their private misgivings, technical or political, sought in this way to accomplish the survey's major aims without becoming too argumentative or defensive. A few, however, either because of rigidity springing from incompetent inability to separate the essential from the trimmings, or because of rigidity springing from over-identification with the survey or the agency, were unable to "give."

Even when one has catalogued all these difficulties, however, it is not clear what they amounted to "on the record." Would briefing have seriously cut down the number of respondents (one in seven in our mail questionnaires) who stated that in the course of the survey they gave up making qualifications because they concluded they were not being asked for subtle differentiations? Moreover, even those respondents who felt qualifications definitely not wanted, when asked for an over-all judgment, usually declared that they had managed to get their main story across—perhaps a few in so declaring did not want to appear to have succumbed to the interviewer's limitations, although in fact they did, but in other cases I see no reason to question their conclusion.

What troubles me more than respondents' criticisms are those cases in which, in reading through the protocols college by college, I have seen batches where nary a side-comment appears to the pre-coded questions; and I wonder: was it really quite as uniform as all that, or did the interviewer, inadequately sensitized to possibilities of small variations, fall into a pattern which then

---

disposed, if not to discourage the survey altogether, at least to limit it, a blue-stocking interviewer got the idea that the group-dynamics department should be in her sample, and called her home office to verify this; in contrast, at another school an unsophisticated interviewer was persuaded that cultural anthropology was not a social science (by a cultural anthropologist who preferred not to be interviewed) and, exceptionally for such situations, did not check with her office. (I am omitting my report to the Fund concerning the problem of sampling and of refusals and break-offs, as handled by the interviewers, since this turned out not to be a significant source of error and since, in any case, the representativeness of those interviewed can be independently determined by the authors of the main report.)

became self-confirming? It happened, I am sure, but I now believe it happened less than I might have guessed. In this connection, I want again to emphasize the immense safety factor built into the interview as a research tool: as with nations, organizations, and families, a great deal can go wrong and still the essential tasks get done. As just pointed out, many interviewers went to the colleges quite unprepared: they knew nothing of college life, of social science, or of academic freedom; some of them had done nothing but market research interviews—and some even less than that, a mere handful of training interviews. They felt intimidated by a questionnaire and spex longer and more sophisticated than any they had dealt with before; many quailed before their own anticipations of professorial brilliance, verbosity, or "queerness"; they felt, as they told us again and again, inadequately briefed and woefully alone. Yet they stuck it out—there were no "refusals" there—at whatever cost to their own schedules, their own tensions and self-esteem or their respondents' patience. And here the good will and decency of Americans, coupled with the kind of docile competent conscientiousness of many women interviewers, protected the survey, along with the concern of the academic respondent to prove himself a scholar or a gentleman or occasionally both —all subordinate to the task set by the topic of the study and its intellectual and technical framework.

Some Concluding Remarks

WHILE I have sought in this report to depict the characteristic experiences of the interviewers in the different ranks of academia—and thus indirectly to comment on the degrees of freedom and of apprehension to be found in those ranks—it took more time to spell out difficulties than to summarize over-all ease and expertise. Interviewing, like life itself, seldom goes as well as one hopes or as badly as one fears—but in this study it went better on the whole than I myself, or many other respondents at avant-garde institutions, would have anticipated: better, at any rate, in terms of getting both quantitatively comparable data and qualitatively useful clues to possible syndromes of attitude and portraits of specific college climates of opinion. What is elsewhere reported in this volume is, then, not to be discounted because of poor communication, given the level and mode of analysis employed by the authors.[98]

But communication with human beings is always two-way, and when one gets data from people one also gives it. One gives it when one issues a report to be read by those one has interviewed, or by those who can identify with the latter; and here, I believe, one has a responsibility not to fend off such readers by intended obscurities or by a dead-pan way of categorizing and explaining which implicitly passes a verdict on the vitality of one's own life and that of the "tribe" one has studied. But my concern here is rather with the first step in the chain of communication, namely with the interview itself and what it implicitly communicates to the interviewees. As Mark Benney and I have written elsewhere:

There is the further obligation of trying to give him [the respondent] some psychological satisfaction—some opening of horizons, perhaps—in return for his information, for his time and trouble, and for permitting a potentially threatening encounter. Ideally, every interview should terminate with the informant having advanced his own understanding of the area investigated and feeling an enhanced respect for himself as a human being.[99]

Many social scientists share this perspective, and are humanistically sensitive to the requirement that their human subjects be treated with respect for their subjectivity as well as for their objective comparability. In a national survey such as the one reported in this book, however, this responsibility is divided among the study directors, the agencies (themselves bureaucratized in some measure), and the interviewers.[100] One contribution study directors

---

98. A number of respondents maintained that it would have been better to send trained anthropologists or other social scientists to fewer colleges for longer inquiries. Such a course would have produced a different study—one I would like very much to see undertaken. Each analyst, of course, must do what he can, with the methods he knows how to use; I doubt if we know enough to assert that there is one best method for everybody—though fashion and prestige certainly play a distorting part in the choice of means.

99. "Asking and Answering," *The Journal of Business*, Vol. 29, 1956, pp. 225-36, at p. 236.

100. The leading agencies have an understandable concern with the public relations of the polls—and in America much that is decent gets done in the name of public relations; in my observation many of the leading survey people, underneath their practical preoccupations, are alive to the ethical implications of their enterprise.

can make to this task flows naturally out of their having an interest in problems of profound importance. If they inquire about such problems, as was done here, they will be talking with respondents about matters of interest to them, or helping to educate them to such an interest; their own curiosity will to some degree be contagious. (Correspondingly, it is an abuse of the interview to employ it to get routine data, e.g., on consumption patterns, which could readily be obtained from carloadings or other such sources.) However, on a national survey there is always danger in the assumption that we are in fact one country, and that issues relevant to one part of the population are or could become meaningful to another. In the Teacher Apprehension study, I believe that more could have been done (or, more justly, could be done if another such survey were to be conducted) to provide, in effect, different questionnaires for the cosmopolitan and the 81 traditional colleges, speaking more fully to the themes men in the latter might have chosen as having a bearing on their situation. Obviously there are problems here; since one cannot have two questionnaires for the cost and time of one, it would have been necessary either to sacrifice something of comparability by not having a uniform schedule, or to sacrifice some of the questions of special relevance to leading institutions and accordingly to the national climate of freedom.

Moreover, matters become still more complicated when we realize that even a fairly routinized interview, in terms of the relevance of the questions, often provided a valuable break in routine precisely in the poorer colleges (just as bored children are grateful for a psychological test which permits an escape from classes). Thus, an encounter that some professors in the avant-garde experienced as depersonalizing sometimes brought a certain freshness to people in the rear guard accustomed to conventionalized contacts. And in the middle ranks of academia, even where the interviewer was herself mechanical, many respondents were grateful for the survey itself as a sign that "somebody cared," and as a chance, if an oblique one, to talk back in the face of felt constraints on freedom. When Mark Benney and I arrived on such a campus in July or August to discuss an interview that had occurred the previous March or April, we were often inundated with respondents who still cared, and who were eager to discuss the topics the survey had broached.

On avant-garde campuses, and occasionally in the upper-middle ranks, it was rather objections to the questionnaire or the interviewer that made angry respondents grateful for an opportunity to voice their complaints.[101] Some of the boredom certain avant-garde respondents found in the encounter was, in my opinion, due to a wish to push troublesome issues of academic freedom to the periphery of awareness. But there were some respondents who were angry for a different reason: academic freedom was a salient preoccupation for them, both because of who they were and where they were, and they were tantalized by a questionnaire which seemed to raise questions it did not permit them to follow up in their own way, and by an interviewer who was an automaton where they would have wanted a colleague. Such men appeared to feel themselves exploited by the study: they wanted to be co-participants, not people in a queue waiting to be interrogated on behalf of a distant authority. Such men frequently said to us that the interviewer did not appear to them to be sufficiently interested in or committed to the support of academic freedom; they referred to her as a recording machine—and not always a very good one.

Yet, at the same time, being social scientists, some of them also did not trust their own reactions of this sort: they "knew" that good interviewers were supposed to be "neutral" or "objective" (i.e., not colleagues in the same boat), and not to express any personal points of view. In such cases, the most they would sometimes ask of interviewers, in addition to recording skills, was that they be "pleasant" or "courteous"—the qualities of an airline hostess, let us say. They would, in effect, place on the questionnaire itself all the burdens of communication, rather than implicitly asking of the interviewer that she make the questionnaire "accessible" to them both in emotional tone and in encouraging their own detailed revision of it. A few respondents recognized the dilemmas lurking in such demands. Thus, one professor at a leading private university wrote:

An interviewer, in my opinion, should transmit expressed ideas into the permanent record. Hence complete objectivity is desirable. In this

---

101. Likewise, the amount of free-answer material in mail questionnaire returns from such men testifies to much resentment, as well as to curiosity and to good will.

instance I happen to classify myself as a "liberal." . . . Had the interviewer made clear to me that she shared my prejudices I probably would have spoken at greater length but not with more freedom. . . . Similarly I would have felt more secure with another historian or social scientist; less time would have been wasted in translating my ideas or language. Yet to another person in a different field, such an interviewer would seem less sympathetic than the one employed in this survey. This interviewer struck me as a good tape-recording machine, and that is probably most desirable.

The N.O.R.C. interviewer who worked at this university was actually a very professional market research type, quite intelligent but neither familiar with nor concerned about academic and intellectual matters. One wonders whether, in not sharing the academic culture and its "prejudices," she didn't appear, in her very manner, to share the anti-academic ones—at least for respondents sensitive to pressures on intellectual freedom?

Indeed, we have some evidence that even when social scientists as respondents declared that an objective professional interviewer was the right kind to have, they did not always treat their own as simply a note-taker. Thus, at elite private colleges from which we have mail questionnaire replies, 82 per cent said they had criticized the questionnaire, in whole or part, to their interviewer. No doubt, many were speaking over her head to Professor Lazarsfeld, but many others were certainly taking her into account as a co-adjutor with them—were, in fact, objecting to her that they did not feel made sufficiently part of the enterprise, and were rewriting questions or reframing perspectives to give themselves a more active role. And the interviewers who insisted on confining them to their role as *respondents,* not permitting them to rise to the status of *informants,* gave these men in the avant-garde a kind of claustrophobia: they did not want to be fenced in.

From another college—one notable for its distinction and its freedom—we have further testimony about the ambiguities among some social scientists concerning the relation between their interviewer's technique and objectivity and her over-all adequacy. As one man wrote:

The interviewer was a middle-aged lady of apparently good education who did exactly what she was supposed to. Nevertheless I found the cultivated attitude of neutrality in questioning concerning such vital

issues, and the absence of outer response to my statements, quite unnatural—despite the fact that I am supposed to be a social scientist.

This same interviewer was described by other respondents as "more
interested in her reporting task than in me as a person," and some
felt they could have talked more freely to a colleague. To understand this, we must realize that the survey helped remind these
men of the air-conditioned climate in which they personally lived,
in comparison with the dire fate of some professors at nearby
state-controlled universities. Partisans of freedom themselves, they
felt some discomfort in the very fact of their own security, and I
believe that they wanted from the interviewer some acknowledge-
ment of their special and perhaps paradoxical situation—they wanted
something from her at any rate, some response, and not the neutrality and task-orientation which appeared to take them and their
world for granted.[102]

There is irony here, for as we discovered later, this interviewer
was extremely alert to that world, if not to each respondent as an
individual. She cared deeply about civil liberties and was herself
the graduate of a "bluestocking" college very like the one at which
she worked, and she was proud of the record of both colleges in
defending academic freedom. But she had learned to sublimate
her zeal into her professional work as an interviewer—work which
in this case was admirable in terms of fullness and accuracy of reporting.[103] Her trained and conscientious restraint forbade her from
granting her respondents an acknowledgment of their distinction

---

102. Some support for this interpretation can be gleaned from a comparison of reactions to this highly professional interviewer and to her co-worker at
this college, a well-educated amateur, recruited from the League of Women
Voters; respondents felt more at home with the latter, despite or perhaps because of her awkwardness, though several doubted her competence and doubted
that she got down a full record of their views. (Both interviewers, in our typology, were clearly bluestockings—both worked for N.O.R.C.)

103. Stephen A. Richardson did a study at Cornell of the training of interviewers which indicates that the best research interviewers are not the most
dispassionate and "objective," but rather those who more frequently express
value judgments and then learn to transmute that concern into obedience to
scientific procedures—as against interviewers who begin with greater detachment. See Richardson, *Selected Personality Characteristics of Social Science
Field Workers*, unpublished Ph.D. dissertation, Department of Sociology, Cornell University, 1954; and Richardson and Barbara Dohrenwend, *The Non-
Scheduled Interview* (New York: Basic Books, forthcoming).

or their situation—something which her neophyte co-worker gave without reserve.[104]

Let me cite a contrasting instance to illustrate the complexity of these processes. An interviewer who was indubitably of the market research type worked at another leading college which has been in the news because of pressure by alumni and one of the Congressional committees against several faculty members. A woman of limited education, wife of a salesman, she read nothing more serious than *Redbook, Our Sunday Visitor,* and the local paper; she had gone to the college with the prejudices of her class and station, irritated, for instance, at the objection of these professors to a teachers' oath—"They have our youngsters in their hands, don't they?" Knowing this, I was surprised to discover how well she had been received; all but a few of the most apprehensive respondents among the younger men (several of whom were Jewish) felt that they had been understood and had gotten their story across. How are we to explain this? It certainly helped that the interviewer was unabashedly feminine; a demure, trim woman with wide blue eyes that made her look nearer thirty than her actual 42 years.[105] It helped, too, that she was impressed by the courtesy and gentlemanly qualities of her first respondents (the very first of whom turned out to be an admirer of Elmo Roper); these men put her at her ease, and allowed her own considerable suavity to appear. But I suspect that it helped at least as much that the interviewer found herself being slowly converted to a greater appreciation of the academic viewpoint; thus, she discovered that men who had been accused of subversion before an investigating committee were not ogres, but charming and sympathetic. I don't, of course, mean to suggest that her twenty-five respondents conspired to take the interviewer into camp; most of them were as unaware of her original hostility as of her later change of view. Rather, I do suggest that her responsiveness did commu-

104. It should in fairness be added that the amateur interviewer also did an adequate job of gathering information, despite the anxiety on this score of some of her respondents; she was intelligent enough, and experienced enough in analogous tasks, to master the assignment with very little previous experience in interviewing.

105. Interviewers in general look younger than their chronological years: only women with a great deal of energy can stand it—and the work keeps them young.

nicate—did give the professor the feeling he was being listened to as a person (and certainly as a man), and not as a number.

And yet that is not the whole story, even at this college. One might well contend that the three-quarters of her respondents who found the interviewer "friendly" and who were satisfied with the encounter were too complacent—conceivably, they were satisfied to hold forth without challenge, to opine without dialectic. Such self-respect as they may have gained must have been in large measure transitory: the interview may have served to make them neither more critical nor more self-critical. The dissenters at this college—who were also the young dissenters from its traditional genteel qualities (more likely than the latter, for example, to see the alumni as caring more for the college's social and athletic than for its intellectual prowess)—did not enjoy the interview, but may have learned more from it. Certainly, the social scientist whom we quoted earlier as finding his "objective" interview "quite unnatural—despite the fact that I am supposed to be a social scientist," may have learned much more: may have learned something of what it is like, in the phrase of J. B. S. Haldane, to be "one's own rabbit."

APPENDICES

APPENDICES

1. Sampling Procedures

THE POPULATION sampled consisted of the teachers of undergraduate social science courses in all the four-year colleges in the United States which were accredited by one of the six regional accrediting associations, or by a teachers college accrediting association. Professors teaching only in professional divisions such as business schools or journalism schools were not included.

The sampling was done in two steps: first, colleges were selected and then, within these, individual professors were designated for interviewing. Probability procedures were used throughout.

To begin with, all accredited American colleges were classified by size of undergraduate enrollment and type of control. To this end the definitions in *American Universities and Colleges, 1952,*[1] were used. When the descriptions there, provided by the schools themselves, were ambiguous concerning type of control (for instance, in not differentiating between religious "control" and "affiliation"), the *Information Please Almanac, 1955,* was used. The schools were stratified into groups by using the following divisions:

(a) Size of undergraduate enrollment in 1952: 800 or less, 801-2,500, 2,501-4,000, 4,001-8,000, 8,001 or larger.

(b) Type of control: Public (city, state, federal), private, Protestant-affiliated, Catholic-affiliated, Protestant-controlled, Catholic-controlled, teachers colleges.

(While these classifications were satisfactory for purposes of stratifying the sample, they were considerably further refined, as explained in Appendix 4, for use as variables in the analysis of our data.)

Certain combinations of size and type of control were infrequent and had to be grouped together. Altogether twenty-one strata of schools were used for sampling. In those where sufficient schools were available, further stratification by region of the country was introduced. Strata containing all-Negro colleges were also further stratified to insure representation of these schools.

---

1. Mary Irwin, ed., Washington, D.C.: American Council on Education.

While government bulletins provided with acceptable accuracy the number of students in accredited colleges, information concerning the number of teachers was unavailable. An estimate of the national ratio of students to social science teachers in accredited colleges was made by a random sampling of college catalogs; from these a figure of 100 students per social science teacher was computed. For a total student enrollment of 1,427,620, this meant an estimated total of approximately 14,000 teachers. An over-all sampling ratio of 0.16 was then set to yield a desired sample of 2,300. Actually the ratio was slightly in error: 2,451 teachers were finally interviewed.

The transition from the size of the student body to the size of the social science faculty was achieved by the following procedure: Colleges were chosen by selecting at random in each stratum enough schools to fill the student quota of that stratum; if a stratum contained 100,000 students, for example, colleges in that stratum were picked one after another until a total student population of 16,000 was obtained. All social science teachers at the chosen colleges were then interviewed.

Actually, this was done only if the stratum involved schools of less than 2,500 students. At larger colleges, since one or two schools could exhaust the stratum's quota, and since the number of important universities represented would be kept overly small, it was decided to *oversample* schools in a proportion of 1/p and then *sample* teachers within these colleges in proportion p. This meant that our sample of large *colleges* would by design over-represent the large schools, but that our sample of *teachers* at large colleges would be in strict proportion. The percentages of the total student bodies sampled in each size group was as follows: schools with 2,500 students or less, 16 per cent; 2,501 to 4,000 students, 31 per cent; 4,001 to 8,000 students, 44 per cent; 8,001 or more students, 56 per cent.[2]

Once the schools were drawn in the home office they were assigned to the interviewing agency which had the best supervisor in the vicinity. If colleges were located more than eighty miles from either a Roper or N.O.R.C. interviewing station, and if more accessible but closely comparable schools in a stratum existed, substitutions were made. Approximately 15 per cent of the schools in the final sample were chosen in this manner.

Altogether 182 colleges were chosen for study. Letters were written to the president of each asking permission for interviewers to visit the college. Twenty schools refused to participate; they included one large private, one small private, three large public, two small public, three

_____

2. A more detailed description of the number of schools and respondents included in our sample will be found in Appendix 4.

teachers college, four Protestant, and six small Catholic institutions. In addition, six other schools were dropped. At one, it developed that no interviewer was available. The State Director of Education in Massachusetts asked the study to choose any two of the state's five teachers colleges, all of which had fallen into the sample, to represent the others. The president of one school wrote that his college was not accredited. Columbia College was deliberately withdrawn from the sample because of its connection with the authors' home university.

Since the refusal letters frequently arrived just as the interviewers were about to go into the field, it was possible to make substitutions only for Columbia College and eight others.[3] In the end, then, interviews took place at 165 institutions.

Despite the fact that large schools were oversampled deliberately, our sample is not unrepresentative of all American colleges in some regards. With respect to region, sex composition of student body, and Negro-white character, our sample closely resembles the characteristics of the 904 accredited colleges listed in the 1952 *American Universities and Colleges*. The detailed figures for region are as follows:

Region	All Colleges	Sample
New England (Me., Vt., N.H., Mass., Conn., R.I.)	8%	12%
Middle Atlantic (N.Y., N.J., Pa.)	17	16
East North Central (Ohio, Ind., Ill., Mich., Wisc.)	16	17
West North Central (Minn., Ia., Mo., Kan., Neb., S.D., N.D.)	13	11
South Atlantic (Del., Md., Va., W.Va., D.C., N.C., S.C., Ga., Fla.)	17	19
East South Central (Ky., Tenn., Ala., Miss.)	8	5
West South Central (Ark., La., Okla., Tex.)	9	8
Mountain (Mont., Wyo., Col., N.M., Ariz., Utah, Nev., Idaho)	4	4
Pacific (Wash., Ore., Calif.)	6	8
	100% (904 schools)	100% (165 schools)

Even when the figures are subdivided like this into nine parts, the largest percentage disagreement is 4 per cent, in New England. This

3. One of these, improperly listed in our records, turned out to be a two-year junior college.

slight disproportion in the sample may reflect the fact that substitute colleges within travelling distance from interviewer stations were most likely frequently chosen from densely settled regions like New England.[4]

The sample contained 72 per cent co-educational schools, 10 per cent mens', and 18 per cent womens', compared respectively to figures of 72 per cent, 11 per cent, and 17 per cent in the total population. Six per cent of the sample colleges were Negro, compared to 8 per cent for the population.[5]

Characteristics of colleges which are more closely related to size, such as budget and size of library, of course show considerable differences when sample and population are compared. When the factor of size is held constant, the following results emerge:

Number of Books in the Library

	UNIVERSE OF COLLEGES			
Number of Books	Schools Under 700 Students	700-2,500	2,500-8,000	8,000 or More
Under 25,000	31%	8%	2%	—%
25,000-60,000	56	44	9	5
60,000-100,000	8	25	15	5
100,000-400,000	5	22	51	28
400,000 plus	—	1	23	62
	(418)	(306)	(124)	(39)

	SAMPLE			
Under 25,000	24%	2%	—%	—%
25,000-60,000	57	39	11	6
60,000-100,000	9	16	11	—
100,000-400,000	9	43	47	31
400,000 plus	1	—	31	63
	(55)	(44)	(45)	(16)

---

4. Our list of colleges was scrutinized subsequently by several experts. The general feeling was that we had a good "microcosm." One Southern educator regretted that sampling chance had excluded some of the major institutions like the University of Texas and the University of North Carolina, thus, perhaps, underrating the level of Southern higher education. Actually regional comparisons do not appear in our chapters. Historical circumstances make the organization of colleges in various parts of the country very different. We could not find any regional difference which could not easily be explained by the other major college characteristics used in our study.

5. Data in the 1955 *Information Please Almanac* make possible these comparisons.

Size of School Budget*

UNIVERSE OF COLLEGES

Total Budget, 1951-52	Schools Under 700 Students	700-2,500	2,500-8,000	8,000 or More
Under $300,000	28%	2%	—%	—%
$300,000-$750,000	60	26	2	—
$750,000-$3 million	11	67	34	8
$3 million-$10 million	—	5	48	27
$10 million or more	1	—	16	65
	(379)	(299)	(120)	(37)

SAMPLE

Under $300,000	22%	2%	—%	—%
$300,000-$750,000	58	26	—	—
$750,000-$3 million	18	60	32	—
$3 million-$10 million	—	12	45	31
$10 million or more	2	—	23	69
	(50)	(43)	(44)	(16)

* It will be noted that the totals in the budget table show slight discrepancies with corresponding totals in the library table. This is due to the fact that for some schools information is available on one characteristic but not on the other.

There exists a slight but consistent bias of sample schools to have larger libraries and larger budgets than are generally found in the universe of colleges of comparable size. Further study may show that this bias was introduced by a predominance of poorly endowed schools among refusal colleges. But in general, within size groups, our sample is quite representative of the total college universe.

It should be remembered that throughout our report all major results are reported separately either for different groups of colleges or for different groups of professors. It can therefore confidently be asserted that the college sampling procedure was adequate for the purpose of the study.

The sampling of teachers within schools was of course much more direct and did not engender any major problems. For each school the interviewers were provided with a dittoed list of all teachers described in the catalog as presenting social science courses.[6] At schools with

6. Our definition of social science included the following topics: anthropology, economics (including those agricultural economics courses which dealt with agricultural economic policy rather than farm management), human geography, history, international relations, industrial relations, political science, government, public law, social psychology (all courses entitled social psychology, human relations, or group dynamics were included), sociology (including branches such as criminology, demography, etc.), and social science or social studies.

less than 2,500 students, interviewers were instructed to bring these lists up to date upon arrival on campus and then to interview all teachers on the list. Our records indicate that interviewers were in general extremely conscientious in up-dating their "blue sheets" at these colleges. At larger schools, as described above, only a proportion of the social science faculty was to be interviewed; here the proper number of names were chosen at random by the home staff and indicated with an arrowhead mark ($>$) on the list given to interviewers. Here, inter-viewers were not instructed to bring the list up to date before beginning to interview, since particularly at the largest schools, this might have been an extremely time-consuming and difficult task, and substitutes for designated but unavailable respondents could readily be taken from the blue sheet. This means that at these schools, teachers contracting to teach social science courses between the last printing of the school catalog and the beginning of the spring, 1955, semester were unlikely to be interviewed, except in certain circumstances to be noted.

When arrowhead-indicated teachers had left the school, were away or sick for the nine-day interviewing period, or refused to participate, standardized substitution procedures were detailed for interviewers in their instructions (a 30-page document dealing in detail with the entire operating procedure). First, they were to substitute a professor of the same rank in the same department; in many cases a recent replacement not listed in the catalog was interviewed in this way. Second, fail-ing this, a numbered list of randomly chosen substitutes in all depart-ments was provided, to be exhausted in sequence. Finally, any other teacher in the same department was to be chosen, regardless of rank. Altogether 392 of the 2,451 professors interviewed were substitutes; 193 of these had the same rank as the individual replaced, and 283 were in the same department.

A careful check of interviewer reports shows that 4 per cent of the arrowhead-designated teachers who fell into the sample of indi-viduals currently teaching (that is, excluding those known not to be teaching because of departure or leave of absence) either refused to be interviewed, were "too busy," were ill, or could not be contacted despite repeated efforts. An additional set of these names was ambiguous; interviewers' reports failed to make clear whether they had been ex-cluded as not teaching or had simply not been reached. They include at the very outside another 9 per cent of the intended sample. If a realistic guess is made that roughly half of them were not teaching, altogether about 8 per cent to 10 per cent of the originally selected sample did not get interviewed. These, and replacements for individuals not in residence, account for the 392 substitutes.

In sum, while for schools the sample is by design not representative, for teachers it definitely is so. By interviewing proportionately fewer social scientists in colleges for which we had drawn disproportionately large school samples, we achieved in principle the correct representation of the universe of college professors we were aiming at. Whatever deviation our sample shows from this universe is undoubtedly small and due to the usual problems of substituting for inaccessible schools and respondents.

2. The Questionnaire

(Page references are given for questions which have been quoted in full in the text.)

			Number of Cases
1a.	Is it your impression that there is greater concern these days than 6 or 7 years ago on the part of the public and groups outside the college over teachers' political opinions and what political matters are taught in the classroom, or not?	Greater concern	1946
		Not greater concern	435
		Don't know	68
		NA (no answer) to 1a	2

1b.　(Is greater public concern harmful? Page 36)

(If "harmful effects" in 1b, ask:)

1c.　In what ways does this greater concern cause harmful effects? Any others?　　　FREE ANSWER

(If "charge of harmful effects is overdone" in 1b)

1d.　Can you tell me any advantages in this greater concern on the part of the public? Any others?　　　FREE ANSWER

(If "greater public concern" in 1a)

1e.　Now, while there may be disagreement over the seriousness of the　　　It impairs the intellectual role a col-

Number of Cases

effects of this greater concern, let's talk for a moment about the areas that some people say might be affected in a harmful way. Here is a list of such areas. (HAND RESPONDENT CARD) If you had to make a choice, can you tell me the one area on the list where you think the most harmful effects might be felt?

lege should play in a democracy	747
It discourages constructive public discussion of important issues	656
It degrades the academic profession	60
It prepares the ground for totalitarianism	180
It really has no serious effects	130
NA to 1e	39
DNA (Does not apply: not expected to answer 1e)	639

2a. In the past few years, have you felt that your own academic freedom has been threatened in any way or not?

Threatened	499
Not threatened	1920
Don't know	22
NA to 2a	10

(If "threatened" in 2a)

2b. In what way or ways do you feel your academic freedom has been threatened?   FREE ANSWER

3a. (Threat to American intellectual activity. Page 35)

(If "present threat greater" in 3a)

3b. What is that greater threat? Anything else?   FREE ANSWER

4a. (Personal approval of student debate on Red China admission to the United Nations. Page 93)

(If "approve debate" in 4a)

4b. Suppose you were a faculty advisor to the debating team right here and the President told you he wouldn't allow the team to debate the admission of Red China issue, would

Protest vigorously	1357
Just say disagree and leave it at that	726
Not say anything	113
Don't know	124

Number of Cases

you protest vigorously to him, or just   NA to 4b   22
say you disagreed and leave it at   DNA   109
that, or would you accept his order
and not say anything?

(If "disapprove debate" in 4a)

4c.   Suppose the President of this college   Yes   23
(university) said that he wanted the   No   38
team to debate the admission of Red   Don't know   —
China issue, would you do anything   NA to 4c   5
about it?   DNA   2385

(If "yes" in 4c)

4d.   What would you do? Anything else?   FREE ANSWER

5a.   (Personal approval of Owen Lattimore speech. Page 93)

(If "approve" in 5a)

5b.   Suppose the President did ban Latti-   Protest vigorously   970
more from speaking and the students   Just say disagree and
who invited him asked you to join   leave it at that   721
with them in protesting the ban.   Not say anything   125
Would you protest the ban vigor-   Don't know   125
ously, or just say you disagree and   NA to 5b   15
leave it at that, or would you ac-   DNA   495
cept his ban and not say anything?

(If "disapprove" in 5a)

5c.   Suppose the President of this college   Yes   127
(university) said that he would not   No   191
interfere with the invitation to Lat-   Don't know   13
timore, would you do anything to   NA to 5c   11
try to prevent his appearance on this   DNA   2109
campus?

(If "yes" in 5c)

5d.   What would you do? Anything else?   FREE ANSWER

6.   Here is a list of things that some
people say have happened to social
science faculty members. I wish you
would run down the list and then tell
me for each whether or not this has

Number
of Cases

happened to you or crossed your
mind here at (name of college/uni-
versity). (HAND RESPONDENT
LIST)

6/1	Have some colleagues here on the campus ever given you advice on how to avoid getting into political trouble at this college?	Yes	356
		No	2073
		Don't know	13
		Never encountered	6
		NA to 6/1	3

6/2 (More careful not to embarrass colleagues. Page 78)

6/3	Have you noticed more of a tendency lately in social gatherings on the campus to avoid controversial political topics?	Yes	445
		No	1801
		Don't know	159
		Never encountered	35
		NA to 6/3	11

6/4 (More careful with class reference material. Page 78)

6/5	Have you ever wanted to join an organization, and despite the possibility of personal criticism for joining it, you went ahead and became a member anyway?	Yes	532
		No	1688
		Don't know	96
		Never encountered	122
		NA to 6/5	13

6/6	Do you find in your conversations with your fellow faculty members that there's lots more talk these days about teacher firings and other political security problems?	Yes	1081
		No	1264
		Don't know	82
		Never encountered	12
		NA to 6/6	12

6/7	Do you feel more inclined these days to advise student political groups not to take extreme positions for their own future well-being?	Yes	465
		No	993
		Don't know	78
		Never encountered	899
		NA to 6/7	16

6/8 (Wondered if political opinions have affected job security.
Page 76)

6/9 (Thought administration might keep political dossier.
Page 76)

Number of Cases

6/10 Do you find you are more hesitant today to sponsor a student political group that advocates unpopular ideas?

Yes	467
No	771
Don't know	76
Never encountered	1124
NA to 6/10	13

6/11 (Wondered about local gossip. Page 76)

6/12 (Describe student's past to F.B.I. Page 208-209)

6/13 If you were to hire a teaching assistant, would you wonder if his political background might possibly be embarrassing to you?

Yes	987
No	1302
Don't know	102
Never encountered	43
NA to 6/13	17

6/14 (Wondered if political views affect future job opportunities. Page 76)

6/15 (Has toned down recent writing. Page 78)

6/16 (Worried that student's warped reports could cause trouble. Page 76)

6/17 When you have private talks outside of the classroom with a student whose views are unpopular, do you try to help him conform to the prevailing views on the campus?

Yes	264
No	1653
Don't know	86
Never encountered	427
NA to 6/17	21

6/18 (Wondered if politics offend school alumni. Page 76)

6/19 (Avoid expressing views that could embarrass administration. Page 78)

6/20 (Express opinion despite possible repercussions. Page 102)

6/21 (Deliberately mention lack of personal extremism. Page 78)

7a. Have you signed any loyalty oath here at this college in which you pledged to disavow all subversive activities and ideologies?

Yes	491
No	1861
Don't know	96
NA to 7a	3

*Number
of Cases*

(If "yes" to 7a)

7b. Did you welcome the chance to sign   Welcomed chance   42
the oath, or did you feel some reluc-   Reluctant about it   242
tance about signing it, or didn't you   No feelings
have any strong feelings one way or   either way   203
the other?   NA to 7b   4
DNA   1960

(If "reluctant" about signing in 7b)

7c. Why did you sign it—because you   FREE ANSWER
felt your job was at stake or that it
wasn't worth making an issue over
this, or what?

(If "No" to 7a)

7d. Suppose you were asked to sign an   Refuse   311
oath in which you pledged to dis-   Sign with reluctance 811
avow all subversive activities and   Welcome
ideologies, would you refuse, sign   opportunity   382
it with some reluctance, or welcome   Don't know   303
the opportunity?   NA to 7d   54
DNA   590

(If "would refuse" in 7d)

7e. What's the main reason you feel this   FREE ANSWER
way? Any other reasons?

(If "sign with reluctance" in 7d.)

7f. Why would you sign it—because you   FREE ANSWER
would feel that your job was at stake
or that it wasn't worth making an
issue over this, or what?

8a. Have you ever worked on a project,   Yes   974
or received a government grant, or   No   1399
worked for the government in a job   Don't know   72
in which security clearance from the   NA to 8a   6
government was necessary?

(If not "yes" to 8a)

8b. Have you ever been turned down for   Have been
a government job or for work on a   turned down   35
government project on what you   Hasn't happened   1394

Number of Cases

suspect might have been political grounds, or hasn't this happened to you?

Don't know	20
NA to 8b	22
DNA	980

9a. Can you tell me which periodicals dealing with politics or public affairs you generally read (here we don't mean technical journals)? Any others? — FREE ANSWER

9b. I wonder if you would tell me what political groups or organizations interested in public affairs you belong to or make contributions to? Any others? — FREE ANSWER

10a. Do you usually express your own personal views on the subjects you teach, or do you usually try to avoid expressing your point of view?

Usually express own view	1767
Avoid expressing own view	554
Don't know	121
NA to 10a	9

(If "usually express" in 10a)
10b. After expressing your own point of view, have you ever wondered afterwards whether you should have said it or not?

Wondered	658
Never wondered	1084
Don't know	17
NA to 10b	8
DNA	684

(If "wondered" in 10b)
10c. Can you tell me more about it (that time, etc.)? — FREE ANSWER

11a. Have you ever felt your point of view on a political subject was reported unfavorably to any higher authorities or hasn't this happened to you?

Yes	394
No	1960
Don't know	91
NA to 11a	6

(If "yes" in 11a)
11b. Can you tell me more about it? Anything else? — FREE ANSWER

Number of Cases

(Ask all)

11c. Have you ever felt that you were being watched in a classroom?

Yes	288
No	2120
Don't know	16
NA to 11c	27

(If "yes" to 11c)

11d. Can you tell me more about it? Anything else? FREE ANSWER

12a. Leaving aside Communist groups, are there any groups that teachers like you might belong to that you feel are likely to be attacked as being subversive? Any others? FREE ANSWER

12b. (Publications that might be attacked as subversive. Page 95)

13a. Have you ever been a member of a political group which advocated a program or a cause which has been unpopular or controversial, or haven't you been a member of any such group?

Been a member	743
Never been a member	1690
Don't know	12
NA to 13a	6

(If "been a member" in 13a)

13b. Has anyone ever criticized you for belonging to such a group, or not?

Yes	339
No	376
Don't know	28
NA to 13b	—
DNA	1708

(If "yes" in 13b)

13c. Can you tell me more about that criticism? Anything else? FREE ANSWER

(If "yes" in 13b)

13d. Do you think your having belonged to this political group adversely affected your academic career, or don't you think it had any bearing on it?

Adversely affected	43
No bearing on it	284
Don't know	9
NA to 13d	3
DNA	2112

Number
of Cases

(If "yes" in 13a and not "adversely affected" in 13d)

13e. Even though nothing has happened so far, are you very worried that this past association might some day have an effect on your academic career, only a little worried, or aren't you concerned about it?

Very worried	11
A little worried	106
Not concerned	537
Don't know	5
NA to 13e	41
DNA	1751

14a. If someone accused you of leftist leanings, would you expect most, some, only a few, or hardly any of your colleagues to rally to your support?

Most	1613
Some	392
Only a few	199
Hardly any	95
Don't know	134
NA to 14a	18

14b. (Administration support in event of accusation. Page 175)

15a. (Discuss controversial issues in class. Page 135)

15b. Have you always generally held this point of view or have you come to feel this way in the past few years?

Always held this view	2210
Come to feel this way in the past few years	186
Not sure	23
NA to 15b	32

16. (Argue own point of view in class. Page 135)

17. (Emphasize facts or problems in classes. Page 140)

18. (Importance of training for betterment of society. Page 138)

19. Do you feel your philosophy on how to teach is pretty typical of that of most of your colleagues on the social science faculty here, or do you feel your philosophy is slightly different or very much different from that of your colleagues?

Pretty typical	1373
Slightly different	651
Very much different	199
Don't know	218
NA to 19	10

Number of Cases

20a. (Follows civil liberties news. Page 107)

20b. Can you tell me which specific cases,
      if any, came to your mind when I   FREE ANSWER
      asked you this last question? Any
      others?

20c. Apart from any cases here in this col-
      lege, what civil liberties or academic
      freedom cases, if any, have occurred   FREE ANSWER
      around here in this area even though
      they may not have been in the na-
      tional news? Any others?

20d. (Discuss civil liberties cases. Page 107)

21.   Compared to 6 or 7 years ago, is it
      your impression that individual stu-
      dents are less willing to express un-
      popular political views (in the class-
      room, etc.), more willing, or hasn't
      there been much change?

a. In the classroom	Less	893
	More	174
	No change	1130
	Don't know	236
	NA to 21a	18
b. In private talks with faculty	Less	456
members outside the classroom	More	186
	No change	1437
	Don't know	327
	NA to 21b	45

22.   Compared to 6 to 7 years ago, is it   Less willing   1113
      your impression that students seem   More willing   35
      to be less willing to form and to join   No change   623
      student political organizations advo-   Don't know   346
      cating what might be unpopular po-   No such groups here
      litical beliefs, or are they more will-   (volunteered)   306
      ing, or would you say there has been   NA to 22   28
      no appreciable change?

*Number
of Cases*

23. In your judgment, what are the things that could make a member of the social science faculty here controversial? Anything else?   FREE ANSWER

24. Is it your impression that members of the social science faculty here are less willing (to express unpopular political views, etc.) than they were 6 or 7 years ago, more willing, or hasn't there been much change?

 a. To express unpopular political views in the classroom

Less willing	502
More willing	68
Not much change	1425
Don't know	442
NA to 24a	14

 b. To express unpopular political views publicly in the community

Less willing	877
More willing	51
Not much change	1035
Don't know	465
NA to 24b	23

 c. To express unpopular political views privately among friends

Less willing	271
More willing	105
Not much change	1701
Don't know	356
NA to 24c	18

 d. To serve as faculty advisors to student political groups that might advocate unpopular causes.

Less willing	634
More willing	26
Not much change	766
Don't know	794
NA to 24d	231

25a. Do you have the impression that compared to 6 or 7 years ago, some members of the faculty here are more worried about possible attacks and accusations on their political beliefs and activities, less worried, or don't you think there has been much change?

More worried	1056
Less worried	79
Not much change	1074
Don't know	227
NA to 25a	15

Number
of Cases

(If "more worried" in 25a)

25b. From what sources do they think the   FREE ANSWER
      attacks might come? Anywhere else?

26a. Now I'd like to ask you about the   Avoid subjects more   415
      research your colleagues do, the pa- Avoid subjects less   53
      pers they publish, or the books they   No change   1571
      write, and the speeches they make.   Don't know   391
      In any or all of these, do you feel   NA to 26a   21
      that some of your social science col-
      leagues here have avoided subjects
      which might have political reper-
      cussion more than they might have
      had six or seven years ago, less than
      they might have had then, or don't
      you think there has been much
      change?

      (If "avoid subjects more" in 26a)
26b. Without naming names of individ-
      uals, can you give me some specific   FREE ANSWER
      illustrations of the sort of thing they
      have done in these cases? Anything
      else?

27.   (Colleagues more careful with reference lists in classes.
      Page 193)

28a. (Threat to colleagues' academic freedom. Page 171)

      (If "colleagues' freedom threatened"
      in 28a)
28b. Can you tell me about it? (them?)   FREE ANSWER
      Any others?

28c. What effect did the incident(s) have
      on the rest of the faculty here? Any- FREE ANSWER
      thing else?

29a. Has any group or person accused   Yes   1122
      anyone on this faculty here of being No   1185
      subversive or of engaging in any un- Don't know   133
      American activities in the past few   NA to 29a   11
      years?

Number
of Cases

(If "yes" in 29a)

29b. Can you tell me about it? (them?)   FREE ANSWER
Anything else?

(If "yes" in 29a)

29c. What did you think of the whole af-   FREE ANSWER
fair(s)?

(If "yes" in 29a)

29d. Do you feel the Administration handled the incident in a way which
(protected the reputation of the
college [university] etc.) or not?

1. Protected the reputation of the college (university) with the public at large	Yes	767
	No	107
	Don't know	160
	NA to 29d(1)	88
	DNA	1329
2. Protected the rights of the faculty	Yes	717
	No	167
	Don't know	154
	NA to 29d(2)	84
	DNA	1329
3. Protected the educational standards of the college (university)	Yes	712
	No	140
	Don't know	180
	NA to 29d(3)	90
	DNA	1329

30. (Protect faculty rights or school's reputation. Page 141)

31a. Thinking back over the past few years, do you know of any cases of teachers here who probably would have been added to the staff if they hadn't had controversial political views, or don't you know of any such cases?	Know of such a case	284
	Don't know of any case	2156
	NA to 31a	11
31b. Do you know of anyone who is no longer teaching here as a result of	Know of such a case here	585

Number of Cases

his political views, or don't you know of any such cases?	Don't know of any 1847
	NA to 31b 19

31c. Do you think it is possible at this college (university) that a man with slightly greater merit but who is unconventional could be passed over for a permanent appointment in favor of a man with somewhat less merit who is conventional, or don't you think that could happen here?

Could happen here 1428
Could not happen
  here 733
Don't know 267
NA to 31c 23

(If "could happen here" in 31c)
31d. Can you tell me about any cases here such as this—again without mentioning names? Any others?

FREE ANSWER

32. Compared to what you know about other academic institutions, would you say that working conditions here (teaching load, salaries, and so on) are: Unusually good; good, but could be improved; fair; or not good, but could be worse; or unusually bad?

Unusually good 422
Good, but could be
  improved 1280
Fair 511
Not good, but could
  be worse 175
Unusually bad 20
No opinion 30
NA to 32 13

33a. Compared to what you know about other academic institutions, by and large, would you say that relations among faculty members here are: unusually good; good, but could be improved; fair; or not good, but could be worse; or unusually bad?

Unusually good 951
Good, but could
  be improved 1084
Fair 304
Not good, but could
  be worse 57
Unusually bad 10
No opinion 36
NA to 33a 9

33b. Compared to what you know about other academic institutions, by and large, would you say that relations between the faculty and the administration of this college (university)

Unusually good 694
Good, but could be
  improved 1023
Fair 469
Not good, but could

		Number of Cases
are: unusually good; good, but could be improved; fair; or not good, but could be worse; or unusually bad?	be worse	164
	Unusally bad	39
	No opinion	52
	NA to 33b	10

34a. (Faculty-administration discussions of academic freedom. Page 169)

34b. (Administration stand on academic freedom. Page 169)

34c. How would you describe the administration's stand on matters of academic freedom? Anything else?   FREE ANSWER

35a.	Of course it is possible to have events that stir up strong feelings on the *local* or *state* as well as the *national* level. Which would you say you have had *more* of around here—local, state, or national controversies?	Local	472
		State	365
		National	1233
		Don't know	350
		NA to 35a	31

35b. Can you tell me about any *local* events that have created strong pro and con feelings here in the past few years?   FREE ANSWER

36a-d. (Pressures on the school administration. Page 38)

37. (Most powerful campus voice in academic freedom matters. Page 170)

38. Now, I should like to ask you some questions about a man *who admits he is a Communist.*

38a.	Suppose he is working in a defense plant. Should he be fired, or not?	Yes	1608
		No	408
		Don't know	406
		NA to 38a	29

38b.	Suppose he is a clerk in a store. Should he be fired, or not?	Yes	227
		No	2014
		Don't know	194
		NA to 38b	16

Number of Cases

38c.	Suppose he is teaching in a college. Should he be fired, or not?	Yes	1093
		No	861
		Don't know	451
		NA to 38c	46

39. Now I would like you to think of another person. (HAND RESPOND-ENT CARD) A man whose loyalty has been questioned before a Congressional Committee, but who swears under oath he has never been a Communist.

39a.	Suppose he has been working in a defense plant. Should he be fired, or not?	Yes	177
		No	1950
		Don't know	299
		NA to 39a	25
39b.	Suppose he is a clerk in a store. Should he be fired, or not?	Yes	26
		No	2308
		Don't know	100
		NA to 39b	17
39c.	Suppose he is teaching in a college or university. Should he be fired, or not?	Yes	88
		No	2135
		Don't know	196
		NA to 39c	32

40.	How great a danger do you feel that American Communists are to this country at the present time—a very great danger, a great danger, some danger, hardly any danger, or no danger?	A very great danger	146
		A great danger	211
		Some danger	1001
		Hardly any danger	859
		No danger	168
		Don't know	50
		NA to 40	16

41. If there are students who want to join it, do you think that a (Young Democratic Club, etc.) ought to be allowed on this campus, or not?

		Number of Cases
Young Democratic Club	Allowed	2276
	Not allowed	97
	Depends (vol.)	30
	Don't know	36
	NA to Y.D.C.	12
Young Republican Club	Allowed	2277
	Not allowed	97
	Depends (vol.)	30
	Don't know	35
	NA to Y.R.C.	12
Students for Democratic Action	Allowed	1845
	Not allowed	230
	Depends (vol.)	88
	Don't know	274
	NA to S.D.A.	14
Young Socialist League	Allowed	1905
	Not allowed	355
	Depends (vol.)	69
	Don't know	109
	NA to Y.S.L.	13
Young Communist League	Allowed	929
	Not allowed	1303
	Depends (vol.)	109
	Don't know	94
	NA to Y.C.L.	16

42. In general, how do you feel about a social science teacher who is an admitted Communist? Do you or don't you feel that (he is not very different from any other teacher with unorthodox views, etc.)?*

a. He is not very different from any other teacher with unorthodox views

Yes	733
No	1405
Don't know	234
NA to 42(a)	79

---

* The answer categories to these questions should have read "Agree" and "Disagree," but a typing error making them "Yes" and "No" was not detected.

		Number of Cases
b. He is troublesome mainly as a source of embarrassment to the college	Yes	921
	No	1304
	Don't know	178
	NA to 42(b)	48
c. He is not fit to be a teacher	Yes	1241
	No	806
	Don't know	327
	NA to 42(c)	77
d. He is a dangerous person to have students exposed to	Yes	1085
	No	1076
	Don't know	244
	NA to 42(d)	46

43.   (Radical teacher a campus asset. Page 120)

44.   On political matters, do you feel that you are **more** liberal or more conservative **than**
    a) Most of the trustees here at this college
    b) Most of the administration here
    c) Most of the faculty here
    d) Most of the alumni of this college
    e) Most people in the community in which the college is located.
    (The answers to this question appear in Chapter VI, Footnote 3, page 133.)

(If "more liberal" or "more conservative" in 44a, b, c, d, or e)

44f.   Have you felt some pressures—direct or indirect—to conform to the prevailing political pattern or haven't you felt any of these pressures?

Have felt	496
Have not felt	1596
Don't know	16
NA to 44f	36
DNA	307

(If "felt pressures" in 44f)

44g.   How have these pressures shown   FREE ANSWER
       themselves? Any other ways?

Number
of Cases

45. Here is a list of four occupations.
(HAND RESPONDENT CARD)

45a. Now suppose a typical businessman were to rank these
four occupations by the prestige he holds for each—
in what order do you think he would rank each?

Rank	Manager of a Branch Bank	Account Executive of an Advertising Agency	A Lawyer	A College Professor
First	947	404	700	192
Second	532	677	751	283
Third	498	627	680	438
Fourth	266	535	112	1330

Don't know, or no answer, to 45a: 208

45b. How do you think a typical Congressman would rank them?

Rank				
First	322	143	1634	107
Second	851	542	337	476
Third	690	860	201	455
Fourth	343	661	34	1168

Don't know, or no answer, to 45b: 245

45c. Finally, how do you think the typical trustee of your
college (university) would rank them?

Rank				
First	538	192	821	493
Second	371	377	737	559
Third	697	589	378	380
Fourth	438	886	108	612

Don't know, or no answer, to 45c: 407

FACTUAL DATA

F1. How long have you been teaching
in colleges or universities?

Less than 5 years	382
5 up to 10 years	832
10 up to 20 years	545
20 up to 30 years	404
30 years or more	282
NA to F1	6

			Number of Cases
F2.	How long have you been teaching at *this* college or university?	Less than 5 years	809
		5 up to 10 years	876
		10 up to 20 years	349
		20 up to 30 years	274
		30 years or more	136
		NA to F2	7
F3a.	Do you have a permanent or rotating chairman of your department?	Permanent chairman	1779
		Rotating chairman	585
		NA to F3a	87
F3b.	Are you now or have you been a department head here?	Yes	758
		No	1668
		Don't know	4
		NA to F3b	21
F3c.	(Do you) (Does your department chairman) (department head) have a considerable amount of latitude and authority in making policy decisions or would you say (you) he (are) is essentially concerned with administrative details?	Considerable amount of latitude and authority	1115
		Essentially concerned with administrative details	1129
		Don't know	156
		NA to F3c	51
F4.	Can you tell me what degrees you hold?	B.A.	1871
		B.S.	381
		M.A.	1882
		M.S.	163
		Ph.D.	1697
		Other	336
		NA to F4	10
F5a.	(Respondent's department. Page 4)		
F5b.	What courses do you now teach?	FREE ANSWER	
F5c.	Do you get a great deal of opportunity in the courses you teach to discuss controversial issues, only lit-	Great deal of opportunity	1701
		Only little op-	

		Number of Cases
tle opportunity, or hardly any at all?	portunity	516
	Hardly any at all	200
	Don't know	18
	NA to F5c	16

F6.	Will you tell me what rank you hold —instructor, lecturer, assistant professor, associate professor, or full professor?	Instructor	334
		Lecturer	53
		Assistant Professor	630
		Associate Professor	516
		Full Professor	881
		Don't know	5
		Does not have a rank	22
		NA to F6	10

F7.	Do you have a permanent appointment here on this faculty or not?	Yes	1662
		No	743
		Don't know	26
		NA to F7	20

F8.	Have you ever hired any teaching assistants?	Yes	970
		No	1455
		Don't know	11
		NA to F8	15

F9a.	Have you written a dissertation?	Yes	2003
		No	438
		NA to F9a	10

	(If "yes" on F9a)		
F9b.	Has it been published in full or in part?	In full	617
		In part	598
		Not been published	779
		NA to F9b, DNA	457

	(Ask all)		
F9c.	Have you published any (other) papers?	Yes	1758
		No	680
		NA to F9c	13

	(If "yes" on F9c)		
F9d.	How many?	2 or less	363
		3 or more	1377
		NA to F9d, DNA	711

Number of Cases

(Ask all)

F9e.	Have you published any (other) books?	Yes	861
		No	1559
		NA to F9e	31

F10a.	Can you tell me any academic honors which have been bestowed on you?	FREE ANSWER	

F10b.	Have you served on any college or university committees?	Yes	2078
		No	361
		NA to F10b	12

F10c.	Have you held office in any professional or academic societies?	Yes	1210
		No	1231
		NA to F10c	10

F10d.	Have you delivered any papers at the meetings of any professional or academic societies?	None	839
		1 or 2	624
		3 or more	977
		NA to F10d	11

F11.	Have you ever applied for a Fulbright lecturer or scholar award?	Yes	359
		No	2074
		Don't know	3
		NA to F11	15

F12.	Have you served as a consultant to industry or any other organizations excluding the federal government?	Yes	857
		No	1587
		Don't know	—
		NA to F12	7

F13a.	Is your salary today higher than it was 5 years ago?	Yes	2216
		No	137
		NA to F13a	98

(If "yes" on F13a)

F13b.	By what per cent has it gone up?	Less than 5%	52
		5 to 10%	238
		10 to 20%	517
		20 to 30%	491
		30% or more	810
		Don't know	88
		NA to F13b, DNA	255

Number of Cases

(Ask all)

F13c. Do you have any outside source of income besides your salary?

Yes	1491
No	922
NA to F13c	38

F14. Are you a member of the American Association of University Professors?

Yes	1227
No	1207
NA to F14	17

F15a. Are you married, single, widowed, or divorced?

Married	1972
Single	396
Widowed	36
Divorced	40
NA to F15a	7

(If "married," "widowed," or "divorced" in F15a)

F15b. Do you have any children?

Yes	1632
No	414
NA to F15b, DNA	405

(If "yes" in 15b)

F15c. How many?

1	462
2	667
3	352
4	106
5	34
6 or more	11
NA to F15c	—
DNA	819

F16. Have you (your husband) ever served in any branch of the armed forces?

Yes	1321
No	1105
NA to F16	25

F17. Sex:

Male	2158
Female	264
NA to F17	29

F18. What is your age?

30 or under	202
31-40	936
41-50	632
51-60	465

		Number of Cases
	61 or older	202
	NA to F18	14
F19. Race:	White	2330
	Negro	74
	Other	13
	NA to F19	34
F20. Do you mind telling me where your grandparents were born?	United States	1702
	Canada	109
	Great Britain (England, Scotland, Wales)	272
	Ireland	194
	Germany	344
	Scandinavia (Norway, Sweden, Denmark)	134
	Italy	33
	Other Western Europe (Netherlands, Belgium, France, Switzerland, Spain, Portugal)	114
	Poland	55
	Other Eastern Europe (Austria, Hungary, Czechoslovakia, Rumania, Bulgaria, Greece, Yugoslavia, Albania, Russia, Finland, Latvia, Lithuania, Estonia)	234
	All other	38
	Don't know	12
	NA to F20	8

Number of Cases

F21. Can you tell me your father's occupation?

High School or Grade School Teacher	70
College or University Teacher	111
Other Professional	565
Semi-professional	66
Proprietors, Managers, Officials	617
Clerical	93
Sales	198
Farmers, Farm Managers	326
Skilled Workers	285
Protective Workers	22
Operatives, Laborers	66
Other	14
NA to F21	18

F22. Do you mind telling me your religious preference?

Protestant	1642
Catholic	291
Jewish	108
Other	64
None	323
Don't know	9
NA to F22	14

F23. How many times in the past year, if at all, has a representative from the F.B.I. talked with you—for any purpose?

None	950
1 or 2	676
3 or more	808
NA to F23	17

F24. Are the people you see the most of socially mainly from your department, from the faculty generally, or from the community?

Own department	306
Faculty generally	1197
Community	745
Don't know	152
NA to F24	51

F25. Would you classify yourself politically as a Republican, Democrat, Independent, or what?

Republican	384
Democrat	1129
Independent	881
Other	22
Don't know	19
NA to F25	16

Number of Cases

F26.	Do you mind telling me whom you voted for in 1952 for President?	Eisenhower	737
		Stevenson	1414
		Other	13
		Did not vote	253
		Don't remember	4
		NA to F26	30
F27.	Do you mind telling me whom you voted for in 1948 for President?	Dewey	548
		Truman	1229
		Wallace	81
		Thurmond	12
		Other	71
		Did not vote	439
		Don't remember	38
		NA to F27	33

3. Comments on the Nature of Classification in Social Research

AT THE BEGINNING of Chapter III we sketched the general considerations on which the indices used in this study are based. Because they play such a basic role in the whole analysis the procedure deserves some additional discussion.

To illustrate, we shall use the productivity index introduced in Chapter I. We wished to classify social scientists according to something which might be called their "eminence." Such an intended classification is necessarily vague. A concept like "eminence," taken over from everyday language, can be translated into a research instrument in many ways. We can think of a long list of items which would serve as indicators; but for practical purposes we usually want to settle on a small number of them. A heated debate over which items to include in the final index often occurs. But what difference would various choices actually make? To clarify the issue the following experiment was undertaken.

In addition to the productivity index used in the text a second index was constructed using as indicators also external achievements, such as holding office in a professional society or acting as a consultant for business or government agencies. We call this the honors index and compare it in the following list item by item with our main productivity index.

Honors Index	Productivity Index
1a. Has a Ph.D.	1b. Has written a dissertation
2a. Has published three or more papers	2b. Has published at least one paper
3a. Has held office in a professional society	3b. Has read three or more papers at meetings
4a. Has worked as a consultant	4b. Has published at least one book

By intention the indices have two partially overlapping items: 1a and 1b differ only to the extent that there are respondents who have finished a dissertation but not fulfilled other Ph.D. requirements; we have 271 such cases.[1] 2b has a lower requirement than 2a: 363 respondents have published either one paper or two. The remaining pairs of items differ in manifest content. These deal with honors, rather than with other kinds of publications, as indicators of eminence.

Table A3-1 classifies all respondents in two ways: according to their productivity scores and to their scores on the new honors index.

Table A3-1
Interrelation between Two Indices of Eminence

PRODUCTIVITY SCORE	HONORS SCORE			
	4, 3 (High)	2	0, 1 (Low)	Total
4, 3 (High)	789	261	64	1114
2	196	214	201	611
0, 1 (Low)	20	134	535	689
Total	1005	609	800	2414*

* The remaining thirty-seven respondents did not answer all of the questions on which the two scores are based.

In the main diagonal, reading from upper left to lower right, we find all the people (789 + 214 + 535) who have the same level of eminence on either index. The remainder, 36 per cent of the total, are classified differently by the two indices. At first sight this looks like a discouraging result; the "eminence" measured by one index is quite often not the same as that measured by another.

---

1. Another six are recorded as having a Ph.D. without a dissertation— probably a result of interviewing and coding mistakes. Some respondents may have written a "dissertation" for the Masters degree.

This outcome, however, is both unavoidable and of limited consequence. It is unavoidable because indicators can at best have only an inferential relation to the underlying factor sought after. Whether a man is liberal, whether he has status in the community, whether an armed unit has morale, or whether an educational system is a success—all these questions can never be answered explicitly, because one cannot measure morale or status with the kind of agreement and precision that one can measure weight or length of an object. This has nothing to do with the fact that some of the things we might want to classify are mental or psychological intangibles. Whether two men are friends is indeed often a matter of external observation, but friendship itself is not a concrete object to be perceived directly. Indicators are still needed to make an inference of its existence. One might tag the whole procedure "diagnostic process."

Indicators will of course vary in how well they reveal the characteristics we seek. To study a person's anxiety, we might show him a set of pictures which are somewhat ambiguous in content and ask him to interpret them. If his answers repeatedly refer to dangerous situations, we could conclude that the person is quite anxiety-ridden. Such an inference from a Thematic Apperception Test undoubtedly seems more complex and less certain than, say, an inference of mathematical ability based on a test of mathematical performance.

The certainty of the inference from manifest data to latent characteristic depends upon many factors. One of these is the degree to which an indicator question permits varied interpretation. It is not possible to formulate a question whose answers allow of only one interpretation. Respondents' experiences immediately prior to the interview may enter in. A man who belongs, by and large, in the middle range of permissiveness might give very restrictive answers one particular morning when his children have irked him a great deal, and unusually permissive ones another time just after an excellent dinner. In short, indicators are only related to an intended underlying classification with a certain probability. The latent characteristic can never, therefore, be reached with certainty. All classifications of this kind in social research have to be "impure."

The consequences of this fact are twofold. One of these is encouraging. If we have a reasonable collection of indicator items, then it does not matter much for most purposes which subset we use to form our index. This is true so long as we are aiming at finding statistical relations between a number of variables, not at the correct classification of each individual person. The idea is best explained by a concrete example. We shall raise a problem in which "eminence" is one of the characteristics involved. We shall then look at the actual data twice:

first using the productivity index and then the honors index as a measure of eminence. The purpose of the comparison will be to see what difference this makes in the final result.

Our problem will be to weigh the relative importance of eminence and age in a teacher's chances for reaching success in the professional hierarchy by becoming a full professor. How do age and eminence together affect promotion? Table A3-2 gives the answer we get if we use our productivity index as the measure of eminence.

Table A3-2
Percentages Who Are Full Professors According to Age and Eminence (Productivity Index)*

EMINENCE IN TERMS OF PRODUCTIVITY SCORE	AGE		
	Under 40	41-50	51 or More
4, 3 (High)	15% (324)	63% (358)	87% (421)
2	7% (349)	39% (131)	65% (122)
0, 1 (Low)	2% (439)	23% (126)	45% (108)

* In this and all following tables in the Appendices, the total numbers of cases on which percentages are based are given in parenthesis. For example, 15 per cent of the 324 teachers under forty and with high productivity were full professors.

In Tables A3-2 and A3-3, lecturers and respondents saying they have no formal rank are not included.

Table A3-2 tells a rather interesting story. Reading across each row, we see that regardless of their eminence the proportion of full professors increases sharply with age. Within the columns, we then learn that teachers who are more eminent in terms of productivity have more often been made full professors. The table also suggests that age and productivity can compensate for each other. On the highest productivity level about two-thirds have already become full professors below the age of fifty, whereas in the middle productivity range the same proportion is reached only in the oldest age group. On the other hand, even in the lowest productivity group almost half the respondents past the age of fifty have become full professors. Many of these men and women doubtless earn their promotion to top rank by their excellent service as teachers.

What would have happened if we had used the honors index as a measure of eminence? Table A3-3 gives the answer. The result is much like the one before. Again age is more important than eminence. Only in the second row is there a noticeable difference between Tables A3-2 and A3-3. Productivity seems to be more helpful in the 41-to-50 age group; honors play more of a role among the oldest people.

In spite of the fact that, as shown by Table A3-1, the two indices are not highly correlated with one another, when they are related to an outside variable they produce much the same result. This "interchangeability of indices" reappears again and again in empirical social research. Studies have shown, for instance, that different social strata have sharply contrasting attitudes on economic and political matters. But what are "social strata," and how should they be measured? We could use as indicators such things as peoples' possessions, their income, or their education. In most such studies it has turned out that whichever index is used, the correlation between strata and any given attitude is about the same. In other words, the findings of empirical social research are to a considerable extent invariant when reasonable substitutions from one index to another are made.

Table A3-3
Table A3-2 Repeated Using the Honors Index of Eminence

EMINENCE IN TERMS OF HONORS SCORE	AGE		
	Under 40	41-50	50 or More
4, 3 (High)	18% (312)	65% (308)	88% (368)
2	6% (298)	28% (149)	73% (148)
0, 1 (Low)	2% (488)	22% (150)	44% (132)

This then is the general rule based on very diversified research practice. To translate a rather broad but non-concrete concept into an empirical research instrument, there will always be a large number of indicators eligible for a classificatory index. A relatively small number of such items is practicably more manageable. If we choose two sets of reasonable items to form two alternative indices, the following two facts will usually be found:

a. The two indices will be related, but they will not classify all the people in a study in precisely the same way.

b. The two indices will usually lead to very similar empirical results if they are separately cross-tabulated against a third outside variable.

While this rule of the "interchangeability of indices" is one of the foundations of empirical social research, its beneficial consequences are paid for by a serious but unavoidable price. Because we can never reach "pure" classifications, a certain number of cases must always be misclassified, and therefore the empirical findings are less clear than if we could somehow have precise measures for the variables with which a study is concerned.

In Chapter VI, for instance, we describe a number of differences between conservative and permissive teachers. These differences would undoubtedly be even greater if we could look into the souls of the professors and classify them according to what we find there. But because we must be satisfied with outward manifestations, our statistical results are always somewhat attenuated. This leads to a need for the study of "deviant cases": cautious professors who are not worried, conservatives who will permit a Young Communist League. Sometimes these are so few that only a case-by-case inspection is possible. Sometimes there are enough to permit statistical refinement by the introduction of qualifying variables. The reader will find examples of this process all through the present report.[2]

4. The Classification of Colleges

THE THREE BASIC CHARACTERISTICS of colleges for which classifications have been developed in this study are type of control, size of student enrollment, and academic quality. Our procedures for forming these classifications are described in this Appendix. The categories presented in Appendix I were used as the basis for stratification of our sample, but for the subsequent analysis, the refined classifications developed here were employed.

Type of Control

WHAT WE HAVE CALLED type of control actually involves two characteristics: curriculum and control. With respect to curriculum, teachers colleges have been distinguished from all others. The remaining schools—including university colleges and technical schools with liberal arts departments—have been subdivided into four groups: public, private nondenominational, Catholic, and Protestant.

Many of the colleges devoted to the training of teachers in this country are undergoing a process of evolution. Originally set up as two-year normal schools, they grew into four-year teachers colleges, and then in some cases, began to develop a liberal arts program. Examination of *American Universities and Colleges*, 1952 (referred to hereafter as

---

2. For a more detailed discussion of concept and index formation see Paul F. Lazarsfeld and Morris Rosenberg, *The Language of Social Research* (Glencoe, Ill.: The Free Press, 1955).

Colleges) shows that there are two types of four-year teachers colleges, a pure type concerned exclusively with the preparation of teachers, and a mixed type which also has a liberal arts program. The latter are identified in *Colleges* as both teachers *and* liberal arts colleges. Many of the mixed type still retain the phrase "teachers college" in their names, and study of their curriculum reveals that the main emphasis is still on the training of teachers. Therefore we have classified both the pure and the mixed type as teachers colleges. Of the twenty-nine teachers colleges in our sample, four have a liberal arts program as well. With two exceptions, one private and one Catholic school, all the teachers colleges in the sample are publicly controlled.

We have classified as public schools all non-teachers colleges that are under the control of either city, county, state, or federal government. There was no difficulty in placing the schools which fall in this category.

Distinguishing nondenominational private schools from Protestant colleges was more troublesome.[1] While most of the private colleges in the United States were founded by religious groups, there has been a long-range trend away from religious control, and many of these colleges have either broken completely or retain only nominal ties with the founding church. Our problem of classification stemmed from the fact that these schools vary considerably in their present degree of secularization. Criteria had to be found to distinguish schools which retain a sufficiently religious atmosphere for us to call them religiously controlled from those which have broken more completely with early ties.

The literature on higher education offers little help, for there are no standard criteria. Some investigators, such as Knapp and Greenbaum,[2] rely exclusively on the college's designation of itself as reported in *Colleges*. But this usually fails to distinguish only nominally affiliated schools from those under the strict control of a religious body. Ostheimer, in a publication for the Commission on Financing Higher Education,[3] relies

---

1. The problem of religious control applies only to the Protestant colleges. Many of the Protestant colleges are listed as related to or affiliated with a religious body rather than as controlled by a church. Catholic colleges on the other hand are listed as being controlled by one or another order of the Catholic Church. Among other things this means that the administrators of the college (and in many instances the faculty) are members of the church hierarchy. All of our Catholic schools satisfy the criteria described in the following paragraphs.

2. Robert Knapp and Joseph Greenbaum, *The Younger American Scholar* (Chicago: University of Chicago Press, 1953).

3. Richard Ostheimer, *A Statistical Analysis of the Organization of Higher Education in the United States, 1948-49* (New York: Columbia University Press, 1951), p. 36.

mainly on data compiled by the federal Department of Health, Welfare, and Education, which defines control in terms of legal responsibility for the school; but he points out shortcomings, and modifies the government's classification in terms of the college's self-description given in *Colleges*. We have therefore formed an independent classification. Several indicators of religious control and religious atmosphere come to mind:

1. A minister as a president of the college.
2. Church representation on the governing board.
3. Financial support from a church.
4. Religion as a criterion of faculty recruitment.
5. Religion as a criterion of student recruitment.
6. Compulsory chapel.
7. Compulsory religious courses.
8. Restrictions on social activities (e.g., dancing).

Unfortunately, systematic current data were available on only some of these items. The 1952 *Colleges* provides the following information:

1. Whether the institution is related to or controlled by a church.
2. Whether church representation is required on the governing board.
3. Whether chapel attendance on the part of students is compulsory.
4. Whether students are required to take courses in religion.

No one of these, by itself, is an acceptable basis for classifying schools. There are some colleges listed as related to a church, or as having church representation on the board, which appear in all other respects to be nondenominational. And a course in religion, or attendance at chapel, are sometimes compulsory at otherwise nondenominational schools. For instance, in a study by Cuninggim,[4] it was found that chapel attendance was required in 56 per cent of nondenominational liberal arts colleges, compared to 91 per cent of church-related colleges.

To separate out the secularized schools, an index of religious control was constructed using three concretely factual items. We gave a school a score of 1 for each of the following: a religious body is represented on the governing board of the school, chapel is compulsory, a course in the Bible or religion is compulsory. Colleges having any two or all three of these characteristics were then classified as Protestant-controlled, the remainder as privately-controlled. All of the former, it should be added, describe themselves as church-related.

---

4. Merrimon Cuninggim, *The College Seeks Religion* (New Haven: Yale University Press, 1947).

Size of School

THE CLASSIFICATION OF SCHOOLS by size is based on student enrollment data compiled by the federal government[5] for the academic year 1954-55, the year in which the field work for this study was conducted.

Our size figure for a school includes full-time undergraduate, part-time undergraduate, professional, and graduate students. This means that colleges which are part of larger universities have been classified according to the total size of the principal student bodies of the university. We feel that the atmosphere of such undergraduate colleges is determined more by the over-all size of their parent institutions than simply by the extent of their particular enrollments. At our own university, for instance, it would seem ridiculous to neglect the fact that Columbia College (not interviewed in our study) with its 2,500 students is part of one of the largest universities in the nation.

The number of part-time students was converted to a full-time equivalent, counting each 3.5 part-time students as one full-time. This figure is taken from Ostheimer, whose data show that the average full-time student takes fourteen credit hours per semester, against four for the part-time student.

Only "resident students" were counted. These are defined in the government bulletin as taking courses of college grade, that is, courses carrying credit toward a degree. Thus extension students and those enrolled in adult education courses of non-college grade were excluded. Extension students are not clearly defined either by most schools nor in this bulletin; typically they are part-time students, taking courses at the lower levels of undergraduate work, or courses which are not of college grade, often at a branch campus or extension center.

The size categories most often used in the text were the following:

Size Category		Number of Students
Very small	(Size 1)	Up to 700
Small	(Size 2)	700-2,500
Large	(Size 3)	2,500-9,000
Very large	(Size 4)	9,000 or more

The Distribution of the Sample

THE DISTRIBUTION of colleges and of respondents according to the type of control and school size categories just described was as follows:

5. *Resident, Extension, and Adult Education Enrollment in Institutions of Higher Education: November, 1954*, Circular No. 454, U. S. Department of Health, Education, and Welfare, September, 1955.

Number of Colleges

TYPE OF ORGANIZATION

	Private	Public	Teachers College	Protestant	Catholic	Total
Size 1	7	3	14	20	6	50
Size 2	15	7	13	12	6	43
Size 3	17	19	2	2	6	56
Size 4	5	11	—	—	—	16
Total	44	40	29	34	18	165

Number of Respondents

	Private	Public	Teachers College	Protestant	Catholic	Total
Size 1	62	20	77	111	33	303
Size 2	264	93	102	152	82	693
Size 3	341	390	16	28	93	868
Size 4	156	431	—	—	—	587
Total	823	934	195	291	208	2,451

The Quality of Colleges

THE INDEX of academic quality was constructed from the following six items available from source books:

1. Total number of volumes in the college library.
2. Ratio of library books to number of students.
3. Ratio of annual budget (1951-1952) to number of students.
4. Proportion of Ph.D.'s on the faculty.
5. Production of scholars.
6. Tuition fees.

With one exception, our information came again from the 1952 *Colleges*. Figures for production of scholars were taken from the Knapp and Greenbaum study cited above.

Each of these items has bearing for the intellectual quality or status of colleges. The absolute size of the library (1) is a valid indicator of quality since library books are in principle available to all students and the sheer number of books suggests the breadth of scholarship possible. At the same time, the larger the ratio of books to students (2), the more accessible are library materials to each individual. Hence we felt that this ratio should also be included as part of our final index.

The size of a school's budget in terms of dollars-per-student (3) is of obvious importance. The proportion of Ph.D.'s on the faculty (4) was computed on the basis of the total faculty, including part-time instructors. It was not possible to obtain this ratio with complete accuracy for a number of large universities, since the figures given for faculty "doctoral" degrees sometimes include holders of the M.D. and other professional degrees.

The Knapp and Greenbaum index of productivity of scholars for a school (5) describes the proportion of all students graduating between 1946 and 1951 who went on to receive graduate fellowships, scholarships, or Ph.D.'s. A high index score presumably testifies to the high standards of recruitment and training of the undergraduate institution. Knapp and Greenbaum give separate index scores for male and female scholars at a school. Since the male scores are almost always higher than the female, we used male index scores in ranking our colleges when both were given. We also computed a male score equivalent to make the scores for women's colleges comparable, multiplying them by the over-all ratio of the average male to the average female score. Scores for about 100 of our sample of 165 colleges are given in the Knapp and Greenbaum book; we have assumed that our remaining colleges produced very few scholars in the years covered by this study. This may be somewhat in error for two reasons. First, Knapp and Greenbaum limited their study to scholars attending the twenty-five leading graduate centers in the country. Possibly some sample colleges produced scholars enrolled in other graduate institutions. Secondly, the authors tell us that they had to discard nineteen schools because of inadequate data; it is possible that some of our sample schools were among these.

Tuition fees (6) are related to quality on two counts. Principally, tuition is a major source of income; the more economic resources a school has at its disposal, the more educational facilities it can provide. In addition, tuition to some extent indicates the demand for a college's educational "product." Certainly, expensive schools that do not offer a superior education can seldom compete successfully for the better students. Empirical support for the use of tuition as an indicator of quality is provided by two recent studies. Knapp and Greenbaum found tuition to be highly related to their index of production of scholars. An unpublished study by Natalie Rogoff, sponsored by the College Entrance Examination Board, shows that tuition is the best single indicator of quality as measured by a variety of other items including College Entrance Examination Board membership.[6]

On each of these six items, every college was given a score ranging from 1 to 5, depending on its location in the total distribution for the

6. Natalie Rogoff, "Board Member Colleges: a Comparative Analysis," Bureau of Applied Social Research, May, 1957.

item. For each item five groups of roughly equal size were set up. It should be noted that the intervals between scores on a single item are therefore not equally distant in this type of rank-order scale; the "quality" measured is relative, not absolute. In the case of tuition fees, because of large differences between even the nonresident fees of the public schools and the tuition costs of the private, public and non-public schools were separately ranked. The final quality score for each college was its average on the various items; these composite scores ranged in value from a low of 1.0 to a high of 5.0. For most of the schools data were available on all six items. In a very few cases, the final status score had to be based on four items or less.

The scoring and distribution for the six individual items, and the distribution of the final quality score, follow:

Distribution of Schools on the Six Quality Items

	Score Assigned	Number of Schools
1. Size of Library		
8,000 to 30,000 books	1 (low)	36
35,000 to 57,000	2	33
60,000 to 126,000	3	32
130,000 to 300,000	4	30
340,000 or larger	5 (High)	29
Information not available		5
2. Books per Student		
6 to 37	1	34
38 to 50	2	33
54 to 72	3	32
75 to 115	4	31
116 or more	5	30
Information not available		5
3. Budget per Student		
$300 to $600	1	33
$650 to $950	2	33
$1,000 to $1,200	3	32
$1,250 to $1,700	4	29
$1,750 or higher	5	28
Information not available		10
4. Proportion of Ph.D.'s on Faculty		
8% to 18%	1	30
19% to 24%	2	31
25% to 34%	3	35
35% to 44%	4	27
45% or more	5	18
Information not available*		24

Distribution of Schools on the Six Quality Items (continued)

	Score Assigned	Number of Schools
5. Production of Scholars		
(Knapp and Greenbaum Index)		
No scholars (school not listed)	1	56
0.3 to 1.9 per cent of graduates	2	30
2.0 to 3.9	3	30
4.0 to 8.3	4	24
9.1 to 61.2	5	25
6. Tuition Fees		
Non-Public Colleges		
$100 to $300	1	19
$320 to $390	2	21
$400 to $480	3	20
$500 to $575	4	18
$600 or more	5	19
Public Colleges		
$0 to $100	1	12
$116 to $192	2	12
$200 to $261	3	13
$300 to $350	4	14
$360 to $520	5	12
Information not available		5

* Includes some large universities where accurate data were not available because those holding professional degrees were included in published figures.

A final quality score was obtained for each school by averaging together the six scores assigned to it above.

Distribution of Schools on the Quality Index

Quality Score	Number of Schools	Quality Score	Number of Schools
1.00-1.49 (Low)	11	3.00-3.49	23
1.50-1.99	21	3.50-3.99	16
2.00-2.49	34	4.00-4.49	12
2.50-2.99	29	4.50-5.00 (High)	19
			165

5. Some Problems of Verification: The Credibility of Teachers' Reports about Their Colleagues and Their Schools

EVERY SCIENTIFIC STUDY must face the problem of verifying its obtained data as well as possible within the limitations of available information. In this project, two kinds of data were collected from each respondent: factual and attitudinal material about the teacher himself, and descriptions of his surroundings—campus events, colleague attitudes, administrative performance, and the like.

The accuracy of information about respondents themselves can be reinforced, in principle, in a number of ways. Certain facts about teachers are a matter of record—their age, their length of residence at the school, their rank, their publications, and so on. Overt behavior patterns in general can be checked by objective observation and study. But if information concerning a state of mind is desired, without observable external correlates, it becomes necessary, of course, to rely solely on the reports of subjects themselves. Even with these, however, we can make internal checks to some extent: we noted, for instance, whether teachers were reasonably consistent in answering closely related questions, or whether the spontaneous comments volunteered as they decided how to answer a checklist question supported their choice. Also, we can expect to find certain common-sense linkages borne out—as when we anticipate that, other things being equal, teachers who have undergone sharp personal attack will usually describe more signs of apprehension than those who have not.

Since we have gone to considerable pains in our report to establish the credibility of the main personal characteristics discussed, and since there is a voluminous literature on this problem, we shall not dwell further on it here. The problem of the validity of subjects' reports on their environment, however, as contrasted to descriptions of themselves, is relatively less well explored. And so when we have reported teachers' descriptions of events and attitudes in their surroundings, the reader has consistently been referred to this appendix. The particular question we wish to raise concerns the extent to which the reports of respondents in a large-scale survey such as this one can be accepted.

It is premature to attempt a systematic answer to this question. We shall be content to present here some of the relevant problems which have arisen in this study, and a few devices we have employed in attempting to resolve them.

The cases to be discussed illustrate a type of verification problem which might be called internal or "intrinsic" verification, in which the only source of evidence is the observations and attitudes of participants in the study, exclusive of "extrinsic" materials such as newspaper reports or college records. To deal with it one special tool is available, the fact that at each of our schools a number of teachers were observing and passing judgment on the same events.

Teachers' reports and evaluations of their campuses have been used at three points in this book: in the discussion of the post-war wave of attacks and accusations against college teachers in Chapter II, in the analysis of administration performance in Chapter VII, and in the establishment of a framework for the case illustrations of constraint and withdrawal in Chapters VIII and IX. In each case, we can profitably focus on certain special problems of the particular subject matter.

Singly-Reported Incidents

IN CHAPTER II we described the incidents reported by our sample of respondents in which they or their colleagues had been the subject of criticism, accusation, or attack during the post-war decade. Since we have not attempted to authenticate these incidents from outside sources, such as newspaper reports, A.A.U.P. records, and the like, the question naturally arises whether these reports from teachers are to be believed. In the case of incidents reported by two or more respondents at a school, there would seem to be little question that the episode actually occurred; our respondents themselves corroborate the descriptions provided by their colleagues. Unless there was collusion among colleagues (and David Riesman in his follow-up study found no evidence of this on the campuses he visited) there is little reason to doubt these joint accounts. But, as Table 2-3 in Chapter II showed, 62 per cent of the incidents were reported by a single respondent. In the absence of any corroboration, it is possible that some or all of these descriptions were improvised by respondents. A teacher who hoped to cover the incompetence which prevented his promotion by inventing vague charges of leftism against himself, one who wished to convince the Fund for the Republic of the vulnerability of his faculty, a respondent who mistakenly described an unfounded rumor as actual fact—all might end up by describing spurious incidents to their interviewers. Nevertheless, there is considerable inferential evidence which supports a decision to accept these reports.

The first strand of evidence lies in the accuracy of a common-sense expectation and its implications. It would seem likely that the interplay of two important factors should affect the extent of corroboration of incidents at a school: the size of the school, and the size of the teacher

Table A5-1
Size of School Held Constant:
Variation of Percentage of Corroboration with Sample Size

Over-all School Size	Size of Respondent Sample	Number of Schools	Total Number of Incidents	Average Number of Incidents per School	Percentage of Incidents Which Are Corroborated
0 (under 500 students	5 teachers or less	21	18	0.86	22%
	6 or more	6	19	3.17	37%
1 (501-700)	8 or less	14	19	1.36	21%
	9 or more	9	34	3.78	32%
2 (701-1,000)	9 or less	14	40	2.86	33%
	10 or more	8	35	4.38	46%
3 (1,001-1,400)	14 or less	7	38	5.43	26%
	15 or more	5	38	7.60	45%
4 (1,401-2,500)	15 or less	11	53	4.82	30%
	16 or more	8	54	6.75	37%
5 (2,501-4,000)	13 or less	9	43	4.78	44%
	14 or more	4	31	7.75	39%
6 (4,001-6,000)	21 or less	6	51	8.50	33%
	22 or more	6	49	8.17	39%
7 (6,001-9,000)	23 or less	14	107	7.64	35%
	24 or more	7	117	16.71	40%
8 (9,001-11,000)	50 or less	3	34	11.33	38%
	51 or more	1	25	25.00	76%
9 (Over 11,000)	42 or less	8	94	11.75	43%
	43 or more	4	91	22.75	41%

sample interviewed at the school. In schools of the same over-all size, do we find that, as we would expect, larger samples of respondents result in pooled accounts which give more frequent confirmation to the incidents reported?

To study this question it is desirable to hold the factor of school size constant in considerable detail, and yet to minimize the possibility that sampling idiosyncrasies at individual schools might distort results. Accordingly, the schools were separated into ten groups according to over-all size, a sufficiently refined division to put into each group a set of colleges quite homogeneous in size. Within each group the schools were then simply subdivided into those with comparatively smaller and larger teacher samples. The dividing point varies from group to group; in each it has been chosen so that the number of incidents in the two subgroups will be as nearly equal as possible. Then for each subgroup the percentage of corroborated episodes, those described by at least two respondents at a school, is computed; these figures are given in the right hand column of Table A5-1. For instance, there were altogether 107 incidents reported by respondents at all schools of over-all size "4" (1,401 to 2,500 student enrollment); in this case, the most nearly equal incident subgroups are obtained by separating the eleven schools (fifty-three incidents) where there were fifteen or less respondents, from the eight schools (fifty-four incidents) with sixteen or more respondents. At the former, the table shows, 30 per cent of all incidents received colleague corroboration, and at the latter, 37 per cent.

When all ten such comparisons are set up, it turns out that in eight of the ten, the schools with larger teacher samples have a larger over-all percentage of corroborated incidents.[1] On the whole, as expected, having more respondents produces a better verification record. This means that, implicitly, the credibility of the uncorroborated incidents is reinforced. For the table clearly suggests that we have many uncorroborated incidents in large part because insufficiently large samples were interviewed at schools to guarantee widespread corroboration.[2]

We can, in passing, also raise the reverse question to that just discussed: when all schools having approximately the same teacher sample are considered, what differences do we find between schools of larger and smaller over-all size? In this case, our common-sense expectations are less clear: it could be that larger schools would have more of the kind of widely noted incidents which show up in our

1. Table A5-1 also shows the average number of incidents per school for each of the twenty subgroups. In nine of ten comparisons, larger samples mean more reported incidents, at schools of comparable size. Altogether, then, larger samples mean both more reported incidents and better corroboration of the reports.

2. Since at a number of schools our sample of teachers was large, another way to check on the effect of sample size on the degree of corroboration—as well as on the total number of incidents reported—would be to artificially construct within our sample at these schools smaller "samples" of varying sizes and study the incident patterns resulting. It should also be instructive to study the effect on incident patterns if only a subsample of social science *departments* had provided informants; this would provide a clue about the limitations caused by our original decision to interview only social scientists rather than entire faculties.

records as "corroborated," or, on the contrary, it seems equally tenable that at larger schools the limited teacher sample would be spread out and increasingly inadequate to describe events on campus. When eight groups of schools having approximately the same sample size are formed, using a procedure analogous to that of Table A5-1, in five instances the smaller schools have a larger proportion of corroborated incidents, but in the remaining three the larger schools do. Perhaps both of our expectations are to some degree correct.

An additional line of evidence is offered by study, not of the characteristics of schools, but of individual teachers, and in particular those who report uncorroborated incidents. Altogether, 40 per cent of the 990 incidents are unconfirmed reports made by respondents of an attack against a colleague. An important source of confidence in these reports is the fact that teachers who report them are likely also to be more alert in noticing the corroborated incidents. In Table A5-2, respondents are grouped according to the number of corroborated incidents they

Table A5-2

Size of Sample	Number of Corroborated Incidents Respondent Notices	Number of Respondents	Percentage Reporting Uncorroborated Accusations Against Colleagues
Up to 10 teachers	0	(380)	10%
	1	(107)	18%
	2 or more	(34)	32%
11 to 20	0	(356)	13%
	1	(190)	21%
	2 or more	(99)	22%
21 to 30	0	(248)	10%
	1	(202)	15%
	2	(70)	19%
	3 or more	(48)	21%
31 to 45	0	(116)	5%
	1	(149)	7%
	2	(115)	10%
	3 or more	(63)	25%
46 or more	0, 1	(100)	11%
	2	(53)	13%
	3 or more	(121)	12%

report—that is, instances which are described by at least one other respondent at their school—and then the frequency with which uncorroborated incidents are reported is given for each group. Since the proportion of uncorroborated episodes declines at schools with larger samples[3] it is necessary to present the results separately for each sample size group.

Table A5-2 shows that, within each of the five sample-size groups, respondents who notice and report the most corroborated incidents are also those who most often report uncorroborated cases. It is exactly from those teachers who were most alert to and interested in campus episodes and whose reports were in general most frequently corroborated by colleagues that we also most often obtained accounts of incidents no one else discussed. In short, the most observant and reliable teachers account particularly often for the uncorroborated cases.

Along similar lines, additional figures show that both corroborated and uncorroborated reports of attacks on others are particularly frequent among teachers interested in academic freedom and civil liberties matters. Table A5-4 demonstrates that the greater a teacher's general civil liberties concern, the more of both types of incidents he reports. The same is true of the A.A.U.P., an organization devoted among other things to the protection of teachers' rights; its members notice more incidents than nonmembers do.

Table A5-4

	Per Cent Reporting Uncorroborated Attacks on Colleagues	Per Cent Reporting Corroborated Attacks on Colleagues	Number of Cases
Concern with civil liberties			
High	18%	62%	(556)
Moderate	15%	55%	(815)
Low	10%	48%	(1080)
A.A.U.P			
Member	17%	58%	(1227)
Nonmember	11%	49%	(1207)

3. While uncorroborated reports of attacks against colleagues compose a smaller share of incidents at schools with larger respondent samples, the relative frequency of uncorroborated incidents in which teachers report themselves as targets changes little with sample size:

Table A5-3

	SAMPLE SIZE				
	Up to 10 Teachers	11 to 20	21 to 30	31 to 45	46 or more
Uncorroborated attacks on colleagues	44%	43%	42%	32%	35%
Uncorroborated attacks on respondent	23	21	20	24	21
Corroborated incidents	33	36	38	44	44
Total number of incidents (= 100% in each column)	(183)	(305)	(211)	(176)	(115)

The grounds, then, for accepting these uncorroborated reports are twofold: they come particularly from the teachers who are demonstrably reliable, and from the kind of professor who would be expected to notice them.

Similar tables, in addition, show that teachers who are in a situation which might make it possible for them to notice more incidents, minor as well as important, in fact do so. One set of figures, not given here, demonstrates that teachers who have been at a school for at least five years report both more uncorroborated and corroborated incidents than more recently arrived colleagues do; the same holds for members of school committees when compared to nonmembers.

There is still one set of incidents which requires our attention. This is the other group of unconfirmed incidents, 22 per cent of the total 990, which were described only by the teachers who claimed to have been the target themselves of the attack or accusation. Table A5-5 demonstrates that the same *kinds* of teachers who are most often the target of corroborated personal attacks are also most often reporters of uncorroborated ones. (Since there are only sixty corroborated personal incidents, percentages of these are very small, and a rate per 1,000 teachers is given instead.) Both, that is, are more likely to belong to those groups of professors whom we would expect to be vulnerable: those who read the left-of-center magazines which reflected the more controversial views of the post-war decade, who have past or present controversial political affiliations, who consider themselves politically "more liberal" than the community in which they reside, or who believe that controversial issues should be vigorously debated in the

Table A5-5

	Report Uncorroborated Personal Attacks (Percentage)		Report Personal Attacks, Corroborated by Colleagues (Rate per 1,000 Teachers)
Read *Nation, New Republic,*			
or *Reporter*	12%	(1085)	34
Do not	6%	(1366)	15
Members, past or present, of			
controversial political group	14%	(310)	39
Not members	8%	(2141)	21
Politically more liberal than			
community	10%	(1642)	29
Same, or more conservative	4%	(514)	6
Favor class discussion of			
controversial issues	10%	(1701)	27
Do not favor	6%	(670)	18

classroom. If singly-reported personal incidents are valid, they should be more frequent among exactly those groups which were more vulnerable during the difficult years. Table A5-5 proves this to be the case.

In sum, while we cannot, of course, prove that the uncorroborated incidents actually took place, short of obtaining outside information about them, we have presented a variety of findings which go together to build a plausible case for their acceptance. Statistically, at least, things we should expect to be true of uncorroborated but factual incident reports are true of these reports.

The Perception of School Affairs

IN CHAPTER VII it was indicated that respondents' evaluations of school events are likely in some respects to be colored by their own attitudes and feelings. In particular, apprehensive teachers, more alert to potential difficulties and more observant than the non-apprehensive, tended to paint a darker picture of their school. Figure 7-2 gave an example of this difference, showing that apprehensive teachers are in general more likely to report accusations of subversion or un-Americanism against colleagues. But, nevertheless, the Figure showed that this coloring did not affect an important result: regardless of whether apprehensive professors or their non-apprehensive colleagues were taken as the group of informants, such reports of accusations were increasingly frequent at higher quality schools. It can be shown that even the more complex tables in the chapter are unaffected by similar refinement. For instance, Table A5-6 is a duplication of the bottom part of Figure 7-7,

Table A5-6
Duplication of Figure 7-7, Chapter VII, Separating Reports of Apprehensive and Non-Apprehensive Teachers

	SCHOOL QUALITY			
	High	Medium High	Medium Low	Low
APPREHENSIVE TEACHERS ONLY				
1. Percentage reporting accusations	71%	56%	37%	27%
2. Percentage reporting threats	45%	42%	28%	25%
3. Difference between 1 and 2	26%	14%	9%	2%
	(405)	(366)	(240)	(98)
NON-APPREHENSIVE TEACHERS ONLY				
1. Percentage reporting accusations	57%	45%	16%	13%
2. Percentage reporting threats	26%	24%	11%	10%
3. Difference between 1 and 2	31%	21%	5%	3%
	(475)	(386)	(349)	(132)

with the observations of apprehensive and non-apprehensive respondents now given separately.

In each case, whether we accept the views of apprehensive or of non-apprehensive respondents, the rather complex result in the third line is the same. While apprehensive teachers do see things differently than others, the difference is on the whole much the same at all types of schools, and so, since we are only interested in comparisons between schools, it does not disturb our results.

A more stringent test is to make a school-by-school comparison of apprehensive and non-apprehensive teachers. To take an important example, do we find that when individual schools are ranked separately according to the levels of administrative support expected by apprehensive and by non-apprehensive teachers, the two sets of rankings agree satisfactorily? If not, then we are not justified in using over-all support rates to describe the school as a whole, for the relative proportions of apprehensive and non-apprehensive respondents vary greatly from school to school, and what might seem to be an over-all estimate of the protection provided by the administration at a school could in actuality be little more than a reflection of the relative prevalence of apprehensive teachers there. To investigate this matter, it is necessary to limit attention to schools at which there are both enough apprehensive and non-apprehensive teachers for group rates to have acceptable statistical meaning. As it turns out, in twenty-eight schools the sample includes at least ten apprehensive and ten non-apprehensive professors. In Figure A5-7 two pieces of information are given for each of the twenty-eight: the percentage of apprehensive teachers at the school who would expect wholehearted support from the administration in case of an accusation of leftism, and a like figure for the non-apprehensive.

Several points should be made about Figure A5-7. First of all, the general tendency of apprehensive teachers to view their schools in darker tones is shown again by the fact that the great majority of the twenty-eight schools fall below the line A-B, showing that at most schools the apprehensive respondents are generally less likely to anticipate full administration support than are the non-apprehensive. But for the question raised here it is especially important to notice that with a very few exceptions, the schools all lie in a belt which parallels the line A-B and is centered somewhat below it. Since this belt, the cross-hatched area between the lines C-D and E-F, is quite narrow in comparison to its length, we can say that on the whole the relative placement of individual schools tends to be the same whether the views of apprehensive or non-apprehensive teachers are used as the basis.

To be precise, the rank correlation between the two sets of ratings is
.71 for the twenty-eight schools; the ranking given a school by its
apprehensive teachers, that is, will on the average be quite close to
that given the school by its non-apprehensive teachers. Even when
the more stringent test of a school-by-school comparison is used,
placements by the two groups of reporters thus tend by and large to
agree quite satisfactorily.

It is clear from the Figure that the two rankings would coincide
even more closely if the four schools falling below the belt were left
out of consideration. Without them, the rank correlation for the remaining twenty-four schools becomes .87. Of particular interest is the

Figure A5-7
**The Perception of Administration Support by Apprehensive and
Non-Apprehensive Respondents at Twenty-eight Schools**

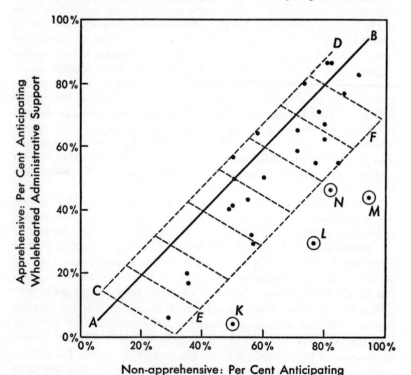

Non-apprehensive: Per Cent Anticipating
Wholehearted Administrative Support

fact that these four schools, differing widely as they do in level of expected support, nevertheless have one thing in common: their apprehensive teachers are unusually more pessimistic about support than the non-apprehensive. So to speak, the apprehensive do not just take a darker view of things than others, they take a much darker view.

Since these four schools lower an otherwise extraordinarily high correlation, at the same time sharing the same pattern of deviation, it is worth while briefly to examine them separately. Tabulations[4] of checklist answers reveal no common factors which could account for the divergence of the four schools; for instance, they do not show an unusual concentration of professors anticipating little administrative support because of such things as exceptionally permissive orientations or particularly controversial past political affiliations.[5]

A more intensive study of the interviews from the four schools, however, produced suggestive information about three of them. School K in Figure A5-7 is a large Midwestern state university. Its faculty, in comparison with others among the twenty-eight, was unusually apprehensive, and also, on the whole, exceptionally pessimistic about chances of personally obtaining administration protection if trouble should arise. Almost all the professors at the school spoke disapprovingly of the recent firing of a colleague who had refused to testify before a Congressional committee; their discomfort, it appeared from their interviews, arose mainly from the sense that in handling the case the president of the school had allowed himself to be dominated by a group of aggressively narrow-minded and suspicious trustees. The general insecurity, however, was not shared by a group of older professors, all of whom had been teaching at the institution twenty years or more. Having safely weathered previous upheavals, these men were almost unanimously sure of administration backing, and so were completely lacking in apprehension. School K, then, appears to have fallen out of line because its older faculty members were unusually more secure than their younger colleagues.

School L is a state college in the Mississippi Valley. During World War II it was the scene of a protracted episode in which the appearance in a professional journal of an article by a faculty member on the merits of butter substitutes created a bitter campus-wide conflict which eventually ended in a considerable number of firings and resignations.

---

4. The study was carried out by Robert H. Somers of the Bureau of Applied Social Research. This discussion draws from his report.

5. Interestingly enough, all four colleges are state-supported institutions; this coincidence, however, does not appear to enter into their distinctive behavior.

The economics department, at the center of the controversy, had been rebuilt after the war, to such an extent that at the time of our study it was by far the largest department represented in our study. In fact, our interviews suggest, it now held the status of administration favorite; most of its faculty reported themselves both unworried and confident of administration protection. But teachers in other departments were less sanguine; even though they were often not apprehensive—perhaps feeling that accusations of leftism against them were highly unlikely— they were nevertheless generally uncertain about the degree of administration support they could expect if attacks ever should materialize. School L, in sum, seems to differ from others because an unusually large and dominant department felt particularly sure of its good standing with the administration.

In sharp contrast to the first two colleges, School M has experienced no incidents at all which have aroused anything like campus-wide attention and concern. Of the large sample of respondents at this distinguished state university, an unusual number are confident of administration support if trouble should arise. In their interviews, several refer to a long-standing tradition of freedom of thought and opinion for the faculty, a tradition supported by a series of vigorous statements by successive presidents of the school. This university, as Figure A5-7 shows, provides the non-apprehensive group most unequivocal of all twenty-eight in its faith in the administration. But a smaller number of teachers, concentrated in two departments, describe episodes which do not seem to be known to the others; in these the administration has quietly denied promotion or tenure to colleagues, apparently on account of their left-of-center political proclivities. Two or three of these teachers point out that no real case has ever come up to put the professed liberal stand of the administration to test, and they are worried that it may some day be their turn for a skillfully quiet by-passing. At this school, then, a majority of the faculty feels quite serenely secure, relying on strong formal administration statements and the apparent complete absence of past trouble, while a smaller segment suspect the administration of deftly deterring certain colleagues and are considerably less confident.

A study of the interviews from School N, a border-state Southern university, offers no help in explaining its deviant attitude pattern (which is, we note, in fact less extreme than those of the other three schools).

Apart from the four exceptional colleges, it is apparent from Figure A5-7 that even when the unit for comparison is no larger than our largest-sample schools, apprehension colors expectations of administration support so uniformly that when schools are separately ranked according to the judgments of apprehensive and non-apprehensive teachers the over-all standing of individual colleges changes very little. When the unit is larger, as for example when it includes all respondents at schools in one of the four quality groups in Table A5-6 above, the distorting effect is necessarily even smaller. On the other hand, study of the sixty-six colleges at which there were a minimum of only five apprehensive and five non-apprehensive teachers revealed a very poor correlation between the rankings based on the two sets of judgments. This suggests that there is a minimum number of informants for which a pooled judgment of an external situation (here, perception of the quality of an administration's protective performance) can be reliably employed for comparison of social "units" (schools, quality groups, etc.) when it is known that a characteristic of individual informants (here, apprehension) which varies in spread from unit to unit can affect perception of the external situation.[6]

The Perception of Apprehension among Colleagues

CHAPTER IX presents a number of questions in which respondents were asked about signs of precautionary activity among their colleagues. If apprehension can color teachers' view of their administrations, should it not be even more likely to affect the perception of precautionary activity, an aspect of apprehension itself? While the matter could be studied by using an analogue of Figure A5-7, comparing the perception of colleague apprehension among apprehensive and non-apprehensive respondents at large-sample schools, it will be presented instead in a somewhat different form, to permit the separa-

---

6. The reader may have noticed that in this Appendix we speak of the relationship between apprehension and the perception of administration support in language which implies that the causal relation is always that of apprehension affecting the expectation of support. Of course (for instance, as we present it throughout Chapter VII) the reverse sequence, in which watching an administration behave poorly leads a teacher to become apprehensive, is perhaps even more likely the true one. But our purpose here is not to separate cause and effect—almost impossible in any case in a single survey like this one—but to demonstrate that the relationship between apprehension and perception of support, whatever the causal sequence, does not affect the validity of the pooled support evaluations sufficiently to distort the findings reported in Chapter VII and elsewhere in the main text.

The poor correlation between rankings for the 66 schools doubtless also reflects variations caused by the very small number of cases (as low as five) on which ratings were based.

tion of two components entering into the perception response. This is given in Table A5-8.

Table A5-8
Colleague Apprehension in Different Colleges as Perceived by Informants Who Are Classified by the Degree of Their Own Apprehension

APPREHENSION RATE OF COLLEGE (PERCENTAGE OF APPREHENSIVE INDIVIDUALS AT A SCHOOL)	APPREHENSION OF THE INDIVIDUAL INFORMANTS			Number of Colleges
	Low (0)	Moderate (1, 2)	High (3 or more)	
0-29%	3% (37)	21% (53)	60% (10)	6
30-39	14% (210)	33% (242)	62% (108)	19
40-49	16% (100)	39% (140)	68% (86)	12
50-59	23% (114)	42% (224)	71% (191)	22
60-69	29% (51)	48% (122)	71% (104)	14
70-89	40% (5)	63% (19)	82% (38)	4

In this table, our *respondents* are divided into three groups: the unapprehensive who have an apprehension score of zero, a middle group with a score of 1 or 2, and the highly apprehensive with a score of 3 or more. The *colleges* in which they teach are classified by their apprehension rate. We have included here only the seventy-seven colleges having thirteen or more interviews. The figures in the table give the proportion of teachers in each group who reported noticeable colleague apprehension,[7] or "intimidation" as we shall call it to avoid confusion. Among teachers, for instance, who are unapprehensive themselves, and who teach in colleges where only a few other respondents are apprehensive, only 3 per cent have the impression that their colleagues are intimidated; this can be seen from the left upper corner figure of Table A5-8. In the right lower corner of the table we find 82 per cent of the cell reporting considerable intimidation; these are the respondents who themselves are highly apprehensive and who teach in colleges where the large majority of their colleagues are also uneasy.

---

7. A rough index of perceived colleague apprehension was formed for each respondent by combining answers to six questions (Nos. 24a-c, 25a, 26a, 27) asking if increased precautionary behavior in various matters, or worry over possible attacks, had been noticed. Each respondent could report from 0 to 6 signs of apprehension among his colleagues. For Table A5-8, we will assume that a teacher who notes 2 or more such signs considers his colleagues apprehensive.

A college's apprehension rate in this Table is the percentage of respondents at the school scoring 2 or higher on the apprehension index.

The two components of respondents' answers are revealed as follows: If we read the figures along each row, it is clearly shown that teachers' own attitudes do affect what they notice about their colleagues; within each line the figures increase considerably from left to right. Given a certain true level of apprehension in a school, teachers' reports of intimidation increase proportionately with their own apprehension. In part we undoubtedly deal here with what psychologists call "projection," the tendency of people to impute to others their own feelings. But this is not the only reason for our result. Since the occupational apprehension we are measuring is, among other things, a sign of alertness and sensitivity to academic freedom matters, the professors with a higher score probably know more about the pressures under which some of their colleagues work and notice more of their subtle reactions.

Secondly, and more important for our argument here, if we read the figures up and down columns we are reassured that, taken together, these answers involve more than projection and individual alertness. Irrespective of their own attitudes, the more apprehension there is in a faculty, the more teachers correctly notice and report it, for the frequency of perceived intimidation increases sharply from top to bottom in each column.

Thus our knowledge of the true situation based on respondents' own interviews shows that their estimates of colleagues' precautionary withdrawal and worry are responsive to the facts. Because of the large element of projection and alertness in these estimates, however, we have limited our use of them to a brief presentation of the over-all total figures in Chapter VIII. Even then, we have offered them as having principally suggestive value except when they are compared among themselves; in this case any elements of distortion, affecting all sides of the comparison equally, no longer matter.

6. Teachers' Attitudes Toward Communism

As EXPLAINED in Chapter V, college teachers' opinions about Communism and Communists, while important to our study, were not for us a central focus of detailed investigation. Our interview, however, did contain several questions on the topic. We have two interesting sets of data in this connection which deserve separate mention.

A number of these questions were taken verbatim from the interview schedule used by Samuel Stouffer in the summer of 1954 for his study of American opinion toward Communists and related issues.[1] Direct comparison is thus possible of the answers given to these questions by our 2,451 college teachers with those of Professor Stouffer's respondents. The latter included a nation-wide cross-section of 4,933 adults, and also 1,500 selected community leaders chosen from a sample of middle-sized American cities.[2] The complete set of answers given by the three groups is shown in Table A6-1.

The college teachers clearly were consistently less inclined than either of Stouffer's groups to see Communists fired from their jobs, and were also less convinced that they were a serious threat to the nation.

It is true, as the Stouffer study shows, that better educated individuals are considerably more often willing to tolerate Communists and other nonconformist groups. However, even the best-educated among the general public are exactly on a par with the sample of community leaders in these matters.[3] The figures given here indicate that college teachers as a whole are considerably more willing to let a Communist hold on to his job than even the best-educated segments of the outside community. (For further comment, see pp. 115-6.)

This conclusion assumes, however, that the opinions of the public did not change significantly between the summer of 1954, when Stouffer recorded them, and the late spring of 1955, when our teachers answered the questions. If the public's tendency toward blanket condemnation of all things Communist had lessened in this interval, then the differences between the teaching profession and the larger community would actually be less great than the figures given above would suggest.

The second set of data concern the impact of the issue of Communism on the outcome of the presidential election in 1952. In Table A6-2 our respondents have been divided according to their voting pattern for the 1948 and 1952 elections. Also, since religious affiliation is closely associated with voting, our two main religious groups, Protestant and Catholic professors, are treated separately. The table divides the two according to how great a danger to the country they considered

---

1. *Communism, Conformity, and Civil Liberties* (Garden City, L. I.: Doubleday, 1955).

2. Fourteen leading citizens in each community, including the mayor, the commander of the largest local American Legion Post, the publisher of the largest local newspaper, etc., were interviewed in a sample of cities of 10,000 to 150,000 population.

3. Compare the figures given on pages 51 and 90 in the Stouffer report.

American Communists to be, and then tabulates their voting patterns in the 1948 and 1952 elections. The figures clearly show that teachers who considered Communists particularly dangerous were noticeably likely to have switched from a Democratic vote in 1948 to a Republican one in 1952, while those who felt Communism was a more remote threat had less often changed their vote in this way. This voting trend was particularly apparent among Catholic professors. In short, the table strongly suggests that the issue of Communism may have contributed in no small way to the widespread switch to the Republican Party in 1952.

Table A6-1

		STOUFFER STUDY		TEACHER STUDY
		National Cross-section (4,933)	Community Leaders (1,500)	(2,451)
Should a man who holds a job as a defense worker and who is an admitted Communist be fired?	Fired	90%	93%	65%
	No opinion (Don't know, no answer)	4	2	18
	Not fired	6	5	17
Should a college teacher who is an admitted Communist be fired?	Fired	89%	86%	45%
	No opinion	5	3	20
	Not fired	6	11	35
Should a clerk in a store who is an admitted Communist be fired?	Fired	68%	51%	9%
	No opinion	6	4	9
	Not fired	26	45	82
Should a defense worker whose loyalty has been questioned before a Congressional committee, but who swears innocence, be fired?	Fired	18%	13%	7%
	No opinion	10	5	13
	Not fired	72	82	80
Should a college teacher whose loyalty has been questioned . . . be fired?	Fired	22%	15%	4%
	No opinion	9	4	9
	Not fired	69	81	87
Should a clerk in a store whose loyalty has been questioned . . . be fired?	Fired	11%	4%	1%
	No opinion	8	3	5
	Not fired	81	93	94
How great a danger do you feel that American Communists are to this country at the present time?	A great or very great danger	43%	37%	14%
	Some danger	38	45	41
	Hardly any or none	11	17	32
	Don't know, no answer	8	1	3

Table A6-2

PROTESTANTS

1948 and 1952 Vote	Communists a Very Great or Great Danger	Some Danger	Hardly Any or No Danger
Republican-Republican	57%	28%	16%
Republican-Democrat	3	7	10
Democrat-Republican	18	12	8
Democrat-Democrat	22	53	66
100%	(161)	(533)	(449)

CATHOLICS

Republican-Republican	36%	23%	6%
Republican-Democrat	2	3	21
Democrat-Republican	34	20	9
Democrat-Democrat	28	54	64
100%	(93)	(87)	(34)

7. The 165 Participating Colleges

Number of Teachers Interviewed	Name of College	Location
	LARGE AND VERY LARGE PRIVATE COLLEGES	
8	Bridgeport, University of	Bridgeport, Conn.
18	Carnegie Institute of Technology	Pittsburgh, Pa.
46	Chicago, University of	Chicago, Ill.
23	Cornell University	Ithaca, N. Y.
33	Dartmouth	Hanover, N. H.
15	Denver, University of	Denver, Colo.
7	Drake University	Des Moines, Iowa
7	Drexel Institute of Technology	Philadelphia, Pa.
21	George Washington University	Washington, D. C.
58	Harvard University	Cambridge, Mass.
6	Johns Hopkins University	Baltimore, Md.
23	Miami, University of	Coral Gables, Fla.
23	Massachusetts Institute of Technology	Cambridge, Mass.
9	Northeastern University	Boston, Mass.

Number of Teachers Interviewed	Name of College	Location
26	Northwestern University	Evanston, Ill.
8	Rensselaer Polytechnic Institute	Troy, N. Y.
32	Syracuse University	Syracuse, N. Y.
24	Temple University	Philadelphia, Pa.
25	Tulane University	New Orleans, La.
16	Washington University	Saint Louis, Mo.
15	Western Reserve University	Cleveland, Ohio
54	Yale University	New Haven, Conn.

SMALL PRIVATE COLLEGES

13	Antioch	Yellow Springs, Ohio
21	Bowdoin	Brunswick, Maine
5	Converse	Spartanburg, S. C.
10	Fisk University	Nashville, Tenn.
11	Goucher	Baltimore, Md.
13	Grinnell	Grinnell, Iowa
20	Lafayette	Easton, Pa.
9	Newcomb	New Orleans, La.
14	Randolph-Macon Woman's College	Lynchburg, Va.
14	Rice Institute	Houston, Texas
14	Roosevelt University	Chicago, Ill.
5	Russell Sage	Troy, N. Y.
35	Smith	Northampton, Mass.
20	Swarthmore	Swarthmore, Pa.
10	Sweet Briar	Sweet Briar, Va.
10	Tampa, University of	Tampa, Fla.
5	Taylor University	Upland, Ind.
9	Tuskegee Institute	Tuskegee, Ala.
28	Vassar	Poughkeepsie, N. Y.
8	Washington	Chestertown, Md.
27	Wellesley	Wellesley, Mass.
25	Williams	Williamstown, Mass.

VERY LARGE PUBLIC COLLEGES

55	California, University of: Berkeley Campus	Berkeley, Calif.
41	California, University of: Los Angeles Campus	Los Angeles, Calif.

Number of Teachers Interviewed	Name of College	Location
31	Maryland, University of	College Park, Md.
61	Michigan, University of	Ann Arbor, Mich.
44	Minnesota, University of	Mineapolis, Minn.
44	Ohio State University	Columbus, Ohio
20	Oklahoma Agricultural and Mechanical	Stillwater, Okla.
31	Oklahoma, University of	Norman, Okla.
25	Purdue University	Lafayette, Ind.
40	Washington, University of	Seattle, Wash.
39	Wisconsin, University of	Madison, Wisc.

LARGE PUBLIC COLLEGES

14	Akron, University of	Akron, Ohio
15	Cincinnati, University of	Cincinnati, Ohio
8	Colorado Agricultural and Mechanical	Fort Collins, Colo.
24	Colorado, University of	Boulder, Colo.
28	Connecticut, University of	Storrs, Conn.
24	Hunter	New York, N. Y.
40	Iowa State College of Agriculture and Mechanic Arts	Ames, Iowa
33	Kansas, University of	Lawrence, Kansas
25	Kent State University	Kent, Ohio
13	*Los Angeles City	Los Angeles, Calif.
13	Louisiana Polytechnic Institute	Ruston, La.
10	Louisville, University of	Louisville, Ky.
19	Miami University	Oxford, Ohio
17	Mississippi State	State College, Miss.
19	Nebraska, University of	Lincoln, Neb.
19	San Francisco State	San Francisco, Calif.
19	San Jose State	San Jose, Calif.
26	Virginia, University of	Charlottesville, Va.
24	West Virginia University	Morgantown, W. Va.

SMALL PUBLIC COLLEGES

11	Clemson Agricultural	Clemson, S. C.

* An accredited 2-year junior college, included in error as a last-minute substitution college.

Number of Teachers Interviewed	Name of College	Location
4	Lander	Greenwood, S. C.
9	Longwood	Farmville, Va.
3	Mississippi State College for Women	Columbus, Miss.
9	North Carolina Agricultural and Technical	Greensboro, N. C.
22	North Carolina Woman's	Greensboro, N. C.
7	Oklahoma College for Women	Chickasha, Okla.
24	South Dakota State College of Agriculture and Mechanic Arts	Brookings, S. D.
14	Texas Southern University	Houston, Texas
10	Texas State College for Women	Denton, Texas

TEACHERS COLLEGES

13	Ball State Teachers	Muncie, Ind.
3	Chicago Teachers	Chicago, Ill.
5	Danbury State Teachers	Danbury, Conn.
8	East Central State	Ada, Okla.
5	Farmington State Teachers	Farmington, Maine
3	General Beadle State Teachers	Madison, S. D.
6	Glenville State	Glenville, W. Va.
6	Emporia State Teachers	Emporia, Kansas
3	Mayville State Teachers	Mayville, N. D.
8	Moorhead State Teachers	Moorhead, Minn.
6	†Miner Teachers	Washington, D. C.
3	National College of Education	Evanston, Ill.
8	Newark State Teachers	Newark, N. J.
9	New Haven State Teachers	New Haven, Conn.
9	New Paltz State Teachers	New Paltz, N. Y.
9	Paterson State Teachers	Paterson, N. J.
6	State Teachers	California, Pa.
5	St. John	Cleveland, Ohio
9	Salem State Teachers	Salem, Mass.
5	Shippensburg State Teachers	Shippensburg, Pa.
13	Framingham State Teachers	Framingham, Mass.
11	Stephen F. Austin State	Nacogdoches, Texas
9	Trenton State Teachers	Trenton, N. J.

† Merged in July, 1955 to become District of Columbia Teachers College.

Number of Teachers Interviewed	Name of College	Location
3	Wheelock	Boston, Mass.
2	Willimantic State Teachers	Willimantic, Conn.
5	†Wilson Teachers	Washington, D. C.
6	Winston-Salem Teachers	Winston-Salem, N. C.
8	Wisconsin State	Superior, Wisc.
9	Wisconsin State	Whitewater, Wisc.

PROTESTANT COLLEGES

5	Atlantic Union	South Lancaster, Mass
1	Barber-Scotia	Concord, N. C.
11	Baylor University	Waco, Texas
7	Beaver	Jenkintown, Pa.
2	Columbia	Columbia, S. C.
16	Davidson	Davidson, N. C.
6	Drew University	Madison, N. J.
4	Dubuque, University of	Dubuque, Iowa
4	Emporia, College of	Emporia, Kansas
7	Greenville	Greenville, Ill.
9	Gustavus Adolphus	St. Peter, Minn.
7	Heidelberg	Tiffin, Ohio
6	Idaho, College of	Caldwell, Idaho
15	Stetson University	DeLand, Fla.
5	Johnson C. Smith University	Charlotte, N. C.
2	LaGrange	LaGrange, Ga.
9	Linfield	McMinnville, Ore.
12	Lynchburg	Lynchburg, Va.
9	Millsaps	Jackson, Miss.
8	Morehouse	Atlanta, Ga.
7	Morris Brown	Atlanta, Ga.
13	Muhlenberg	Allentown, Pa.
6	Northwest Nazarene	Nampa, Idaho
14	Occidental	Los Angeles, Calif.
5	Park	Parkville, Mo.
17	Southern Methodist University	Dallas, Texas
2	Union University	Jackson, Tenn.
13	Upsala	East Orange, N. J.
10	Wagner Lutheran	Staten Island, N. Y.

† Merged in July, 1955 to become District of Columbia Teachers College.

Number of Teachers Interviewed	Name of College	Location
3	Washington Missionary	Washington, D. C.
15	Whittier	Whittier, Calif.
16	Willamette University	Salem, Ore.
9	William Jewell	Liberty, Mo.
16	Wooster, College of	Wooster, Ohio

LARGE CATHOLIC COLLEGES

7	DePaul University	Chicago, Ill.
18	Duquesne University	Pittsburgh, Pa.
21	Loyola	Chicago, Ill.
27	Notre Dame, University of	Notre Dame, Ind.
13	St. John's University	Brooklyn, N. Y.
7	Seton Hall University	South Orange, N. J.

SMALL CATHOLIC COLLEGES

11	Gonzaga University	Spokane, Wash.
23	Holy Cross, College of the	Worcester, Mass.
4	Holy Names	Spokane, Wash.
18	John Carroll University	Cleveland, Ohio
7	Loras	Dubuque, Iowa
10	Mount St. Mary's	Los Angeles, Calif.
4	Nazareth	Louisville, Ky.
14	New Rochelle, College of	New Rochelle, N. Y.
5	Regis	Denver, Colo.
9	St. Mary's	Notre Dame, Ind.
5	St. Teresa, College of	Kansas City, Mo.
5	San Rafael, Dominican College of	San Rafael, Calif.

8. Additional Data

THIS APPENDIX PRESENTS the details of several results which were summarized in the main text.

A. Age, Rank, Tenure, Length of Teaching (Page 6)

THE DETAILED age distribution of our sample was as follows:

Age	Per Cent
30 or less	8%
31 to 40	38
41 to 50	26
51 to 60	19
61 or more	8
Not obtained	1
	100% = 2451 cases

School rank was divided as follows:

Rank	Per Cent
Instructor	14%
Lecturer	2
Assistant Professor	26
Associate Professor	21
Full Professor	36
No rank assigned, or information not obtained	1
	100% = 2451 cases

Possession of tenure ("a permanent appointment on this faculty" was the question's wording) varied according to rank as follows:[1]

Rank	Per Cent Having Tenure
Instructor	21%
Assistant Professor	47%
Associate Professor	86%
Full Professor	94%

1. Lecturers and undesignated teachers are omitted.

The length of respondents' over-all college teaching careers, and their length of residence at their present colleges, are summarized below.

Number of Years	Length Teaching in Colleges or Universities	Length at Present School
5 or less	16%	33%
5 to 10	34	36
10 to 20	22	14
20 to 30	16	11
30 or more	12	6
(2451 cases)	100%	100%

Using these questions, a rough measure of professional mobility can be obtained by cross-tabulating how long a respondent has been teaching altogether against the time he has spent at his present job.

TEACHING HERE	TEACHING IN COLLEGES						
	−5 Yrs.	5-10	10-20	20-30	30 +	No Answer	Total
Up to 5 yrs.	381	335	55	30	8		809
5 to 10		497	270	83	26		876
10 to 20			220	101	28		349
20 to 30				190	84		274
30 or more yrs.					136		136
No answer	1					6	7
Total	382	832	545	404	282	6	2451

We can combine all the cases in the main diagonal into a "stable" group. They have spent practically all their teaching career at the same college.[2] More than half of all our respondents fall in this group. This stable proportion is actually 66 per cent for the teachers below the age of forty—these are the ones who are still at their first job. The largest amount of mobility is in the age group 41-to-50, where only 47 per cent have taught most of their lives at the same college. The figure increases to 56 per cent again in the age group above 50. This is a strange result; it suggests that in this oldest age group there are really two types of teachers, those who have matured in what one might call a normal academic career, and also those who entered teaching a long time ago when standards of employment were much lower and who were never sought out by another institution later in their career.

---

2. This is not strictly true due to the combination of cases into larger classes. A man who is in the "20 to 30 year" class in both directions might well have taught twenty-nine years but been at his present post only twenty-one years. Still, for a rough assessment, this "measure of stability" is instructive.

B. *The Patterning of Incidents* (Pages 68, 69)

Sources Instigating Incidents

Not connected with the school		9%
Government committees and investigative agencies		
(state or national)	13%	
Right-of-center community political groups	3	
Local special interest groups	6	
Left-of-center political groups (no cases)	—	
Unorganized community groups and individuals	12	
Mass media	5	
Connected with school		36
Formally constituted regulatory bodies (trustees,		
Board of Education, etc.)	2	
College administration	13	
Alumni	3	
Colleagues	6	
Students and student groups	9	
Relatives of students	3	
No information about originator		25
		100% (990 cases)

Types of Charges Made by Different Sources

	INSTIGATOR				
CHARGE	Govern-ment Committees	Other "Off-Campus" Sources	Admin-istration	Other "On-Campus" Sources	No Answer re Instigator
Communist Party membership	24%	2%	2%	2%	1%
Other extremist politics and disloyalty	50	56	9	41	27
All other political	13	17	18	28	19
Specific issues	2	17	27	15	17
Personal idiosyncrasy	—	—	7	1	17
Intramural	—	—	15	4	6
Issues without charges	9	1	19	2	2
No answer	2	6	3	8	11
Incident totals	(131)	(259)	(131)	(221)	(248)

The Distribution of Charges in Different Types of Schools*

	Extremist Politics and Disloyalty	All Other Political	Specific Issues	Personal Idiosyncrasy, etc.	Intra-mural Issues	Issues Without Charges	No Answer re Charge	Number of Incidents
Private								
Large	56	16	11	4	4	2	7	(219)
Small	52	23	13	6	3	1	2	(129)
Public								
Very large	44	21	9	3	5	11	7	(175)
Large	38	20	20	6	4	4	8	(204)
Small	24	10	28	3	10	11	14	(29)
Teachers Colleges	38	21	16	5	5	12	3	(61)
Protestant	30	21	25	9	6	3	6	(135)
Catholic	29	24	21	5	5	5	11	(38)

* Percentages add to 100 reading across each row. Also, because of the small number of incidents, the large and small Catholic colleges are combined.

C. Per Cents Who Have Toned Down Their Recent Writings, among Groups Divided According to Age and Productivity Score (Page 79)

	PRODUCTIVITY SCORE				
AGE	4 (High)	3	2	1	0 (Low)
40 or under	12% (106)	11% (219)	14% (349)	8% (281)	5% (166)
41 to 50	13% (172)	7% (189)	10% (136)	7% (98)	0% (30)
51 or over	8% (248)	6% (178)	4% (124)	5% (86)	0% (27)

D. Replication of Figures 4-2 to 4-4, Chapter IV, Using Caution in Place of Apprehension

	CAUTION SCORE				
	0 (1174)	1 (729)	2 (311)	3 (168)	4, 5 (69)
Table 4-2					
Would vigorously protest ban on the controversial speaker	39%	40%	41%	43%	38%
Would vigorously protest China debate ban	54%	56%	57%	59%	46%
Table 4-3					
Read *The Nation*	14%	16%	21%	19%	22%
Read *The New Republic*	15%	19%	26%	26%	32%
Read *The Reporter*	28%	33%	31%	39%	41%
Table 4-4					
Reads at least one magazine which he feels is likely to be attacked as being subversive	18%	26%	34%	33%	35%
Is member of at least one political organization he considers likely to be attacked as subversive	9%	12%	21%	18%	23%

E. Appointments to School Position (Page 152)

IN EACH AGE GROUP, it is not the most permissive teachers who are made department heads or appointed to school committees.

PER CENT WHO ARE OR HAVE BEEN DEPARTMENT HEADS

AGE	Highly Permissive	Quite Permissive	Somewhat Permissive	Somewhat Conservative	Clearly Conservative
40 or less	7% (328)	11% (258)	12% (299)	18% (127)	23% (126)
41 to 50	34% (125)	32% (132)	44% (188)	43% (86)	42% (101)
51 or more	58% (90)	57% (115)	54% (201)	51% (140)	59% (121)

PER CENT WHO HAVE BEEN ON A SCHOOL COMMITTEE

AGE					
40 or less	67% (328)	72% (258)	78% (299)	83% (127)	80% (126)
41 to 50	94% (125)	96% (132)	96% (188)	92% (86)	86% (101)
51 or more	95% (90)	94% (115)	97% (201)	98% (140)	94% (121)

However, the highly permissive are most often called in as consultants.

PER CENT WHO HAVE BEEN CALLED IN AS A CONSULTANT TO BUSINESS

AGE					
40 or less	39% (328)	34% (258)	32% (299)	29% (127)	31% (126)
41 to 50	42% (125)	41% (132)	39% (188)	36% (86)	24% (101)
51 or more	41% (90)	33% (115)	37% (201)	36% (140)	26% (121)

Figure 6-13 gives the relevant data concerning productivity.

F. The Detailed Cross-tabulation of Permissiveness and Apprehension (Page 153)

LEVEL OF PERMISSIVENESS	APPREHENSION SCORE						Total
	0	1	2	3	4	5, 6	
Highly Permissive	101	112	112	108	62	48	543
Quite Permissive	140	113	107	72	46	27	505
Somewhat Permissive	207	183	128	98	51	30	697
Somewhat Conservative	136	87	57	36	23	15	354
Clearly Conservative	158	105	50	22	11	6	352
Total	742	600	454	336	193	126	2,451

G. Comparison with Figure 10-6, Chapter X: Congressman and School Trustee

PER CENTS OF APPREHENSIVE RESPONDENTS

CONGRESSMAN'S IMPUTED ESTEEM FOR PROFESSORS	Clearly Permissive	Somewhat Permissive	Conservative	Average Per Cent Apprehensive
Low (Ranks 3, 4)	60% (717)	49% (462)	36% (444)	48%
High (Ranks 1, 2)	50% (235)	38% (157)	24% (191)	37%
TRUSTEE'S IMPUTED ESTEEM FOR PROFESSORS				
Low	63% (427)	52% (293)	40% (272)	52%
High	52% (451)	43% (271)	28% (330)	41%

9. List of Indices

ALTOGETHER ten indices are used in this book. Eight of these characterize individual teachers; the remaining two characterize colleges.

For seven of the eight indices used to describe individual respondents, a simple, uniform scoring procedure has been used. Response categories for each item in an index are dichotomized; the "positive" response (e.g., the answer to an apprehension-index item which indicates apprehension) is given a score of 1, the remaining answers a score of 0. An individual's final index score is the sum of his positive replies; if four items are used in the index, his score may vary from 0 to 4.

The seven indices follow, with a reference to the page in the book at which they first appear, the range of possible scores, and the list of "positive" responses. The original number of each item in the questionnaire is also given, in parentheses, so that its complete wording and position in the questionnaire can be examined in Appendix 2.

1. Index of productivity (Page 8). Score may range from 0 to 4.
   Has written a dissertation (F9a)
   Has published papers (F9c)
   Has published a book (F9e)
   Has delivered three or more papers at professional meetings (F10d)

2. Index of pressures on the college administration (Page 39). Score range: 0 to 4.
More pressure from the trustees (36a)
More pressure from the alumni (36b)
More pressure from the community (36c)
More pressure from the politicians (36d)

3. Index of worry (Page 76). Score range: 0 to 6.
Worry about student misinterpretation causing trouble (6/16)
Wondered if move to another college could be affected by his politics (6/14)
Wondered if a subject of local gossip (6/11)
Wondered if his politics affected his job security (6/8)
Wondered if alumni disliked his politics (6/18)
Thought about possibility of administration political dossiers (6/9)

4. Index of caution (Page 78). Score range: 0 to 5.
Makes clear he has no extremist leanings (6/21)
Avoids embarrassing trustees and administration (6/19)
More careful not to embarrass colleagues in conversations (6/2)
More careful when recommending class reference material (6/4)
Toned down recent writing to avoid controversy (6/15)

5. Apprehension index (Page 81). Score range: 0 to 6.
More careful when recommending class reference material (6/4)
Wondered if his politics affected his job security (6/8)
Wondered if a subject of local gossip (6/11)
Wondered if move to another college could be affected by his politics (6/14)
Toned down recent writing to avoid controversy (6/15)
Worried about student misinterpretation causing trouble (6/16)

6. Index of concern with civil liberties (Page 107). Score range: 0 to 2.
Follows civil liberties news more closely than other news (20a)
Discusses civil liberties issues fairly often with friends (20d)

7. Index of faculty intimidation (Appendix 5, page 428). Score range: 0 to 6.

Colleagues less willing to express unpopular views in class-
room (24a)
Colleagues less willing to express views in community (24b)
Colleagues less willing to express views among friends (24c)
Colleagues worried about possible attacks (25a)
Colleagues avoid controversial subjects in research (26a)
Colleagues keep controversial material out of reference lists
(27)

8. The permissiveness index, page 127, is formed by combining
answers to two indicators of a permissive orientation with replies to
four indicators of a conservative orientation. The detailed procedure is
shown on page 125.
Indicators of a permissive orientation (Page 114).
Would not fire a teacher who admittedly is a Communist (38c)
Would allow Young Communist League on campus (41/5)
Indicators of a conservative orientation (Pages 119-120).
Would not allow Lattimore to speak on campus (5a)
Would fire a store clerk who admittedly is a Communist (38b)
Would not allow the Young Socialist League on campus (41/4)
Considers a radical teacher a luxury for the college (43)

The two indices characterizing colleges deal with their quality and
their "procedural adequacy" in handling issues of academic freedom.
The construction of the quality index (page 20) is given in detail
in Appendix 4. Taken into consideration for each school are:
Size of library
Number of books per student
Budget per student
Proportion of Ph.D.'s on the faculty
Production of scholars (Knapp-Greenbaum index)
Tuition fees
The data were obtained from independent sources.
The index of procedural adequacy is derived from an interview
question (37) asking which campus groups had the most powerful voice
in matters of academic freedom; scores assigned to the answers of indi-
vidual teachers are summarized and averaged for each school. The
details are given on page 171.

INDEX